Up Front!

Becoming the Complete
Choral Conductor

Guy B. Webb, Editor

Twelve Essays by

Ray Robinson
Timothy W. Sharp
Gordon Paine
Melinda O'Neal
Jameson Marvin
Donald Neuen
Paul Brandvik
Richard Cox
James Jordan
Guy B. Webb
G. Roberts Kolb
Scott W. Dorsey

ECS Publishing
Boston

ISBN 0-911318-19-4

ECS Publishing Catalog No. 4638
10 9 8 7 6 5 4 3 2

For Barbara

Preface

The idea for this book orginated at a Youth and Student Activities Committee roundtable breakfast meeting during the 1991 National Convention of the American Choral Directors Association in Phoenix, Arizona. The subject that early March morning was "Training Our Future Choral Directors," and several of us on the committee felt it could form the basis for a journal article or monograph. Sr. Sharon Breden, Chair of the ACDA Repertoire and Standards Committee, was of invaluable help in her encouragement, as was Ray Robinson, who suggested that the subject might well become the basis for a book.

While many fine volumes have already been written on the subject, it soon became evident that singing in a college choir, taking one or two courses in conducting and a choral techniques class is all too frequently the extent of a choral conductor's training. Also, the path to conducting a choir is often approached from different areas of expertise — from one's keyboard skills or instrumental background, leaving many conductors without a concept of diction or choral tone. So much is involved in the learning process to become an effective choral director. A publication which would articulate basic concepts would be an invaluable research tool in the training of choral musicians.

The learning process is the sum total of many things — courses taken, books read, conventions attended, and, most importantly, **on-the-job training.** Though this book is written for the student, it is written for every choral director who is still striving to grow in the profession. It is not limited to those who have yet to find their first choral position.

I wish to thank the chapter authors who so promptly and graciously agreed to participate in this project. Their succinct views on their respective topics were requested, in a manner that would speak directly to choral students. They have each brought considerable uniqueness to the approach of their subject. The reader may find within these twelve chapters some repetition of the various aspects of rehearsal techniques, score study, resource materials, etc. Yet such duplication, if viewed from different perspectives, can be illuminating. If through reading these pages the reader gains some new concepts, a desire to grow, to look anew at what is involved as a choral musician — to listen, search, and perhaps even question old habits or ways of doing things — this book will have served its purpose.

— Guy B. Webb
Southwest Missouri State University
Summer, 1993

About the Authors:

RAY ROBINSON, author of five books and numerous articles on the choral art, is distinguished professor of choral studies at Palm Beach Atlantic College. Since 1986 he has been chair of the Research and Publications Committee of the American Choral Directors Association of the United States. He served as president of Westminster Choir College, Princeton, New Jersey from 1969 to 1987, and as dean of The Peabody Conservatory of Music, Baltimore, Maryland from 1963 to 1969.

TIMOTHY W. SHARP is scholar in residence at Belmont University, Nashville, Tennessee, and he writes the "Research Reports" for the *Choral Journal* and edits the church music periodical *Leadership in Church Music*. He has chaired the music departments at Taylor University, Indiana, and The King's College, New York. He currently serves on the Research and Publications Committee and the Editorial Board of the American Choral Directors Association.

GORDON PAINE is vice chairman and coordinator of graduate studies and choral conducting at California State University, Fullerton. He is chorusmaster of the Oregon Bach Festival in Eugene, Oregon, and has published two books and numerous articles. He has served on the Editorial Board of the *Choral Journal*, has chaired the Don Malin Award Committee and currently serves as a member of the Research and Publications Committee of the American Choral Directors Association.

MELINDA O'NEAL is professor of music and former chair of the music department at Dartmouth College, New Hampshire, where she conducts the Handel Society, the Concertato Singers, and the Chamber Singers. She founded the college's foreign music study program in London and the Dartmouth Conducting Institute. In 1990 she was awarded the American Choral Directors Association's Julius Hereford Outstanding Dissertation Award for her "Berlioz's *L'enfance du Christ:* A Conductor's Analysis for Performance." She currently serves on the Research and Publications Committee of the American Choral Directors Association.

JAMESON MARVIN has been senior lecturer of music and director of choral activities at Harvard University, Cambridge, Massachusetts since 1978. He is conductor of the Harvard-Radcliffe Collegium Musicum and the Harvard Glee Club. He has served as choral director at Vassar College, Bard College, Lehigh University, and the University of Illinois, and has been a visiting scholar at Stanford University and Trinity College, Cambridge, England. He has edited and arranged numerous Renaissance works and folk songs for male chorus.

DONALD NEUEN is currently professor of conducting and director of choral activities at the University of California, Los Angeles following a tenure of twelve years as professor of conducting and director of choral activities at the Eastman School of Music, Rochester, New York. He previously served as choral director at the University of Tennessee, the University of Wisconsin, and Ball State University, Muncie, Indiana. He was assistant conductor for Robert Shaw and the Atlanta Symphony Orchestra, director of choral and orchestral activities at Georgia State University, conductor of the Oak Ridge Symphony Orchestra, assistant conductor of the Knoxville Symphony, and guest conductor for the Rochester Philharmonic Orchestra.

PAUL BRANDVIK has been director of choral activities at Bemidji State University, Minnesota since 1967. He was awarded the Burlington Northern Foundation Distinguished Teaching Award in 1991. His choirs have toured intenationally, and he has served as guest conductor and lecturer for state and national conventions of the Music Educator's National Conference and the American Choral Directors Association. He has composed, edited and arranged over fifty choral works and is the author of *The Compleet Madrigal Dinner Booke* and seventeen madrigal dinner scripts.

RICHARD COX has been chair of the division of vocal studies and conductor of the University Chorale at the University of North Carolina at Greensboro since 1960. He is author of *The Singer's Manual of German and French Diction*, and *Singing in English*. He has been editor of "Research Reports" in the *Choral Journal* and has chaired the American Choral Directors Association's reviewing committee for the Julius Hereford Outstanding Dissertation Award.

JAMES JORDAN is presently conductor of the Westminster Chapel Choir and associate professor of conducting at the Westminster Choir College, Princeton, New Jersey. He was previously chair of music education at the Hartt School of Music, Hartford, Connecticut, where he conducted the Hartt Symphonic Choir and the Hartford Youth Chorale. He has also held choral positions at The Pennsylvania State University and the Lewisburg, Pennsylvania, High School. He has collaborated with the late Frauke Haasemann on a book, video and vocalise cards, and has contributed to *Readings in Music Learning Theory.*

GUY B. WEBB is both general editor and contributor to this book. He is currently coordinator of choral studies at Southwest Missouri State University in Springfield, and also national chair of Youth and Student Activities for the Repertoire and Standards Committee of the American Choral Directors Association. He has held choral positions at the University of Florida, State University of New York at Cortland, and New Mexico State University.

G. ROBERTS KOLB has been director of choral music and chair of the faculty at Hamilton College, New York since 1980. He has taught at Smith College, Northampton, Massachusetts. He is currently musical director of the Syracuse Vocal Ensemble and director of music at the Stone Presbyterian church in Clinton, New York. In 1988 he was awarded the American Choral Directors Association's Julius Herford Outstanding Dissertation Award for his doctoral study on the music of the early seventeenth century composer Guillaume Bouzignac. He is a member of the Research and Publication Committee of the American Choral Directors Association.

SCOTT W. DORSEY is director of choral activities at Montana State University, Billings. He previously served in similar positions at Vennard College (Iowa), and the University of Northern Iowa. He has recently authored *The Choral Journal: An Index to Volumes 19–32* for the American Choral Directors Association, and he has been a contributing author to the *Choral Journal* and *The Music Educator's Journal.* He is editor of *The Student Times* and is a member of the American Choral Directors Association's Youth and Student Activities Committee.

Credits

Contents

The Challenge of Choral Leadership in the Twenty-First Century

Ray Robinson

In a world of political, economic, and personal disintegration, music is not a luxury but a necessity, not simply because it is therapeutic nor because it is the "universal language," but because it is the persistent focus of man's intelligence, aspiration and good will.[1]

We live in an extraordinary time in world history, but it is a period that is not without its difficulties for choral musicians: support for the choral art is waning in the schools; entire segments of the church across denominational lines have declared choral programs and choral literature irrelevant as a meaningful vehicle of congregational worship; college and university curricula no longer consider the arts an integral core requirement for all students; and a difficult economy has reduced public and private financial support for professional and community choruses to the extent that many are actually struggling for survival. As we begin to write the final chapter on the twentieth century, it is painfully clear that the next generation of choral conductors will have a much more difficult time than did its predecessors.

Yet when we really stop and think about it, choral musicians have always existed in a state of tension. We only need to read the letters of Johann Sebastian Bach to the Leipzig Town Council[2] or conduct some research on Felix Mendelssohn's frustrations with the religious establishment at the *Berliner Dom* during his years as Kapellmeister[3] to realize that little has changed in the last two hundred years for those choral musicians who wish to produce a high quality choral experience for their singers and the audiences they reach.

In the millennium that is about to dawn, a new generation of choral artists will emerge to face many of the same problems that frustrated Bach and Mendelssohn, as they accept the challenge of choral leadership in a new century. Those who are the primary audience of this volume represent the vanguard of this new wave. However theirs will not be the pioneer role of the great choral conductors of the twentieth century — F. Melius Christiansen, Wilhelm Ehmann, Eric Ericson, Helmuth Rilling, Robert Shaw, John Smallman, Roger Wagner,

---

[1] Robert Shaw, quoted in: Robinson, Ray and Allen Winold, *The Choral Experience.* Prospect Heights, Illinois: Waveland Press, 1992, (re-issue of Harper-Collins, 1976) p. xvii.

[2] David, Hans T. and Arthur Mendel, *The Bach Reader.* New York: W. W. Norton and Co., 1966.

[3] Werner, Eric, *Mendelssohn: A New Image of the Composer and His Age.* Translated by Dika Newlin. New York: Free Press, 1963. His appointment as Kapellmeister in 1842 at the Berlin Cathedral by King Friedrich Wilhelm IV proved to be the only church music post that Mendelssohn ever held, and it was a very unhappy experience for him.

David Willcocks, and John Finley Williamson. Rather theirs will be the task of consolidating gains that have been made by their predecessors and, perhaps even more importantly, meeting the challenge of bringing the choral experience[4] into a new relationship with the world-wide cultural diversity that their generation will inherit. It is always more difficult to maintain than to build, but this will be one of the formidable tasks facing those who accept the challenge of choral leadership in the twenty-first century.

Any musician who wishes to be effective in the service of the choral art today or in the next century will be required to make some basic commitments. These are fundamental to successful choral leadership, and it is to these commitments that this essay is dedicated. We begin this discussion with one of the most important requisites for the choral musician:

Commitment to a Quality Choral Experience for Every Singer

The following statement may shock some readers, but it is advice well worth heeding: *Do not pursue a career in choral music if you can or want to do anything else with your life!* You might ask why this essay would open with such a dogmatic statement. The answer is simple! In thirty-five years of college teaching this writer has observed that many students select a career in choral leadership for the wrong reasons: because they consider it (choral singing) "fun" or because they enjoy the "ego" trip of standing on the podium in front of a choir and "making music." And they are right, to a certain extent. Making music with good singers *is* fun and choral leadership *is indeed* a wonderful and exhilarating experience. But it is also just plain *hard work*. Not only is the job of the choral conductor more than a full-time occupation if it is done right, the choral art is a hard taskmaster as well. To be effective as a choral musician one must make a serious, life-long commitment.

There was a time when one could "dabble" in choral music — conduct a church choir, direct a madrigal group, or lead a community chorus without learning much about the business. But this is no longer the case. The demands of the profession are simply too great, and the jobs for choral conductors are far too scarce. With the possible exception of the person pursuing another career who wants to maintain a part-time church position, and such a role can be spiritually rewarding and musically satisfying to a certain level of involvement,[5] a commitment to pursue a career in choral music must be taken very seriously. The reasons are simple and should be fairly obvious. First of all, you owe it to yourself to be the very best you can be at what you do. Achieving excellence

---

[4] In this context, the "choral experience" can be defined as "an interaction between a singer and a piece of music within a group setting under the guidance of a capable conductor." Robinson and Winold, *Op.Cit.,* p. 2.

[5] The place of choral music in the church has changed a great deal in recent years. The role of musical leadership in many churches across denominational lines is moving away from the model of a choral director and a choir and in the direction of a "worship leader" who interacts with the congregation in conjunction with a "band" or small vocal group which "leads" the people in the corporate worship experience. Except for special religious holidays such as Advent, Christmas, and Easter, the choirs of the church, and especially the youth choirs, are becoming obsolete in many places as desired vehicles for worship leadership.

requires a serious decision, first, to become a consummate musician, one whose musicianship and understanding of the art of music is as thorough as possible. It also demands a lifetime study of choral literature and familiarity with languages, at least French, German, and Italian, and others if you wish to specialize in the music of eastern Europe, Latin America, or the Orient. A career in choral music also requires an in-depth understanding of musical styles and performance practices. People travel a great deal today, and audiences are much better educated than ever before. A choral conductor can no longer get away with poor choral diction in any language, including English. Likewise, one cannot stand before an audience at any level of sophistication and perform a motet by Victoria in the same manner as one by Bach, or a coronation anthem by Handel in the same style as one by Vaughan Williams. Everyone knows too much. The world-wide information explosion, the television set, the compact disc, and the music video have made the performances of Gardiner, Harnoncourt, Hogwood, Leonhardt, and Pinnock the property of people in every culture. Finally, we must make a commitment to a quality choral experience because our singers deserve the very best we can give them.

For a number of years this writer had the opportunity to observe Robert Shaw in rehearsals and performances on the Westminster Choir College campus in Princeton. On rare occasions we would have lunch together and discuss various topics related to the choral art. At one such meeting the question arose: "Why are there not a lot of young conductors out there who are emerging as successors to Robert Shaw?" Mr. Shaw's answer: "There are few young conductors who are willing to work hard enough to achieve success!" This writer has never forgotten that response. By this statement, Mr. Shaw was reinforcing the idea that a commitment to choral leadership results in a prescription for hard work. Those who have the ability and are willing to pay the price for success will undoubtedly achieve it.

Commitment to an Effective Leadership Role

The simplest definition of leadership in any area of endeavor — whether corporate, political, or academic — is the accomplishment of a predetermined goal through the direction of human resources. The person who is able to marshal human collaborators for the purpose of achieving a particular end is a leader. A great leader at any level of activity — from kindergarten or Sunday School teaching through the presidency of the country — is one who can be effective day after day, week after week, month after month, and year after year, while facing and adapting to a wide range of changing circumstances. The great choral leaders of ours and past generations have all demonstrated this ability.

Nicholas Murray Butler, a former president of Columbia University, identifies one characteristic of leadership when he says:

> There are three kinds of people in the world: those who don't know what's happening; those who watch what' s happening; and those who make things happen.[6]

---

[6] Quoted in: Engstrom, Ted W., *The Making of a Christian Leader*. Grand Rapids: Zondervan Publishing House, 1976, p. 20.

We are appointed to positions of choral leadership in the school, church, university or community by those who expect us to define the thrust of the program, recruit singers, improve the situation musically, and eventually attract the attention of the community-at-large; in short, to take the human resources we have been given and to turn them into a capable choral ensemble. When we do this in a careful and systematic manner, we make things happen!

The Merriam Webster Dictionary defines a leader as "one who guides or conducts; who directs in action, thought, opinion; who instructs . . . directs by influence, good or bad."[7] Notice the emphasis here on the subtle aspect of leadership: to direct by action, thought or opinion. In short, anyone who influences a group of people, and thereby is able to accomplish a defined purpose through the efforts of the group, is a leader.

Interestingly enough, a conductor of a musical organization can be one of the best models of leadership in any human enterprise — whether business, education, or industrial management. For the conductor to be a successful "leader," four important prerequisites are necessary:

1. The conductor must take charge. No stone can be left unturned to insure the success of the musical enterprise. Ultimately singers respond positively to discipline and order. It often takes young conductors a while to accept this premise. But a conductor who walks into a position and establishes himself or herself as a strong leader from the very first day *will* be successful, all other things being equal.

2. A psychological setting must be created to establish the proper environment for the common task. Beginning with the first rehearsal, the conductor must create ground rules of attendance, appoint section leaders to take the roll and energize their sections, and devise an organizational structure to ensure that the notes will be learned, deadlines for learning individual works will be met, and methods of operation will not get in the way of the musical result. In other words, the administrative expectations of the conductor must be clearly defined early in the process. Organizational clarity is the second important step toward successful choral leadership.

3. Obvious enough, but not always recognized, is the fact that singers or instrumental performers must have the requisite skills and training to fulfill their roles satisfactorily. If they do not possess these skills, then the conductor must work with them until they gain them. Here is another place where the choral conductor must make something happen. It is the task of the leader — through daily vocalization, rhythm and sight-singing drills, musicianship studies, attention to musical details, reference to historical and stylistic matters, and any other means at his disposal — to ensure that a high standard of performance is established and maintained. In short, the choral conductor must build the choral ensemble into a first-rate musical organization.

Over the years this writer has heard conductors say, "I do not believe in choral warmups; I just want to make music!" Well, it is fine to take this attitude if one is working with professionals (although this writer would recommend

[7] *Webster's New International Dictionary of the English Language.* Second Edition. Springfield, Massachusetts: G. & C. Merriam Company Publishers, 1945, p. 1045.

appropriate warm-up exercises for professional singers as well; no athletic coach would dare take football, basketball, or baseball players into a practice or game without putting them through their warm-up drills!), but most choral conductors work with amateurs. Amateur choirs need regular (daily if possible) vocal, rhythmic, sight-singing, and stylistic drills if they are to develop their full potential as choral ensembles. Howard Swan, the noted choral pedagogue, often has been heard to say: "There are no bad choirs, only *bad conductors.*" This writer would paraphrase this statement as follows: "There are no bad choirs, only choirs which are led by conductors who are not willing to take the time and make the effort to ensure that their singers have the necessary vocal and musical skills to meet the demands of the literature being studied and performed." This is a challenge of choral leadership that cannot be neglected.

Often young conductors approach this writer after a class, concert, or workshop and say, "I really want to be the best choral conductor that I can be, but I do not know where to go or what to read to improve myself as a choral musician." Fortunately, today there is a wide range of reference material available to the intellectually curious choral conductor. Some are included in Scott Dorsey's contribution to this volume; additional ones can be found in other essays in this volume.

4. Finally, and perhaps most importantly of all, singers and instrumentalists must share satisfaction with their conductor as they prepare a musical performance. Unless each member of the ensemble achieves a sense of accomplishment or even fulfillment in their rehearsals and concerts, the leader has failed, and great performances will not result.

A vital aspect of choral leadership then is to instill in singers the conviction that they are part of a quality musical experience that could only take place under *your* leadership. Conductors must use those musical skills and human insights with which they are endowed to capture a strong sense of individual satisfaction and to create an environment of self-fulfillment that will motivate each singer to become a more productive member of the choral ensemble. The effective choral leader will make this happen.

Commitment to People

With all the other demands the choral conductor faces, it may sound a little strange for this writer to suggest that one of the important commitments that the choral musician must make today is a commitment to people. "Why," you may ask, "is this so important?" For one reason, the choral art is a "people" business. Choral singing is dominated by the amateur who joins a choral ensemble for the love of singing. Because extensive and serious musical study is not an essential prerequisite for a satisfying choral experience, children, teenagers, and adults around the world find delight and fulfillment as regular participants in this form of musical endeavor. It is the one art form that can provide for the non-professional that glimpse of transcendental beauty and musical self-fulfillment that is usually reserved for those who have devoted years of practice and study to their instrumental or vocal specialization.

One of the most exciting things about choral singing is that it touches directly on the entire life of the individual singer. From birth to death we are vocal, rhythmic creatures. Our rhythms are synonymous with nature's rhythms — the heartbeat, the seasons, the tides, the weather. We celebrate our lives vocally when we laugh, cry, shout, sing, or talk. We are endowed with a natural means of communicating our spiritual state. Our physical bodies cultivate life at the same time that they sustain art. As distinct from orchestral or band players, choral singers bring their instrument (their bodies) and their problems with them to every rehearsal, and they take them home with them at night.

Consequently, one of the many things a choral conductor must come to understand about the choral art is that its unique achievement often has as much or more to do with human and social concerns as it does with musical ones. This statement is not meant to imply that a choral conductor is not first and foremost a fine musician, conducting technician, and scholar. On the contrary, this thought is interjected at this point to reinforce the idea that the choral leader is always working with people, and what one is able to accomplish musically is often very closely related to the empathetic[8] relationship that the conductor is able to establish with singers. This association is an outgrowth of the conductor's understanding of the musical and personal needs of individuals and their relationship to the goals of the choral ensemble. The necessity of this kind of sensitivity is not a new phenomenon in choral music, but it is a more significant part of the conductor's overall approach than it was, say, three decades ago. Today we live in a much more complex society, and the personal difficulties singers bring to the choral rehearsal — just because they live in this period of human history — are a reflection of the problematic and sometimes unfriendly world in which they find themselves.

Many of these problems are the result of three decades of social ferment during which our country has experienced significant societal change. The implications of this revolution are now being felt in all sorts of leadership roles, including the school, the church, and the community organization. Many of these new social values — affluence, self, short-term commitments and superficial involvements — will also affect tomorrow's social institutions. The skepticism about other people and organizations, the lack of respect for traditions, and the general uncertainty concerning relationships will make it more, rather than less, difficult for leaders to lead in the years to come. The new forms of family relationships will also complicate peoples' lives, and this phenomenon will continue to proliferate in the decades ahead with new family units — single family parents, blended families, cohabitating adults, and student gangs — changing the way individuals view the world in which they live, work, and play. Divorce and multiple marriages will become the norm. Loneliness among teenagers and adults will become more widespread, as the usual sources for developing friendships (church, school, and traditional social organizations) are displaced, and their skills at creating and maintaining friendships erode.

---

[8] *Empathy* might be defined as "understandings so intimate that the thoughts, intentions and motives of one are communicated intuitively to another." This relationship between conductor and singer is a special characteristic of choral singing.

All these factors will provide wonderful opportunities for musical organizations and those involved in the choral art to serve society, not only in the traditional ways we know so well, but in new ways which will meet special needs in the lives of those with whom we work in these musical settings. The importance of this kind of extra-musical role is wonderfully identified by the humanist psychologist Abraham H. Maslow:

> Let people realize clearly that every time they threaten someone or humiliate or hurt unnecessarily or dominate or reject another human being, they become forces for the creation of psychotherapy, even if these be small forces. Let them [also] recognize that every person who is kind, helpful, decent, psychologically democratic, affectionate, and warm, is a psychotherapeutic force even though a small one.[9]

A sensitivity to this aspect of choral leadership is necessary if choral musicians are to accomplish their musical goals through the people they serve.

Commitment to Teaching

In the most basic sense, every choral conductor is a teacher, a transmitter of knowledge and experience from one generation to another. This role not only presents an exciting opportunity for the choral musician, it creates an awesome responsibility as well. Teaching is a high calling. When we teach, we hold the potential of influencing lives for good or evil in our very hands. Students look to us as authority figures and often as personal counselors as well. Therefore when we assume the role of a teacher we must take our responsibility very seriously.

When we stop to think about it, teaching is not only a demanding role, it is a very complex activity as well. As such its boundaries are very difficult to define. This writer likes the definition of teaching which Pullias and Young offer:

> Teaching is many things. The teacher is many persons. Teaching is sometimes instructing, explaining or telling, yet very little can be "taught" in this sense. Teaching is waiting, but there is a time for action. Teaching involves demands that externally imposed standards be met, yet the best standards are self-made. The teacher is "learned" — he should know more than his students — but he is aware of deep ignorance and is in essence a learner. The teacher is, in the nature of the teaching-learning process, an example, yet he is stumblingly faulty; he has feet of clay. A teacher should be objective and detached, but probably the best teaching is [unpredictably] very much like a love affair.[10]

This writer views teaching as both a craft and an art. Clearly there is a great deal the "choral" teacher must know in order to be effective: the body of knowledge that makes up the field of choral music; the nature of the music learning process as practiced in rehearsals; something about human psychology and working successfully with people; and the social context in which the

---

[9] Quoted in: Pullias, Earl V. and James D. Young, *A Teacher is Many Things*. Bloomington: Indiana University Press, 1977, p. 90.

[10] *Ibid.,* p. 6.

learning takes place. These skills might be considered the "craft" of choral leadership. But one may know all of this and much more and still not be a successful teacher. Teaching is an art that demands a delicate balance of many factors: knowledge, skill, and traits of personality and character.

If we pause for a moment to draw an analogy from the field of musical performance, we discover that a great concert artist may possess a consummate knowledge of his craft and perform brilliantly as a soloist, but that knowledge alone does not necessarily make him an effective teacher nor does it guarantee that he will be a great conductor. There is something intangible involved here. The innate ability of the conductor to conceptualize the essence of the musical score and to communicate the musical symbols on the page in an effective non-verbal manner to a group of singers and/or instrumentalists, and through the musical ensemble to an audience, is the result of talent, insight, intelligence, musicianship, and a keen sense of musical style. In his monograph on *The Musical Experience*, Roger Sessions suggests that the agent of this recreation is the imagination of the conductor, or, if you will, his "personality."

> It is his task, and I believe his whole task, to apply his imagination to discovering the music [elements] inherent in the composer's own text, and then to reproducing them according to his own lights; that is, with the fullest partici-pation on his own part. This is only another way of saying that, having discovered as well as he can the composer's intentions, he must then apply himself to the task of reproducing them with the utmost conviction.[11]

The same can be said of teaching. It is fairly well recognized that there is a certain intangible element in the rehearsal experience that transforms knowledge into artistry. Knowledge can be achieved by careful and systematic study; but artistry involves imagination and personal style.

Knowledge and imagination then might be considered basic elements in the teacher-student relationship as it unfolds in the choral classroom. There is also one other, and it is one to which we have alluded earlier in this essay. To be effective the teacher must understand and respect the human personalities of the students, or in the case of those who do not work in an academic setting, the singers. The teaching-learning process involves a spirit of cooperation which goes beyond the narrow confines of the music-making event. It includes an intimate, articulate relation; the teacher (the presumably somewhat more mature learner); the student (the somewhat less mature learner); and the whole of life, which Alfred North Whitehead suggests is the true subject matter for all learning:

> The solution which I am urging is to eradicate the fatal disconnection of subjects which kills the vitality of our modern curriculum. There is only one subject-matter for education, and that is Life in all its manifestations.[12]

---

[11] Sessions, Roger, *The Musical Experience of Composer, Performer, Listener*. Princeton: Princeton University Press, 1950.

[12] Whitehead, Alfred North, *The Aims of Education and Other Essays*. New York: Mentor Books, 1957, p. 18.

What Whitehead is suggesting here is that all teaching is reinforcement, and for only one purpose: to prepare the student for a life-time of learning.

In the choral rehearsal the teacher must take great care to apply appropriate aspects of the subject matter she is teaching to a broader context so that it does, in fact, reinforce knowledge gained beyond the strict narrowness of the music field. For example, when rehearsing a specific piece of music the choral director is obliged to place the work in its general historical context, to deal with the text, its source and meaning, to discuss the style of the composition by relating appropriate information such as where the piece was first performed and for what purpose, etc. In an academic environment, the conductor must go further and use the rehearsal as a forum to teach about the elements of musical form, contrapuntal techniques, harmonic structure, and the more technical aspects of musical style. When this is done in a careful and systematic manner, the leader is a *teacher* as well as a *conductor*.

Commitment to Multi-Cultural Education

As we anticipate the demands of the twenty-first century it is clear that a central task of every choral conductor will be to provide a learning environment that will make all singers feel at home in the world, in all aspects of the culture in which they live. From the beginning of its history, America has been a "melting pot" of cultural diversity. It has been the one great world-wide experiment of cultural integration, where the oppressed and disenfranchised have sought and found refuge and come with dreams of personal fulfillment. They have come in waves since the seventeenth century, when the basic issue was freedom of religious expression. Each wave of new emigrants has created a distinctive need for new societal adjustments. In some cases our country has not handled these changes very well. Yet, on balance, we have probably done as well as any other country which has chosen to take the responsibility of emigration upon itself.

But the world in which we live today is a very different place than it was, for example, in the mid-twentieth century. Wars, political repression, the information explosion, world-wide satellite television, and MTV have brought other cultural practices to our very doorstep. We are now part of a "world" culture, whether we like it or not, and the choral art is a world-wide phenomenon. As a result, we must begin to assume a broader role than the one for which our undergraduate and graduate schools prepared us. The Western European model, while still a necessary and worthy context for the training of the choral musician, is no longer sufficient by itself to provide the only context for effective training and leadership. One only needs to visit cities like Los Angeles or Miami to learn very quickly that the majority population in these metropolitan areas is no longer Caucasian, but rather Hispanic. The same is true of towns along the Mexican border in Texas, New Mexico and Arizona. In Northern California the fastest growing minority population is, surprisingly enough, not Hispanic, but Asian. Consequently, we do not have to look very far or hard to discover "multiculturalism," even in our own country and among our own people. But the more important question is not that it exists, but how we, as leaders of the choral art in the twenty-first century will deal with this phenomenon. It is an issue that can no longer be ignored. Therefore let us consider some of the issues that are involved and then perhaps we can establish some basic guidelines for dealing with them.[13]

First, our approach must be positive and affirmative. Consequently, we should consider the multicultural issue as neither one of confrontation nor of redress. In a pluralistic society, the challenge of a multicultural choral program cannot be viewed as a matter of the music of one culture versus another. Nor can it be thought to mean only that the art of a repressed culture will finally gain its voice. It should not be the issue of a new chauvinism of emergence over the older one of dominance. This approach is doomed from the start because its fundamental premise is based on a *plus* versus *minus* mentality — my culture has this insight or that cognitive sensitivity, and yours does not. This point of view only prolongs the awkward ineffectiveness of confrontation and of cultural provincialism. As conductors of the choral art our first responsibility is to make our singers feel at home in a world where choral music is the right, privilege and natural expression of all people. Therefore we must accept our role as world citizens in the twenty-first century and make every effort to deal with this issue in a positive and affirmative manner.

The second concern that we must address is that multiculturalism in choral music is neither a matter of getting to know everything there is to know about the music of another culture nor of selective narrowness. This is a necessary principle for choral musicians to understand and apply. There are simply too many artistic languages out there — thousands of them — to bring even the most gifted scholar to factual fullness of even a few of them. Therefore, to attempt to make "ethnomusicologists" or "musical encyclopedists" out of our singers in the short period we spend with them is to perpetuate the error of learning as data transfer. No choral conductor should embrace this kind of superficiality. As to narrowness, the term "multiculturalism" means to many the selection of only one or two cultural expressions, primarily from preponderant minorities: Blacks, Hispanics, and certain Asians because they live in an area where these minorities predominate. This solution to the problem is flawed because it represents prescription over insight, formula over flexibility. Such efforts can be just as dogmatic and open to challenge as the school administrator's belief that the only literature worthy of study today is that of the contemporary "pop" idiom.

Multiculturalism in the choral art is not properly addressed until it fosters a positive spirit that encourages cultural nuance and diversity, instead of simply activating this or that vocabulary: a piece in this style, a work in that idiom. There will always be fewer units than there are cultures. Consequently the most important factor in any kind of sensitivity to multiculturalism is the attitude and openness one brings to this topic. Are we prepared to foster cultural diversity for the right reasons? If we say we are, we must then ask ourselves the next question: How really serious are we to take the time and make the effort to

---

[13] The author's thoughts on this subject have been influenced by Harold M. Best's article, "Arts Education: Culture, the Media, and the Church," in *Arts in Education*, September-October, 1988, pp. 2-10.

ensure that we have done all we can to provide our students with a true "multicultural" choral experience? If our answer to these questions is positive, then we must be prepared to move beyond superficial solutions in both the identification and performance of this music. The beneficiaries will be both ourselves and our singers!

The third principle for the choral musician who is really serious about this matter is that multiculturalism in the choral art is not the outgrowth of guilt feelings about another culture for what has been done to its people. As much as any decent human being should be indignant over maltreatment and oppression, there are other, more compelling reasons for the recognition of multiculturalism in the choral curriculum. If we are to accept the creative worth of someone else, we must do so as celebrators, increasingly coming to the understanding that love for another artistic vocabulary is hypocritical unless it is driven by a genuine love for the people who generate it. There is simply no substitute for this. If we truly love the people of other cultural backgrounds, we will love their art as well.

Finally, we must come to understand that multiculturalism is not cultural ambiguity. In the rush for inclusivity in the choral art — and there will be legitimate pressure to do so in the twenty-first century — there is the temptation to embrace the music of other cultures from an acentric point of view. It is here that Harold Best has some thoughtful advice for us:

> Centrism has needlessly become a tainted suffix. To be ethno- or culturally-centric need not be the same as to be prejudiced. Prejudice is an attitude about centrism — what's mine is mine, and what's your's is negotiable. But ethnocentrism can and should be something else: a consciousness of and love for one's own ways, so secure that their centrality becomes a guiding, organizing, and integrative force, of such peaceable resilience as to cry out for, and be nurtured by, the ways of others. The best multicultural education will of necessity distinguish between bias and prejudice, between centrism and superiority. It will help students understand that as individuals and citizens they can show preference without dominating and can reject without oppressing.[14]

This does not mean that the multiculturally sensitive choral musician is blind to quality. Cultural relationalism should never mean an absence of appraisal. Rather, when choices are made, however conductors and singers are taught to make them, a sense of excellence coupled with a pursuit for superior results should dominate the decision.

Once we have made our decision to perform a specific piece of multicultural choral literature, we are obliged to perform this music as authentically as possible. This is very important! We must put the same effort into the stylistic interpretation of this music as we do when we perform so-called "early music." For example, when we introduce the music of Black Americans to our choirs, we must be careful to make a basic distinction between the performance of a spiritual and a gospel song. This seems so basic when it appears in print, but

---

[14] Ibid., p. 10

there are choral programs in this country where even this most basic of all performance practice distinctions is not made. While emerging from the same cultural roots, the spiritual and the gospel song represent two very different art forms, and the historical integrity of each must be honored. If we do not seriously search for this kind of authenticity in our approach to the music of other cultures, we run the risk of having our singers accuse us of perpetuating a double standard (a kind of musical hypocrisy, if you will). We spend years of study in the performance of Western music (taking workshops; running around the world looking at European churches, castles, and concert halls; sitting at the feet of "performance practice gurus" — and it is important that we do this), yet we often make no serious attempt to apply this same standard of performance to the music of another culture. Little wonder that we look a little silly to our singers. This is an indictment that no choral musician should have to face in a multicultural society.

What we are saying here is that the choral music of any culture is indeed fit for inclusion in a choral program if it meets the same universal standard of excellence that we apply to all the music we place in front of our singers. And we are saying something else as well: in today's choral programs the choral art of no one culture can be considered superior to another in its readiness to speak to us and our audiences. Any artistic language is capable of expressing musical ideas with integrity. This is a very important principle for contemporary choral musicians to understand and practice. It is also one of the significant opportunities the choral conductor will face in the twenty-first century.

Commitment to a Vision of Greatness for Our Singers

Why is it necessary for a choral ensemble to perform the "best" music? This is a question that really should not have to be asked. The answer is obvious. But if it needs to be raised, it would seem to have a logical answer in something like this: because studying the finest choral literature brings the singer into contact with inspired works of art, profound texts from the Bible and other great works of literature — from which one can learn and grow — and provides the opportunity to express musical ideas which are the product of exceptionally fine minds. The problem is that fewer and fewer choral directors in our society are encouraged to make their rehearsal rooms the center of great teaching and learning.

At the risk of alienating the educational establishment, it must be stated by anyone who has any insight whatsoever into the schooling of our children that there is a virtual crisis in the average learning community today. And it is particularly acute in the field of music education. Somewhere along the line the arts have lost their role as academic disciplines and have become, in the minds of many school administrators and school boards, frills which exist for a purpose other than to become an integral part of a child's education. The result of this situation is an attitude on the part of administrators and boards of education that places the arts in a precarious position: "Since serious work is not taking place in the music rehearsal room, then why should this aspect of the curriculum be funded when school budgets are tight?"

Whether this circumstance has come about because 1) musicians have projected a helpful and cooperative spirit by providing "pop" choirs, "show" choirs, "jazz" choirs, and even "caroling" groups for public relations, fund raising, and community efforts; 2) it has been necessary in building our programs to support the athletic activities of our schools with marching bands, drill teams, and "pep" bands; or 3) our society is so overtaken with contemporary culture and MTV that it has forgotten the role that aesthetic education has played in the past in public and private education — somehow we have lost sight of the purpose of music in the education of our children. *We, as choral leaders at all levels of musical activity, must take a leadership role in turning this situation around.* We simply must become a pro-active force for change in our communities. This is a challenge of choral leadership that cannot be ignored.

Throughout the ages an important ingredient in this process has been the study of the products of the great minds of the past in the fields of art, sculpture, literature, and music: the writings of Chaucer, Shakespeare, and Langston Hughes; the sculptures of Bernini and Michelangelo; the paintings of Leonardo, Picasso, and Diego Rivera; and might we even say, the music of Bach, Mozart and Burleigh. We have gone to school to learn what we cannot or will not learn on our own.

What should constitute the curriculum of the liberally educated person in the twenty-first century? This is a question that has baffled educational administrators for centuries, beginning with those of classical Greece. When faced with a similar inquiry in his day, Plato expressed the following opinion:

> When a Greek Boy has learned his letters and is beginning to understand what is written, [his teachers] put into his hands the works of the great poets, and he reads them on his bench at school; and they contain many admonitions and stories and praise of famous men of old, which he is required to learn by heart, in order that he may imitate or emulate them.[15]

It is this principle that Alfred North Whitehead seeks to reinforce when he writes:

> Moral education is impossible without the habitual vision of greatness . . . . An atmosphere of excitement, arising from imaginative consideration [of greatness] transforms knowledge. A fact is no longer a bare fact: it is invested with all its possibilities. It is no longer a burden on the memory: it is energized as the poet of our dreams, and as the architect of our purposes.[16]

This vision of greatness is a necessary ingredient in our choral programs today. The importance of music as an academic discipline must be re-established in the minds of administrators, board members, and parents. What better place is there to start than in the choral classroom?

---

15 Plato, *The Republic.*

16 Whitehead, Alfred North, *The Aims of Education and Other Essays.* London: Williams and Northgate Ltd., 1929, pp. 139-140.

One word of caution must be raised at this point in the discussion. We make a mistake in music education when we look only to Western Civilization for our exemplars of quality. This vision of greatness about which Whitehead speaks is found in every culture. Our task as choral musicians is to discover these models within multicultural resources as well as from our traditional repertory. Remember, one of the goals of choral leadership is to create the environment that will make our students feel at home in the world in which they live.

Commitment to Festivals and Celebrations

Thus far in this chapter we have concentrated on the multi-faceted challenge of choral leadership. Admittedly it has been a rather heavy discussion because the responsibilities of choral leadership are important ones. In these closing paragraphs, however, it might be a good change of pace to share a different kind of thought: the importance of putting the choral experience in its proper perspective by ensuring that we and our singers have fun at what we do — that we learn the importance of "celebrating" what we accomplish together.

Choral musicians are the hardest working people in the music profession, or so it seems. There is always so much to be done, and we often have limited resources — both human and fiscal — with which to achieve the results, so we work and work and work! Hard work is critical to success in choral music, but we also must take time to have some fun together.

Have you ever wondered why choral festivals normally take place at the end of the year? It is not only because it takes the entire year for us to learn our music. It is that festivals and celebrations serve as a kind of capstone to the experience of singing together. The final concert of the year accomplishes the same purpose for collegiate and community choruses.

Festivals have had a close relationship with music and the arts since prehistoric times. They have been special times in the history of the church, the school, and the community. In the Genesis narrative we are told that even the Creator rested from his labors on the seventh day and contemplated with joy the work he had done. And we are also told that when he sat back and contemplated what he had created, he discovered that it was "good!" Might we even speculate that the angels celebrated this event with a *Gloria in excelsis* of their own? This was probably the first festival of any kind. After the Creator had completed his work, he rested — he contemplated — and he rewarded himself with a celebration, a "festival" if you please. Therefore, contemplation is a necessary part of the choral experience.

Joseph Pieper, a twentieth century German theologian, has written extensively about the importance of celebration as a means of putting things in perspective. He suggests that festivals and periods of contemplation help us keep in tune with the world:

> The day of rest is not just a neutral interval inserted as a link in the chain of a workaday life. It entails a loss of utilitarian profit. In voluntarily keeping the holiday, men renounce the yield of a day's labor. This renunciation has from time to time immemorial been regarded as an essential element of festivity. As an animal for sacrifice was taken from the herd, so a piece of available time was

expressly withdrawn from utility. The day of rest, then, meant not only that no work was done, but also that an offering was being made of the yield of labor. This, then, unexpectedly brings us to a new aspect of a holiday. A festival is essentially a phenomenon of wealth, not, to be sure, the wealth of money, but of existential richness.[17]

From this it follows that some kind of corporate contemplation of work accomplished should become a regular event in the life of every choral ensemble; a time when the group sits back, has fun, travels together, and celebrates what it has accomplished. Every choral group should experience the joy of a choral festival, perhaps even annually. These are events that can be marked by a kind of self-forgetting delirium. Festivals take us out of our regular routine — and really out of ourselves — and place what we do in a larger context. Without the power to celebrate, to contemplate what we have accomplished, to perform before others, to demonstrate what we have learned, what we do as a group can be greatly diminished. On the other hand, the fruit of festivity is the rebirth or transformation or renewal of the participants.

However, simply taking time off from a regular rehearsal is something that we cannot do without sufficient reason. The idea of "valuable working time" is, after all, not just idle talk; something quite real is involved. Why should we do this if there is not a good reason? If we probe a little more deeply for a purpose, we discover a curious relationship to the other, the contemplative aspect of the day of rest, to which we have just referred. The achievement of contemplation — the art of stepping back and enjoying what has been accomplished — is a recognition of our state of satisfaction with what we do and another aspect of being at home in the world, if you please. Precisely in the same way, the act of freely giving of oneself cannot take place unless it grows from the root of a comprehensive affirmation of what we do — for which no better term can be found than "love." We do not renounce things, then, except for love. Joy is an expression of love. The joy of the choral experience comes from the love of it. This is the overall goal for which every choral conductor at every level of activity should strive: to create the rehearsal and performance environment that will cause each member of the choral ensemble to feel so at home that they truly love what they do.

The inner structure of real festivity has been captured in a profound way by Chrysostom in a little phrase that we have come to know through a lovely motet by Maurice Duruflé:

Ubi caritas gaudet, ibi est festivas.

Where love rejoices, there is festivity.

To truly love what we do and to communicate this love to those with whom we work is the ultimate challenge of choral leadership!

---

[17] Pieper, Joseph, *An Anthology*. San Francisco: Ignatius Press, 1989, p. 151.

Choral Literature: Research References, Current Sources, and Future Directions

Timothy W. Sharp

Introduction

The search for accurate choral sources is similar to studying maps. Maps, like choral sources, come in different types. If you are visiting an area where you must know street names to find a specific address, a grid map outlining every street is very helpful. It is also possible to look at a topographical map of the exact area you are going to visit on the street map. The topographical map, however, would not have street names or crossings, but would rather have bodies of water, land elevations, and other geographical features. Both maps would offer a description of the area, but from two very different perspectives.

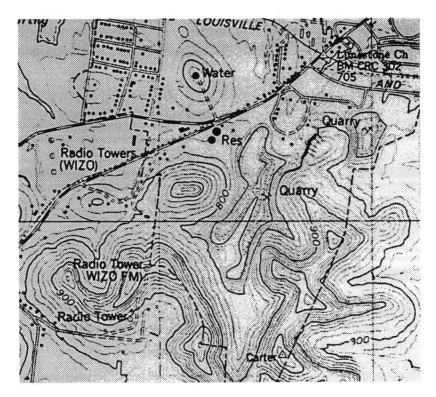

Topographical Map

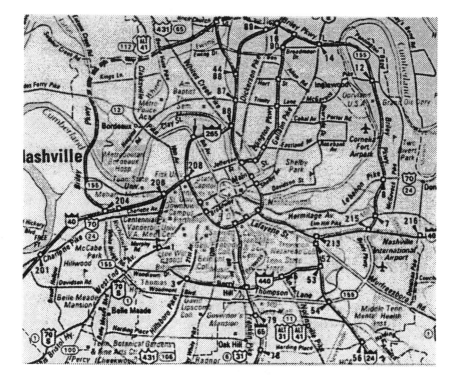

Street Grid Map

The search for accurate editions of choral music is similar to choosing a map for studying a geographical location. One edition may give a picture of the choral work, while another edition may be based on the same music, but marked quite differently. Both are representations of the music, but, like maps, describe the musical landscape from two different perspectives. The map itself is obviously not a destination or place, and similarly, the musical score is not the music.

They both describe an environment through printed symbols — the map describes land space, while the musical score describes sound space. A map uses lines, spaces, and circles. Similarly, the musical score uses lines, spaces, and circles. In the year 1492 the navigator Columbus charted a course on a map. In the same year, the composer Josquin charted compositions on a musical score. And today in jazz compositions, musical scores are actually called "charts," a term which makes the comparison to a map reasonable.

When looking at a street map we are often looking for very specific information. For example, we want to know how to get to the center of town. When looking at a musical score, we also need very specific information. Not only do we need to know the correct notes to sing or play, but we also look for the desired degree of loudness or softness to play, indications of tempo, and other important interpretive musical characteristics as intended by the composer.

Returning to the map analogy, if we want to know why a street takes the direction that it takes or why a series of streets suddenly come to a dead end, a street map may be inadequate for explanation. In these instances, a topographical map may show a river, a mountain, or a cliff which explains the reason the street map looks the way it looks. Similarly, one musical source may give a fair representation of the sound of a piece of music, but that representation may not be complete. In order to find the complete description of the music through a printed score, a more accurate or complete source may need to be consulted. Like the topographical map, there are some musical sources that present a more complete picture than others.

The challenge to cartographers is to project the three-dimensional reality of geography onto a flat surface—a process that leads inevitably to distortion. The challenge to composers is to project the representation of sound onto the soundless medium of the musical score—a seemingly impossible concept. This chapter will describe the sources available to help the choral conductor more accurately discover the musical intentions of the composer, and it will identify the most commonly used sources for finding choral literature.

Choral Sources

Where do you go to find ideas for a program of Renaissance choral music? How do you know if the edition is reliable? Where do you go to find a choral piece written on a particular text? Where can you find a complete listing of a composer's choral works? How can you find out if a choral piece is still in print? Before you leave on your choral journey, you must first know where you are headed. This chapter is written to give answers to the above practical questions as well as to outline a research system to discover sources for choral literature.

It stands to reason that on any journey the more you know about the lay of the land, the more you will understand and appreciate what you see on the journey. Similarly, a broader view of choral musical sources leads to greater understanding, informed choices, and greater appreciation of the music chosen.

Choral musicians often know choral music literature the same way they know about anything—by what they have experienced in the past. This bank of knowledge begins early through choral experiences in school, community, or church. Beginning with what we have been taught and from what we already know is a very important and valuable starting place. It is also important to realize that inherited knowledge of choral literature may have been appropriate for the ensemble in which one was performing at an earlier time, but a particular literature's appropriateness may not apply to other ensembles. For this reason, the study and understanding of choral literature sources is a very important part of the choral musician's education.

Identifying Sources

In order to choose choral literature that will give confidence in the building of a program, the type of choral literature you want to study or perform must first be identified. The questions you will want to ask are the following:

1. What is the desired musical period or periods for the program?
2. Who is the composer of the music and what is the source for the text?

3. What is the desired voicing ?

4. Is the choral piece a major work or smaller in scope ?

After these questions have been considered, the next area of questioning is in regard to the type of source you want to consult. Source materials used by the choral researcher like sources used by the historiographer are approached from two levels: primary and secondary sources.[1]

Primary and Secondary Sources

Primary sources are original documents and are considered to be the most reliable sources of research information. This is "firsthand" information. When data are not original to the researcher they become "secondhand," or secondary sources. Secondary sources represent varying degrees of likeness to primary sources. They also vary in degrees of reliability due to increased levels of remoteness from the original sources and the various levels of the strength of scholarship used in the editing of the secondary sources. If the data are even further removed from the originals, tertiary documents may exist. The distinctions between primary sources, secondary sources, and tertiary sources require that we consider the following questions before beginning the search for the desired choral edition:

• Does the choral literature sought merit the study of original sources?
• If so, is it possible to view the original manuscript or a facsimile?
• If not, are scholarly secondary editions available?
• Are reliable editions available for use in performance?

Understanding the Nature of Choral Sources

The information we know about choral music comes from four principle sources:

• Documents of record—such as programs or newspaper accounts.
• Essays and treatises on the theory and practice of music.
• Composer biographies or contemporary accounts.
• The musical score itself.[2]

Choral conductors and performers would seem to be working with the most important source, the actual musical score. However as has been stated, all musical sources are not the same. The choral score in the hands of the choral singer is by the very nature of the publication process at least one step removed, if not many steps removed, from the primary source—the composer's original manuscript.

The fact of the matter is, some choral editions are more accurate than others. The most correct edition of a choral score is the one that most precisely conveys the final intentions of the composer. Friedrich Hänssler, senior editor of the publishing firm Hänssler-Verlag of Stuttgart, states that the ideal edition

---

[1] Phelps, Roger, *A Guide to Research in Music Education.* 2nd Ed., New Jersey: The Scarecrow Press, Inc., 1980, p. 125.

[2] Westrup, Jack, *An Introduction to Musical History.* 2nd Ed., London: Hutchinson and Co., Ltd., 1978, p. 20.

is one that "seeks to accurately present the composer's last wish for the composition."[3]

However, determining the exact intentions of the composer is not as simple as rendering an exact duplication of the original manuscript. Such a rendering would fail to convey to the modern audience matters such as the reconciliation of differences in possible duplicate versions of the original manuscript, differences in notation practice between the time of the original manuscript and today, and questions regarding original performance practice. Therefore, to understand the nature of editions, we must have an understanding of music editing and printing.

Music Printing

Simply stated, the process of editing music is the art of preparing a manuscript for publication. Prior to the advent of personal desktop printing and personal computer notation software, composers depended on publishers and engravers to typeset and publish an accurate rendering of their musical composition.

The process of musical printing was developed at the turn of the sixteenth century by Petrucci, whose first publication appeared in 1501.[4] Prior to this, musical scores were copied by hand. The earliest musical scores that we know today originally existed in manuscript form only. Multiple copies frequently are found for the same music, but those editions were copies from other editions, which sometimes can be traced back to the original manuscript.

It took some time before music printing was a universal process. Many of the choral pieces from English sources in the sixteenth and even into the seventeenth centuries are found only in manuscript. There are many compositions of early periods that have never been printed. Practically all of J. S. Bach's cantatas and Passions were not printed until after his death. Of the hundreds of compositions by Mozart, only seventy were published during the composer's lifetime.

Commercial music printing has always been a costly process and remains so today. In earlier times, manuscripts were passed back and forth and along within a community of composers. It was not until the eighteenth century that collections of printed music were more generally available. The scope of the publication was defined by the laws of supply and demand, a law which still governs the publication process.

The publication of a full choral score as we know today began in the late 1500's with the four-part madrigals of de Rore.[5] This publication process enabled all parts of a work to be visible—for an organist to play or for study as an exercise in music theory. In time, the more performers involved in the performance of a work the more it was necessary for the conductor to see a full score. This need eventually led to multiple publication of the full choral score.

---

[3] Friedrich H. Hänssler, President, Hänssler-Verlag, Stuttgart. Interview, Minneapolis: October 13, 1990.

[4] Westrup, p. 20.

[5] Westrup, p. 22.

Editorial Process

Choral editions are only as good as the scholarship that led to their publication. The ideal that any editor is working toward is a trustworthy representation of the musical intentions of the original composer. In modern times, if the composer is living, the published edition has the opportunity to accurately represent the composer's musical intentions. However, even under these conditions mistakes are made in the printing process. These are often corrected in a second printing, but many original printings of the incorrect score will be available and widely distributed before a choral publication is reprinted.

If the published choral score is from an earlier musical period, the editorial process is critical to an accurate publication. Editorial methods may vary greatly. The importance of the editor in the process cannot be overstressed; the results are crucial. The motivation to publish historical works is to get worthy music to the attention of the choral community. Therefore, any form of simplification which makes the music immediately accessible to the greatest number of people is desirable.[6] But whatever form simplification of notation may take, the overriding caveat is to convey accuracy.

Therefore, the most important editorial marking is that indication which distinguishes between what is original and what has been supplied or emended by the editor. Any information provided by the editor is valid, as long as the editor demonstrates the original musical markings and explains what has happened in regard to the original. The choral scholar must be certain that nothing has been changed from the original without some indication in the score. The use of editorial brackets or parentheses is the common indicator of information supplied by the editor to distinguish it from original material.

Toward Ideal Sources

The ideal for every choral conductor is to have scholarly scores informed by the original choral manuscript. The opportunity to see the exact musical markings made by the composer brings great understanding and confidence to the research, interpretation, and performance process. However, original scores before the 1500's are extremely rare. This is true of all early editions and in diminishing levels of rarity as the process of music printing progressed through the centuries.

Therefore, choral conductors, like researchers of any music, must depend upon editions of the original manuscript for study and performance. Fortunately for choral musicians, much of the choral music of earlier times remained in use well beyond its time of composition due to its relationship to the church and the relatively stable nature of the liturgy and consistent core of text sources.

In the latter part of the eighteenth century choral musicians began to be very interested in music of earlier periods. Prior to this, publications were primarily devoted to new compositions. This growing awareness of the choral music of earlier times led to the availability of great choral pieces from bygone eras. This interest was paralleled by advances in music printing and publication. The music

---

[6] Westrup, p. 28.

of Bach, Handel, Mozart, and Haydn proliferated due to such interest and printing advances. The attention to music from the past was accompanied by an equal interest in accurate editions of historical music. Unsuccessful attempts were made as early as 1760 at preparing complete editions of the works of early composers. These attempts paved the way for later successful complete editions of early composer's works, such as the publication of the Bach-Gesellschaft in 1850.[7]

The Bach-Gesellschaft set new standards of scholarship for historical editions. By 1900, complete historical editions became the rule rather than the exception, with complete editions being published or begun for the works of Mendelssohn, Palestrina, Mozart, di Lassus, Schütz, Schubert, Victoria, Brahms, Buxtehude, Haydn, and other important choral composers.

Furthermore, the publication of complete scholarly editions of the major composers brought attention to lesser known composers which have contributed masterpieces to the choral repertoire. Series of volumes devoted to single works by individual composers or to selections from the works of several composers exist today from several sources. The most significant of these series have been published by scholarly societies.

The Search for the Right Source

In order to begin the search for choral literature, you should ask the following questions at the outset of every choral music choice:

1. What kind of literature do I want to study or program?
2. What is the best source for the choral literature identified?
3. What process do I follow in order to review the source identified?

In general, the term historical edition may be applied to any music publication that is devoted to a past repertory.[8] The serious choral investigator and/or performer is interested in investigating scholarly editions, also termed critical editions. Such published historical editions are based upon an editorial process which involves comparing and contrasting the original composer's manuscript or other historical editions based upon the original manuscript.

The alternative to the historical/critical edition is the performance edition. The performance edition involves an editorial process which may, but does not necessarily use primary or scholarly secondary sources. The performance edition often does not footnote or reference its sources, and often incorporates editorial markings designed to assist in a modern performance.

Going back to the map analogy used at the beginning of this chapter, the street map differs from the topographical map in many ways, even though they may depict the same land area. Similarly, the historical or critical edition and the performance edition need not be mutually exclusive in editorial process, but the fact that they are intended for two different audiences usually determines the choices made in the editorial process. The scholar expects the historical or

---

[7] Westrup, p. 27.

[8] Sadie, Stanley, ed., *The New Grove Dictionary of Music and Musicians.* London: MacMillan Publishers Ltd., 1980. "Editions," p. 848.

critical choral edition to indicate through verbal description and footnotes research relative to the understanding of the original manuscript. The performer on the other hand expects the performance edition to render a score which is honest to the intentions of the composer, yet easily readable in a performance setting. The performance edition does not distract the performer with possibly confusing notation alternatives and descriptions printed in the musical score.

The historical edition is found in either a collected edition which contains a composer's complete compositional output, or in an anthology which contains a variety of works of a similar genre. A facsimile in which the primary source is reproduced with or without scholarly commentary is considered a category of

Grant to me, O God, a Pure Heart
Schaffe in mir, Gott ein reines Herz
Psalm 51:10-12

English Translation by
Bradley Greenwald and Paul Oakley

Andreas Hammerschmidt
1612-1675

For rehearsal only

Piano reduction by Paul Oakley

Urtext Edition of Andreas Hammerschmidt's
Schaffe in mir, Gott, ein reines Herz.

the collected edition. Collected editions, anthologies, and facsimiles are usually available in ongoing series published by musicological societies and usually found in libraries.

Performance editions exist separately as independent publications due to their practical function as a performance copy for either conductor or performer. Performance editions are pubished in large quantities because of the needs of the choral performing ensembles for which they are intended. Performance editions are usually found by searching the catalogs of music publishers.

As stated above, historical editions are based upon primary and secondary sources. Performance editions may also be based upon primary or secondary sources, as in the case of the "Urtext" edition. "Urtext" is a term applied to a modern printed edition of earlier music in which the aim is to present a literal

Autograph Copy of Manuscript, C. P. E. Bach's *Magnificat.*

rendering of the original score without editorial additions or alterations.[9]

Although it is greatly preferred for editors to include references to source materials, many performance editions do not indicate sources. If sources are not referenced, the performer must either take the responsibility of comparing the performance edition to critical source materials, or trust the scholarship of the editor to be true to the original intentions of the composer.

Acquiring Sources

After determining the literature type and the source desired, the final step is to acquire the edition of the choral musical score. In some instances, more than one source may be identified. In other instances, the desired choral score may not be available. When beginning the quest for the source and edition desired, it is important to note the descriptive elements regarding the composition:

1. Title of composition
2. Composer and author or text source
3. Editor
4. Vocal setting
5. Publisher and/or Distributor
6. Item number
7. Copyright date or publication date

It is the rare and privileged one who has the opportunity to view original manuscripts of early music, especially if the musical score is a choral classic. It is important to know that such works are indeed available and can be viewed. As you would expect, rare and important original documents are kept under lock and key and behind glass or in environmentally protected libraries or vaults. These are typically found at the important research libraries, national libraries, and national archives. However, under special conditions, such material can be viewed.

When the viewing of the original document is either difficult or impossible, it is quite possible for the choral researcher to refer to a photographic facsimile. Manuscripts dating from as early as medieval works are available through facsimile editions.

If a facsimile is not available for the desired choral score, the study of a primary source is still possible through photostats specially ordered, or through microfilm or microfiche copies. Libraries and archives which have acquired historical manuscripts often make these resources available through copy services. Such formats are relatively inexpensive to acquire and are excellent sources for study. The availability of important works through photostat copies, microfilm, and microfiche have made scholarship possible on a much broader scale, allowing researchers to command the resources of libraries around the world.

The next step for study beyond photographed likenesses of the originals comes through scholarly historical editions. Typically, such editions describe the

---

[9] Apel, Willi, ed., *Harvard Dictionary of Music.* 2nd ed., Cambridge: Belknap Press, 1969, p. 471.

original sources on which the modern edition is based as well as other sources for information employed. Information regarding modern scholarly editions has been consistently chronicled through journals and other periodicals dealing with historical musicology. Information about the primary sources on which modern editions are based is best obtained from the editions themselves, but this information may need to be amplified by consulting the catalogs of printed and manuscript music in a major research library.

Indispensable reference books, dissertations, and catalogs exist today for locating both historical editions and performance editions of choral scores. Such reference materials are available in libraries which focus on music research.

Due to the expense involved in preparing and publishing historical editions, libraries are generally the only place historical collections are found. Performance editions, on the other hand, are affordable for individuals interested in collecting and studying specific compositions. Performance editions are published with the intention of making them available to choirs and conductors on a mass scale for performance. Libraries are less likely to shelve individual performing editions of small choral compositions. However, major works such as oratorios and cantatas are often found in libraries. The performer interested in locating performing editions of smaller choral works must contact publishers or retail choral music suppliers directly to secure a particular composition. Only the most popular of performing editions stay in print for extended periods.

References for Finding Sources

The most thorough and accessible list of historical editions in English is found in A. H. Heyer's *Historical Sets, Collected Editions, and Monuments of Music: A Guide to Their Contents.*[10] The most recent edition of Heyer's monumental work includes the complete editions of the music of individual composers and the major collections of music that have been published or are in the process of publication. The form of each entry follows the form of the Library of Congress card. Each entry contains the composer or compiler of the collection, the title, the place of publication, the publisher, the date of publication, the paging or number of volumes, and a brief description of illustrative material. After any special notes, a listing of the contents is given.

Three other English language works are also very helpful for identifying historical editions. These are the bibliography listing in *Historical Musicology* by L. B. Spiess,[11] the list of historical editions published in ongoing series found in Willi Apel's *Harvard Dictionary of Music*[12] under the entry "Editions, historical," and a similar listing found in *The New Grove Dictionary of Music and Musicians*[13] edited by Stanley Sadie. The German musical encyclopedia *Die Musik in Geschichte und Gegenwart* is another standard reference for scholars seeking historical editions. Collected editions and their contents are listed in this

---

[10] Heyer, A. H., *Historical Sets, Collected Editions, and Monuments of Music: A Guide to Their Contents.* Chicago: American Library Association, 1980.

[11] Spiess, L. B., *Historical Musicology.* 1963.

[12] Apel.

[13] Sadie.

German language reference under the heading "Denkmäler," meaning "monuments." At the end of this chapter is a selected list from the many historical sets and editions found in the above references. The annotation for this list gives an indication of the type of contents that will be found in the actual edition and collection.

```
BACH, JOHANN SEBASTIAN (1685-1750)
   Aeolus Appeased  *see
        Zufriedengestellte Aeolus, Der

   Air
      (Asti) SATB oct VOLKWEIN VB7711
         $.45                        (B85)

   All Nature Is Smiling (from Cantata
        "Weichet Nur")
      unis cor NOVELLO 48.1866.00 f.s.
                                    (B86)
   Allsvaldige, Ditt Lov Forkunna
      mix cor NORDISKA 4386 f.s.    (B87)

   Allt Ar Redo, Kom Att Njuta
      mix cor NORDISKA 3620 f.s.    (B88)

   Amore Traditore (Cantata No. 203) BWV
        203
      [Ger] cor,pno voc sc KALMUS 6639
         $1.25                      (B89)

   Auf, Schmetternde Tone (Cantata No.
        207) BWV 207
      "Auf, Schmetternde Tone" [Ger] cor,
        pno voc sc KALMUS 6643 $1.25
                                    (B90)
      (Todt, B.) mix cor,SATB soli,hpsd,
        2fl,3ob,bsn,3trp,strings,timp voc
        sc BREITKOPF-L EB7207A $1.25, ipr
                                    (B91)
   Auf, Schmetternde Tone  *see Auf,
      Schmetternde Tone

   Auf, Schmetternde Tone Der Muntern
        Trompeten  *BWV 207a, cant
      mix cor,SATB soli,cont,2fl,3ob,
        3trp,strings,timp cor pts
        BREITKOPF-W CHB 5087 f.s., cmplt
        ed BREITKOPF-W rent, pno red
        BREITKOPF-W EB6971           (B92)

   August, Lebe, Lebe Konig
      (Tillinghast) "May You Ever, Ever
        Prosper!" [Eng/Ger] SSA WARNER
        W3575 $.30                   (B93)

   Ausgewahlte Choralsatze  *CCU
      (Burkhardt, H.; Lipphardt, W.)
        [Ger] SATB,cont,opt treb inst/
        bass inst (easy) BAREN. BA 873
        f.s.                         (B94)
```

Excerpt from listing in *Secular Choral Music in Print*. Used by permission, Musicdata, Inc., Philadelphia, Pennsylvania.

Similarly, the most complete reference for locating available performing editions is the multi-volume *Choral Music in Print* series.[14] *Choral Music in Print* includes all published choral music intended for performance by choral ensembles. The series is an ongoing effort to locate and catalog all music in print throughout the world. The intention is to cover all areas of music as rapidly as

---

[14] *Choral Music in Print.* 2nd ed., Philadelphia: Musicdata, Inc.

resources permit, as well as to provide a mechanism for keeping the information up to date. The *Choral Music in Print* series is divided into two parts, *Sacred Choral Music in Print*[15] and *Secular Choral Music in Print*.[16] Since 1973 this series has solicited catalogs and listings from music publishers throughout the world. Using the information supplied by cooperating publishers, the series lists specific editions which are available from a publisher either for sale or on a rental basis in appropriate categories.

Many other listings of performing editions exist by type of music. *Canadian Music for Women's Voices* edited by Apfelstadt,[17] *American Choral Music for Women's Chorus Since 1960* edited by Crews,[18] and *Christian Music Directories: Print Music* published by Resource Publications[19] are three of the many listings available for locating currently available performing editions by specific choral literature type.

The technology exists today and is being used in a limited commercial arena for viewing printed editions through images delivered electronically and viewed on a computer screen. In this process, printed editions are scanned and transferred into a digital format on CD ROM. Images stored on the CD ROM can be viewed on screen or printed. This process is now in full commercial use with popular performing editions.[20] This technology can be adapted for future scholarly editions which would allow a full library of scholarly and performing editions to be available to the widest possible audience.

Laser technology allows the transference of more than eight thousand pages of information to one three and one-half inch compact disc.[21] When this process becomes completely economical for all users, the printing of editions as we now know them may become irrelevant.

Elements Contributing to an Excellent Edition

It is entirely possible to edit an historical manuscript oneself. In fact, the best way to understand the process that contributes to an edition is to work through the various steps necessary for producing an accurate historical edition. The first step is to seek out the best sources for the work one is to edit. This step requires securing primary or secondary sources and assessing the accuracy and reliability of these sources.[22] This task is less difficult if there is only a single source for the desired composition.

---

[15] Daugherty, F. Mark and Eslinger, Gary S., eds., *Sacred Choral Music in Print.* 2nd ed., Philadelphia: Musicdata, Inc., 1985.

[16] Daugherty, F. Mark and Eslinger, Gary S., eds., *Secular Choral Music in Print.* 2nd ed., Philadelphia: Musicdata, Inc., 1985.

[17] Apfelstadt, Hilary, *Canadian Music for Women's Voices.* Spectrum Music, 1989.

[18] Crews, Thomas, Jr., *American Choral Music for Women's Chorus Since 1960.* University of Washington, unpublished doctoral dissertation, 1987.

[19] Guentert, Kenneth, ed., *Christian Music Directories: Print and Recorded Music.* San Jose: Resource Publications, 1990.

[20] Breeden, Frank, President, Keynotes. FAX memorandum, Nashville, July 31, 1992.

[21] Barker, Joel Arthur, *Future Edge.* New York: William Morrow, 1992, p. 145.

[22] Sadie, "Editing," pp.839–840.

The second step in the editorial process is to compare and take into account all versions deemed reliable for the desired work. If there are several sources for the desired composition, the editor must compare and contrast these sources, always keeping in mind that the intent is to discover as best as one can how carefully the source mirrors the composer's final intentions.

The next step in the editorial process is to consider the notation devices used in the original work, and then make decisions how best to convey the original markings into notation that has meaning to the modern reader. For early music, this is a particularly difficult task. Even as late as the eighteenth and nineteenth centuries, notation markings conveyed meanings that are interpreted differently today. The modern editor must decide whether to keep the original marking and explain the modern difference for interpretation in footnotes, or change the marking to convey modern meaning, again noting the editorial change by way of footnotes.

The fourth step in the editorial process is to consider the performance practice factor. The editor must consider how the work was intended to sound during the period in which it was written. What implications do these facts have upon a modern performing edition? Composers in earlier times often left some notation or interpretive markings off their manuscript, leaving some decisions to the performer. This meant that there was a difference between how the manuscript looked and how it actually sounded. For example, in the Baroque period composers used a formula called figured bass to indicate the harmony desired for a composition. The informed keyboard player knew to render the indicated figured bass into a correct performance. However, what does the modern editor do with such markings? This is one example of the performance practice considerations every historical editor must face.

Finally, the editor must decide who is the intended audience for the edition. In other words, is the edition intended to be a performing edition, or is the final work an historical critical edition intended for scholarly study. Or, is the final edition intended to satisfy both performance and scholarly study? The Urtext edition attempts to convey the original composer's composition without editorial markings. Such an edition translates into modern notation all the notes and details of the original manuscript. At the other extreme is a heavily edited performance edition. Characteristics of the pragmatic performance edition are exact markings for various interpretive characteristics. Such an edition makes the work immediately available for a wide group of performers. These two extremes in types of editions do not need to be mutually exclusive. If the editor is careful to clearly indicate editorial additions and interpretations from what was in the original manuscript, an edition can be both a scholarly edition and a performance edition.

Summary

This chapter began by comparing cartography to choral musicology. Both the map and the musical score are two-dimensional descriptions of environments that are seemingly impossible to represent with complete accuracy. Neither the map nor the choral score take the place of what is being represented.

The map points the way to a location; the musical score reveals, in a limited way, the aural intentions of the composer.

After determining the type of choral literature desired — along with essential descriptive information such as composer, type of work, and author of text — the quest for the most appropriate study and performance source can begin. Sources are divided into two types: primary sources and secondary sources. Primary sources are regarded as the most accurate and dependable sources. Such sources are rare to view, but not impossible. Secondary sources are based upon original manuscripts, but are by the nature of the copying, printing, and publishing process, at least one step removed from the originals. Secondary sources may come in the form of copies of the original manuscript, facsimiles, or photocopies of the original manuscript.

Included under the category of secondary sources are scholarly editions and performance editions. Such editions convey the material as seen through primary sources, and also document the rationale and source for any editorial changes made to the original documents. Scholarly editions are helpful in the research process only to the degree that they thoroughly document any and all changes made to the original documents. Performance editions allow a wide audience access to the music through an easily readable choral score. A third type of source may exist when an edition of a choral work is made from a secondary source. The value of such a source is only as good as the editor's indications of what is original material and what has been added or changed.

Conclusion

In the analogy of the map to the musical score, a map which demonstrates mountains, plains, and valleys, as well as rivers, lakes and oceans, enables the reader to better understand all that revolves around the surrounding geography. Similarly, the inquiry into the varying levels of choral musical sources throws the essential musical material into relief, casting light on what scholarship has already been accomplished and pointing out the existing shadows where choral scholarship is still needed.

Sample Listing of Historical Edition Series[23]

L'Arte musicale in italia. Ed. L. Torchi. 7 vols., 1897-1908; reprinted with corrections, n.d. c. 1958.

Biblioteca de Catalunya: Bilioteca central. Publicaciones de la seccion de musica, Barcelona. Ed. H. Angles and others, 1921-.

I Classici della musica italiana. Ed. in chief G. d'Annunzio, 36 vols, 1918-21.

I Classici musicali italiani. Ed. G. Benvenuti and others, vols. 1-13, 15, 1941-43; vol 14, 1956.

Corpus mensurabilis musicae. Ed. in chief A. Carapetyan, 1947-; mostly collected works of 15th and 16th century composers, in process of publication.

---

[23] Apel, pp. 253-282.

Denkmäler deutscher Tonkunst ("DdT"). 65 vols., Ed. R. Liliencron, 1892–1912, H. Kretzschmar to 1924, H. Albert to 1927, A. Schering to 1931; new revised edition ed. H. J. Moser, 1957–1961.

Denkmäler der Tonkunst in Österreich ("DTO"). 115 vols. to date, ed. G. Adler to vol. 83, ed. E. Schenk from vol. 85; new ed. of vols. 1–83, 1959–.

The English Madrigal School. 36 vols., ed. E. H. Fellowes, 3 edtions, 1913–24; new revised edition, *The English Madrigalists*, 27 vols. to date, ed. T. Dart, c. 1958–.

Early American Imprints. American publications through the nineteenth century; American Antiquarian Society.

Das Erbe Deutscher Musik. Continuation of DdT, various editors, 1935–; earlier vols. in the process of being reprinted.

Hispaniae schola musica sacra. 8 vols, 4–7 may be bound together; ed. F. Pedrell, 1894–98, subtitle to series: *Opera varia.*

Musica Britannica. Various editors, 1951–; rev. ed., 1958–, only a few vols. are unnumbered. Has been reprinted.

Musical Antiquarian Society (publications of). 19 vols, c. 1840–c. 1848; vols. are unnumbered; has been reprinted.

Musikalische Denkmäler. 6 vols, Kommission für Musikwissenschaft, Akademie der Wissenschaften und der Literatur in Mainz, 1955–.

The Old English Edition. 25 vols., ed. G. E. P. Arkwright, 1889–1902; reprinted 1965, bound together or individually.

Plainsong and Mediaeval Musical Society. 1890–. The publications are not issued as a set and are unnumbered.

Tudor Church Music. 10 vols. and 1 supplementary vol., various editors, 1922–29, 1948; vocal church music of sixteenth and seventeenth century England.

Score Selection, Study, and Interpretation

Gordon Paine

The thousand-year history of musical notation is the story of composers' attempts to communicate musical ideas on paper. It is also the history of performers' attempts to transform that notation into sound. This art and craft of the performer is known as "interpretation."

Notation in the Middle Ages and most of the Renaissance conveyed nothing more than pitch and rhythm, but since that time composers have increasingly sought to become closer partners in the realization of their works through the use of instructions to the performer. By the late nineteenth century, composers had filled their scores with instructions, not just on tempo and dynamics, but on articulation, phrasing, mood, and sound color as well. In our own time, a few composers have attempted to prescribe performance in such detail that the performer seems reduced to the role of a CD player. Most modern composers, however, realize what generations of their predecessors knew: no matter how refined the art and science of musical notation might become, a score can never be more than a skeletal outline of a performance. It cannot possibly indicate all aspects of musical expression that live performers must produce at any given moment. This is the principal reason that performers must "interpret" scores.

The key to musical interpretation is score study and analysis — a systematic attempt to discover how the composer constructed the music and what "makes it work." Through analysis the conductor must decide *how* — via the technical means available to him (phrasing, dynamics, articulation, tempo, and tone quality) — to underscore what the composer has written and communicate the composition to an audience.

Interpretation is a mixture of both subjective and objective ingredients, including intuition, analysis, and historical understanding. Musical intuition is important, but it must be nurtured by experience and study, since performance based on untrained intuition runs the danger of being capricious. The more a performer bases his ideas on analysis and historical knowledge, however, the more he focuses his intuition. Only through score study can the conductor "learn" the music, and only through learning the music is one equipped to "interpret" it.

The exploration of "interpretation" and the issues surrounding it will be the focus of this chapter.[1] Score selection will be the first topic to be examined, followed by a method of interpretive score study. Finally, Victoria's motet "O magnum mysterium" will be analyzed using the techniques that have been discussed.

---

[1] The author is indebted to Howard Swan and Helmuth Rilling for many of the ideas expressed in this chapter. Thanks are also due to the members of the CSU, Fullerton Choral Literature and Interpretation class (Fall, 1992) for their insights, and to Father Philip of St. Michael's Abbey (Silverado, CA) for assistance with liturgical questions.

Score Selection

Responsibilities of the Editor

The foundation of a good performance is a score that accurately communicates the composer's desires. Accuracy is reasonably assured if the composer was alive during the publication process and had the opportunity to approve the final product. But composers of the past often left divergent sources that must be reconciled and obsolete notation that now requires translation. They also may have presumed performance conventions that were self-understood in their day but must be made explicit for today's performers. These are the challenges that face the modern editor, who serves as a musicological intermediary between the composer and the performer. Conservative editors set as their goal the preparation of a score that presents an accurate text of the composer's work in modern notation. Their scores will generally be "clean," with little visible sign of editorial contribution. Another philosophy of editing, however, is to provide the performer with performance suggestions, which may range from sparse to copious. While both philosophies are to be found in all sorts of musical publications, the first is most typical of "scholarly" or "critical" editions such as collected works, while the latter is usually embodied in "performance" or "practical" editions, including octavos meant for use by choruses.

In the nineteenth century and much of the twentieth as well, editors often produced highly personal, romantically influenced performance scores in which the contribution of the editor sometimes rivaled that of the composer. Since World War II, editors have tended toward conservatism and less editorial intrusion. Regardless of the editor's philosophy, however, he is responsible for observing two fundamental principles:

- The edition must accurately represent the composer's intentions.
- The editor must make explicitly clear what in the score stems from the composer and what stems from the editor.

Only in this way can the performer know which markings should be honored and which may be subject to other interpretations.

Choosing an Edition

Editions vary not only in the quantity and quality of expressive indications provided by the editor. The piece may have been transposed; the original text may have been deleted or placed below a poor or unsingable translation; portions of the work may have been rearranged or even omitted; the accompaniment may be unstylistic or unplayable by people possessing fewer than three hands; and so on. The best way to choose an edition is thus to compare everything available. The first step is to winnow out those scores that misrepresent the composer or are otherwise problematic. From those remaining, the director can select the edition that best suits his needs and taste. Unfortunately, time and expense usually make this process impractical, especially when it comes to octavo music. Instead, one must often rely on the recommendations of informed retailers and colleagues, and on the reputations of individual editors and publishing firms. It thus behooves every choral conductor to establish a close relationship with a knowledgeable retailer and to become familiar with the philosophy and products of the various choral music publishing houses. One should, however, try to examine a single copy before ordering an octavo in quantity. All may be well — or the translation may be in Welsh and the key a third higher than anticipated.

Sometimes the best publication is out of print, is too expensive, or cannot be imported in time. Indeed, there may be no choice at all, as the piece may exist in only one edition, or only one edition may be available to you (e.g., you already have 100 copies in your church choir library). In these cases the best solution is to compare the edition you *do* have with a scholarly edition, and then make corrections as necessary.

Collected-works editions (Library of Congress "M3") and "historical collections" (LC "M2") usually contain editions of high scholarly quality that can be used as standards of reference. If a collected-works edition exists for the composer in question, the "works" list at the end of the appropriate *New Grove* article will often lead the reader directly to the desired composition. Anna Harriet Heyer's *Historical Sets, Collected Editions, and Monuments of Music: A Guide to Their Contents*, (3d ed., 2 vols. Chicago: American Library Association, 1980) may also be helpful in finding reliable reference editions.

A Case Study: Palestrina's "Alma redemptoris Mater"

To understand the value of consulting a scholarly source, it would be helpful to explore a specific case. Palestrina's motet "Alma redemptoris Mater" has enjoyed popularity in the United States for over half a century, thanks largely to the out-of-print McLaughlin and Reilly octavo (ed. Leo Rowlands, © 1936; henceforth "M&R"), as well as Roger Wagner's sensitive recording of it (*Echoes from a 16th Century Cathedral,* Angel S-36013, ca. 1960). It is interesting to compare this performance edition with a critical source.

Two editions of the complete works of Palestrina have been published:
- *Giovanni Pierluigi da Palestrinas Werke*. F. X. Haberl and others, eds. (Leipzig: Breitkopf and Härtel, 1862–1903).
- *Giovanni Pierluigi da Palestrina: Le opere complete*. R. Casimiri and others, eds. (Rome: Instituto Italiano per la storia della musica, 1939–).

The Breitkopf publication is a "diplomatic" transcription of the original partbooks into score form; i.e., note values, mensuration signs, etc. have not been changed. Despite its age, it is reliable and superior in many ways to the newer edition.

The comprehensive list of Palestrina's works in *The New Grove* lists four "Alma redemptoris mater" motets, two for four voices and two for eight. On consulting the scholarly editions, one discovers that neither of the four-voice motets resembles the M&R edition, which is, however, identical to the *eight-voice, double-chorus* motet printed in the Breitkopf set, vol. 7: 73–75. (It has yet to be printed in the newer edition.) This piece is typical of Palestrina's polychoral writing in that the two choirs have the same music when they sing together. It is thus possible for the motet to be sung by a single, four-part choir, which is how M&R published it, *but without informing us of the change.* Further examination shows other tacit alterations in the M&R edition — some benign, some not:
- The piece has been transposed down a major second. This is reasonable, as the tenors would otherwise have numerous high As.

- The unmeasured chant incipit has been moved from the tenor to the bass and written out rhythmically.
- The editor has altered the original rhythms in mm. 4–5 (SATB), m. 12 (ATB), and m. 14 (B).
- The text underlay in the bass has been altered in mm. 3, 14, and 26–27. An accidental shown as editorial (T, m. 11) is actually original, and another given as original (S, m. 14) is in fact editorial.
- The first chord in m. 22 should be C minor (C–C–E flat–G) rather than the E-flat major shown in the accompaniment (E flat–B flat–E flat–G) or the C dominant seventh (C–B flat–E flat–G) show in the vocal parts.

Palestrinas Werke

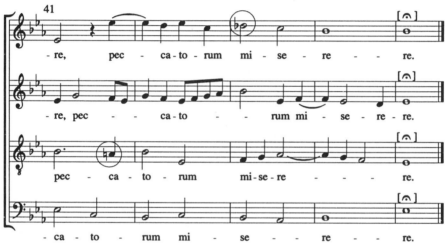

M + R Edition

Example 1

philosophy and products of the various choral music publishing houses. One should, however, try to examine a single copy before ordering an octavo in quantity. All may be well — or the translation may be in Welsh and the key a third higher than anticipated.

Sometimes the best publication is out of print, is too expensive, or cannot be imported in time. Indeed, there may be no choice at all, as the piece may exist in only one edition, or only one edition may be available to you (e.g., you already have 100 copies in your church choir library). In these cases the best solution is to compare the edition you *do* have with a scholarly edition, and then make corrections as necessary.

Collected-works editions (Library of Congress "M3") and "historical collections" (LC "M2") usually contain editions of high scholarly quality that can be used as standards of reference. If a collected-works edition exists for the composer in question, the "works" list at the end of the appropriate *New Grove* article will often lead the reader directly to the desired composition. Anna Harriet Heyer's *Historical Sets, Collected Editions, and Monuments of Music: A Guide to Their Contents*, (3d ed., 2 vols. Chicago: American Library Association, 1980) may also be helpful in finding reliable reference editions.

A Case Study: Palestrina's "Alma redemptoris Mater"

To understand the value of consulting a scholarly source, it would be helpful to explore a specific case. Palestrina's motet "Alma redemptoris Mater" has enjoyed popularity in the United States for over half a century, thanks largely to the out-of-print McLaughlin and Reilly octavo (ed. Leo Rowlands, © 1936; henceforth "M&R"), as well as Roger Wagner's sensitive recording of it (*Echoes from a 16th Century Cathedral*, Angel S-36013, ca. 1960). It is interesting to compare this performance edition with a critical source.

Two editions of the complete works of Palestrina have been published:

- *Giovanni Pierluigi da Palestrinas Werke*. F. X. Haberl and others, eds. (Leipzig: Breitkopf and Härtel, 1862–1903).
- *Giovanni Pierluigi da Palestrina: Le opere complete*. R. Casimiri and others, eds. (Rome: Instituto Italiano per la storia della musica, 1939–).

The Breitkopf publication is a "diplomatic" transcription of the original partbooks into score form; i.e., note values, mensuration signs, etc. have not been changed. Despite its age, it is reliable and superior in many ways to the newer edition.

The comprehensive list of Palestrina's works in *The New Grove* lists four "Alma redemptoris mater" motets, two for four voices and two for eight. On consulting the scholarly editions, one discovers that neither of the four-voice motets resembles the M&R edition, which is, however, identical to the *eight-voice, double-chorus* motet printed in the Breitkopf set, vol. 7: 73–75. (It has yet to be printed in the newer edition.) This piece is typical of Palestrina's polychoral writing in that the two choirs have the same music when they sing together. It is thus possible for the motet to be sung by a single, four-part choir, which is how M&R published it, *but without informing us of the change*. Further examination shows other tacit alterations in the M&R edition — some benign, some not:

- The piece has been transposed down a major second. This is reasonable, as the tenors would otherwise have numerous high As.

- The unmeasured chant incipit has been moved from the tenor to the bass and written out rhythmically.
- The editor has altered the original rhythms in mm. 4–5 (SATB), m. 12 (ATB), and m. 14 (B).
- The text underlay in the bass has been altered in mm. 3, 14, and 26–27. An accidental shown as editorial (T, m. 11) is actually original, and another given as original (S, m. 14) is in fact editorial.
- The first chord in m. 22 should be C minor (C–C–E flat–G) rather than the E-flat major shown in the accompaniment (E flat–B flat–E flat–G) or the C dominant seventh (C–B flat–E flat–G) show in the vocal parts.

Palestrinas Werke

M + R Edition

Example 1

- The character of the ending is distorted by the omission of two of the only four original accidentals in the piece. Compare the final five measures as given in the collected works (transposed downward and note values halved) with the parallel passage in the M&R edition (Example 1).[2]

It should be clear that an editor can profoundly affect how the music will eventually sound, and that the conductor therefore ought to make sure that his performance materials do not misrepresent what the composer wrote.

Choral-Orchestral Works

The chance to conduct a choral-orchestral work is a great opportunity. It will usually involve substantial investment of time, effort, and money — all of which can be squandered through the use of flawed performance materials. Works by twentieth century composers are usually available in only one edition, but earlier works may be available from several publishers in editions ranging from excellent to abysmal.

In general, the most reliable performance materials will be from the publisher of the most recent edition of the composer's complete works. Not all publishers of complete works editions issue performance materials, however, and even if they do, they may be expensive, available only on rental, out of stock, or out of print. If it is necessary to turn to other sources, try to obtain the full score, piano-vocal scores, and orchestral parts from the same publisher to assure internal consistency (especially movement numbers, measure numbers, and rehearsal letters). If materials from different publishers must be used, try to check them out carefully before buying them. As with the purchase of octavos, advice from experienced colleagues and retailers can be invaluable in finding suitable choral/orchestral scores and parts.

Many older European editions are now in the public domain in the USA, and companies such as Dover Publications (full scores only) and Edwin F. Kalmus (complete performance materials) reissue them at attractive prices. Nearly the entire Kalmus catalogue of Bach materials, for example, has been reprinted from the *Bach Gesellschaft* complete-works edition (Breitkopf & Härtel, 1851–99) and the Breitkopf orchestral parts derived from it. (If requested, Kalmus will provide information on the origin of its publications.) In many cases savings can be significant when using old materials, but *caveat emptor:* full scores copied from old complete-works editions may contain vocal parts in C clefs, and many early

---

[2] Following the principles of *musica ficta*, a performer of Palestrina's time, reading from a single-voice part, would have raised the lower-neighbor in the tenor, m. 41, to A natural. Hearing a forbidden tritone with the soprano E flat, however, the tenor would have returned to the notated A flat. But Palestrina *intended the dissonance* as a depiction of the word *pec-catorum* (sin) and provided the accidental to make sure it occured. The M&R edition eliminates this poignant word-painting. (The fact that Palestrina employs the raised lower neighbor here, where it would otherwise be avoided, implies its use as well in the two earlier, consonant presentations of this point of imitation.) Two measures later Palestrina notated a D flat in the soprano, creating an affective, B-flat minor chord on the word *miserere* (have mercy). Once again, the M&R edition ignores this explicit accidental, weakening the ending.

publications contain tacit revisions, cuts, re-orchestrations, and other head-
aches.

A word about rental might be helpful. The author's personal preference is
to avoid rental, as the materials (including the full score) are available only for
a limited time and may be in dismal condition, filled with markings from earlier
performances. Purchase can sometimes be less expensive, as a student learned
several years ago when he rented the Schubert *Magnificat* in C from a major
domestic publisher. When he received the parts, weeks after the contractual date
and just four days before the recital, he discovered that everything had been
photocopied from the public-domain Kalmus edition — which he could have
purchased for a fraction of the rental fee.

Score Study

Overview

A conductor studies a score for three basic reasons: 1) to determine whether
or not to perform the piece, 2) to learn the music and determine how to interpret
it, and 3) to help him to rehearse it and conduct it effectively.

Preliminary score study assesses the quality, appropriateness, and practicality
of the composition in question:
- Is it of high musical quality and worth performing?
- Is the text appropriate for the intended singers, audience, and occasion?
- Is the piece within the emotional grasp of the singers and the intended
  audience, and within the technical (range, tessitura, dynamics, phrasing,
  vocal endurance, etc.) abilities of the choir?

Once the conductor has decided to perform the piece, he begins *interpretive
score study*, through which he also "learns" the score. Interpretive score study
consists of:
- gathering background information (including score selection)
- studying of the text
- studying of the music and its relationship to the text
- making interpretive decisions

Once the score is learned, *pedagogical score study* begins, through which the
conductor seeks to:
- locate potential problem spots for the performers and determine effective
  ways to teach them
- find and solve the conducting challenges of the piece (starts, stops,
  transitions, cues, dynamic changes, etc.)
- develop an overall strategy for rehearsing the work

For a beginner, thorough score study can be arduous and time consuming,
even for a short piece, but practice and experience speed the process. It is helpful
to begin score study early, so that the music can be well learned for the first
rehearsal. While a director with superior musicianship can sometimes learn the
music with the choir, this is bad practice. Rehearsal time will be lost, and the
director's poor example will teach the singers that they need not take seriously
their learning of the music.

Interpretive Score Study

The gathering of background information is an important and often neglected part of learning a work. A composer lives a real life with real problems, challenges, and joys, and his compositions and their realization in sound are influenced by the aesthetics and artistic currents of the day. A performer must have knowledge of these things in order to understand the music and realize it sympathetically.

- *Learn about the composer and the period in which he lived.*
- *Learn about the composer's works and how the piece in question fits into the composer's total output.*
- *Learn about the compositional aesthetics, musical styles, and performance practices of the time and place involved.* Even if one does not have or does not wish to have "historically authentic" performance forces, it is always possible to take into account appropriate musical style and sound character. This issue will be discussed in more detail under the heading "Historical Performance."
- *Determine the genre of the piece* (motet, madrigal, cantata, part song, concerto-chorus, etc.). Each genre from each period is characterized by common features of construction, aesthetics, style, and performance practices. Knowing the genre will provide a helpful framework for understanding the piece and interpreting it.

The study of the text is a logical place to begin the actual study of a work, since composers of vocal music are inspired by words and write music to express those words. In a fine composition, the union of text and music is usually greater than the sum of the parts.

- *What is the origin of the text* and what, if anything, does this suggest about the composition? Is it a lament, a song of praise, a love poem? Is it from the Bible, a Shakespeare play, or perhaps from the pen of the composer himself?
- *Is the text sacred or secular?* Throughout history, musical settings of sacred texts have usually been subject to various limitations of length, style, and performance forces because they were to be sung in worship services to the glory of God. Musical settings of secular texts, on the other hand, were for the enjoyment of man and were not necessarily as conservative.
- *What is the meaning of the text* – both word for word and sentence by sentence — and what are the moods or characters of it as a whole and of its individual parts? Is there perhaps more than one level of meaning to the words? Many Renaissance madrigals that center on death, for example, are less concerned with mortality than sensuality.
- *What is the structure of the text?* Is it a rhyming poem, a bar-form (AAB) hymn, a passage in prose? The structure of the text suggests or even dictates the form of the music. An understanding of the way the text is constructed will give the conductor a framework for understanding the musical structure.
- *How is the text pronounced,* and what is its resulting sound character? What sounds are peculiar to the language involved? It is tedious to listen to a

concert in which German, French, and Italian are all delivered with the same American accent. The conductor therefore must be an amateur linguist and strive to master the sounds of the languages in which he performs.

- *What words of particular importance, strength, or intensity might one want to bring out* in some way via diction, dynamics, articulation, or vocal color? "Love," for example, sounds much more believable and urgent if the "L" is stressed and lengthened. Onomatopoetic words — words whose sound embodies their meaning — should be of particular interest.
- *What is the natural stress of the words* and how can this inherent contouring of the text be used to help shape the musical line?
- *Are there any special circumstances surrounding the text?* Performers preparing the Britten *War Requiem*, for example, will identify more profoundly with the words if they know that the poet, Wilfred Owen, wrote them from the trenches during World War I and that he perished in battle just days before the armistice.

The study of the music and its relationship to the text is where one's analytical skills come into play. By this point in score study, the director will know the period of the composition and its genre, and these will suggest ideas about the structure of the music and how to investigate it. In addition to text, the major structural elements in all musical styles will be harmony, melody, texture, rhythm, and use of performance forces. These will vary in relative importance, however, according to the period, genre, and style in question, and one therefore needs to find an analytical approach appropriate to the music being studied. Mozart and Haydn, for example, constructed their choral/orchestral works according to the same principles as their instrumental music, and many of the same forms (e.g., sonata-allegro, rondo) are represented, but with the added structural element of text. Thus, the same type of harmonic/thematic analysis one would use for their instrumental music will be suitable for their choral/orchestral works. On the other hand, an imitative Renaissance motet, in which harmony usually plays a minor role, will require a text- and counterpoint-oriented analytical approach. A fugue from any period will require the conductor to isolate expositions and episodes and to see how they are individually constructed and combine together into a musical unit.

It is beyond the scope of this article to discuss the technique of analysis in detail, but the following principles will provide a sound analytical framework for any piece from any period:

Start by exploring the large-scale organization of the piece.
- How is the piece divided into large sections? In a choral work, the large-scale musical structure will almost always correspond to the large-scale structure of the text.
- How do the sections relate to each other musically?
- To what extent are they musically unified vs. independently constructed?
- What is the flow of energy from one section to another — which sections build energy and which relax it?

- How can the performer best make these elements of the music come alive in sound?

Proceed next to lower levels of structure – subsections or periods.

- How has the composer delineated one from another, and how are they connected?
- What is the flow of energy from one to another?
- Where does the music intensify and where does it relax?
- How can the above be brought out in sound?

Examine the individual musical phrases.

- How is each phrase shaped?
- Where is its climax and how does the composer create that climax?
- Where and how does the composer create musical relaxation?
- What is the special quality or characteristic of each phrase, and what musical elements give it that quality?
- What does the composer do in the music to reinforce or even depict the words, and how can these musical ideas be projected to the audience in terms of dynamics, phrasing, articulation, tempo, and tone quality?
- Is there any conflict between the words and the corresponding music? If so, *why* does the conflict exist, and what do you think the composer is trying to say? How can the conflict be resolved? (Real conflicts of words and music are generally best resolved in favor of the music.)

Finally, having studied the composition at all levels, go back and look at the piece as a whole.

- Have you developed any new insights?
- How do the many individual phrases, periods, subsections, and sections unite into a coherent musical unit, and what can the director do to make this clear in performance?

The making of interpretive decisions began with studying the score. If you have followed the process described above, you will know the piece quite well and will already have made most of your interpretive decisions, because they will have evolved from your analysis. Now is the time to review, to polish your interpretive ideas, and to consider how you will go about teaching the piece and building your interpretation into the learning process.

Preparation under Pressure

Sooner or later you will have to conduct an unknown piece extemporaneously and will have no time to follow normal score-study procedures. Remember that the conductor's most basic role is that of a traffic cop — keeping the ensemble together. What little time *is* available for preparation will be valuable, so use it wisely.

- *Where are the potential "train wrecks"* (e.g., changes of tempo, fermatas, changes of meter, sectional changes)? Mark these prominently in your score and figure out how you will conduct them. Practice each spot a couple of times if possible.
- *What is the voicing of the piece, and where, if at all, does that voicing change?* Remember to assign voice parts before you begin to rehearse.

- If the work is accompanied, of how much help — or hindrance — is the accompaniment to both you and your singers?
- *Where will the choir need your help* in initial rehearsal in order to master the music?
- *What is the basic articulation required* for the piece and of its individual sections? Keeping this in mind will help you to shape the music immediately.

These suggestions should get you through the first rehearsal, after which you will have time to learn the piece under less hectic circumstances.

The preceding pages have explored the process of score study and the development of interpretive ideas. Let us now look at the various means by which the conductor shapes the music and communicates interpretive ideas.

Phrasing

"Phrasing" is perhaps the most misused word in the choral vocabulary. Most singers think of phrasing in terms of where they breathe, but this is only part of the story. Real phrasing is the shaping of the music *between* breaths. Musical phrasing consists of three basic elements:
- good voice production and singing with focused energy
- sensitivity to the meaning and natural stress of the text
- sensitivity to the natural ebb and flow of energy in the music

Every musical line in every composition needs to contain an undefinable but undeniable intensity that pushes the music forward and gives it life. This concept of energy should be trained into every singer from the earliest age, for this more than anything else makes singing sound "natural" and "musical." As a conductor you yourself must learn to sing with energy and a beautiful, sensitive musical line; you must develop your own singing voice so that you can demonstrate accurately and musically what you want to hear from your singers. You should also learn as much as you can about vocal production and how to teach it in a choral rehearsal.

Musical line can be achieved in many ways with a chorus. Some directors approach this skill through the development of vocal production. Others — Robert Shaw prominent among them — energize the phrase primarily through rhythm. Whatever techniques you find helpful, they cannot be learned passively from an article or a book. Instead, they require active analysis, listening, and practice.
- Listen to outstanding ensembles, both live and recorded, and analyze the phrasing you hear. Which groups do you find to be the most pleasing? What do they do that you find to be satisfying? How can you achieve similar results?
- Attend and study the rehearsals of various conductors whose music exhibits energetic singing and musical phrasing, and practice the tecniques you observe. Find those that work best for *you* as an individual.

One of the most important jobs of the choral conductor is to identify the natural shape of each phrase and to help the singers realize it in their singing.

The best conductors teach their singers how to recognize the shapes of phrases independently, so that the singers themselves can take responsibility for their phrasing. This makes the conductor's job more gratifying and is more rewarding for the singers than being taught by rote.

The text is a good place to start, since that is where the composer began. Good composers set text in musically sensitive and logical ways. Stressed syllables will generally receive longer and/or higher notes than the unstressed syllables that surround them, and the rhythm of the music will reinforce the natural rhythm of the words. Important words also may be underlined or depicted through the music.

The shape of the musical phrase is determined by musical elements as well as by the text. Composers control the building and dissipation of energy in a musical phrase through melody, harmony, rhythm, texture, dynamics, and the use of performance forces. It is the conductor's job to discover what the composer has done on paper and to translate that into sound. Nearly all phrases will contain some degree of intensification and subsequent relaxation, but the exact shape and degree of the resultant arch will differ with style and compositional period. In Romantic music, for example, the natural contour of the phrase is often accompanied by dynamics that reinforce the flow of energy already inherent in the music. In Renaissance music, however, composers never provided such hints as to phrasing, and the style calls for much more subtle shaping of the phrase according to the natural shape of the melody and the accentuation of the text. Make no mistake about it, however: even when the composer provides no "phrasing" dynamics, the conductor must be sure that the phrase has a clear and expressive shape.

Dynamics

Composers provide dynamics in their music for several reasons. Dynamics within a composition can be used to:
- make audible how the piece is shaped or constructed
- bring out expressively the tension-relaxation scheme of the piece (e.g., phrase shaping)
- underscore the meaning of the text
- provide musical beauty, interest, and variety

Most composers, however, do not and have not indicated every appropriate dynamic nuance. In fact, as one looks back into music history, the expressive indications provided by composers become progressively sketchier, and by 1600 they disappear almost completely. The conductor must therefore decide what unwritten dynamic changes are needed to shape the composition and make it communicate effectively to the listener. The fewer the indications left by the composer, the more decisions the conductor must make.

How much unwritten dynamic variation is appropriate depends on the musical period, the style, the composer, and the individual piece. In general, earlier music — particularly sacred works — should be handled more conservatively than later music. The appropriate dynamic shaping of a Renaissance motet, for example, will be confined largely to phrase shaping; an early Baroque concertato might benefit from terraced dynamics and echo effects; and a

Romantic part song might be subject to almost constant dynamic fluctuation. In a Baroque fugue, dynamic variation can be used to highlight the alternation of expositions and episodes and to keep prominent the musical material that forms the basis of the fugue. In Classical music, dynamics can help to underline the tension and relaxation that are inherent in the melodic and harmonic shape of each phrase, period, and section.

Intelligent musicians will not always agree on whether dynamic variation is desirable or appropriate in a given instance. Some performers feel that one should play or sing the notes "just as the composer wrote them." On the other extreme are performers whose liberties with dynamics distort the musical style. How does one decide what to do?

A musician must study history, style, and performance practices to develop the personal concepts of style and expression that will guide his interpretations. This study will establish a sense of the boundaries of appropriate and stylistic expression in different types of music. Once the musician has developed these concepts, he can make use of hints to be found in the music of all periods — musical events that singly or in combination with others suggest that an increase or decrease of dynamics might be appropriate. When a composer specifies a dynamic change, analysis will usually reveal the corresponding presence of one or more of these "internal dynamic markings" that are a part of the structure of the music. A thoughtful conductor will search out these events and determine whether or not dynamic reinforcement of them would be appropriate to the style and beneficial to performance.

The table below summarizes some of the musical devices that subjectively create intensification or relaxation and that might be underscored by dynamic changes. Of course, these devices only *suggest* dynamic emphasis; they do not mandate it.

Composed Intensification	Composed Relaxation
1. Thickening of texture (adding parts)	1. Thinning of texture (subtracting parts)
2. Building of harmonic tension	2. Relaxation of harmonic tension
3. Upward melodic movement (particularly sequence)	3. Downward melodic movement (particularly sequence)
4. Stretto (decreased interval of time between imitations)	4. (No corresponding event)
5. Moving toward the climax of a phrase, subsection, or section	5. Moving away from the climax of a phrase, subsection, or section
6. Repetition (particularly motivic), especially when accompanied by other indications of intensification	6. Repetition (particularly motivic), when accompanied by other indications of relaxation
7. Outward expansion of the outer voices	7. Inward contraction of the outer voices
8. Increasing rhythmic activity	8. Decreasing rhythmic activity

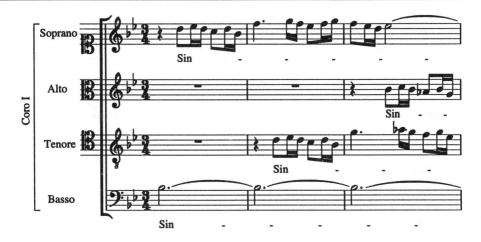

Example 2

1) Begin the initial "n" very early and push it to the downbeat (marcato). Close to the second "n" on beat 2 (staccato).

2) Strong, short consonants. Glottal stop on "es." "Ist nicht" may be pronounced "iss nicht" to avoid slowing.

3) Glottal stop on "aus-." Pronounce both the "s" and the "z" (="ts") if possible but eliminate the "Z" if necessary. Close to the "m" early and push it into beat 3.

4) Eliminate the "t" in "mit den" if need be to avoid slowing. Short vowels on "Leu-ten."

Example 3

5) Close to "l" on beat 2 and push to beat 3. Close immediately to "s" in "wissen."

6) Short, strong "s" (="z") in "sie so." Close to "f" and "g" early on "gif-tig."

7) Glottal stop on "aus-." "Aus-zu" may be simplified to "au-su" if need be. "Deu-ten" with short vowels like "Leu-ten."

Example 3, conclusion

Articulation

The ability to sing with a variety of articulations — e.g., legato, staccato, marcato — is one of the most powerful of interpretive tools and it is also one of the least used. On one hand, this is understandable, because a conductor's first job is to teach good, basic singing technique, and this is best taught with a continuous air flow that is only lightly interrupted by consonants — i.e., legato articulation. A great deal of choral (and solo) literature demands articulations other than legato, however. The conductor therefore needs to integrate articulation skills into the teaching of vocal technique. Although a great variety of articulations may be called for in both vocal and instrumental music, they all fall into one of two basic classifications: *legato* and *non legato*. Non-legato articulation will involve a degree of shortness, accent, or a combination of the two.

The most fundamental non-legato articulation is the staccato, and in vocal music there are, again, two basic types: melismatic and syllabic. "Melismatic staccato" is often called for in musical styles that treat the voice instrumentally (e.g., Bach and Mozart). Consider, for example, the opening measures of the first chorus part to the Bach motet *Singet dem Herrn*, BWV 225 (Example 2). This passage is written idiomatically for strings and double reeds, which would have no trouble playing the short, instrumental articulation required. For human voices, however, these measures require great flexibility and vocal skill. There is no shortcut to mastering the vocal technique required to sing such literature. For this reason it is important that voice teachers and conductors emphasize flexibility along with the production of a beautiful legato.

"Syllabic staccato" is less technically demanding. Intensity and prominence of consonants can create an illusion of staccato without the singer being called upon to chop off the flow of air *unnaturally*. Two basic principles are involved in "healthy" syllabic-staccato singing:

- *Unvoiced consonants should be short and crisp.*
- *Vowels should be shortened in ways that are natural for the language.* Vowels before plosive and semiplosive consonants can be shortened by stopping the vowel early in preparation for the consonant. Vowels preceding voiced consonants (and sibilants in some circumstances) can be shortened by lengthening ("singing on") the consonant. If the beginning of the consonant is sung softly and the end is emphasized, an illusion of staccato is created. Double, voiced consonants can be made to sound short using the same principle: close to the consonant early on the first syllable and push it vigorously into the vowel of the second syllable. The early closing to the first consonant shortens the preceding vowel, and the intensity of the second strengthens the illusion of staccato: e.g., Al-le-lu-ia.

Example 3 shows these principles applied to the beginning of no. 11 of the Brahms op. 52 *Liebeslieder Waltzes*, "Nein, es ist nicht auszukommen," a piece that requires a combination of marcato and staccato articulations. Notice that the accompaniment contains articulation marks that are not in the voice parts: Brahms assumed that the singers' diction would produce the desired effect without instruction, or that the singers would follow the instrumental articulation. This example illustrates how accompanimental articulation can often provide guidance in the absence of explicit vocal articulation.

One must be careful in using these energetic articulations with inexperienced singers, as they will tend to overdo them to the detriment of their basic vocal production. While intensity is desirable, tension is not, and the conductor must be aware of the borderline between the two.

In example 3 Brahms indicated much of the articulation he desired; in example 2, however, Bach assumed that the performers would figure things out for themselves. Since the latter situation is more common than the former, the conductor must often determine the articulation appropriate to a particular passage. These decisions should be based on:
- the meaning and character of the text
- the character of the music
- the need for clarity in performance (In order to achieve a given articulation, a choir must always sing with more marcato and with more intense enunciation than would a singer performing alone.)
- the character of the language

Artistic articulation is intimately related to the knowledge of language. Different languages have different characters of articulation, and this must be audible in singing. The Romance languages, for example, are largely legato languages in which elision of words is practiced in normal speech as well as in song. German, on the other hand, avoids most elision, especially between a word ending in a consonant and the following word beginning with a vowel. German speech and singing are thus filled with glottal stops that are *a natural part of the articulation of the language.* German and the Romance languages also have different articulatory characters with regard to consonants, those in German generally being stronger. The pervasiveness of nasalized consonants in French gives its special, unique sound. Finally, vowels as well differ among languages, and the appropriate choral tone for any particular piece must take into account the proper vowel sounds of the language.

Since choral music is set to words, and words come in many languages, choral directors must be able to deal with the demands of multiple languages — traditionally English, Latin, German, Italian, and French. Diction classes are a good way of learning basic pronunciation, but *actual study* of a language is yet better, as it permits one to *understand* the language as opposed to merely approximating its sounds. With the growing internationalization of this country and the opening of Eastern Europe, new literature in strange and wonderful languages will be entering the repertoire, and with it will come additional challenges for choral conductors and singers.

While the development of foreign-language diction skills is important, so is proper English. It is easy to become complacent regarding the diction of one's native language. The result, however, is often incomprehensible singing, dialectical or regional coloration, or both. The conductor who takes the same care with English diction as he does with a foreign language will be rewarded by better overall tone (unified vowels) and intonation.

Tempo

Finding an appropriate tempo is perhaps the most crucial interpretive decision facing the conductor, since a performance at the wrong tempo stands little chance of success. If the music is too slow, the singers' endurance (and perhaps that of the listeners as well) will be strained; if too fast, the piece will sound hectic and may even fall apart. Finding an appropriate tempo for a piece thus means considering 1) the technical and expressive demands of the music itself and 2) the ability of the ensemble.

Decisions about tempo are best made after the conductor has thoroughly studied the score and knows its technical and expressive demands. The fastest *possible* tempo will be determined by the fastest ornamental note values of the piece or the fastest syllabic movement; the slowest *possible* tempo will be the slowest speed at which the piece still has a sense of moving forward musically (harmonic and melodic rhythm). Although a wide range of tempos is possible for any piece, the range of tempos that actually "works" may be rather narrow. Some experimentation is thus in order to find the appropriate tempo spectrum. This is a subjective and personal matter for each conductor, and what works for one may not be to another's taste. The technical skill of the choir must also enter into the equation; the tempo must work for both the music and the choir. *If the tempo required by the music and the tempo at which the choir can sing it are too different, it would be advisable to select different literature.*

In setting tempo one must also take into account the performance practices and styles of the period in which the music was written. In the Renaissance, for example, there existed the concept of a *tempo giusto* or standard tempo (*tactus*) for sacred music. This dictated a tempo of ca. mm. 50–80 to the whole note (in most modern scores with reduced note values, the half note). Performers thus thought of this music "in two." Modern performances that are slow enough to require a quarter-note beat may thus be too slow from the historical point of view.

Prior to the invention of the metronome (ca. 1800), tempo could not be notated and reproduced precisely. Italian or vernacular words were used to indicate the character of the music, part of which was, of course, its tempo. Notwithstanding their presence on many metronomes, *these terms did not necessarily denote specific tempos or ranges of tempo.* Indeed, the meanings of many of these terms have evolved since their first use early in the seventeenth century. For example, the words *adagio* and *presto* were used at that time to denote "relatively slow" or "relatively fast" but they did not indicate *how* slow or *how* fast. In the late Baroque and Classical periods, many more descriptive words came into use as composers strove to make their ideas ever clearer, and the resulting complex of terms has been in use with continuous additions and refinements since that time. "Tempo words" and metronome markings in the score — sometimes from the composer, sometimes from the editor — can thus provide a helpful starting point for setting tempo, but each individual conductor must still determine what is right for his situation.

A final consideration that enters into selection of tempo is the acoustical environment: a large, live hall (a stone church, for example) may require slower than normal tempos to preserve clarity. Choruses in this country do not often face this situation, as performance spaces here are usually acoustically dry. If your choir takes a European tour and sings in large churches, however, you may need to slow down your faster pieces to keep them from becoming a blur of sound.

Flexibility of tempo or rubato is appropriate — indeed necessary — to much Romantic and Romantic-style music. The Brahms *Liebeslieder Waltzes*, for example, demand a constant give and take of tempo. Such freedom is not appropriate to most earlier music, however, and will make it sound sentimental. In Renaissance or Baroque music, however, "terraced" changes of tempo may be effective and appropriate with the introduction of a new, contrasting section of music.

Tone Quality and Vocal Production

There are many different concepts of good choral tone and even more ideas about how to achieve it. Regardless of personal preference, however, there is one universal truth: *pleasing choral tone is achieved by teaching choristers to sing well and adapting the resulting sound to the music being performed.*

The sound of a given choir can be changed only to a limited degree. For example, high school singers cannot possibly achieve the richness of tone that an adult choir can, and trying to make them do so will lead to artificially dark, heavy, and ultimately unhealthy vocal production. *A director should not approach his chorus with a preconceived sound ideal that is incompatible with the choir's abilities or age.*

That said, however, the director *does* need to approach each composition with an understanding of its musical style and the technique of singing best suited to it. A Renaissance motet or madrigal will require a clear, light production with emphasis on use of head voice and lack of excessive breath pressure. This type of singing will also tend to minimize vibrato naturally. A similar vocal style, but with more rhythmic energy and perhaps more weight, will be required for instrumentally conceived Baroque and Classical music. Repertoire from the time of Schubert to the present will require a wide range of vocal productions — from light and floating to vigorous, full-throated, and soloistic — often within the same piece (e.g., Brahms *Requiem*, "Wie lieblich sind deine Wohnungen"). *Thus, if a choir is to sing a wide variety of musical styles, the singers must be taught to master the singing techniques needed to produce the required spectrum of sounds.* Wise directors will select challenging literature that their singers can sing beautifully and that will develop their singing skills, but that does not exceed their vocal abilities.

Historical Performance

One of the most exciting musical trends of today is historical performance. Research over the past thirty years has revealed a great deal about the way music was performed in earlier times ("performance practices") and has enabled modern performers to attempt reconstructions of performances as they might have sounded hundreds of years ago. These have opened our ears and our thinking about musical sound and aesthetics. When this writer was in college in the 1960s, many of the standard recordings of early music — indeed, sometimes the only recordings — were well-intentioned but ultimately dismal and poorly recorded performances from the 78 r.p.m. age. At that time it was often argued that historical performances were impractical because "primitive" instruments could not be played musically and in tune. Brilliant specialist musicians like the late David Munrow soon disproved that idea. Today, numerous choral and instrumental ensembles specializing in historical performance continue to demonstrate that early music played and sung with musicality and attention to original performance practices can please our ears and move us emotionally just as much as the more outwardly "expressive" music of the Romantic period.

Historical reconstruction should not be an end in itself, however, and it does not guarantee that the performance will be musically satisfying. Even though our knowledge of early music performance practices continues to grow, we can never hope to possess but a fragmentary understanding of what music sounded like centuries ago. We also cannot recreate the audience, to whose ears Stravinsky, Brahms, Mozart, or even Bach were unknown. An "authentic" performance is thus ephemeral, and dogmatism on the subject is inappropriate. In addition, most practical situations thwart efforts at "authenticity." While it would be nice for schools, churches, and community choirs to have several consorts of early winds and strings (and the people to play them), multiple continuo instruments, boy sopranos, countertenors, and the like, this is impractical. Most modern choral conductors are thus faced with the task of performing early music with forces not historically suited to the literature. The conductor should not be embarrassed for doing so, however. Even when the external trappings of historical performance are absent, it is still possible to perform early music with integrity. What matters most is that the conductor possesses a concept of the *style* of the music and a sympathy for the sound that is appropriate to it. Then he should pursue those goals as far as possible *with the forces available to him and with literature suited to those forces.*

Of course, it should be clear that certain literature is best avoided by some performance groups. A light, quick madrigal originally composed for five soloists will sound like a parody with a festival choir of 200, but it might still work beautifully with a sensitive, well-trained choir of twelve, twenty, or even forty. While Byrd would have heard his motets sung by all-male choirs, they still can be rendered pleasingly by a mixed choir that sings with sensitive phrasing, clean intonation, and attention to the meaning and accentuation of the text.

In summary, although historical performance is an area of great importance, worthy of study by all performers, in the real world the pursuit of "authenticity" is less important than musicality blended with knowledge of musical style.

Language is perhaps the "final frontier" of historical performance. Much attention has been paid to ensemble size and constitution, performance practices, and appropriate sound ideals, but little work has been done with regard to authentic language. English pronunciation in the Renaissance, for example, was quite different from what we speak today, although it was apparently closer in many ways to modern American speech than to British English. It is not often, however, that one hears sixteenth century English sung, except by professional specialist groups.[3]

One aspect of historical language of which all choral musicians should be aware is that Italianate church Latin is inappropriate to many Latin-language compositions. Some composers, such as Carl Orff, have set Classical texts that demand Classical Latin pronunciation. Even more important is the difference between Italianate and Germanic Latin. Mozart, Beethoven, Haydn, and other Germanic composers who set Latin texts would have heard them sung in a type of Latin with a distinctly Teutonic accent, a dialect that is still in use today in German-speaking countries.[4] Is it any more acceptable to use Italianate Latin in singing these compositions than it would be to use a piano for basso continuo in the B-minor Mass?

Victoria's "O magnum mysterium": An Interpretive Analysis

In the following pages we will study this magnificent motet within the framework that has been proposed in this chapter. First we will explore background information and selection of an edition. We will then analyze the composition and consider the interpretive consequences of that analysis, section by section. For visual clarity, discussions of interpretation are enclosed in boxes. The entire motet is presented in the form of three musical examples, and facsimiles of the original parts are provided for the reader's reference.[5]

---

[3] The early English carols on EMI CDC 7498092, "The Carol Album" (dir. Andrew Parrott) provide a hair-raising example of the effect that authentic pronunciation can have on choral tone and overall musical impression.

[4] For a concise guide to the pronunciation of Latin, both Italianate and Germanic, see Ron Jeffers, *Translations and Annotations of Choral Repertoire. Volume 1: Sacred Latin Texts* (Corvallis, OR: earthsongs, 1989), 36–44.

[5] *Thomæ Lvdovici de Victoria, Abvlensis, Motecta qv[a]e partim, quaternis, partim, qvinis, alia, senis, alia, octonis vocibus concinuntur.* Venice: Sons of Antonio Gardano, 1572 (RISM V1421). The author is grateful to Walter S. Collins for making available his photocopies of the source, and to the administration of the Bibliothek des Priesterseminars u. Santini-Sammlung (Münster, Germany) for permission to reproduce them.

The 1572 original contains a few typographical errors:
1) B: m. 38/4. Colored (black) semibreve should be a white minim.
2) T & B: m. 23, T: m. 25. Erroneously *viderunt*.
3) S: m. 57/3. Erroneously colored. In normal practice, m. 56/2 would be colored but not m. 57/3. (See also note 8.)

The score presented here is a transcription of the 1572 partbooks in which 1) note values have been halved, 2) clefs and time signatures have been modernized, 3) bar lines have been added, 4) coloration of notes has been replaced by bracket corners above the notes, and 5) ligatures (two notes bound together to indicate that they are to be sung on a single syllable) have been shown by brackets (ex., T: m.15). Editorial accidentals appear above the staff; they are suggested for the following reasons:

Part: M.#	1572 Reading	Comment
A: m. 8/4+	B flat	B natural needed to avoid the B flat–C sharp augmented second.
S: m. 13/4	F (natural)	Modern notation requires an accidental to cancel the preceding sharp on beat 2. *(Continued next page)*

Background

Victoria (1548–1611), a Spanish priest and one of the greatest composers of the late Renaissance, spent nearly twenty years of his student and adult life in Rome as a singer, organist, composer, and *maestro di cappella*. There he mastered the style of Palestrina, with whom he may have studied, and published many of his collections of masses and motets, including the first book of motets (1572), which contains "O magnum mysterium." Victoria's compositional output was small compared with that of Palestrina and Lassus, and he is not known to have composed any secular music. While his style is similar to that of Palestrina, it is not as strict and is more intense, particularly in terms of harmonic expression.

> The fact that Victoria was a Renaissance composer suggests several things in terms of appropriate style of performance. The choirs with which he worked were small and invariably all male, with boys singing the soprano and alto parts. "Expressive" singing as we think of it today was unknown: singers were prized not for the individuality of their voices and their beautiful vibratos, but rather for their flexibility, clarity, accuracy, and their ability to deliver the text clearly and naturally. Clarity of sound is also suggested by the linear, polyphonic nature of much Renaissance music. With a modern mixed chorus, the director thus needs to emphasize light production, unobtrusive vibrato, and phrasing based on proper pronunciation and word stress. The "expressivity" or "intensity" of Victoria's music should not lead the conductor to over-interpret it. The expression is largely built into the composition and does not have to be superimposed upon it. As we shall see, there are times when a slight underlining of Victoria's ideas might be desirable, but exaggeration will make the piece sound out of style.

"O magnum mysterium" appears in both of the Victoria collected-works editions.[6] Several American octavos of the work are available, the best of which

Part: M.#	1572 Reading	Comment
A: m. 16/2	F	A sharp is required to make a leading-tone cadence to G. Victoria usually provides it in such a context (ex., m. 56).
A: m. 26/1-2	F sharp	The restatement of the sharp is required by modern notation.
S: m. 41/1	F sharp	As immediately above.
T: m. 58/3	F	In the first "alleluia" phrase (mm. 53/3–57/1), both Fs leading to G are given in the original as F sharps. The same accidentals have been applied to subsequent, parallel phrases.
A: m. 62/3	F	See explanation of T: m. 58/3.
T: m. 64/3	F	See explanation of T: m. 58/3.

[6] These, and the location of the present motet within them, are as follows:

Tomás Luis de Victoria: Opera omnia, ed. P. Pedrell (Leipzig: Breitkopf und Härtel, 1902–1913) 1:11.

Tomás Luis de Victoria: Opera omnia, ed. P. Pedrell, rev., and corr. H. Anglès, in *Monumentos de la musica Española* (Rome: Consejo Superior de Investigationes Cientficas, 1965–1968) 26:7.

(Continued next page)

is Hinshaw Music HMC-960, edited by Walter S. Collins. The musical text is reliable, the transposition a minor third upward is sensible, and the editor is conservative in his addition of expression marks. The Shaw-Parker edition (G. Schirmer 10193), while not as accurate, contains expressive suggestions that might make it attractive to a conductor seeking interpretive assistance.[7]

Text

"O magnum mysterium" is a motet that in Victoria's time would have been sung on January 1, the Feast of the Circumcision. This feast and the Passion are the two observances of the shedding of Christ's blood, a fact that may have occasioned some musical references to the Passion. In the modern Catholic liturgy these words are sung on Christmas Day as the first part of the Responsory following the fourth Lesson of the Second Nocturn of Matins. The text and its translation below are adapted from *Translations and Annotations of Choral Repertoire*, vol. 1, 175.

Latin Text and Word-for-Word Translation	Translation
I *O mágnum mystérium* O great mystery	O great mystery and wondrous sacrament,
et admirábile sacraméntum and wondrous sacrament,	

ut   animália   viderunt   Dóminum   nátum,
      that animals should see   Lord   born
      jacéntem   in   praesépio!
      lying   in   manger!
	that animals should see the new-born Lord lying in their manger!

II *[O] Beáta Vírgo, cújus víscera meruérunt* [O] Blessed Virgin, whose womb was worthy	[O] Blessed Virgin whose womb was worthy to bear the Lord [Jesus] Christ.
portáre Dóminum [Jésum] Chrístum. to bear Lord [Jesus] Christ.	
III *[Alleluia!]*	[Alleluia!]

The Breitkopf score is based on the 1572 edition, but it conflicts with the original with regard to several accidentals. The same is true of the later collected-works edition, but the inconsistencies differ.

[7] The Shaw-Parker edition differs from the 1572 source as shown in the following table (Shaw-Parker transposition in parentheses):

Part: M.#	1572 Reading	S-P Reading	Comment
A: m. 8/4+	B flat	B natural (D natural)	B natural needed to avoid the B flat-C sharp augmented second.
T: m. 20/2+	F sharp	F natural (A flat)	
A: m. 25/2– 26/2	F sharp	F natural (A flat)	
S: m. 27/2	2 sixteenths	2 eighths	
T: m. 58/3	F	same (A flat)	Ed. F sharp recommended. (See S: m. 54)
A m. 62/3	F	F sharp (A nat.)	Ed. F sharp recommended. (See A: m. 56)
T: m. 64/3	F	same (A flat)	Ed. F sharp recommended. (See S: m. 54)

How miraculous and fitting it was, that the mortal incarnation of God was born not before kings, but in the presence of humble creatures! The words express the awe of mankind before that miracle and before the Virgin Mother. The conductor must embody this character of wonder into the singing of the choir. Victoria altered the liturgical text on three occasions (brackets above), each time heightening his expressive possibilities:

- His addition of the vocative *O* changes *Beata Virgo* from a simple statement of "Blessed is the Virgin" to a personal evocation: "O Blessed Virgin."
- The first name *Jesum* personalizes the title *Christum.*
- The addition of the "alleluia" provided Victoria with the opportunity to conclude the motet with joy and strength.[8]

The Music and Its Relationship to the Text

Victoria's composition appears to owe no debt to the "O magnum mysterium" chant given in the *Liber usualis.* The chant is used neither as a *cantus firmus* nor as a source of melodic ideas for points of imitation. It is possible, however, that the upper-neighbor figure that gives this motet much of its character might have its origins in the B–C–B figure that appears several times at the beginning of the chant.

At first glance the motet appears to be written in transposed (G) Dorian. The E flat and leading-tone F sharp are used so pervasively, however, that the result is almost tonal; in many ways it is more accurate to classify the piece as G minor, partaking of both the melodic and harmonic scales. Within the contrasting dominant (D-major) harmonies, the F sharp functions as the major third, while the E flat provides for solemn, quasi-Phrygian cadential motion (E flat–D). The alternation of major and minor harmonies is one of the most powerful expressive aspects of the composition.

The division of the text into three sections suggests a three-section musical setting, which is how Victoria constructed the motet:

I. mm. 1–39:   "O great mystery . . . ."
II. mm. 40–53/2: "O Blessed Virgin . . . ."
III. mm. 53/3–end: "Alleluia!"

---

[8] The "O magnum mysterium" chant is responsorial and thus consists of a "respond" followed by a "verse," the latter of which seems to have varied with time and place. The *Liber usualis* (Benedictines of Solesmes [Tournai: Desclée, *Imprimatur* 1956], 382) gives the text of the "Ave Maria" as the verse, while liturgical books of the later Middle Ages and Renaissance present a variety of other texts.

A motet could be used either liturgically (in place of the speaking or chanting of a required text) or extra-liturgically (as an addition to the liturgy, independent of the liturgical text). To be used liturgically, it had to present the words of the liturgy intact. Victoria's additions to the text and his substitution of the word "alleluia" for the verse indicate that this motet was to be used as extra-liturgical music (ex., as a processional).

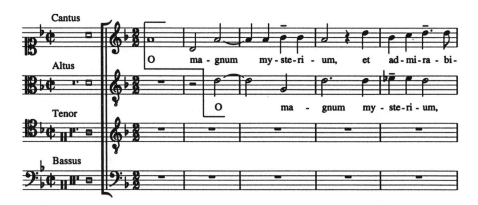

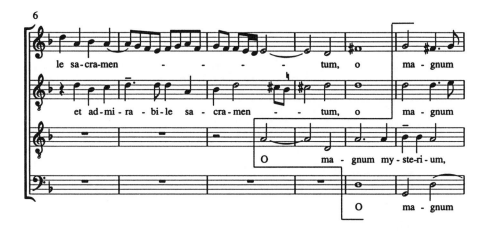

Example 4

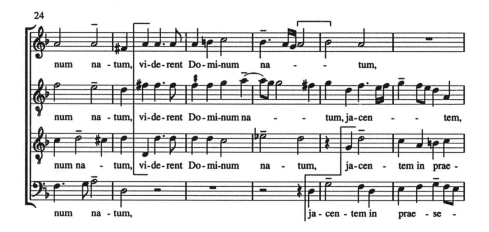

Example 4, continued

Example 4, conclusion

Section I. Victoria set the beginning in a manner so typical for motets that it is often called "motet style": each phrase of text receives its own motive or "point of imitation," which is taken up in turn by all the parts. Sections are built by linking together these settings of individual phrases. Phrases may be elided to each other or come to a general conclusion. Homorhythm and the lack of elision create stronger and more final cadences than a polyphony and elision.

The first subsection or period consists of a three-phrase setting of the words *O magnum mysterium et admirabile sacramentum.* The first two phrases contain identical imitative duets — first for the women and then for the men, the latter accompanied by the women on free musical material. The second phrase of the duet is elided to the first and has a brighter character, owing to the D-major harmony and the use of all four voices. In m. 14 Victoria breaks off the men's canonic imitation of the women to permit him to cadence in G minor instead of the previous D minor. The third phrase, a climactic, homorhythmic acclamation that ends this subsection, restates the last three words and concludes with an elided, perfect-authentic cadence in G minor.

This period is restrained yet highly expressive, owing to the minor harmonies, the descending fifth that depicts the word *magnum*, and the half-step, upper-neighbor figures (A–B flat-A, D–E flat–D). Many Renaissance and early Baroque composers recognized the emotional power of these motives. Compare, for example, the opening point of imitation in Victoria's motet with the beginning of the Luther's chorale melody "Aus tiefer Not" and the opening subject of Schütz's St. John Passion:

Example 5

The mood of awe can be established at the beginning by a restrained dynamic level (*p*, *mp*). The opening point of imitation requires tension leading to the flatted upper-neighbor tone, followed by relaxation. Likewise, the numerous B flat–A and E flat–D melodic cadences throughout the motet need to be prominent. This descending half-step cadence is melodically like the lower voice of the Phrygian cadence, which was thought to express sadness and supplication (Zarlino, 1588). The E flat–D motion is particularly effective, as it throws an unexpected shadow on the surrounding D-major harmonies.

Each phrase should be shaped to follow the natural accentuation of the text, with the climax of the phrase occurring where the tenutos are marked in the score. One must not use too much crescendo and diminuendo in shaping these phrases, however; loudness should never be substituted for energy. In mm. 8 and 9 the women must relax the end of their elided phrase to let the male duet predominate, and in their following accompanimental measures they must continue to remain in the background.

The homorhythmic statement that concludes this subsection is a climax and should be preceded by a general breath (m. 16/4). In m. 17 the composed intensification (homophony, expansion of outer voices) could be underscored with a slight crescendo, followed by a natural relaxation of the phrase in m. 19.

The second period or subsection extends from m. 19/4 to m. 39 and treats the following text:

1) *ut animalia*   2) *viderent   Dominum   natum,*   3) *jacentem in praesepio!*
that animals   should see the new-born Lord   lying in their manger!
As a contrast to the previous polyphony, and perhaps in depiction of the simplicity and innocence of the animals, Victoria set the first two word groups in homophony before closing with polyphony. He combined the words in three ways (1, 1+2, and 2+3), each of which permitted a different emphasis: first on the *animals*, then on the beholding of the *Lord*, and finally on the *lying in the manger*.

The first depiction of the animals is a simple, one-and-one-half-measure male duet in thirds that is elided to a soprano-alto-tenor trio on the same words but one step higher. The contrary motion of the outer parts (m. 22) sets up the entrance of the bass, who joins in a four-part, homophonic climax (mm. 23–24). The next phrase, on word groups two and three, begins as another high-voice trio that constitutes one of the most poignant moments in the motet — particularly when sung with the F sharps that are missing from most editions. The optimism of the D-major harmonies is suddenly clouded in m. 27, first by the soprano-alto suspension on *natum*, and then by the Phrygian motion (E flat–D) in the tenor. Here, even as the baby lies in the manger, the music foreshadows the crucifixion like the Golgotha scenes in many Renaissance nativity paintings.

The Phrygian motion in the tenor and the F sharp–G cadential figure in the alto (m. 27) provide melodic cadences, but there is no general cadence. Instead, the trio is elided to the final text group through the continuation of the alto part. The final phrase of text is characterized by four elided duets that alternate between low- and high-voice pairings. At the entrance of the final duet (mm. 34–35), all four parts sing together, bringing the section to a climax with the ascending swell of the upper three parts, supported by contrary motion in the bass (m. 36).

> The "animals" duet should begin lightly and simply, and the following four-part homophonic acclamation of the Lord should have a sense of climax at the word *natum*. This could be underscored with some crescendo leading to the first syllable. There should be no breath after the second *animalia*, as the thought continues and is treated as a single musical phrase. The *viderent Dominum* trio (m. 25) represents a relaxation and a change of thought. This could be considered the beginning of the following idea rather than the end of the one preceding. The elision can be made clear by having the alto carry through m. 28 without a breath, despite the comma. (The original print provides no punctuation whatsoever.) Three elements combine to create a climactic close for this section that could be underlined with increased intensity and dynamic: the coalescing of all four parts into the same text and rhythm in m. 36, the strong contrary motion of the outer voices, and the upward movement of the inner parts. The subsequent, natural relaxation that closes this section in mm. 37–39 could be reinforced by a diminuendo and a slight ritard and fermata.

Section II. The brief (14 mm.) middle section begins with a homophonic evocation of Mary, the unexpected D-major harmony of which is reminiscent of the halos surrounding Baroque statues of the Virgin. Almost immediately, however, the harmonies revert to G minor, and the somber upper-neighbor motive returns. Here Victoria refers again to the Passion: in his motet for Maundy Thursday entitled "Vere languores" (also from the 1572 book of motets), he used precisely the same music for the words *sustinere regem*: "Gentle cross and gentle nails that bore so sweet a burden; you alone were *worthy of bearing* the King of Heaven and the Lord." The Virgin's womb alone was worthy to bear the Christ child, and the cross alone was worthy to bear the King of Heaven.

The passage begins with two measures of calm, long-note homophony that is subsequently energized by the soprano-bass melisma in parallel thirds. The delayed entrance of the alto on *cujus viscera* (m. 44) begins an intensification that is urged forward by the ascending chain of eighth notes in the inner parts on the word *meruerunt* in mm. 45–46. In m. 48 Victoria cadences to B flat on the same word — the only time in the motet that he does not cadence to G or D. This has the character of a half-cadence and creates no real sense of arrival, since the upper three parts continue seamlessly onward in homophony. The two-measure omission of the bass and the simultaneous soprano-alto descent (mm. 48/3–

50/2) create a relaxation that sets the stage for the majestic statement of the name *Jesum Christum*. Victoria probably decided to add the word *Jesum* to personalize the title *Christum* and to give him more time to create a climax through staggered entrances and cross-rhythms.

Example 6

This section should begin softly, as suggested by the worshipful text, the suspended harmony, the static rhythm, and the low range. The melismas in mm. 42–43 should be shaped as arches, with the repeated notes in both voices distinctly separated. The composed intensification in mm. 45–47 might be underlined with some crescendo, just as the composed relaxation in mm. 49–50 might be complemented by diminuendo. Victoria's rhythmically vigorous setting of the name *Jesum Christum* suggests that it should be delivered triumphantly, with a growth of intensity and dynamic through m. 51, and with light accents to bring out the interplay of the cross rhythms. A softening at the end should be avoided, as it would negate the composed contrast with the restrained beginning of the "alleluia" that follows. The last note could be given more finality by a slight hold before the "alleluia" is begun.

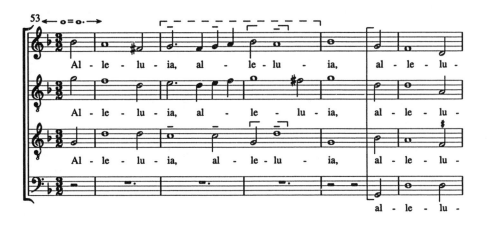

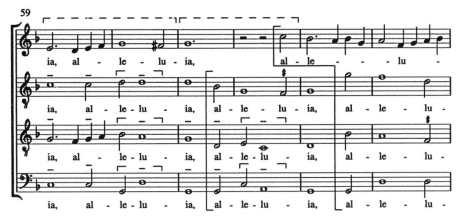

Example 7

Example 7, conclusion

Section III. The "alleluia" is simply and strictly constructed. It is composed in two parts, the first in triple meter and the second — a quasi-codetta — in duple meter. The triple-meter section consists of four parallel phrases, the first, second, and fourth of which are four measures in length. The third phrase, abbreviated to two measures, is used as a bridge to relax tension (the lower three parts are in their low ranges) in preparation for the climactic last phrase. Each of the four-measure phrases contains the same melodic and rhythmic structure, with the two central measures written in hemiola counter-rhythm in all but one voice. (Two measures of 3/2 become the rhythmic equivalent of a measure of 3/1.)[9] The two-measure "bridge" to the fourth phrase is also hemiolic in all but one part.

---

[9] Victoria and his contemporaries often explicitly notated hemiola by blackening ("coloring") the last two notes of each hemiolic rhythm. This can be seen in the facsimiles of the partbooks reproduced as example 8 at the end of this chapter. In the score, notes that were colored in the original print are enclosed by bracket corners above the staff (ex., S, T, and B: m. 56), and the hemiolic combining of two measures is indicated by the elimination of bar lines and the use of broken brackets above the affected measures.

The concluding, duple-meter section of the "alleluia" is triumphant and abounds with rhythmic activity. The initial stretto-like imitation from bottom to top establishes this character. In a manner typical of Renaissance compositions, Victoria composes a ritard in the last three measures by having the soprano sustain its final note while the rhythmic activity of the other voices slows; this suggests that little additional ritard is required. The use of the picardy third on the final chord is typical of Renaissance compositions in a minor mode.

As indicated in the Shaw-Parker edition, the concluding "alleluia" is usually performed in fast compound meter, with two measures of triple time approximately equal to one measure of duple time. Research into *tactus*, tempo, and proportion in the late Renaissance suggests, however, that the solution offered in the Collins edition is more accurate: this section should be performed in a slower three, with a triple bar approximately equal in duration to a duple bar. While an exactly proportional relationship is not absolutely necessary, and a somewhat faster triple meter is possible, on no account should the triple section be taken fast enough to be conducted "in two."[10]

The relatively slow tempo makes it all the more important that the hemiola rhythm be emphasized to provide rhythmic interest. The notes shown with tenuto marks in the score should be stressed, and a genuine Italianate (frontal, dental) pronunciation of the double "l" will help. While Americans tend to pronounce this word with weak "l"s, as "ah-leh-lu-yuh," Italian pronunciation of double consonants calls for the "l" to be closed at the end of the first syllable and opened on the second: "al-leh-lu-yah" This provides the opportunity to stress the second "l." It also shortens and lightens the upbeat, providing additional rhythmic interest.

The reduction of the texture to three parts at the beginning suggests a restrained dynamic. The final triple-meter phrase, however, has a climactic quality created by its placement at the end of the section, the early entrance of the soprano, the use of all four voices, and the expanded vocal range. If one accepts this analysis, the question that follows is how to bring out this intensification in performance. This writer would propose beginning at a *piano* dynamic level and increasing the dynamic of each phrase in terraced fashion, with the climax occurring in m. 66. Of course, this must be done subtly in order not to sound inappropriately romantic.

The transition into the second section of the "alleluia" often presents difficulties for conductors. A simple and musical solution would be to make a slight ritard in m. 66, with the last beat of triple meter equal to the half-note beat in the following duple meter. This will permit the chorus to anticipate the new tempo accurately.

The method of analysis and the interpretive ideas presented above are those of the author. Others might follow different procedures and reach other conclusions just as valid as those given here. This is not necessarily a question

---

[10] The solution the author advocates here is known as *sesquialtera* proportion, which was the standard triple-meter proportion in sixteenth-century sacred music. *Tripla* proportion, which would yield the fast triple meter indicated in the Shaw-Parker edition, was very rare in Renaissance motet literature, and is not indicated by Victoria's notation.

of right or wrong, but rather of taking different paths toward the same goal. The point is that all performers need to go through a careful, systematic process of inquiry in reaching their interpretive decisions, so that they might present with beauty and integrity the music with which they have been entrusted.

Facsimile. *O magnum mysterium*, 1572 edition.

Facsimile, continued

In Circumcifione Domini.   4. Voc.   5   ALTVS

Magnũ mifterium   & admirabile facramen-

tum O magnum mifte   rium & admi-

rabile facramen tum & admirabile facramentum ut animalia   ui-

derunt dominũ natum uiderũt dominũ na   tum iacen   tem

iacentẽ in pre fe   pi o iacentẽ in pre-

fe   pio O Beata Virgo cuius vifcera me-

ruerunt portare do   minũ Ie   fum Chriftum allelu-

ia al li leluya   alleluya alleluya alleluya alleluya al-

alle   lu   ya alle   lu   ya.

Facsimile, continued

Facsimile, conclusion

Coming to Terms with Historical Performance Practices

Melinda O'Neal

I. Introduction

Musicians know that a serious effort must be made to understand a composer's musical intentions starting with the context of a work within its historical style period. For the conductor, this avenue of inquiry presents an extraordinary, even bewildering, array of topics to investigate, including: 1) the circumstances and audience for whom the work was composed; 2) the size and shape of the hall and disposition (stage setup) of the instrumental and vocal forces; 3) the tuning system, the local pitch level, types of instruments and their construction (e.g. use of gut or metal strings, valve or natural horns); 4) the tone colors of the voices and instruments; 5) the variations of metrical stress within measures and phrases and principles of articulation; 6) the meaning of the text, sentence syntax as well as regional pronunciations. These are just *some* of the questions the conductor should ask concerning performance practices in order to be prepared for the first rehearsal.

For the student of conducting who must secure a plethora of new information and skills, addressing every one of these issues is an impossible charge, perhaps even an unfair one. Reticence to incorporate an informed perspective on performance practices may be more deeply ensconced, however, in those of us who have not addressed the issue in our own training. If we are conducting community organizations or teaching in the primary or secondary schools, or even conducting at the college and university levels, many of us simply do not consider active application of historical performance practices to be within the scope of our responsibilities. Some may think performances using such an approach will fail in their potential for making expressive, beautiful music. Many contend that such an endeavor is not a realistic pursuit for it requires extreme amounts of effort and time, both of which are at a premium. Resources are limited, the landscape of reliable information is quixotic and subject to fashion, and confirmed irrefutable facts are nearly impossible to locate for a specific work.

But more to the heart of the matter, many conductors do not like to experiment with the process and product of their performances. Whereas within a classroom or in an article one can explore performance questions without jeopardizing an actual performance, the rehearsal process and its resultant concert presentation are always a gamble for the conductor who cares deeply for the music and whose reputation is on the line. To invite additional elements of risk into our own public performances takes more courage than many of us can reasonably be called to muster.

Still, with all these causes for concern, musicians today know that addressing the issue of historical performance practices — the "who, what, why, where, and how" which framed performance at the time of composition — is fundamental to understanding the music itself. The presumption that the notes on the page, of and by themselves, comprise a perfect system whereby we can conclude centuries later we are performing what the composer had in mind, is clearly an insufficient premise.

There is no one answer for the myriad of questions involving performance practices. This chapter will present various perspectives on the topic and some practical suggestions for coming to terms with the issue.

II. Musicology vs. Aesthetics vs. Pedagogy

The claim of authenticity is an arrogant one, especially when it purports to overrule the taste of musicians or listeners by an appeal to scholarship.[1]
                                                    — Nicholas Temperley

Resistance among some conductors to learning more about how music was performed at the time of its composition is caused by a fear of over-intellectualizing music, binding it up in sets of categories and rules. This is not surprising, considering the state of musicology stemming from the 1950s, as Joseph Kerman described it:

> New manuscripts were discovered and described, archives were reported on, dates were established, cantus firmi traced from one work and one composer to another. Musicologists dealt mainly in the verifiable, the objective, the uncontroversial, and the positive.[2]

Facts and new critical editions, not the interpretation of facts or the music, have been the goal and notable achievement of musicology. "Much less attention was paid to the interaction of music history with political, social, and intellectual history. And less attention yet was devoted to the attempt to understand music as an aspect of and in relation to culture in the large."[3] There were (and are) "more and more facts, and less and less confidence in interpreting them."[4]

This positivistic approach is still the dominant mode for much of musicology today. Thus, in the process of identifying the music text and developing virtual sets of fast and firm rules for performers to obey, the assumed freedom which allowed the conductor to perform music in an expressive personal way *before* this information was discovered is seemingly eliminated. Searches for new revelations, spontaneity, meaning, re-creation are crushed underneath the burdensome overlay of designated, obligatory, perceived but not clearly enough defined performance directives.

But musicians know that the music is lost when a performance becomes a documentation of a state of knowledge rather than an expression of musical

---

[1] Temperley, Nicholas, Contribution to "The Limits of Authenticity: A Discussion," *Early Music*, 12 (1984), p. 18.

[2] Kerman, Joseph, *Contemplating Music*, p. 42.

[3] Ibid, p. 43.

[4] Ibid, p. 54.

conviction. Indeed, it is the performer who must bring the facts to life through interpreting them, finding a sure basis for confidence in doing so. This means, therefore, asking questions, doing research, and taking risks.

Unfortunately, there is a troubling separation of the artistic disciplines into two general categories: those who perform versus those who analyze. The underlying assumption is that performers would prefer to simply locate the recommended edition, duplicate the notes aurally, and "make music." A similarly narrow-minded view holds that historians and theorists are unable to perform — or just would rather not. Enlightened interaction within the arts has been seriously undermined by the notion that choosing one specialization absolves or prohibits venturing into other realms.

The chasm between musicology and performance has been further reinforced in many conservatories and academic circles. The student conductor may be led to think of music encountered in history and literature classes in historical terms and therefore as literature in the abstract. Music studied in lessons and in ensembles, however, is more real because it relates to the application of instrumental or vocal pedagogy; it is participatory and allows music to be more deeply assimilated through the experience of rehearsing and performing.

Consequently, some of our educational systems may lead the interpreter (conductor) to falsely believe that absolutism, positivism, the setting down of "rules" of performance practices, and the abstraction of music into facts, history and literature are all incompatible with many dynamic, flexible, spirited elements of performance. But in reality, exploring the non-conventional — that is, trying some of the conventions of previous styles of performance — may lead to a fresh new understanding of the music and, indeed, more compelling performances. Understanding the values, aesthetics, and sounds of a different age can be nurtured through allowing conductors the freedom to experiment with both old and new modes of expression. This is a profoundly affecting benefit of incorporating performance practices into present-day performances, one that offers a vastly enlarged scope of performance choices and possibilities for the conductor.

Many conductors working with young musicians share the conviction that it is impossible to reconstruct what may have been the sound ideal at the time of, for example, the Mozart *Requiem*. Of course, this is true. We will never know exactly how voices sounded in 1791. If, indeed, there were different tone colors, different vocal sound ideals in each region of each province, different Latin pronunciations, different approaches to the voice *passagio*, use of boys' voices with sopranos from the opera house and/or castrati for treble parts, different systems of tuning from what we are accustomed to in the present day, then presenting a survey of music history through a traditional, generalized music ensemble is incompatible with the demands that those differences make. Prevalently, the more important goals of building a good tone and playing or singing in tune seem to be the more reasonable, attainable objectives. Consequently, the potential for a conflict of interest looms ahead forebodingly between the specialized ensemble attempting to perform Mozart's *Requiem* with a light, boy-choir soprano sonority and the studio teacher (or the conductor who comes from the player-singer orientation) desiring a more full-bodied "beauti-ful" tone from those same singers.

Frequently the vocalise-oriented rehearsal is formulated out of context with a work's historical properties or structural aspects. This approach to choral music focuses on developing the vocal instrument, not unlike a group voice lesson. In many contexts, from elementary school upward, the value of having a uniform, "beautiful" vocal-choral tone, even putting the conductor's personal tonal "stamp" on the sound, no matter what the music, overtakes other essential and equally important stylistic and contextual considerations, such as metrical and textual accentuation, articulation and phrasing, proportion of tempos throughout the structure of a work, varieties of tone color from movement to movement, the meaning and potential impact of the text, understanding the composer's socio-political context, or the affect of the music on audiences of the time.

The economizing pedagogical decision made long ago to teach singing to young people in groups versus teaching instrumentalists on a one-to-one basis has produced a number of unfortunate circumstances. First, as previously mentioned, there is the conductor's underlying concern for putting a uniform tonal "stamp" on the sound. Second, the individual's vocal problems are not addressed when the rehearsal is devoted to applying general principles for singing, not to mention the demands of singing in a variety of styles consistent with the varieties of music available. Whereas instrumentalists receive early one-to-one instruction, singers do not receive this kind of attention until much later. This has resulted in the use of a diluted, generalized vocal pedagogy in choruses, leading to a third unfortunate consequence: the individual chorister is marginalized. Whereas the oboe player is playing one- or two-to-a-part, the chorister — who is one of five- or ten- or fifteen-to-a-part — is not dealt with as an individual. The devaluation of vocal ensembles as compared to instrumental ensembles, as seen ultimately in the disparity of pay scale and job security in the professional world, is one of the ultimate consequences.

Just as instrumentalists specialize by learning the demands of playing each instrument, so may singers specialize by learning to vary tone quality, text pronunciation (with the aide of using the International Phonetic Alphabet), procedures for ornamentation, and even different ways to breathe and produce tone. The unrealistic expectation that, in order to be properly prepared as musicians, all singers must sing repertoire from all style periods — yet never vary their approach according to stylistic performance practice differences — must not continue as an underlying principle for vocal ensembles. Treating the singer like a listener in a music history survey class, where covering all the style periods is assumed, necessitates an unrealistic approach technically. Obviously, to perform and to listen are two entirely different artistic functions; the educa-tional objectives for one need not govern those of the other. The age of breadth and generalization, consequently, is not as relevant to the essence of the music, and rightfully so, as is the emerging imperative for focus and specialization which can ultimately reveal the music for what it might have been at inception.

The goal of the music educator and conductor performing music composed prior to the twentieth century (or any music, for that matter) is to offer a life-enriching aesthetic experience and provide an enhanced understanding of self and the world. In this context, the conductor can choose one of several kinds of performance philosophies. One would be a late nineteenth and twentieth century, personalized tradition based on modeling and instinct as is perpetuated in many conducting training programs today. This tradition acknowledges that music is different from style period to style period, but the ways of performing it differ only slightly. Another would entail pursuing a specific body of repertoire, performing it in accordance with the information and resources at hand, and seeking to experiment with the "otherness" of what may have been performed in another day and age. This approach requires additional inquiry into the nature of the work and the composer's sound ideal, and it requires willingness to take risks. Yet another choice could be a combination of the two in varying degrees, allowing for variables in each individual's circumstances and resources. Conductors will be able to make the necessary practical decisions by establishing a clear set of historical, pedagogical, and aesthetic goals.

III. Authenticity — Ideal or Caveat?

I do not recognize that the mode of performance that suited the composer is necessarily the best for all time.[5]

— Nicholas Temperley

The meaning of authenticity has been debated thoroughly in the last twenty years.[6] Despite the distinctively twentieth century notion of absolute right and wrong ways of performing historical music, there will always be decisions to be made for which there will be no patent guidelines, and there will be questions on which authorities in and out of fashion will agree and disagree. Additionally, conductors will inevitably project into a performance mannerisms and traits of which they themselves are unaware.

But how do we get clos*er*, or clos*est* to the composer's original intent? Philip Brett, in an article on two 40-voice motets on the same text by Tallis and Striggio, discusses how the expressive details must relate to the overall design: "I think we need insights into the intentions and the anatomy of early music derived from a close reading of the music itself and related not to some abstract method but to the realities of the matter in hand."[7] He argues that it is wrong "to place a piece in terms of the externals of style rather than structure" because style "tells us nothing about the inner logic of a piece or about the kind of compositional thought it embodies."[8]

Le Huray also recommends the use of analysis as an interpretive tool to grasp overall structure and to focus upon the individual work rather than

---

[5] Temperley, Nicholas, Contribution to "The Limits of Authenticity: A Discussion," *Early Music*, 12 (1984), p. 18.

[6] Authors such as Temperley, Taruskin, Brett, Neumann, Le Huray, and Donington are noted.

[7] Brett, Philip, "Facing the Music," *Early Music*, 10, 1982, p. 349.

[8] Ibid, p. 349.

perceived performance conventions. The performer must "search for the fullest possible picture of the original, a picture that will more clearly define the range of choices that are open to the performer."[9] Then Le Huray points to the crux of the issue: " . . . but until every potential source of information has been checked the player will be in no position to assess the strengths and weaknesses of modern techniques and interpretive approaches."[10] He recommends having the humility to modify accepted assumptions.

IV. Subjectivity or Objectivity; Interpreter or Transmitter

Vaughan Williams once compared a page of music to a railway timetable. The page, he says, tells us no more about the living experience of the music than the timetable tells us about the sights to be enjoyed during the journey.[11]

— Peter Le Huray

How do we balance new performance practice information with a creative approach to interpretation? Stravinsky believed that balance was an ethical matter. He deplored the "exaggerated role accorded to the performer."[12] Hindemith called the performer an "intermediate transformer station."[13] Schoenberg and Messiaen were both aware of notational limitations and the need for respect of the composer's wishes. Le Huray writes: "If, then, composers tend to mean what they write, it is our duty as performers to try to find out as much as possible about that meaning. It is as much a question of ethics as aesthetics."[14] But, he contends, musical "meaning" has no fixed or absolute value. There cannot be only one way of playing a piece. ". . . [A] musical object can be viewed from many angles and yet remain essentially the same piece."[15]

There is the inevitable comparison of historically informed performances referred to earlier which are labelled "sterile" — so objective as to be unmoving — and those which are "deeply committed" — moving because the conductor imbued the music with a personal, subjective interpretation.[16] Yet it seems that

---

[9] Le Huray, *Authenticity in Performance,* 1990, p. 4.

[10] Ibid, p. 4. This statement may pose grave difficulties, for by the time *every* potential source is checked, the conductor may become paralysed with indecision in the face of too many choices. Maintaining a balance between the spirit and the law of this assertion and its application is advised.

[11] Ibid, p. 1.

[12] Ibid, p. 3.

[13] Hindemith, *A Composer's World*, p. 132.

[14] Le Huray, op. cit., p. 3.

[15] Ibid, p. 4.

[16] Leech-Wilkinson, Daniel, Contribution to "The Limits of Authenticity: A Discussion," *Early Music*, 12 (1984), p. 14: Modern performances, in comparison with historically inform-ed ones, incorporate a more "emotional," more a personal "interpretation" of what the performers believe the composer to be "saying;" while the more recent, "authentic" performance is characterized by relatively uniform tempo and dynamics, a "clean" sound and at least an attempt to avoid interpretive gestures beyond those notated or documented as part of period performance practice.

the "deeply committed" or subjective view of interpretation refers only to music performed with those nineteenth century approaches underlying our twentieth century aesthetic, and "objectivity" refers only to historically informed performances of earlier music which then lack some important element of spirit or appeal. Experience suggests that many listeners are still convinced that it is necessary to have a Wagnerian crescendo with a Brahms-sized orchestra in order to get an emotional charge from, say, Mozart's Symphony No. 40.

Equating big, romantic-style sonorities and dynamic contrasts with dramatic excitement is simply superimposing the stylistic traits and performance practices of the nineteenth century retroactively onto the music of the eighteenth and even seventeenth century. In most concert halls, consequently, conductors shape the music according to the needs and desires of modern temperaments instead of guiding audiences toward becoming informed and thus shaped by the nature and design of the music as it was first intended by the composer. Historically informed conductors, just as those of the modern school, will sometimes succeed and sometimes not succeed in capturing a convincing sense of the music. But as more historically informed artists come to the forefront, it is becoming clearer that new (more accurately, re-created) performances, which make an effort to perform the music as it may have sounded when it was composed, are taking on a wholly different aesthetic, a new world of "otherness" which can beguile and charm on its own merits.

Some critics would maintain that since there is not a twentieth century repertory many audiences want to hear, performers and their audiences have harkened back to music of earlier centuries for a safe haven.[17] In fact, modern-style performances of historical music are *necessitated* by our larger concert halls — performances on period instruments in large halls often do not work well enough. For the most part, historically informed performances become feasible only in the recording industry where fewer instrumentalists are playing in smaller halls. To give live performances in a scaled-down concert hall and sell fewer tickets is simply impossible economically. Ironically, successful historical performances are more frequently experienced in the living rooms of ardent audiophiles than in expense driven concert halls.

There may be a strong element of self-delusion in the way we have allowed ourselves as conductors to take a personal, subjective posture toward the music we perform. It is almost as if the interpreter, because he is alive and here, may take away or add to a work whose creator has been long dead. By contrast, when a visual artist takes a guest to look at a painting by a great master, he normally will bring him to a gallery to see the work in natural light, if at all possible, in a quiet place devoted to viewing art. The point is to see the painting *as it is* and *as the artist saw it*. Because music is temporal and requires re-creation in performance, curiously some conductors feel empowered to bring it to life in their own image rather than in the composer's image — as if we know better how to do it

---

[17] Morgan, Robert P., "Tradition, Anxiety, and the Musical Scene" in *Authenticity and Early Music*, Oxford: Oxford University Press, 1988, p. 78: "The music of the twentieth century is too chaotic with no clear lineage of accessible works forming a mainstream repertoire for mainstream audiences."

today than the actual creator did then. In effect, "modern" has been equated with "new and improved" and thus better than the original. If *newer* truly is *better*, then indeed we should be performing only new music.[18]

The question, then, of whether our own performances are objective or subjective becomes far less relevant than: 1) the importance of understanding context and congruity; 2) the question of whether we have started from a fundamental basis of understanding the music; and 3) the importance of making informed rather than unconscious choices about the way we perform music.

As conductors we need to know the extent to which we have unknowingly succumbed to sociological, economic, and pedagogical influences in our modern music making. The reward in taking a fresh look at the music and its context, as Donington has put it, "is experiencing something other than ourselves." It is "in the sheer delight of the music."[19]

V. Context and Congruity

The performers, who may be musicologists themselves, inevitably add many features of style that are too subtle to be described and hence cannot be judged by the criterion of historical accuracy. The resulting mixture may appeal strongly to the desire for a novel but historical-sounding style.[20]

— Nicholas Temperley

Understanding how a musical work was performed at the time it was composed is a fundamental part of the basic text of the music. This is what Donington calls "congruity between music and performance."[21] But who could possibly desire incongruity between music and its performance? When and where did such separation occur, and how did it happen?

Contextual and congruity issues of historical performance practices are brought into heightened relief when viewed in relation to performances of music from other cultures. In a recent effort to broaden the horizons of an undergraduate non-music major singing ensemble, this author invited Dmitri Pokrovsky, a noted folksinger and conductor from Russia, to teach the group several Russian folk songs. He provided music scores with Cyrillic text transcribed into phonetic symbols underneath, and he taught the music to the group by singing the various parts as he would have done in Russia. By the eve of the performance, the ensemble was ready to perform, knowing full well that: 1) the

---

[18] See Jackson, Roland, "Performance Practice and Its Critics — the Debate Goes On" in *Performance Practice Review*, Fall, 1991. This article summarizes the proponent and antagonist positions to use of performance practices directly in reference to subjective, nineteenth-century interpretations.

[19] Donington, "The Present Position of Authenticity," *Performance Practice Review*, Vol. 2, No. 2, (Fall, 1989), p. 123.

[20] Temperley, Nicholas, op. cit., p. 18.

[21] Donington, "The Present Position of Authenticity," *Performance Practice Review*, Vol. 2, No. 2, (Fall, 1989), p. 117.

women could not alter their vocal technique to produce the nasal, coarse chest-tone of the Russian folk singers and then perform the nineteenth and twentieth century Western classical repertoire programmed for the remainder of the program; 2) the songs were out of context — some were processionals, one was a ceremonial song intended to be forty minutes in length rather than the four minutes the concert format required; and 3) the texts were meaningless to performers and audience without performing multiple verses and without extensive explanation. The concert would have turned into a lecture and the chorus would have had far too many Russian words to learn to pronounce.

This illustrates that the modern concert setting — our most prevalent present-day cultural context for performance — is substantially different from contexts for ethnic music and, to take one more step, of historical music. The values of each culture and the reasons for making the music were and are now very different. Our concert clearly *missed the point*. Music is a transmitter of *culture*. The human reasons for making music were and are, in many situations, far more important than the music itself. The display of a modern performer's intellect and skill in the concert hall has far less to do with why music exists than many musicians realize. Our well-intentioned ambition to perform Russian folk songs well, and even the conductor's well-intentioned pedagogical goal of exposing students and audiences to Russian folk music, in fact led the songs, when taken so completely out of context, to lose their most important meaning. This music became a rarefied object, an artifact in the modern concert hall rather than a reflection of the music's significance and function in another culture's way of life. The original meaning and impact were compromised, and thus the music was the first to be improperly served.[22]

In *Mozart's Symphonies*, Neal Zaslaw, one of the few musicologists to treat music as literature in the same breath with performance practice considerations, points to other incongruities. He says music of the Classical period has been given a "spurious uniformity, both within itself and with music of the Romantic period."[23] This spurious uniformity, the application of generalized nineteenth century performance practices to the standard repertory of eighteenth century music, has blurred the distinctiveness of an entire corpus of music. Clearly, without the benefit of recordings, there exist only treatises, chroniclings, scores, instruments, iconography, and performance rooms to provide a physical or written record of an ephemeral, aural experience. Consequently, nineteenth century traditions which were viewed then and now as superior, were passed on orally, by role-modelling and by demonstration in nineteenth and twentieth

---

[22] One could rightfully argue that the students and the audience most certainly did gain something valuable from this venture into Russian folk music performance. While the cultural context and tone quality were missing, everyone did experience harmonies, textures, and language which were different and rewarding in their own way. To identify to the audience where our efforts fell short of the goal to re-live the music would have been helpful, and framing the music more carefully, rather than programming it as another set of selections in a concert, would have been well advised.

[23] Zaslaw, *Performance Practice after 1600*, p. 211.

century private studios, classrooms, and concert halls. As pointed out previously, most nineteenth century instrumental and vocal performance practices are nearly synonymous with modern ones and are still applied retroactively to the music of earlier eras.[24]

In fact, present-day conductors are already twice-removed from the composer when performing historical music: first by time period; and second by function. What Elizabeth Green aptly calls the "modern conductor" was an unknown entity until the 1820's and 30's. Even in those years, if the first violinist was not leading the ensemble from his chair or the keyboard player from the console, it was the conductor — the one *not* holding an instrument yet standing in front of the group — who faced the audience rather than the performers. Until very recently, composers themselves most frequently led or conducted their music; Byrd, Bach, Mozart, Haydn, Berlioz, Mendelssohn, Liszt, Brahms, Wagner did not use intermediaries. Mendelssohn, and particularly Berlioz in his treatise on instrumentation and conducting, were most influential in turning conducting into the highly visible performance practice and art form it is today. This role of conductor, then, is a modern phenomenon out of context with the performance circumstances of much pre-nineteenth century music. Whether to dispense with the silent, gesticulating leader of earlier style periods must remain a decision for the conductor, of course. To know that he or she is to some degree dispensable is valuable information, indeed.

Often the structure of the musical organization and other extra-musical considerations take precedence over the demands of the music itself. For example, choosing to perform the Mozart *Requiem* with 150-plus choristers, soloists from the Verdi/Puccini operatic tradition, in a concert hall that seats 2,000 or more was hardly what Mozart had in mind. We might do this, however, for a commemorative occasion such as the anniversary of Mozart's death, box office demand, or to establish the pre-eminence of the performance group or a conductor. In these instances, however, most of the audience is seated so far away that the performers are like little specks, effectively removing the listeners from the palpable, sensual realities of attending a live performance. By contrast, Mozart's commemorative performance of Handel's *Messiah* probably employed 16 choristers, soloists from the opera house who also sang with the chorus, an orchestra with probably just four or five first violins[25] in a hall that was perhaps 59 feet by 36 feet.[26] The use of compact-sized halls in the eighteenth century confirms that early composers were counting on an intimacy and immediacy

---

[24] The behavior of audiences and the makeup of concert programs in the nineteenth-century are significantly different now than in the nineteenth century. Since, however, most of the orchestral instruments were "improved" in the nineteenth century and have remained virtually unchanged since, there is a strong basis for this statement.

[25] Maunder, Richard, *Mozart's* Requiem: *On Preparing a New Edition*, pp. 199-200.

[26] Zaslaw, Neal, *Mozart's Symphonies*, pp. 471–472. Other sources note expanded forces up to forty choristers. The 1784 commemorative performances in Westminster Abbey are universally acknowledged to be special occasions, not the norm.

rarely available today.[27] Surely listeners deserve to feel the sound and to sense its physical impact. Modern conventions have altered dramatically this music and its context.

Looking back even further to Bach's time, we see that a wholly different dynamic prevailed for the educator-manager-conductor and his pupils. The cantor was the director of music at a church as well as the chief administrator of its instructional institution. Students were taught to sing, play several instruments, and compose. Versatility in all areas was assumed, as is illustrated by the following quotation from a recommendation written by J.S. Bach on behalf of one of his pupils:

> To give you a slight foretaste, he is thoroughly expert as a composer and has given various samples of his work here with good acclaim. Furthermore he plays a good organ and clavier, is accomplished on the violin, violoncello, and other instruments, sings a bass that is, though not too strong, quite stylish, and his qualities in general are such that I believe he could well be employed for the vacant post.[28]

The importance of multiple skills and the cross-fertilization of singing and playing techniques was common in the Lutheran music tradition at this time. "We might expect, then, that string players possessed much the same musical knowledge as singers and that they interpreted the music in a similar fashion."[29] Often singers would be asked to play instruments when the regular players were absent from the chapel. Later, Leopold Mozart demanded deep musical knowledge from the player, a "great insight into the whole art of musical composition and into the variety of characters."[30] Performers were asked to deal with music on a different level from today: they were asked to think as composer, theologian, and humanist. Singers now, it seems, are required merely to pay attention, sight read exactly what is on the page, make a beautiful tone, and ardently (and at times blindly) follow the instructions of the conductor.

The question must be raised: Which entity is most important and to what degree — the organization, tradition, pedagogy, conductor, scholarship, composition? Careful thought given to the impact each of these matters have on repertoire choices and approaches to performance will lead the conductor to explore the use of performance practices, and all will benefit from the resulting lively spirit of experimentation. Most importantly, performers and audience alike will advance toward meeting the true goal: realizing the quality and convincingness of a work of art.

---

[27] This need for not just hearing but feeling the sound is undoubtedly one major element of success for the recording industry. With a recording the listener can feel as though he is inside the sound to the limits the volume dial or button and human aural capacity will permit.

[28] Butt, John, *Bach Interpretation*. Cambridge University Press, 1990, pp. 35–36.

[29] Ibid, p. 37.

[30] Ibid, p. 37, from Leopold Mozart's *Versuch einer gründlichen Violinschule* of 1756, p. 254.

VI. Topics of Inquiry

Performers want scholars to tell them what is right; scholars should tell them what they know, and emphasize that the rest is a matter of taste.[31]

— Nicholas Temperley

While the landscape of information and resources is ever-widening, and while scholarly arguments continue to complicate the scenario, the conductor must continue to do the necessary research, ask questions among colleagues, and draw independent conclusions. Good library skills, a bent for exploration, and planning ahead are essential.

The following are suggested topics for inquiry and some suggested practical approaches to performing historical music in an informed, thoughtful, and persuasive manner.

1. Edition selection. After conducting a thorough search for all available editions of a work in a music library, identify a good music retailer (preferably with an 800 telephone number) with whom you can establish a friendly working relationship. This person can list additional editions of works in their various formats and provide the all-important cost comparison of available full scores, piano-vocal scores, and instrumental parts. Determine retail or rental status of the performance materials and the time required for delivery. Borrowing performance materials from another institution is a cost saving option, though ideally conductors should assemble their own personal library not only of full scores and piano-vocal scores but of marked sets of orchestra parts as well. Newer editions are usually more expensive than older editions but not necessarily the best. For example the Maunder edition of the Mozart *Requiem*, in which the editor has recomposed passages left incomplete by Mozart, is not acceptable to many conductors. Perusal and referential use of all available editions, especially the collected works editions held in the reference areas of music libraries,[32] will be invaluable for answering note discrepancy questions, comparison of editorial procedures, and locating important information provided in historical and performance notes. Style of layout and readability are important considerations. Discussion with colleague conductors about their knowledge and experiences with various editions will be essential.

2. Historical background. The conductor is obligated to locate authoritative sources discussing the historical style period, socio-cultural-political-economic context, composer, the composer's overall output, and the work itself. Through assembling performance notes for the audience or rehearsal comments for the performers, a conductor can establish a framework for the original context so that all involved may experience (or at least imagine) the music beyond the limited, out-of-context concert settings of today. It is significant to point out, for example: "Symphonies lacked the prestige of either vocal music

---

[31] Temperley, Nicholas, op. cit., p. 18.

[32] The editorial and performance notes in more recently published collected works editions (e.g. Berlioz) can be extremely informative concerning performance considerations.

or instrumental music intended for elite gatherings of connoisseurs. During Mozart's lifetime his symphonies were not "classics" to be savoured, repeated, and passed on to posterity, but music for use, to be enjoyed and replaced by newer works."[33] Acquiring a sense of the place of music in society is important, indeed. In addition, performers sometimes forget to acknowledge that music does not consist of notes and sounds alone. Music makes referential connections in a strata of levels, as in the associations patriotic and hymn tunes have for Americans in the works of Charles Ives or chorale tunes in a Bach cantata have for Lutherans. Musical references, connections, and the place of music in society is meaningful and essential information to share.

3. **Learn the score, analyze the structure.** Each conductor will formulate an approach which works best for him or her. As this topic is addressed at length elsewhere in this book, suffice it to say that it is essential to examine the following areas: melodic components and thematic connections; key areas and their relationships; harmonic language; cadential structure; styles of texture; instrumentation; orchestration; forms; varieties of color qualities; contrast and continuity of tempi; contrast and continuity of dynamics; sequence of dramatic logic. As the conductor proceeds through these parameters, a secure composite aural image of the composition will emerge. Establishing the "inner-ear" sound ideal is undoubtedly one of the most deeply satisfying steps for the conductor in the process of score preparation.

4. **Performance practice considerations.** The process of incorporating newly discovered sound ideals based on performance practice information, thereby revising earlier aural images of the music, will be exciting and at times frustrating. The first step is conducting a library search for the most recent and authoritative practical information. The following key words are helpful in such a search: historical; style; authentic; performance; traditional name of each style period (e.g. classic, baroque, etc.), century name (e.g. seventeenth, eighteenth), the composer, names of instruments being used; theorists and pedagogical studies of the time period. Journals, prefaces to editions, and essay collections are especially helpful in documenting more recent thought. Caution and skepticism are warranted while reading all materials, as even the most authoritative authors may change their minds over time. Checking the reception of new sources by reading reviews of them in current periodicals is recommended.

The following is a partial list of sources which may serve as a starting point for research. The most current research will be presented in journals:

Journals
Performance Practice Review[34]
Early Music
Historical Performance: The Journal of Early Music America
Nineteenth-Century Music
Journal of the Conductor's Guild

---

[33] Zaslaw, *Mozart's Symphonies*, p. 511.
[34] This journal publishes annually an updated bibliography which is most helpfully categorized by topic.

Journal of the American Musicological Society
The Musical Quarterly

The following are suggested books and articles:

General

Brown, Howard Mayer and Stanley Sadie, ed., *The New Grove Handbooks in Music: Performance Practice Music after 1600*. London: Macmillan Press, 1989.

Donington, Robert, *The Interpretation of Early Music*, London: Faber and Faber, 1974; rev. New York: Norton, 1992.

Galkin, Elliott W, *A History of Orchestral Conducting: In Theory and Practice*. New York: Pendragon Press, 1988.

Jackson, Roland, *Performance Practice, Medieval to Contemporary: A Bibliographic Guide*. New York: Garland, 1988.

Kenyon, Nicholas, ed., *Authenticity and Early Music*. Oxford University Press, 1988. Articles by Philip Brett, Howard Mayer Brown, Will Crutchfield, Robert P. Morgan, Gary Tomlinson, Richard Taruskin.

Kerman, Joseph, "The Historical Performance Movement." *Contemplating Music: Challenges to Musicology*. Cambridge, Massachusetts: Harvard University Press, 1985, pp. 182–217.

Neumann, Frederick, *Essays in Performance Practice*. Ann Arbor, Michigan: UMI Research Press, 1982.

Neumann, Frederick, *New Essays on Performance Practice*. Ann Arbor, Michigan: UMI Research Press, 1989.

MacClintock, Catherine, *Readings in the History of Music in Performance*. Bloomington, Indiana: Indiana University Press, 1979.

Rosenblum, Susan, "Potholes in the Road to Critical Editions," *Journal of the Conductors' Guild*, Vol. 10, No. 3 and 4 (Summer/Fall) 1989, p. 81–87.

Weiss, Piero and Taruskin, Richard, *Music in the Western World: A History of Documents*. London: Collier Macmillan, 1984.

Seventeenth and Eighteenth Century

Butt, John, *Bach Interpretation: Articulation Marks in Primary Sources of J.S. Bach*. Cambridge: Cambridge University Press, 1990.

Dreyfus, Laurence, *Bach's Continuo Group*. Harvard University Press, Cambridge, 1987.

Donington, Robert, *Baroque Music: Style and Performance*. New York: Norton, 1982.

Donington, Robert, *A Performer's Guide to Baroque Music*. New York: Charles Scribner's Sons, 1973.

Harnoncourt, Nikolaus, *Baroque Music Today: Music as Speech: Ways to a New Understanding of Music*. Trans. Mary O'Neill. Portland, Oregon: Amadeus Press, 1988.

Harnoncourt, Nikolaus, *The Musical Dialogue: Thoughts About Monteverdi, Bach and Mozart*. Trans. Mary O'Neill. Portland, Oregon: Amadeus Press, 1989.

Houle, George, *Meter in Music, 1600–1800*. Bloomington, Indiana: Indiana University Press, 1987.

Houle, George, "Meter and Performance in Seventeenth and Eighteenth Centuries," *The Journal of Early Music America*. Vol. 2. no. 1 (Spring, 1989).

Le Huray, Peter, *Authenticity in Performance. Eighteenth-Century Case Studies*. Cambridge: Cambridge University Press, 1990.

Le Huray, Peter and James Day, *Music and Aesthetics in the Eighteenth and Early-Nineteenth Centuries*. Cambridge: Cambridge University Press, 1981.

Neumann, Frederick, *Ornamentation and Improvisation in Mozart*. Princeton: Princeton University Press, 1986.

Neumann, Frederick, *Ornamentation in Baroque and Post-Baroque Music: with a Special Emphasis on J. S. Bach*. Princeton, New Jersey: Princeton University Press, 1970.

Newman, Anthony, *Bach and the Baroque: a Performing Guide to Baroque Music with Special Emphasis on the Music of J. S. Bach*. New York: Pendragon Press, 1985.

Marty, Jean-Pierre, *The Tempo Indications of Mozart*. New Haven: Yale University Press, 1988.

Ratner, Leonard G., *Classic Music: Expression, Form, and Style*. New York: Schirmer Books, 1980.

Shrock, Dennis, "Aspects of Performance Practice During the Classic Era," *Five Centuries of Choral Music*, ed. Gordon Paine. Stuyvesant, NY: Pendragon Press, 1988.

Stowell, Robin, *Violin Technique and Performance Practice in the Late Eighteenth and Early Nineteenth Centuries*. Cambridge: Cambridge University Press, 1985.

Zaslaw, Neal, *Mozart's Symphonies: Context, Performance Practice, Reception*. Oxford: Clarendon Press, 1989.

Zaslaw, Neal, "Mozart's Orchestras: Applying Historical knowledge to Modern Performances," *Early Music*, May 1992, Vol. 20, no. 2, pp. 197–205.

Nineteenth Century

Koury, Daniel J., *Orchestral Performance Practices in the Nineteenth Century, Size, Proportions, and Seating*. Ann Arbor, Michigan. UMI Research Press (Studies in Musicology), 1986.

Mostovoy, Marc, "The Modern Orchestra and Period Performance Practice," *Journal of the Conductors' Guild*, Vol. 10, No. 3 and 4, 1989, pp. 97–110.

Text

Jeffers, Ron, *Translations and Annotations of Choral Repertoire; Vol 1: Sacred Latin Texts*. Corvallis, Oregon: Earthsongs, 1988.

Copeman, Harold, *Singing in Latin*. Printed privately at 22 Tawney Street, Oxford 4 1NJ, United Kingdom, 1990.

Moriarty, John, *Diction: Italian, Latin, French, German*. Boston: E. C. Schirmer Music Company, 1975.

The following topics pertaining to performance practices will be essential to investigate:

A. Choice of instruments and pitch: period or modern. The decision of what kind of instruments to use, and, consequently, whether to use "old pitch" (@A=415 for Baroque style and @A=431 for Classical style)[35] or "modern pitch" (@A=440–442) is predicated on budget and availability of qualified players and instruments. The complaint that period instruments continually squeak, squawk and play out of tune has been voiced less and less frequently as the reproduction of instruments, knowledge of how to play them, and skills of the players have improved. If qualified period players are not available locally, a university program within the region or players clustered near metropolitan centers may be invited to participate. In general, experienced period players are willing to provide information to the conductor unfamiliar with period instruments, and most players look forward to traveling out-of-town for performances. Establishing a friendly, constructive rapport is essential for the conductor to gain the most from the project. The orchestra contractor can be very helpful in discussing choice of continuo instruments (violone or doublebass; theorbo, harpsichord or organ?) and discussing amounts of rehearsal time needed.

If the use of modern instruments, and therefore modern pitch, is the only option, adjustments can still be made in the overall sound of the resulting orchestra. There may be less use of vibrato, a lighter bowing technique, more space between selected notes, more contrast in metric accentuation within the bar, adjustment of tuning to lower sevenths and thirds in seventeenth and eighteenth century music, the readjustment of balances between the winds and strings, and a re-examination of tempi. It follows that the choice of vocal soloists and type of choral tone should complement the instruments and size of ensemble.

B. Number and disposition of performing forces. The arrangement of present-day orchestras is a modern phenomenon. Seating charts and drawings of instrumental and vocal ensembles in the Baroque, Classical and even nineteenth century periods show players standing as they perform, often in church balconies or in rows, with only the keyboard player or first violinist taking charge. In the nineteenth century, as in the Classical period, first violins were generally to stage-right, and second violins to stage-left; cellos in the center and contrabasses toward the back, two or three on each side. Berlioz recommended softer instruments (strings and harp) toward the front, and louder instruments, particularly brass, toward the back. The entire ensemble was to be tiered with at least five to eight rows, to create "maximum acoustical balance and projection and maximum visual contact for optimum ensemble."[36] The Harnoncourt, Koury, Galkin and Zaslaw texts, referred to above, are especially helpful in providing concrete evidence of seating arrangements and number of players in

---

[35] There was no prevailing standard of pitch — it varied by region and by time. The pitch levels offered here are generally in use today in performances using period instruments.

[36] Matesky, Michael Paul, *Berlioz on Conducting*, DMA thesis, University of Washington, 1974, p. 77.

the eighteenth and nineteenth centuries.

C. Size and ambiance of performance space. Choosing music appropriate to the space and choosing the ensemble size in accordance with both the space and the demands of the music presents the conductor with some exciting opportunities. While Mozart's music was offered in a variety of locations,[37] "[I]n general, performance spaces of the period were resonant with small, narrow, rectangular dimensions (e.g., 79 feet by 32 feet, or 59 by 36, or 76 by 38) and with high ceilings."[38] Since both string and wind amplitudes were more soft and the tone qualities less projected and brilliant, and since there was an apparent close-quarters proximity of the performers to the audience, the intimacy and immediacy of the music could hardly have failed to be alluring.

Similarly, the intricate phrases and the brisk harmonic rhythm of the Bach *B-minor Mass* will be consumed and lost in the multiple reverberations of a large, resonant cathedral, a space more suited to performance of the Fauré *Requiem*. When my own group recently performed Berlioz's "Veni Creator Spiritus" in an enormous New York city cathedral, the simple, supple harmonies and clear timbre of the chorus resulted in far more clarity of musical thought and textual meaning than in a much smaller chapel setting. A conductor's first priority is to select music for spaces which will allow it to sound to its optimum potential.

D. Text and vocal tone. Generally a conductor is relieved when the chorus achieves uniform pronunciation of consonances and vowels in English or Italian-liturgical Latin. Re-educating the conductor and singers to regional pronunciations of Latin and other foreign languages may seem not only daunting but extreme in all but professional situations. Unquestionably, pronunciation of language has a fundamental effect on phrasing, articulation, accentuation, and tone quality. One need only attempt to sing, for example, the English translation of Honegger's *King David* and then try a few solos or choruses in French to understand that the entire color and quality of both text and music are inextricably tied together and far more affecting in the original French. The music comes alive when text and music are united in this way. Similarly, using the British vowels and consonants for, say, William Byrd's "Ave Maria" where the closed "e" vowels are more closed than American ones, or Mozart's *Requiem* in Austro-Germanic Latin where the "g" in "Agnus Dei" is a hard "k" sound,[39] the music acquires greater pungency and a new-to-modern-ears kind of timbre. The difference created by replacing the standard Italian-Latin pronunciation with a regional variation is the contrast between a blur of sheer lyricism and power versus a distinctive clarity of sound produced by greater awareness of vowel timbre and articulation.

Information about vocal tone in various historical periods and regions is sparse. Descriptions in treatises and concert reports using words such as "pleasing" and "clear" do not complete the picture, to say the least. However,

---

[37] Zaslaw, *Mozart's Symphonies*, p. 471. "Mozart's symphonies were performed in private rooms, in great halls, in theatres, and in churches."

[38] Ibid, pp. 471-2.

[39] See O'Neal, Melinda, "An Introduction to Performance Practice Considerations for the Mozart *Requiem*," *The Choral Journal*, April, 1991, pp. 47–56.

with the knowledge of prevalent use of boys in choruses through the time of Mozart, small performance venues, the use of fewer players and singers and softer-sounding instruments as compared to today, one can conjecture that performers admired a less full-bodied and more transparent sound than is generally used today.

E. Singing in the original language. Presently our society is experiencing a resurgence in interest for understanding and celebrating diversity of culture and origin. Difference has become intriguing rather than isolating; a hallmark rather than a complication. Consequently, previous generations' bent for making editions which are easily accessible and standardized into every-day English translations need no longer continue. To sing music in languages other than English communicates, first, the willingness of the performer to become educated by "otherness," and second, a willingness to bring both composer and audience closer together into the realm of sound. In most vocal ensemble performances, unless the listener already knows the text by heart in English, the text will be largely unintelligible if in anything other than a hymn-style, homophonic texture. A more genuine, direct musical experience may be attained by performing the music as it was originally intended in partnership with the text, regardless of the age or level of ability of the group. For choral and choral-orchestral music, providing the audience that same original text and an English translation in printed form offers listeners far more opportunity for comprehension than singing in translation with no printed text available.

F. Articulation and phrasing. Each conductor must carefully research the composer's context, depending on time-setting and region, in order to make decisions about note length and weight. Decisions regarding tempo, meter, language, rhythm and choice of ornamentation all will affect articulation and phrasing. In nineteenth century Russian music, for example, the prevailing aesthetic is continuous sound. Phrasing is seamless, and the tone is full, vibrant, and projected. By contrast, in the Classic period in Austro-Germanic regions, according to treaties of C.P.E. Bach, Quantz, Türk, Koch and Leopold Mozart, fast movements were played in a detached and more variably accented fashion than today, while in slow movements notes were played with less separation than the fast movements. By the 1780s, notes that were formerly played at half their value were more likely to be played at full value.[40]

G. Rhythm and ornamentation. Principles of rhythm and ornamentation are particularly controversial topics among specialists in the field, notably Neumann, Donington, and Crutchfield. Each musicologist may examine treatises of the period, interpreting content and application in different ways: ". . . improper use of historical treatises, in particular unjustified generalizations of their teachings and their unquestioned and categorical application . . ." is frequently discussed.[41] However, nearly all musicologists do agree that the printed notes on the page are more like a guide or a short hand to what the

---

[40] Zaslaw, "Introduction" from *Performance Practice: Music after 1600*. Ed. Howard Mayer Brown and Stanley Sadie. London, MacMillan Press, p. 213.

[41] Neumann, William, "A New Look at Bach's Ornamentation," *Essays in Performance Practice*. Ann Arbor, Michigan: UMI Press, 1982, p. 197.

composer had in mind. In light of this, then, issues such as *notes inégales*, rubato, descending and ascending appoggiaturas, vibrato, *messa di voce*, other ornaments in all their varieties on or before the beat and from above or below must be researched in relation to each composer, not simply a general style period. Special care must be taken in application of general principles to specific circumstances, and above all, the music must make sense rhetorically. Music of previous periods very likely had a natural, improvisational quality due to familiar procedures of ornamentation and the at-ease, frequent act, whether in church, school or court, of making music on an almost daily basis. Modern tendencies toward slavish adherence to replicating the notes on a page and making the next rendition *the* definitive statement certainly fall short of capturing the essence in performance of, for example, Handel's own ideas in "Behold the Lamb of God" or the transcendent spirit of the hymn "Amazing Grace."

H. Tempo and Meter. Houle, Zaslaw, and Marty address the ramifications of tempo indications in the Classical period (and their frequent absence) in relation to meter. There is continuing debate concerning Mozart's "Ave verum corpus," its tempo and tactus: is it really in 4/4 Adagio or 2/2 Adagio? Does the half note or the quarter receive the *tactus*? What did Adagio really mean then?

The current tendency to think that all earlier music was faster and more detached is a dangerous generalization which ignores a number of equally important considerations such as metrical stress, harmonic rhythm, melodic contours, ornamentation, text, number and skill of players, acoustical properties of the hall, mood and quality of the occasion. Faster speed of and by itself can be empty and stylistically ineffective. Mallock states:

> [W]hat needs to be achieved is a point of balance, the tempo giusto: the place where the work's lyrical and active elements are thrown into highest relief relative to one another. Once such points of balance have been divined, it may often occur that the actual pulses of associated pieces are not dissimilar from one another. The issue is more one of adjusting to internal proportions than of conforming to superimposed external notions of pace.[42]

VII. Components of the Music

We tend to assume that if we can recreate all the external conditions that obtained in the original performance of a piece we will thus recreate the composer's inner experience of the piece and thus allow him to speak for himself.[43]

— Richard Taruskin

If stylistic adjustments are to be made in performance practices for each and every work, then it appears that we must become highly skilled, specialized artists. In 1966, Howard Swan asked, "Can the singer change his vocal produc-

[42] Mallock, William, "Carl Czerny's Metronome Marks for Haydn and Mozart Symphonies," *Early Music*, 16, 1988, p. 76.

[43] Taruskin, Richard, "On Letting the Music Speak for Itself: Some Reflections on Musicology and Performance," *Journal of Musicology*, 1 (1982), p. 341.

tion and his interpretive ideas to suit every new composition? Swan gave a disturbing reason why he thought the choral singer cannot:

> The chorus is under a far greater handicap in this respect than is the soloist, for in front of them stands one who is almost powerless to change the way that he responds to music. The strength of his beat, the nature of attack and release, the duration of vowel and consonant sounds, his response to rhythm, to dynamics, to balance and to every other factor involved with singing is the musical extension of his imagination and his personality. He cannot will himself to change from song to song, and neither can his chorus.[44]

Howard Swan did not hold irrevocably to this view, for earlier he completed a demonstration of five different types of choral tone qualities to use with works of various styles from Palestrina to Brahms. Later, in 1986, he recommended a three-step procedure to approximate the wishes of the composer: 1) listing the performance practices relevant to a particular period of composition; 2) comparing composers within the same period; 3) studying the overall output of a single composer. While one must be dubious of style-trait lists (several items he included are no longer viable), Swan's reversal on this issue is an important one. Surely conductors are not powerless to change the way they respond to music, for this goes against the basic precepts of education. Swan's purpose is clear and the need for it is universal: *to avoid having the music of various historical styles sound the same when performed by the same chorus conducted by the same conductor*.[45] Therefore, "[I]f we accept the premise that the basic sound of a chorus shows little change regardless of what is sung, it follows that the choir cannot perform all music equally well. It is most effective in singing music which in style and structure is best suited to the tone of the group."[46]

According to Swan, then, it appears that the conductor has only one course of action: only perform music for which the ensemble is best suited. This would imply the formation of ensembles which specialize in each of the style periods: Renaissance, Baroque, Classic, Romanticism, Modern. But there is another option, one which is part of the basic premise of this chapter and is preferable to most conductors: research the performance practices of music from various style periods and regions, become re-educated, choose repertoire best suited to the chorus and the performance space, and thus begin to experience a release from conscious and unconscious pre-existing limitations, especially those of the conductor.

In order to achieve variability of style, the conductor's responsibility is to identify the components of the music — its substance and style — and let these elements be the guiding principles for every decision regarding performance: choice of repertory, selection of singers, scheduling of rehearsals, scheduling of personal preparation, rehearsal methods, conducting technique, historical performance practices, text and translation, setup on stage, lighting in the

---

[44] Swan, p. 81.

[45] Swan, p. 71: "Why is it that most choirs sound much the same whether they sing Bach or Palestrina or Brahms?"

[46] Ibid, pp. 81-82.

house, length of the performance, management of business aspects, travel, etc. When these decisions are made on the basis of the music and how it was first envisioned by the composer, there is an enormous difference in the result.

This all sounds simple enough yet may seem nearly impossible to achieve in our own individual situations. A brief comparison of two different organizations' approach to the same work illustrates how, on a very basic level, one may reflect the composer's intentions more effectively and obtain, in the author's view, a more engaging musical result. The work is Berlioz's *La Damnation of Faust*, a nearly three-hour quasi-operatic oratorio written in 1846 for large chorus, children's chorus (only in the conclusion), orchestra, and four soloists. Performances cited are by two similar major metropolitan symphony orchestras with professional soloists and amateur choruses. (Read left to right)

Organization A	Organization B
• harps placed in front, as Berlioz directs in his *Traité*	• harps in back; audience never heard them
• soloists to the conductor's left, close to the audience and easily heard	• soloists seated between the conductor and the orchestra; they had to step out to sing
• brass were balanced with the rest of the ensemble (modern instruments)	• brass were too loud (also modern instruments)
• text in book form, audience able to turn pages quietly, lighting sufficient to follow	• text pages were noisy to turn, pages were falling out, lighting inadequate
• work treated as a complete entity, similar to an opera; not sectionally	• double-bars interpreted as stops; non-continuous
• used children in final chorus as Berlioz directs	• no children
• soloists: two French, two American singers; excellent French pronunciation	• all American singers, one with very poor French pronunciation
• rehearsal schedule effective: rehearsed orchestra movements separately; the dress rehearsal was open to donors	• no dress rehearsal scheduled
• two concerts on the weekend	• 4 concerts, 2 during week; the last on Tuesday began at 7:00 and ended at 9:50
• full house	• partly full house

Without having heard a note of either performance, perhaps a sense of the effect of each can be imagined. In fact, the audience of Organization A's performance did not want to leave — they were enthralled. This was an extraordinary occasion, perhaps just as Berlioz imagined. In Organization B's performance, some of the audience left early. While the conductors were equally skilled, the net result was dramatically different. One conductor understood what Berlioz wrote and acted on that understanding; the other made no attempt to include Berlioz's clearly articulated intentions in either rehearsals or performances. Organization A committed itself to performing Berlioz's *La Damnation of Faust*; the other was performing just another oratorio-style concert. One performance was magical; the other was a puzzlement. While most listeners in each audience could not pinpoint the reasons for their concert's success or failure, they certainly knew when the music was convincing and when it was not.

VIII. Conclusion

The search for an 'authentic' interpretation is not the search for a single hard and fast answer, but for a range of possibilities from which to make performing decisions.[47]

— Peter Le Huray

More than thirty years ago, Paul Henry Lang, while praising the inauguration of the Ford Foundation's Young Conductor's Project at Peabody Conservatory, said modern conducting ". . . demands knowledge and skills far in excess of those the old-line [nineteenth century] *Kapellmeister* needed for a successful career . . . [T]he typical Central European conductor of the old school . . . dealt with a living tradition and convention." And he said, " . . . even Haydn and Mozart call for orchestral balances basically different from Wagner and Tchaikowsky. Nor are seventeenth and eighteenth century dynamics, tempo and accents the same as in more recent music."[48] Lang recommended performance practice studies be included in this training program for professional conductors, and he strongly encouraged conductors to become more aware of the varying quality of available editions. "The conductor is no longer an artisan, he must be a literate and educated musician."

In the same time period, Howard Swan asked, while complaining that too few choral performances are artistically satisfying: "Should [the conductor] not continue the attempt to discover what the composer had in mind as he wrote his music? Can a conductor ignore the important contribution which his own scholarship will make to a performance of integrity and taste?"[49] Recently, Taruskin stated:

But the object is not to duplicate the sounds of the past, for if that were our aim we would never know whether we had succeeded. What we are aiming at, rather, is the startling shock of newness, of immediacy, the sense of rightness that

---

[47] Le Huray, Peter, *Authenticity in Performance. Eighteenth-Century Case Studies.* Cambridge: Cambridge Universtiy Press, 1990, p. 4.

[48] Lang, Paul Henry, "Music and Musicians: In Praise of a Grant." *New York Herald Tribune.* January 29, 1961.

[49] Swan, p. 74.

occurs when after countless frustrating experiments we feel as though we have achieved the identification of performance style with the demands of the music . . .[50]

This "sense of rightness" can be achieved by first establishing the components of the music — its substance and style, and by deciding whom the music will serve.

Dramatically increasing the time devoted to both score study and research is recommended. In the following three steps suggested for the score preparation process, revelations in each will concurrently nurture information gathered in others. Conferring with historians, theorists, literature specialists, linguists — as well as other conductors — will only enhance the process.

Score Study I
Research background, editions, performance practices

Score Study II
Score analysis, sound imaging, part marking

Score Study III
Rehearsal organization and procedures

Finally, separate the conductor's interpretive identity from the composer's creative product. This means, as an experiment or exercise, shedding as many twentieth century constructs and values as possible. Identify the "objective" stance — making decisions based on facts as currently understood. Identify the "subjective" stance — being intuitive and unquestioningly a product of our modern conventions. Establish a well-founded, personal reconciliation of the two.

The composer's purpose in writing music is *to move* the audience and the musicians who bring the music to life. To allow this to happen, we as conductors must not compete with the composer; rather we need to cooperate a little better. As has been stated unequivocally, "interpretation in the hands of the historically ignorant leads to falsification of the composer's intent."[51] Performance must be informed by scholarship and scholarship informed by performance. Naive or intentional separation of these elements seriously compromises the musical arts.

Of course, an absolutely true replication of a composer's work is impossible to achieve and perhaps is even undesirable. However, we can take more steps to draw closer to the composer's intentions and become more informed about the incumbent controversies and compromises. It is the thesis of this chapter that, as we come to a clearer understanding of what the composer composed by studying the music in context, the music will speak for itself — and wonderfully so. Then perhaps the conductor will not seem the same at every concert, nor will the music sound the same, either.

---

[50] R. Taruskin, contribution to "The Limits of Authenticity: A Discussion," *Early Music*, 12 (1984), p. 11.

[51] Serwer, Howard and Paul Traver, "Maryland Handel Festival's Tenth." Maryland Handel Festival Program Book, University of Maryland, 1990, p. 10.

Bibliography

Brett, Philip, "Facing the Music," *Early Music*, 10, 1982, pp. 347–50.

Brown, Howard Mayer and Stanley Sadie, ed., *The New Grove Handbooks in Music: Performance Practice Music after 1600*. London: Macmillan Press, 1989.

Butt, John, *Bach Interpretation: Articulation Marks in Primary Sources of J.S. Bach*. Cambridge: Cambridge University Press, 1990.

Donington, Robert, "The Present Position of Authenticity," *Performance Practice Review*, 2 (1989), pp. 117–125.

Le Huray, Peter and James Day, *Music and Aesthetics in the Eighteenth and Early-Nineteenth Centuries*. Cambridge: Cambridge University Press, 1981.

Le Huray, Peter, *Authenticity in Performance. Eighteenth-Century Case Studies*. Cambridge, Cambridge University Press, 1990.

Kenyon, Nicholas, ed., *Authenticity and Early Music*. Oxford University Press, 1988. Philip Brett, Howard Mayer Brown, Will Crutchfield, Robert P. Morgan, Gary Tomlinson, Richard Taruskin.

Kerman, Joseph, *Contemplating Music: Challenges to Musicology*. Cambridge, Massachusetts: Harvard University Press, 1985.

Lang, Paul Henry, "Music and Musicians: In Praise of a Grant," *New York Herald Tribune*. January 29, 1964.

Leech-Wilkinson, Daniel, "The Limits of Authenticity: A Discussion," *Early Music*, 12 (1984), pp. 13–15.

Mostovoy, Marc, "The Modern Orchestra and Period Performance Practice," *Journal of the Conductors' Guild*, Vol 10, No. 3 and 4, 1989, pp. 97–110.

Neumann, Frederick, *Essays in Performance Practice*. Ann Arbor, Michigan: UMI Research Press, 1982.

Neumann, Frederick, *New Essays on Performance Practice*. Ann Arbor, Michigan: UMI Research Press, 1989.

Rosenblum, Susan, "Potholes in the Road to Critical Editions," *Journal of the Conductors' Guild*, Vol. 10, No. 3 and 4 (Summer/Fall), 1989, pp. 81–87.

Said, Edward W., *Musical Elaborations*. New York: Columbia University Press, 1991.

Swan, Howard, *Conscience of a Profession*. Chapel Hill: Hinshaw Music, 1987.

Taruskin, Richard, "The Limits of Authenticity: A Discussion," *Early Music*, 12 (1984), pp. 3–12.

Taruskin, Richard, "On Letting the Music Speak for Itself: Some Reflections on Musicology and Performance," *Journal of Musicology*, 1 (1982), pp. 338–349.

Temperley, Nicholas, Contribution to "The Limits of Authenticity: A Discussion," *Early Music*, 12 (1984), pp. 16–20.

Zaslaw, Neal, *Mozart's Symphonies: Context, Performance Practice, Reception*. Oxford: Clarendon Press, 1989.

Mastery of Choral Ensemble

Jameson Marvin

A profoundly inspired choral performance provides deep fulfillment and lasting enrichment. When a conductor hears such a performance, a number of provocative questions may emerge: "Why does the choir sound so beautiful? What is it in their singing that moves me so greatly? What precisely is so compelling and inspiring about the choir's interpretation? How has the conductor been able to reveal the structural components of the composition so clearly — the performance elicits the feeling that one is hearing it for the first time! How did the choir achieve such a high level of choral mastery?

The purpose of this article is to provide insight into the process that conductors use to achieve the highest levels of choral performance. Mastering **choral ensemble** — a unified sound image of the whole — is the foundation upon which enlightened, communicative, and inspiring performance takes place. It is a goal toward which serious conductors aspire. The depth and scope of knowledge, musicianship, experience and personal attributes that are required for achieving the highest levels of choral mastery are limited only by the choir's and the conductor's human limitations. Thus, it is truly a humbling experience to meet the challenges ultimately required to perform good music well.

Introduction: An Overview of the Conductor's Process

In rehearsals, conductors ask choral singers to give aural meaning to a set of notational symbols through the mediums of time and pitch. **This process requires thinking.** Before rehearsals, conductors must think about the priorities they choose upon which to base their conceptualization of the score. Their conceptualization forms a *mental-aural image* — a vision of what the music should sound like. It is the "mind's ear."

The foundation for the mental-aural image is score study. Fired by the imagination, the mental-aural image is a powerful motivating agent. In each rehearsal it provides the conductor with an ever-present standard against which to measure the choir's progress. The conduit through which the conductor measures the choir's acquisition of the mental-aural image is *the ear*. The process that conductors use to place their "mind's ear" of the score into the composite mental-aural image of the singers is *rehearsing*.

Over time, in rehearsal after rehearsal, the choir as an *ensemble* begins to mirror back the conductor's conceptualization of the score. Ultimately, the responsibility for projecting this unified sound-picture rests with the singers. The core of the process that conductors use in rehearsal is *teaching* — teaching the singers how to be responsible for providing and maintaining a meaningful, communicative sound-image of the music they sing. In this manner, the choir learns to consistently reflect a **unity of ensemble**, and **mastery** occurs; singers, conductors, and audiences are inspired. Inspiration rejuvenates all participants and activates the compelling desire to "do it again." Through this profoundly creative process choirs and conductors are drawn together to experience the continuing transcendent power of choral music.

Below is a diagram in the form of a circle. It represents the interrelationship of the components of "The Conductor's Process":[1]

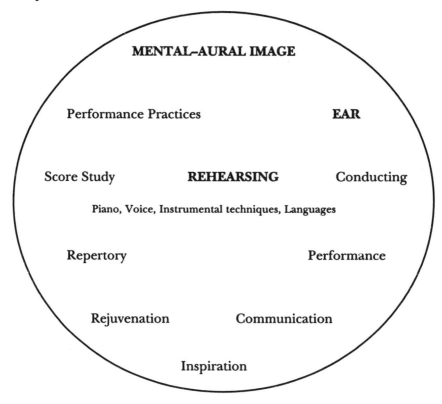

MENTAL–AURAL IMAGE

Performance Practices   **EAR**

Score Study   **REHEARSING**   Conducting

Piano, Voice, Instrumental techniques, Languages

Repertory   Performance

Rejuvenation   Communication

Inspiration

At the center of the "Conductor's Process" is *Rehearsing*. While each part of the conductor's process impacts on several other parts and the composite represents the "ideal conductor," each of the elements cannot be fully realized without the ability to rehearse.

Performance is the ultimate motivating goal for the rehearsal, but it is not the goal of the process. Before the performance occurs, *rehearsing* takes place; and

[1] In 1988, the author wrote an essay entitled "The Conductor's Process" from which many ideas and excerpts are drawn for the present chapter. The essay was published by Pendragon press for a *Festschrift* edited by Gordon Paine entitled *Five Centuries of Choral Music: Essays in Honor of Howard Swan*. All excerpted sections are reprinted with permission of Pendragon press.

before the rehearsal, the *repertory* must be chosen, the *score studied*, and questions concerning style and *performance practices* must be addressed. Through stylistic and structural analysis, the conductor develops a *mental-aural image* that prepares him for *rehearsing*. In the process of rehearsing, the conductor uses his *ear, conducting technique* and rehearsal procedures to lead the choir toward a unified musical conception of the composition.

Specific skills are needed by the conductor to aid in the preparation for rehearsal, as well as in the rehearsal itself: *piano* facility, *language* skills (translation and pronunciation), *voice* training, and for concerted works, a knowledge of *instrumental techniques*. The *complete* conductor aspires to excel in all aspects. It is a life-long process.

The diagram on the previous page illustrates the interrelationship of the elements of the "Conductor's Process." By far the most complex is the relationship of the *mental-aural image*, the *ear*, and *rehearsing*. It is primarily through the ear that the conductor measures his mental-aural image against what the choir is singing. Having an indelible image of the musical concept of the score by the conductor acts as a powerful stimulus in directing the choir toward that image. The degree of mastery of the score by the choir is dependent upon the conductor's aptitude and abilities in rehearsing. The ear provides the information necessary to make the process work. Each element of the process requires a lifetime of study and demands continuous attention. The complete process, by nature, is self-perpetuating. Its essence nourishes *communication*, *inspiration*, and *rejuvenation*, the life-blood of the profound interaction of music and humanity.

Understanding the relationship of the *mental-aural image*, the *ear*, and *rehearsing* (the core of the "Conductor's Process") is the key to understanding the process by which conductors achieve **mastery of choral ensemble**. The author approaches this complex subject through offering the following logical steps; all conductors employ these, to some degree, as they guide their ensembles toward their mental-aural image of the score:

I. Score Study: Catalyst for the Mental-Aural Image
    A. A Suggested Approach to Score Study
    B. Score marking
II. Preparing the Ear for Listening; the Score for Rehearsing
    A. The Four Elements of Music
        1. Duration
            a. Definition and Overview
            b. Specific Principles and Tendencies
        2. Pitch
            a. Definition and Overview
            b. Specific Principles and Tendencies
        3. Timbre
            a. Definition and Overview
            b. Specific Principles and Tendencies
        4. Intensity
            a. Definition and Overview

I. Score Study: Catalyst for the Mental-Aural Image

Notational symbols reveal an enormous amount of information. Realizing them in sound requires conceptualization of all the information that the symbols denote, and of all that they imply. Bringing this composite picture to life in sound requires imagination — the catalyst for spawning the mental-aural image of the music. The deeper the insights into the score, the more clear and profound the mental-aural image becomes. Clarity of insight inspires conductors to attain their vision. Inspired conductors motivate singers to their vision of the composer's intentions. Motivated singers inspire each other and the conductor: the process is self-renewing.

Structural analysis is the core of score study: the understanding of how harmony, melody, rhythm, texture, and instrumentation reveal the total design of a composition and the details that order its architecture. All these elements interact with *text*, and to what degree words inspire or affect these structural building blocks is a particularly important question to ask. Throughout the history of western music, *words* have inspired the masterpieces of choral literature. Words also impose order and prescribe limits. In the hands of one composer, the text may serve as a vehicle for displaying the composer's compositional craftsmanship; in another's, the words may be the impetus that generates each structural and expressive element of the composition. Choral music, when sung without words can be an extremely satisfying and inspiring experience. Music always transcends the text — it amplifies and gives greater meaning to the *affect*, the mood, the individual concepts, and even the specificity of a single word. Once the text-music relationship is understood, the form and structure analyzed, and the kernel of inspiration is perceived, the conductor will have come a long way toward discovering "the truth" of the composition. That is the ultimate goal of score study.

A Suggested Approach To Score Analysis

Conductors will develop insight into a composition by determining how the composer's treatment of text relates to or is enhanced by the musical structure — the harmony, melody, rhythm, and texture. As insights deepen, conductors internalize information. The resulting internalization forms the mental-aural image of the composition. Below is an approach to score analysis — an outline that can be used in developing a clear mental-aural image of the composition:

I. Text. Analyze:
- the relationship of the text to the overall form of the composition, and the relationship of the text to the primary structures that provide structural coherence for the form
- the influence of the text on forming the principal cadences that articulate the primary structures within the large form
- the influence of the text on the sub-structures — the smaller cadential units that occur within the principal one
- the specific relationship of the text to each element of the compositional fabric: harmony, melody, rhythm, texture, instrumentation.

II. Harmony. Understand:
- the influence of the text on mode (major, minor, modal) and key
- the specific influence of the text on passing events
  - chromaticism
  - dissonance
  - harmonic progression(s)
  - specific chord choice
  - modulation

III. Melody. Analyze:
- the relationship of text expression to melodic shape and contour
- the influence of the text on the tessitura and range of the vocal parts
- the influence the text may have on long line; on short line

IV. Rhythm. Understand:
- if there is a relationship of the text to the meter
- the specific relationship of the text and rhythm
- the specific choice of note combinations (long, short, symmetric, asymmetric) that may be related to text

V. Texture. Analyze:
- how high, low, open, closed, dense, opaque textures may reflect some aspect of the text
- how the number of parts and the changes in texture may be influenced by the text
- how texture — polyphonic, homophonic, linear, chordal — may relate to text *affect*

VI. Instrumentation. Understand:
- how text influences the composer's choice of instruments
- how text may relate to changes in instrumentation
- how text may relate to a composer's decisions regarding contrasting or complementing instrumental colors

VII. Style, Performance Practice, Interpretive Considerations
Understand how the text may be related to:
- tempo; tempo fluctuation; tempo markings; mensuration; meter
- phrasing (long note groups; short note groups); linear direction
- articulation
- pitch level, temperament, tuning
- dynamics

- instrumentation, timbre
- rubato
- ornamentation, improvisation
- musica ficta
- basso-continuo realization
- balance, size, make-up of performing forces

Score Marking

The mental-aural (sound) image — developed through analyzing the relationship of the harmony, melody, rhythm, texture, instrumentation, to the text of the composition — provides the foundation for rehearsing. The sound image becomes even more deeply etched in a conductor's mind through marking the score. This process overlaps for most conductors with score study itself, and prepares the ears for listening.

The conductor's mental-aural image can be clarified through categorizing the score-markings by the **four basic elements inherent in music**: duration, pitch, timbre, and intensity. The conductor's interpretive ideas are linked to one or more of these four elements. These ideas are given aural meaning though the **expressive elements of music**: dynamics, phrasing, articulation, rubato, and linear direction. The following outline integrates score analysis with score marking. It does so by organizing score marking — or score preparation — under the four basic elements of music.

I. Duration
- pulse (tempo)
- rhythms; rhythmic groupings
- meter; mensuration
- macro and micro levels of the beat
- harmonic rhythm

II. Pitch
- intonation
- quality – color – timbre
- intensity

III. Timbre
- vocal sound - color - sonority;
- vowels, pitched consonants
- resonance

IV. Intensity
- dynamics
  - structural
  - expressive
- articulation
  - syllabic accentuation or emphasis
  - consonants
  - clarity of quick-passage work
  - articulations of silence

- phrasing
  - note groups
  - short phrases
  - long line(s)
- rubato
  - shifts of intensity in relation to changes in duration
  - cadential influence
  - harmonic/melodic/rhythmic interaction
  - ritards, accelerandos
- linear direction
  - short note-group
  - long line

Marking the score, like taking notes in a course, reinforces learning. The process forces one to see *everything*, and provides visual reminders of the conductor's mental-aural image. It is in marking the score that the conductor begins to prepare for **rehearsal listening**.

To prepare the ears for listening, visually highlight in the score — and aurally highlight in the "mind's ear" — each important element and musical gesture that will contribute to an understanding of the compositional structure. When the structure is defined, the composer's conception is clarified. Through your mental-aural image of the composer's conception, categorize your markings by duration, pitch, timbre, and intensity. Reflect and amplify your interpretive ideas by marking appropriate dynamics, phrasing, articulation, concerns of balance, rubato, and linear direction.

In essence, a conductor must re-edit the score to clarify the composer's sound-image implied by — but not explicit in — the symbolic notation that is used to represent it. The deeply-etched clarity of the conductor's mind's ear will be the foundation upon which to base the "re-edition." Finally, **change** will be an extremely important element to mark and to make clear in the score. A study of *change* reveals *detail*. Look for *change* in 1) harmony, melody, rhythm, texture; 2) pitch, duration, timbre, intensity; 3) dynamics, phrasing, articulation, rubato, and linear direction; 4) text; and 5) instrumentation.

II. Preparing the Ear for Listening; The Score for Rehearsing

The four elements of music

Before offering some specific principles and concepts that will aid the conductor in preparing for rehearsals, it will be important to first understand the interlocking relationship of the four elements of music by which the score markings will be categorized.

Each element — duration, pitch, timbre, and intensity — interacts and affects at least one other. Pitch is perceived through duration, and its quality is identified by timbre. Intensity is felt through the interaction of pitch and duration. Duration provides the medium through which all three elements are given order and sound. Thus, the element of music that plays the greatest role in providing **ensemble unity** is duration. The expressive components of music — dynamics, phrasing, articulation, rubato, linear direction, and text nuance — are integrally connected with one or more of the four elements.[2]

Duration: Pulse (Tempo), Rhythm, Meter, Note Lengths

Definition and Overview

Duration is articulated in music by pulse, rhythm, and meter, and makes possible the expressive components. When our primary objective in choral singing is directed toward unity of duration, we provide an ordered medium through which pitch, timbre, and intensity can be more meaningfully realized.

We achieve unity of duration primarily through establishing *ensemble rhythm*. Ensemble rhythm is the interaction of pulse on the rhythmic-metric-textural fabric of the composition. Teaching a choir to sing with good rhythm means to sensitize choral singers to a unanimous group pulse. Their internal clocks must be taught to perceive sound by the same scale of measure. By sensitizing their physiological responses to it, choir singers internalize pulse. As group pulse internalizes, ensemble rhythm is developed. When ensemble rhythm is established, the expressive components realized through duration — dynamics, phrasing, articulation, rubato, and linear direction — will be given a chance to project their powerful communicative potentials.

Specific Principles and Tendencies

I. *Tendencies* of fast notes and slow notes:

A. Long (held) notes aurally obscure short (moving) notes. Therefore, decide what note value(s) in any given texture are the most important to be heard. Use as a guideline the following ideas:

1. Generally, short moving notes serve expressive purposes; long notes often serve as pedal or "filler" functions.

a. Mark (place) short moving notes in(to) relief with stronger dynamics, and articulation; give them "goal orientation."

b. Mark stationary or long notes that do not serve an expressive function with soft dynamics and/or diminuendos

2. Sometimes, however, long notes create dissonance.

a. Usually dissonance serves an expressive purpose or signals the approach of a cadence.

b. If long (held) notes create dissonance, highlight the dissonance with a quick crescendo to occur at the end of the held note just before the dissonance occurs, and place an articulation of stress on the moving note as it "rubs" against the held note. In this manner

---

[2] Each element of music also contains inherent functions that overlap with characteristics of other elements. Thus the reader may find "variations on familiar themes." **The guidelines offered here approach the process of "marking the score" and "preparing the ear for listening" (and thus for "rehearsing") as a synonomous activity.** Marking the score **does** prepare the ear for listening, as well as rehearsing. Therefore the reader can consider each activity—marking the score, preparing the ear, knowing what to listen for before the rehearsal — as essentially one and the same process.

the dissonance is immediately brought into aural relief.
B. Long notes and short notes in polyphonic textures
    1. Points of imitation (usually fast-moving notes) are structurally impor-
tant and therefore need to be heard. Highlight them by marking
appropriate dynamic shapes, phrasing, and articulation. These are
determined and derived from the:
        a. melodic contour(s)
        b. range and tessitura
    2. Inherent rhythmic groupings:
        a. micro (as in short 2 and 3 note-groups), especially in Renaissance
polyphonic lines (derived in style from chant), and in seventeenth,
eighteenth, and nineteenth century polyphonic or fugal lines that
are derived inherently from the style of Renaissance polyphony
        b. macro (ie. long-note groups); these are larger rhythmic levels
derived from:
            1. a composer's phrase marks
            2. textual strong-weak syllabification
            3. larger levels of phrasing that a conductor wishes to be made
audible in connecting several short (micro) groups together
            4. mensuration signs in Renaissance music
            5. hemiola phrasing occurring at cadences in triple meters in
much music of the sixteenth-nineteenth centuries, such as the
following example:

II. Tempo (pulse)
    A. Decide in advance what tempi you intend to use; sensitize your internal
clock in preparation for rehearsal.
    B. Tendencies:
        1. Choirs typically drag the tempo at the note-learning stages because
singers wait to hear the note before moving to it. While a conductor at
the initial stage may need to be flexible in this regard, it will be important
to be conscious of the comparison of the choir's tempo and one's own
internal-clock tempo.
        2. Notes of consecutive equal value rush
            a. Be aware that any sequence of notes, each of the same time-
duration tend to increase — move ahead — in tempo.
            b. The accumulative energy inherent in singing notes of consecutive
equal value, one after another, inevitably produces rushing. Be
ready to listen for this natural ensemble phenomenon and draw
your singers' attention to it.
    C. Be prepared to rethink tempi that, in rehearsal after rehearsal, seem too
fast or too slow for the chorus and/or for the acoustical situation.
    D. Understand tempo as a function of:
        1. the speed of harmonic rhythm

2. the clarity or opaqueness of the texture

3. the meter signature in Renaissance, Baroque, and Classic repertoire and in certain Romantic repertoire that is based in style upon principles of the past (motets of Brahms, for example)

4. the composer's written *affects* (allegro, adagio, andante, largo, etc.); these Italian words describe mood even more than precise tempi, especially in Baroque and Classic music.

5. the natural speed of the *tactus* in the Renaissance (about 60 MM; no slower than 40, no faster than 80). This tempo is normally related to a half-note in modern editions; modern editions usually halve the composer's original notation

6. the natural speed (*tempo justo*) of duple meter in the Baroque (about 70 MM), unless a specific word-mood *affect* appears

7. the changing meaning of the term *alla breve* . In the fifteenth and to a lesser degree in the sixteenth century, this sign ¢ meant the whole note (the semi-breve) is equal to the breve. In some works of the early sixteenth century and in most works of the late sixteenth century, however, the *alla breve* sign loses this specific meaning; yet, the connotation of "two beats per bar" continues, and should be observed in later eras and styles. Bach and Handel often employ *stile antico* notation (alla-breve sign with large-note notation) to signify their use of old style; *stile antico* strongly implies a tempo of two beats per bar as in the second *Kyrie* of Bach's *B-Minor Mass* or "And with His Stripes" from *Messiah*. In the sacred works of Haydn, Mozart, and Beethoven in which fugal movements (or passages) are written under the *alla breve* sign with large-note notation, the same general (two beats per bar) tempo may be expected.

E. Consonants have a profound impact both on tempo-control and on clarifying textures

1. in contrapuntal textures, especially at points of imitation that initiate new compositional material, strong initial consonants may be employed to clarify the structure

2. consonants "eat up time"; decide if consonants occur on the beat or before it; pitched consonants: m, n, ng, l, v, z, th, and r, require time to be heard.

3. orchestral instruments "eat up consonants"; singers' diction must be more exaggerated in performing choral-orchestral works than in works with no accompaniment

III. Rhythms - prepare phrasing in advance to reveal:

A. The inherent small-note groups

B. The long-line macro phrases

C. The internal dynamic and rubato relationships inherent in

1. some specific rhythmic gestures

2. the subtle changes of direction in vocal line

3. micro note-groups, especially in lines derived in style from Renaissance polyphony

4. many cadential structures

D. Mark "articulations of silence" to better reveal the metric organization of rhythms. In triple meter or with notes in triple groupings, for example, it is necessary to decide upon a hierarchy of importance of most- to least-stressed notes, as well as the phrase groups. Are beats 1-2-3, stressed or grouped as:

1.   1̄, ' 2, 3⏜   1̄, 2,⏜ ' 3   1̄, 2, 3⏜ '

2.   2, ' 3, 1⏜   2, 3,⏜ ' 1   2, 3, 1⏜ '

3.   3, ' 1, 2⏜   3, 1,⏜ ' 2   3, 1, 2⏜ '

E. Visually group asymmetric rhythms that serve an expressive function — especially when rhythmic groupings occur against the natural musical pulse or against the barline

F. *Tendencies* - consider assigning specific dynamics to individual note values; often, simply asking choirs to sing whole-notes "*p*," half-notes, "*mp*", quarter-notes "*mf*", eighth-notes "*f*" in rehearsal will clarify the rhythmic design and the expressive components of the composition. Modify and connect these dynamics somewhat to allow them to sound more natural

G. Be aware of *hemiolia* phrasing that occurs in triple meter at many cadences in music of the Renaissance, Baroque, and Classic eras, as well as in music of the nineteenth/twentieth centuries that is modeled on these eras. A hemiola prepares the listener for the cadence. It beautifies and enhances the preparation by placing the internal rhythmic stress on a higher level of "3," amplifying the dramatic gesture inherent in "arsis" (the preparation) and "thesis" (the cadence)

H. Mark shifts in tempo: i.e., rubato, ritards, accelerandos

    1. Depending upon the absolute tempo, a conductor may choose to initiate tempo change on a number of beats. Each choice will create a particular musical *affect*

    2. Choose to enhance the musical *affect* that best seems to represent the composer's intention for a given moment in time

I. Use articulation of silence:

    1. between vowels and final consonants

    2. to highlight note-groups

    3. to clarify textures, especially when long held notes are pitched in low, thick textures

Pitch

Definition and Overview:

Unifying pitch — singing with good intonation — is one of the most elusive challenges in the choral art. When a choir sings in tune, the listener is allowed to hear more clearly the music's structural components: harmony, melody, rhythm, and texture. Thus, singing in tune heightens the awareness of structure, which facilitates communication.

Good choral intonation is also beautiful. The sound of a choir singing in tune is an experience in hearing extraordinarily compelling sound-images, produced through changing patterns of timbres, textures, and sonorities. In reinforcing the overtone series, good intonation creates a rich sonority that invites the listener into the music and heightens the audience's awareness of the beauty of the choir.

A great many factors affect the achievement of good pitch: acoustical theory and the acoustical environment, weather, health, the structural components of a composition, and most importantly, ear/voice coordination. The voice is the medium for choral music. Healthy voices, housed in healthy bodies, full of energy, have a great capacity to sing in tune. However, a choir will not truly sing in tune until its composite vocal sound achieves a unity of timbre. Pitch and timbre together define intonation. The vowels as well as the pitch must be tuned. When vowels are matched, the pitch can be unified.

Singing in tune requires good ears — conductor's and singers' — and consistent reinforcement. The responsibility for maintaining good pitch lies ultimately with the singers. While the conductor can provide them with a pitch standard initially, acquiring good pitch perception is integrally connected to understanding the process by which it is attained. By teaching choral singers to become conscious of the process they have individually used in attaining the conductor's pitch standard, the responsibility is placed squarely on their shoulders. Once this process becomes clear to them, choir singers are invigorated by the thinking that is required to re-create good pitch each time, and are stimulated by their own abilities (with friendly conductorial prods) to maintain it.

Specific Principles and Tendencies:

I. Mark and prepare to tune and balance all dissonances
    A. Hear them as color nuances - timbral considerations
    B. Mark and be alert to all dissonances that are difficult to hear because of the harmony itself or the denseness of the texture

II. Note problems
    A. Circle harmonic and melodic intervals that tend to cause pitch problems
    B. Mark all unisons, octaves, perfect fifths; these intervals form the important building blocks for tuning cadences or internal consonances
    C. Circle melodic intervals that are difficult to sing
    D. Circle chromatic change
    E. Circle difficult-to-hear or unexpected harmonies

III. In relatively atonal compositions, search for "homing-pigeon chords": chords that, over time, will stick in the memories of singers and will reinforce their security in rehearsals at these points. Build a framework around, and a context between these "homing-pigeon chords," upon which to place the more difficult passages. In time, singers in this way will develop readily-found aurally-accessible points of reference from which to gain security in performance.

IV. Write in reminders of sharps, flats, naturals, when singers are apt to forget the signatures or sing wrong notes because of what they expect to hear. Mark the unexpected, or at least the unexpected at the initial note-learning level.

V. Intonation[5]

    A. Some specific factors in preparing for listening for intonation problems, can be summarized by the following concepts:

        1. Pitch and timbre together define intonation. To sing in tune, therefore, means to unify the pitch — to bring all voices into like frequencies and compatible timbres.

        2. Pitch problems show up in half-step and whole-step relationships. There is good reason to "think high going up" and to "think narrow coming down". Develop a consciousness of hearing and singing wide (to piano equal temperament) ascending half steps and whole steps and narrow descending half and whole steps (see footnote on page 118).

        3. Tune principal cadences to the overtone series; sensitize singers to overtones. Learn to hear perfect 8ves, 5ths (high to the piano), and 3rds (low to the piano); if at each structural point (cadence) the vertical *concentus* is tuned, the music that precedes it will sound in tune.

        4. Proper vocal-breath support and energy-filled singing that affirms and constantly serves the vocal line aids considerably in the acquisition of good intonation.

        5. Pay particular attention to melodic contours that invite pitch problems. Sensitize singers to "rehear" the following formuli by singing narrow (to the piano) descending half and whole steps and 3rds, and wide ascending half and whole steps and 3rds. [Note: x marks the "typical" flat note in the melodic formula; * marks the next note that is apt to flat, if the preceding note is flat.]

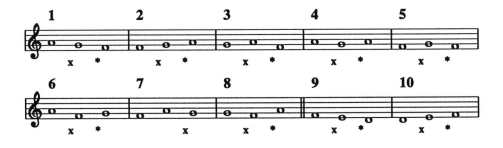

---

[5] The reader is referred to the article "Choral singing In-Tune" written by this author for the December 1991, *Choral Journal*; it explores the topic of intonation in depth. The *Choral Journal* has given the author permission to reprint excerpts from this article. Excerpts appear sporadically throughout this essay.

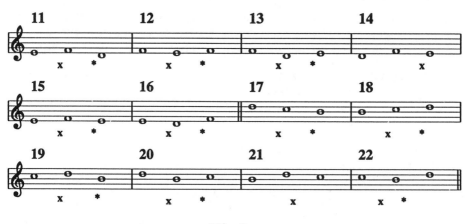

Timbre

Definition and overview:

There is no element in choral music with greater impact upon timbre than the sung word. The enormously colorful sound continuum of the shifting colors produced by passing mosaics of vowel sounds and vocal timbres, sustained through time contributes significantly to the intrinsic beauty of choral sound. The individual vocal timbres of each section needs to be unified. In choral music, this means to match vowels. When the vowel sound of each section projects a unified sonority, the pitch of the choir will improve, and the sheer beauty of the vocal sound will enhance and clarify the musical meaning of the score.

Specific Principles and Tendencies:

I. Text

   A. Search and listen for textual duets, trios, etc. Clarify them by marking parallel articulation and phrasing

   B. Pay attention to principal cadences. If each part sings on the same vowel, the pitch can be unified. If all parts, except one, sing on the same vowel, there are occasions when a conductor may want to change the vowel (of one word) to unify the vowel and timbral sonority, especially at important or final cadences

II. Vowels

   A. Watch for the necessity to modify vowels in extreme ranges

   B. Be ready to hear and guide the choir to pure vowels with matched timbres, especially when they are vertically aligned

   C. Make decisions on diphthong or other vowel combinations before rehearsal; these decisions will relate to timbre as well as duration

III. Consonants: mark those to be voiced, those to be unvoiced, those to be heard, and those that should be silent.

Intensity

Definition and overview:

Intensity serves primarily as an expressive element in music. It affects many agents of expression, including dynamics, articulation, phrasing, rubato, and linear direction. Intensity also serves another function — clarifying balance. Balance plays an extremely important role in projecting musical structure.

Concerning the expressive agents:

1) *Dynamics* illuminate passing musical gestures. They highlight expressive nuances, and to a greater degree than any other expressive agent, they can be a powerful force in emphasizing structure.

2) *Articulation* enhances structural clarity and serves an expressive function as well. Words are given inherent clarity of expression through articulation. Consonants are projected, and strong-weak syllabic relationships are revealed, heightening inherent word expression. Sometimes, however, the *affetti* of words (as opposed to the syllabic accents) are felt more powerfully by emphasizing each syllable equally, an effect that draws the listener into experiencing the emotional quality inherent in the word.

3) *Phrasing* provides cohesion to a series of pitches, and primarily through articulation, it sets into relief specific segments of a musical line. Short phrases or note groups heighten local expression; long phrases enhance continuity and direction. Phrasing is created by a combination of intensity and duration.

4) *Rubato* is produced through fluctuations in duration and intensity. While duration is the primary means through which rubato is realized, shifts in intensity normally accompany it. Cadential structures are heightened when rubato momentarily draws the music behind the pulse, and dramatic gestures are energized as rubato temporarily pushes the music beyond the pulse. Ritards and accelerandos (respectively) achieve similar effects through absolute changes of pulse. Passing events are often heightened by the impact of rubato, especially in the context of illuminating musical line and harmonic color.

5) *Linear direction*. Many styles of music are given meaningful expression through emphasizing the musical line (either the long line or short note groups that form the line). Intensity of direction serves long line; dynamics, articulation, and subtle rubato highlight shorter components of the line.

When we unify each of the expressive functions related to intensity, we develop an arsenal of communicative power to heighten, illuminate, and clarify musical meaning. Of the four elements of music, intensity most directly affects the expressive components of music-making.

Specific principles and tendencies:

    I. Dynamics serve to
        A. clarify structure
        B. improve balances
        C. enhance "expression"
    II. Dynamics and melody:
        A. In determining balance considerations, make a distinction between melodies that "carry the lead" (are harmonized vertically), and those that are inherently equal, as in contrapuntal textures.
        B. In contrapuntal or fugal passages, distinguish between the primary components of the individual lines (the head motifs, subjects,

countersubjects, etc.) and the "filler notes" by assigning appropriate dynamics, phrasing, articulation to enhance (or decrease) their audibility.

C. Mark with appropriate dynamics, melodies that are present in vocal ranges that create balance problems.

D. Be thoughtful in your preparation. Challenge an editor's thinking; know the composer's dynamics. Be aware of how the use of dynamics can amplify every musical nuance, even subtly, but always with some effect.

E. *Tendencies* :

    1. Count on long notes decaying

        a. Let them decay if they are not structurally important.

        b. Mark them with the appropriate dynamics if they serve the structure, i.e. a long line or an expressive purpose.

    2. Music takes place between notes, over time; every held note will require some attention dynamically:

        a. because singers' breaths decay

        b. because the held note may serve an expressive purpose

        c. because it connects to another note or several in a long line in the context of an expressive melodic function

F. In studying the score, marking the score, preparing the ear for rehearsal, look for structural duets — know what vocal parts "go together." Realize, if they are to be in balance, that appropriate dynamic changes may need to be written into the score by the singers.

In summary, differentiate each melodic component dynamically. Highlight melodies that contain notes that are "the most important notes" to be heard, with appropriate dynamics. Notes that serve purely as filler or as pedal functions are "less important notes"; let them recede into the background by marking dynamics accordingly.

III. Dynamics and harmony:

A. Harmonic progressions invite "associative" dynamic response — strong-weak, weak-strong; strong-stronger; weak-weaker, and so on. A series of harmonic progressions will invite a multitude of dynamic changes, from subtle to obvious. Highlight the musical meaning of the harmony by superimposing appropriate (though not necessarily exaggerated) dynamics to illuminate them. Use your mental-aural image of the composer's intentions, and mark accordingly the dynamics that reflect the associative meaning of the harmonies.

B. Tendencies — the interaction of harmonic, melodic, and rhythmic motion produces "pivots of energy"

    1. The pivot is literally the point at which either "release" of energy — at the approach of a cadence for example — or "motion" of energy begins to occur — for example, as the phrase begins to unfold.

        a. As music takes place in time, "release" of energy occurs after a build up (or "motion" of energy); conversely, "motion" ebbs from "release."

        b. In this way, "dynamic motion" precedes "arrival" creating "arsis to thesis" (tension to relaxation).

2. Enhance these gestures with appropriate dynamics and rubato.

IV. Dynamics and balance:

A. Shifts in balance occur when texture change occurs. For example: a momentary three-part texture may result in a four-part texture when one part is doubled at the unison by another.

1. Tendencies — often these changes occur simply because of the rules of voice-leading and are not inherently a part of the composer's intention to make one part louder than another. If your conception of the composer's aural-image makes clear that the composer did not intend one voice to predominate over another, in this context, notes that are doubled at the unison need to be rebalanced. This will be especially true if they are held over a considerable length of time, and/or occur in the context of a slow tempo.

B. Circle balance problems created by the range and tessitura of individual parts.

1. Circle crossed parts

2. Study the importance of a note's function — is it a filler, a pedal, or an important part of the compositional fabric. Mark accordingly

3. In essence, build a hierarchy of dynamics around notes based upon their structural importance.

C. *Tendencies*

1. Low textures are hard to hear; high textures are fatiguing to sing Circle exceptionally low or high textures

2. Balance problems occur when textures change — from horizontal to vertical, open to closed, high to low; number of parts, unison doublings; and the range/tessitura of individual vocal lines. Rebalance the vocal parts within the context of texture change. The composer's musical conception is realized and the structure is clarified when all elements of a composition are heard precisely in balance.

V. Dynamics and duration:

A. Assign gradations of dynamics to those phrases that are marked by the composer with the traditional signs of crescendo and diminuendo

1. Mark these dynamics with "assigned degrees of change"; for example: *mp* to *mp+* to *mf-* to *mf*

2. Link incremental dynamic change to pulse

3. Tendencies - longer notes decay through unthinking entropy (loss of energy)

   a. Mark held (long/slow) notes with dynamic indications that are the same at the beginning and at the end, with a crescendo through-out. This reminds singers that they must add energy to their singing while sustaining, to counteract the natural tendency of running out of breath (entropy).

   b. Held notes invite flat pitch; marking them with dynamics helps to counteract this tendency.

VI. Dynamics — summary:

A. Confirm in your own mind the validity of the dynamic markings you see in the score.

B. Distinguish between those written by the composer and those written by the editor. Seek out primary sources or collected works editions to verify the original dynamic indications of the composer. Choose the most authoritative practical edition available for use in performance.

C. Challenge the editor's dynamics; be sure they make sense on a structural and expressive level.

D. Reevaluate the composer's dynamics.

1. Understand the intentions implied by the specific dynamics used by the composer.

2. In the light of your mental-aural image of the composer's gestures implied by the dynamics, re-mark accordingly.

3. Think about your own choir's vocal make-up; understand if their collective vocal potential can truly realize the composer's dynamic intentions. If necessary, adjust the written dynamics accordingly.

4. Consider the acoustics of the hall in which you will perform the composition. If necessary, adjust the written dynamics.

E. Tendency: often the specific moment at which a written crescendo ends and a written diminuendo begins, does not in fact indicate the precise apex of the phrase. To better serve the composer's implicit intentions of the gesture, the collective energy of the phrase may be better expressed by delaying the diminuendo by one or two beats where the true apex ("dynamic pivot") of the phrase actually takes place.

1. In essence, understand the musical gesture first, and then validate or subtly change the composer's notation of it.

2. Try to honor the composer's dynamics by understanding the reason they were included in the score.

3. Avoid being too literal, yet don't ever ignore the composer's intentions.

VII. *Tendencies* : there is great truth in this rustic statement: sopranos sharp, altos are inaudible, tenors flat, and basses are late.

A. In singing through the vocal break in the soprano-voice high range, sopranos (especially youthful ones without a great deal of experience) tend to push, and therefore sharp.

B. Altos are often not heard because in much of the music they sing, the vocal ranges of their parts are low (compared to the tessitura of other vocal parts); two reasons account for this:

1. Sacred music of the Renaissance, Baroque, and Classic eras was sung by men and boys. Men sang the alto parts either in chest voice or falsetto (depending upon the range); older boys with lower voices also sang alto parts. Thus the range of the parts in much of the music of these eras was not conceived for the range of the modern alto voice.

2. The compositional structure itself and the rules of voice leading,

often produce, as a by-product, a low alto part.

C. A true high, natural tenor is rare. It is simply a voice that is uncommon. It is a rare choral conductor who has enough high tenors. Thus, the vocal range and general tessitura of tenor parts are simply high for the "normal" male voice. Especially over the break f/f#/g — singing in that range and above for any length of time is fatiguing. Fatigue invites flat pitch.

D. Bass voices sing low notes. Low notes vibrate at low frequency. The vocal chords producing the low frequency vibrate more slowly than when they sing high(er) notes. The slow vibrations of vocal chords as they produce low notes invite slow-motion singing — i.e., dragging. It simply takes longer to produce low notes, longer for them to be heard, and it is difficult to move quickly from one to another. Thus, basses often sing (subtly or not so subtly) behind the beat.

Summary

By marking the score — etching the mind, preparing the ear — the musical materials will be brought into conscious relief in the conductor's *mind's ear* and will serve as a foundation for *listening* in rehearsals. This process highlights, illuminates, and therefore rivets the conductor's attention on the four elements of music, setting a complete aural foundation for listening in rehearsals.

Expecting to hear and preparing to listen for these inherent aspects of choral ensemble music-making is the key to the conductor's degree of success in implementing *change*. The score and the ear become one. In rehearsals, make each singer conscious of the process you are using — why they are serving the music by what **you** are asking them to do; why they are serving the inherent meaning of the music by what **they** are doing. By making *conscious* the process they are using to acquire the conductor's mental-aural image, your singers will empower themselves with the knowledge necessary for maintaining *change*. In this manner, singers develop pride in their own abilities as their goal: *mastery of ensemble* becomes apparent. The pride they feel elicits positive and cohesive energy toward realizing their goal, and the results will be inspiring.

III. Ear

Communicating the mental-aural image to singers requires time, patience, discipline, and experience. The process is a circular one. The conductor measures the sound produced by the choir against his mental-aural image; he feeds information back to the choir, and the choir reshapes the sound. As this process continues in rehearsal after rehearsal, inevitably the choir's sound begins more clearly to match the conductor's mental-aural image. The ear is the yardstick — the "truth teller," the intermediary that makes possible the conductor's capacity to realize the conception.

The better the conductor's ear, the more effectively the conductor's mental-aural image will be taught to the choir. Every bit of information is gathered by the ear. The information received can be categorized (as stated before) by the four elements that comprise music: duration, pitch, timbre, and intensity. Each musical element contributes to the composite picture of the whole. The ear has the capacity to hear all four elements at the same time. The mind has the ability to focus selectively on one at a time — also the capacity to assimilate information on all levels simultaneously.

Learning to hear simultaneously on four levels requires natural aptitude, training, and experience. Each rehearsal presents a fresh opportunity to expand the ear's capacities. Concentration is the key. Conductors who possess the capacity to concentrate will reap the rewards of increased auditory perception, and will thus be able to quickly identify information related to duration, pitch, timbre, and intensity. As the ear improves, the conductor's ability to evaluate this information will be greatly enhanced, providing him with the knowledge necessary to implement change.

How to Listen

Picture a dial. While the choir is singing, slowly turn the dial and focus your concentration on one element of music at a time. Spend considerable time listening to one element — *pitch*, for example. Quality, amplitude, accuracy, intonation, balance, dynamics, articulation, phrasing — all of these characteristics may enter into your assessment of the choir's pitch.

Next, picture the dial in your mind and turn it to *timbre* or a combination of both *pitch* and *timbre* , since these two elements can be closely related in function. Vowels, color, sonority, texture — all are facets of *timbre* upon which to concentrate. Then, listen for *duration*. This is a complex activity, because *duration* will overlap with *pitch, timbre,* and *intensity*. Specific aspects of listening to *duration* will be linked inevitably to rhythmic accuracy, to ensemble rhythm, to tempo, to metric structure, and to speed of harmonic rhythm. The *expressive elements* — dynamics, phrasing, articulation, rubato, linear direction — are served by *duration* as well as *intensity*.

Now, turn the dial to *intensity*. Dynamics and color may leap into mind; or balance considerations will become immediately apparent. One may focus on each of the *expressive elements* of music by using "the dial" and listening for articulation or phrasing or line or rubato. *Intensity* serves most substantially, however, dynamics and balance.

Turning the dial focuses the conductor's auditory concentration on one element at a time. The capacity to hear increases when the conductor's full energy is focused like a laser beam, with total concentration on each element, one by one. In this manner, through one rehearsal after another, a conductor can build an acute degree of auditory perception. Conductors can also learn to hear on more than one level at the same time and for longer periods of concentration-time, given accrued experience, sufficient aural aptitude, and the ability to concentrate.

One cannot listen too long, however, without forgetting what one has heard. "Click off" in the brain each element you would like to "fix," each element that needs to be changed, as you measure the choir's sound against your mental-aural image. To avoid breaking the singers' concentration, do not stop to correct them until at least three "problems" have occurred. Stop the choir after hearing three or four or five specifics — or more, if your auditory memory can store them up. By vocal part, measure number, and beat — in that order — describe what you want (positive). Compare it verbally against what the choir did (negative), and describe what you want again (positive). Over time, this sequence will provide the choir with very positive incentives for *change*. If the "why" of "what you want" is clearly explained, you will have provided the choir with invaluable positive imaging to accomplish your goals. In summary, the conductor in this manner motivates the choir to give meaningful aural life to the written composition that symbolically represents through the composer's notation his conceptualization — his sound image.

While correcting specific aspects of a choir's rendition, it will be very important to confirm other aspects of their rendition you hear that you like! For example:

> I liked the way you shaped that phrase in bars x-y-z; however, in the tenor part at bar x on beat 2, the 'g' natural should be sung higher — mark it with an 'up' arrow. Basses, in bar y, beat 3, you need to move the eighth-note more quickly; it is late following the dotted quarter ! Mark it with an arrow moving towards the next note. Altos in bar z beat 4, you need to sing more strongly. You are overbalanced in this particular texture; mark the note mf with a stress on it to give it more presence. Sopranos, in bar y, you need to modify the 'ee' vowel — it is too bright because of the high vocal range. Modify the vowel to 'ih' to give the sound more space. Again choir, these bars x-y-z continue to have excellent line; make these individual modifications, and continue to sing with energy and purpose, giving dynamic shape to your individual parts.

One can listen horizontally or vertically. Both types of listening open conductors' ears to hearing duration, pitch, timbre, and intensity. Thoroughly preparing the score, and therefore the ear, serves as a memory bell in rehearsal, and more importantly is the foundation upon which we organize the way we hear. In rehearsal over time, through listening, measuring the choir's sound against the mental-aural image, and reshaping the sound, the choir's image of the sound grows closer to the conductor's. When the profound experience of "matching conceptualization" occurs, *Ensemble Mastery* will result.

IV. Rehearsing

Introduction and Overview

It is in the rehearsal that each element of the conductor's preparation is drawn together. The conductor will have begun his preparation by studying the score. Score study and stylistic insights will have stimulated a mental-aural image. The rehearsal provides the context in which to realize that mental-aural image. Through the ear the conductor measures the chorus' sound against the mental-aural image and implements *change*. This is rehearsing.

No aspect of the "Conductor's Process" will more directly affect the performance than the conductor's ability to rehearse. Without effective rehearsing, insights into the score will not be realized. No matter how much the conductor is able to hear, no matter how visionary the interpretation, no matter how highly communicative the conducting technique may be, the principal foundation upon which the actualization of the score rests is *rehearsing*.

Some Specific Principles[4]

1. In general, try to have each piece or each movement of a major work at a different stage of development. It will help rejuvenate the singers' energies by contrasting their work on the countless musical demands of a composition if their approach in rehearsing pieces one after another is highly varied.

2. Group your work into two categories — musical and technical — and three stages: 1) **the preliminary stage**, in which the musical gestures and the inherent expressive qualities — the *affetti* of the music — should become clear to the singers. This understanding will provide a very meaningful context in which to teach the notes, the rhythms, and the text; 2) **the technical stage** — getting the choir to sing in tune, in balance, and rhythmically aligned: developing *choral ensemble* . This stage represents about 80 % of the work; and 3) **the final stage,** overlaying the musical ideas introduced in the preliminary stage with the *ensemble* achieved in the technical stage. The inherent expressive qualities of the music can be developed at a more sophisticated level in this final stage as they are placed upon the foundation of *ensemble pitch, rhythm, and balance.*

There are many advantages to this approach: a) Singers will have a meaningful musical context in which to place the technical work, and their motivation for learning the basics — the notes, rhythms, and text, the ensemble pitch, pulse, balance, in depth — will be far greater. b) In developing from the outset a musical understanding of the composer's gestures, the singers will be inspired to serve the technical demands of the composition and will be motivated to follow the conductor's methods for achieving them. c) During the final stage a higher level of attention can be paid to the expressive elements — the dynamics, phrasing, articulation, rubato, linear direction — that shape and give beauty and meaning to the composition.

3. In all that is done in the technical and musical areas, make it clear that the singers are expected to mark their parts. They must realize at the outset that being a part of an *ensemble* is a privilege that brings with it certain responsibilities. When singers feel responsible for marking their individual part they begin to embark upon a learning process that eventually empowers them with the knowledge that **they** can effectively maintain *change* - the core of the rehearsal process.

4. In the technical work, separate text from music. Do this early on in the rehearsal process, because text impinges upon pitch, duration, timbre, and intensity. The variety of vowels in words, placed in vertical and horizontal sonorities, provides no unified sound continuum in which to place an aural foundation for the acquisition of good pitch, ensemble-rhythm, and balance.

---

[4] Rehearsal methods, procedures, and techniques vary greatly from one conductor to another. While it is not the intention of this discussion to suggest specific rehearsal techniques, the author has found the principles here useful. These principles are the product of his experience and represent a composite picture of ideas derived from numerous mentor-conductors, most especially Robert Shaw and Helmuth Rilling.

Once the notes are learned, sing them semi-staccato on "doo." Insist on a pure "oo" vowel. Singers often associate 'oo' with the sound of 'oo' in the word "you," "due," or "dew" — all of which contain automatic diphthong associations of "eeoo." Once choral singers can sing semi-staccato "doo" (or as the author calls it, "legato doo with space between notes") in tune, together, and in balance, they can easily sing true "legato doo," connecting each note very well in tune, together, and in balance. Furthermore, once the fabric of sound and the musical gestures are heard on a beautiful pure "legato doo", over numerous rehearsals the foundation upon which the text can be placed will be set, producing a unified sound-image that greatly improves ensemble intonation, rhythm, and balance. N.B: "oo" used for too long a period of time can produce vocal fatigue. Change to "nah" in legato contexts, and/or move on to another piece that is at another stage of rehearsal.

5. Choral singers learn faulty pitch intonation and imprecise rhythmic habits at the initial sight-reading and note learning stages. Immediately correct the pitch of the notes and rhythmic alignment during these early stages. It is during this time that associative pitch problems develop, i.e., problems related to the subtle ear/voice coordination required in singing. When the voice consistently fails to maintain the proper pitch of a note, poor associative pitch habits arise and singers invariably and unconsciously perpetuate these habits long after notes are learned. So, at the initial stages, correct the notes as well as the intonation of the notes; the rhythms as well as the alignment of the rhythms.

6. Achieving ensemble rhythm will be the foundation upon which ensemble pitch, balance, timbre, intensity, and the expressive elements will be meaningfully placed. There are a number of techniques that can help to sensitize singers to ensemble rhythm. All of them relate to sensitizing a singer to a unanimous group pulse. A unanimous group pulse can be best evoked through *feeling silence* — together; in fact, "hearing silence!" Energy can fill silence; energy can be felt. Energy that is harnessed together, in silence, accumulates unanimous group pulse. From 1) using the "staccato doo or dah" technique, to singing "pum" (sustaining only on the "m"), 2) counting while singing on various levels of the beat, 3) counting inwardly and feeling the rhythms of an individual part and clapping at a point of arrival — all of these techniques, and many others, help to sensitize singers to group pulse.

Overlaying text will impact considerably upon group pulse. Further energy and concentration must be directed towards insuring accuracy of ensemble rhythm when text is sung. Consonants take time. They affect vertical and horizontal alignment. Be alert to keep ensemble rhythm from slowing down when the text is added. Having each part sing on one pitch — perhaps sung a 4th or a 5th apart, with the correct rhythms, vowels, and consonants — will help re-align ensemble rhythm.

7. Do not allow singers to "mix functions." For example, the functions of slow-ing down or singing a diminuendo must be separated from their natural associative tendency: flatting. Counteract these tendencies by separating functions. Make clear that crescendoing is not the same as speeding up or sharping, each time this associative tendency occurs in rehearsal.

8. Avoid singing at extreme dynamic ranges until notes and rhythms are secure. Very soft dynamics require tremendous breath control and often invite flat pitch; loud dynamics sung for great lengths of time invite vocal forcing and fatigue. Sing at a comfortable level: mp-mf. Later, incorporate the proper dynamics.

9. After the notes and gestures are *well* learned, if pitch problems persist, change keys — up or down a half step. This procedure changes the physiological associations of how the notes feel in the voice, and often counteracts many of the "associative pitch" problems that have accrued over time.

10. F major generally goes flat. After the note-learning stage is completed, change to E or F# depending upon vocal/balance/color considerations.

11. Energize singers through exercise, posture, enthusiasm, humor, elation, exuberance, well-intentioned anger, love of the music, positive reinforcement, and inspiration.

12. Rehearse in rooms that have clear non-reverberant acoustics yet with reasonable room ambience. Avoid low ceilings, acoustical tile, rugs, curtains, and low-roofed acoustical shells.

13. Sit/stand in positions that allow each singer to take responsibility for his or her own pitch/rhythm/intensity/etc., without interference from another singer of the same vocal part. Sing in (STAB) (BATS) quartets or in some type of mixed position. This is a prerequisite for the acquisition of good individual pitch habits and developing independent rhythmic security. Singers hear best when placed in concentric circles, facing each other. They also hear well in half-circles, or horseshoes, or so-called "acoustical cup positions." Even out-of-doors, a semicircle or U position acts as a natural "acoustical cup," resonating the choral sound with great warmth and ambience *if* the singers are placed in "mixed" positions and there is considerable space between singers — about an arm-length on either side. Acoustical shells try to compensate for this in concert halls. This conductor has found that placing a choir in an "acoustical cup position" (a semi-circle or horseshoe) is a far more effective manner to aid natural resonance than by simply placing the choir in front of an acoustical shell. Of course, if the shell is placed behind a choir that is already in the "acoustical cup position" the projection of sound, especially in a large, non-resonant concert hall, can be further enhanced.

14. While the piano may be used at the initial stages of rehearsal if it speeds up the process of learning the notes, wean singers early from the piano. When the piano plays, the conductor cannot hear or listen acutely for problems of intonation, rhythm, diction, vowel uniformity, balance, dynamics, phrasing, etc. Also, singers will not hear other sections or their own as acutely when the piano doubles their vocal parts. Furthermore, the piano is tuned to equal-temperament, to accommodate for "the Pythagorean flaw."[5]

---

[5] The "Pythagorean flaw" is a term this author uses for a natural acoustical phenomenon — an irreconcilable "flaw" in acoustics. It is measured by the audible pitch difference between the e (for example) produced by the *fundamental* pitch C at the frequency ratio of 5:4 (the pure major 3rd) and the e produced by tuning a series of perfect 5ths (C-g-d-a-e) at the frequency ratio of 3:2 (the pure fifth). The comparative pitch difference between the two e's is easily

(Continued next page)

Summary of Rehearsal Philosophy

Rehearsing at the highest levels of the choral art is a vastly complex and extraordinarily rewarding process. There is something uncanny about the essence of the rehearsal process — the ability to develop in choral singers a technical and musical concept of the score that matches that of the conductor's mental-aural image. Developing matching conceptualizations is inevitably inspiring, perhaps fundamentally spiritual. How does the conductor draw the choral singers toward the compelling image he or she possesses? Through creating in them a *unanimous vision of it*: a *unity of ensemble* that reflects it.

Rehearsals are the forum in which conductor and choir come together to engage in a creative process that is normally motivated by a concrete goal: the performance. The quality of rehearsing is inevitably measured by the quality of performance. While disagreement concerning details of interpretation and differences of opinion regarding sound ideals are as common as conductors are different, few musicians or knowledgeable listeners fail to recognize an outstanding performance when they hear one.

An outstanding performance communicates. It allows listeners and participants to transcend their common daily experience. Outstanding performance enriches lives and rejuvenates spirits. Good rehearsals do the same thing. How can rehearsals best serve music's ultimate value? By focusing the energy of singers on the inherent elements of music that, when revealed, give meaning to its structure and order as it develops in time. When the *meaning* of a composition is revealed, *communication* occurs, fulfilling music's ultimate purpose.

How do we make clear the elements of music that provide the key to understanding its structure and order? Through *unifying* them. In the process of unifying the elements of music, the medium through which the music is being heard — the choir — absorbs and assimilates a unanimous vision; a *unity of ensemble*.

By achieving unity of ensemble, then, we simultaneously answer both questions: how are the singers drawn toward the compelling image the conductor possesses, and how do we make clear the elements of music? Ensemble unity **is** unity of duration, pitch, timbre, and intensity. When the choir attains **ensemble unity** — the "ideal" — it clarifies the form, the function, and the design of the sound continuum of the music. It reveals the music's total structure, reinforcing meaning and enhancing its capacity to communicate. It is through

---

heard; one needs only only to tune two ranks of a harpsichord to these temperaments to hear "the flaw" — it is not subtle. Pythagorean tuning (the one based upon pure fifths) contains large major 2nds and 3rds and small minor 2nds and 3rds. Mean-tone tuning (the one based upon pure thirds) produces a small fifth, and a pure major 3rd divided into two equal (small) major 2nds. If Pythagorean fifths are used to form the circle of fifths, the 12th of these fifths — the "unison" — is higher (by about one-eighth of a tone). This is called the Pythagorean comma. For further information the reader can refer to the entry "Temperament" on page 757 of the *Norton/Grove Concise Encyclopedia of Music*, edited by Stanley Sadie. Two excellent sources on acoustics and intonation, specifically designed for choral conductors, are *Choral Intonation* by Per-Gunnar Alldahl, Gehrmans Musikforlag 6771, and *Choral Studies* by Lars Edlund, AB Nordiska Musikforlaget.

meaningful communication that music can realize its profound capacity to inspire. The results: **mastery of choral ensemble.**

It is important to point out that all of the principles upon which effective rehearsals are based require two essential ingredients: energy and desire. The quality of the energy that the conductor gives to the singers will be the primary force that stimulates them to implement the conductor's ideas. Singers must be motivated to accomplish the conductor's goals. The conductor who is motivated by the quality of the music, by the conceptual vision of it, and by the joy received in realizing the concept, cannot help but project positive energy. Enthusiasm, encouragement, patience, humor, and positive reinforcement will serve the conductor well as choral singers are engaged in the rehearsal process. The joy that students experience in singing with inspired conductors is transformed into a collective energy that replenishes and inspires both conductors and students. This mutual experience is one of the deepest rewards of the pivotal element of the "Conductor's Process" — rehearsing.

V. Conclusion

A common thread of **energy** runs through each component of the "Conductor's Process" — especially in the remarkable inter-relationship of its core: the *mental-aural image*, the *ear*, and *rehearsing*. Combing through the rich repertory of choral music to discover a profoundly crafted masterpiece can be an extremely exhilarating experience. This compelling process inspires the conductor to imagine how the music will sound in performance. Then upon analyzing the structure and style of the work, an even more powerful image of the score emerges, igniting a sound-vision that in rehearsal energizes the conductor to motivate the choir to attain it. The choir in turn is inspired by the informed, impassioned energy emanating from the conductor.

In rehearsal after rehearsal, as the conductor and choir build an *ensemble* that is able to project a unity of conception through a unity of presentation, their spirits soar as they work together to perfect the process of the multifaceted art of recreating music. **Mastery** results, and in performance, projecting their collective vision of the beauty of the music inspires, rejuvenates, and enriches the lives of the participants. They have engaged in the process of realizing the conductor's vision in sound, and together are rejuvenated by a cycle of energy that emanates from the process itself. Thus, energy is the catalyst for making music transcendent and for breathing spirituality into the interaction of humanity and music.

Conducting

Donald Neuen

Many books have been written on the subject of conducting. To condense this subject into one chapter necessitates a very selective and economical process of *conceptualizing* those thoughts, concepts, and "tools" with which a conductor can further develop the highest levels of conducting excellence. These basic *ideas* must be clearly formulated and established. They are absolutely crucial to the conductor's development and consistently abound in the work of all great conductors.

It will be necessary for the reader to separate the study of this chapter from the typical conducting-class situation in which there is a full-length textbook and the presence of an instructor to explain, demonstrate, and teach each principle, technique, and fundamental. *Concepts* only will be presented — and these will at times be quite general and broad, as well as very specific and direct. However, it is hoped that they will be of great substance and lasting value and that they will form the basis for a lifetime of further study and development.

At the outset, one major point must be established: The subject is *Artistic Musical Conducting*. We are not interested in the age-old misconception that there are major differences and a giant chasm between choral and instrumental conducting. A truly great *musical conductor* finds few things different when working with voices or instrumentalists. Basically, we should envision ourselves as *musical* conductors who conduct *musicians musically*. The manner, style, and overall general appearance of what we do and should look like are, with few exceptions, the same whether we are in front of an orchestra, band, or chorus.

Techniques of musicians differ; and the conductor must have an effective working knowledge of the skills of a clarinetist, violinist, timpanist, trumpeter, etc. — as well as the human voice. When it comes to the physical act of conducting, expressive, clear, and precise conducting movements are consistently effective in *any* ensemble situation.

A fine *instrumental* conductor clearly and effectively communicates precise beats or pulses; expressive melodic lines; driving rhythms; dynamic changes and nuances; significant harmonic moments; and all other musical expressions of a composition. The *choral* conductor should do likewise. *A sensitive expression of the text does not negate the demand to be musical, clear and concise.* To conduct words or syllables, using inconsistent and musically undefinable motions is fortunately becoming a day-gone-by. To spoon-feed the chorus in this manner denies the conductor of musical expression and the singers of intelligence.

For years singers have justifiably earned choruses the reputation of "second-class musicians." They were — and sometimes still are — less well trained than their instrumental counterparts. Choral directors have felt that they must teach and direct in a rather elementary and mundane manner because singers "wouldn't catch on if you didn't." We now know differently, thanks to the example and professionalism of many outstanding conductors. We have come to see that singers *will* respond to artistic musical conducting if given the opportunity. It is the conductor's responsibility to raise the level of performance through the *highest levels of artistic conducting* instead of lowering standards to match the level of a given ensemble. If we are to get rid of a "second-class" category of "choral directing" and strive to be truly fine *conductors* — able to stand in front of choral *or* instrumental forces with ease and confidence — certain concepts must be established.

I. Great conductors have developed great minds and a great depth of musicianship, knowledge, and expression.

Anyone can develop the mind, limitless in its potential for growth and expansion. Those who wish to grow, do so; those who don't, stagnate. The successful conductor must continue to expand both mind and musicianship for as long as life itself lasts.

The presence of what we might call *artistic conducting technique* is often lacking in many highly successful conductors. How, then, did they succeed? It was due to intelligence, knowledge, and expressiveness. The conducting techniques of some of the world's greatest conductors would never be found in a textbook, yet their *minds* have enabled them to produce incredible results with choruses, orchestras, or bands. They *know* what they need to *know*, and they know how to *teach* and *express it*. Does this mean that precise, disciplined, and consistent conducting techniques are not important? Absolutely not. It simply means that they are secondary in importance to a fine, well-developed *mind*. I will hasten to add that "minimal-technique-conductors" frequently have to *over-teach* to compensate for *bad* conducting. Instrumentalists and singers have to *overcome* poor conducting techniques in order to do what has been asked of them. In many situations, even at the top professional level, this results in the musicians purposefully *not* watching the conductor, except in situations where it is absolutely essential.

Thus, we must strive to accomplish 1) the development of a great mind *and* 2) effective conducting techniques. But, we must remember: *intelligence* and *knowledge* must predominate. They are the very essence by which true substance and long-lasting success find their reality. It is especially important that choral conductors — who by definition are involved with text and textual *feeling* — realize that pure emotion, personality, and charisma are, in themselves, not a substitute for intelligence and knowledge — whether it be in areas of "lighter" music or the classics.

II. It is the conductor's full responsibility to know all that can be known about the music.

The conductor must approach the score with deep commitment, dedication, and integrity — whether it be a Broadway tune, folk song, spiritual, motet, or gigantic work for chorus, soloists, and orchestra. It must be our goal *to know everything there is to know* about the score. This includes:

- stylistic interpretation
- structural and harmonic analysis
- compositional techniques and instructions
- phrasing analysis, and conductorial (editorial) markings
- performance problems for singers and/or players
- technical and dramatic understanding
- mastery of conducting problems

Knowledge is the cornerstone of security — for both conductor and singer/player. That which is unknown cannot be taught. That which is not taught seldom happens. The conductor must be able to teach a piece with a comprehensive understanding of its *wholeness*.

Great minds are not so much "born" as they are self-developed. Robert Shaw, when asked the question "How much time do you spend studying the score?" replied, "Every waking hour."

Most conductors are, to varying degrees, involved in things other than music. Each must wrestle with, and successfully find, that "right" solution to the problem of sufficient study time. Whatever the result, it must equate to really *KNOWING THE MUSIC*. To be a conductor is to be a leader. To lead is a privilege that brings with it the responsibility to *know* enough to *do* it.

III. The conductor must understand the techniques involved within the performing forces.

This simply means that if you're conducting *singers*, you must know and understand the art of *singing*. Many choral conductors have been justifiably criticized for not knowing enough about instruments when conducting a combined choral/instrumental work. It is our *responsibility* to *know* and *understand* the *instrumental* aspects of these performances. By the same token, many instrumental conductors fall short when they conduct singers. Those who have majored primarily in a keyboard instrument and find themselves in a position of choral conducting — church, school, or community — must accept the responsibility of knowing and understanding the techniques of *fine singing*.

Strings require a different language — of bowing and articulation — than winds; women's voices present different challenges and problems than men's voices; and young singers must be treated in a very special way. It goes on and on. The main issue is that efficiency of rehearsals and quality of performances must not be limited by technical ignorance on the part of the conductor. We must enable the ensemble to perform better and more effectively because we are there — with the *knowledge* to help them do so, through solid *teaching* — whether they be singers or instrumentalists. It is important to remember that the voice of a singer can be *permanently damaged* by a conductor who does not thoroughly understand the art of singing.

IV. A Great conductor is a true reflection of the score.

The conductor must *become* the *music itself,* which can only be achieved as all aspects of the score are known and understood. Few conductors are able to reach the level where they actually become a *true reflection* of the score. This is not easy. *Complete knowledge of the score* and *total reflection of it* are the two main factors that separate truly great conductors from all others. To reflect the score means several things:

1. All movements should be interpretively appropriate and meaningful without affectations. No gesture should be unnecessary, unmusical, undefined, nor unnatural. None should be obtrusive or distracting or simply for "show." There should be no meaningless, idiosyncratic, or habitual movements/gestures.

2. Every movement/gesture is dictated by a specific musical thought or idea and is consistently accountable to the *score.* Conducting is a *pre-determined,* highly-*developed* artistic *skill,* and its specific characteristics emerge anew with each score. The conductor must *look* and *feel* like the music is sounding or about to sound.

3. A musical line is always a process of continual change — if the composition is one of substantial quality. *There will seldom be even one full measure, let alone a phrase, in which there is only one musical thought, idea, or nuance to express* — such as changes or contrasts in dynamics, rhythm, melodic direction, harmony, instrumentation, voicing, or textual expressivity. *Something of musical or textual interest is constantly happening or changing.* So, too, must the appearance, feeling, and expression of the conductor. To conduct and look the same for several consecutive measures or phrases is simply not *musical conducting.* This would fall into the category of mechanical *time beating.* Time beating is the negating antithesis of musical expression!

4. The conductor must not only *feel comfortable* expressing the full spectrum of emotional feelings, but actually *enjoy* and receive *fulfillment* through it. This is very similar to the visible, dramatic expression of inner emotions by great actors. You actually see, in the expression of their physical being, those emotional feelings which they are experiencing deep within their mind, heart and soul. We must hasten to say that this does not suggest that the conductor should overstate or exaggerate the true and honest expression of the music to the extent of sentimentality or superficial theatrics. It simply means that whether the music is *piano/dolce* or *forte/marcato,* the conductor must be able to *reflect the text* accurately, effectively, and consistently — whether one of simple beauty or heavy dramatic impact.

5. The conductor must develop the *focus* and *concentration* that will enable him or her to figuratively *become the music.* One must become so completely involved and engrossed in the music that nothing else exists at that moment, in the entire universe! So centered in the music that to disturb this focus and concentration — to call them away from their "musical existence" — would cause an immediate state of momentary disorientation. This takes great effort and practice for most conductors to develop. It is one thing for the *great actor* to bring

himself into this state-of-being as he executes the oneness of his role. It is quite another challenge for a conductor to do it and, *at the same time*, retain a consciousness of *technical awareness* that 1) enables what is being produced by the musicians to be continually heard and analyzed, 2) connects with the established concept of what is *supposed* to be produced, and 3) through effective teaching, *establishes the latter*.

6. There will be less such all-consuming focus in the early mechanic-fixing rehearsals than in the later ones. The total, all-encompassing involvement may happen only in the final rehearsal or two and, most effectively, during the *performance*. It is critical to acknowledge that without the prerequisite of *total knowledge of the score*, the conductor's "being" could never be *free* enough to achieve this level of artistic and expressive involvement. Knowledge allows freedom.

V. The development of skilled, refined, and artistic conducting should, for the conductor, be as high a priority as a fine violinist's right arm, hand, and bowing technique.

Most conductors have studied the actual art of physical conducting less than any other discipline in their musical training. Most have spent much more time with their major instrument and in the study of theory, counterpoint, form and analysis, and music history. For many, the serious study of conducting may amount to only one, two, or, at the most, three semesters — seldom on a private lesson basis.

There are two obvious reasons for this: 1) one to three semesters of conducting is all that is offered in most college curriculums, and 2) most musicians who are physically coordinated and possess a good basic sense of rhythm feel very confident to conduct with minimal training. It is often felt that, while it takes a gifted person *years* of rigorous training to become a fine singer, instrumentalist, theorist, or musicologist, "*anyone can conduct*." We see the results of this in many ways: 1) professional singers and instrumentalists who, in their later years, begin a conducting career; 2) organists who, without sufficient conducting or choral techniques training, conduct church choirs; 3) singers and pianists who do the same thing with school and community choirs; and 4) one of the most visible examples — the professional symphony orchestra conductor who began as a pianist, became an opera coach, then an opera conductor, and finally a symphony orchestra conductor — and in some cases, never studied conducting at all!

These examples, together with the fact that choruses, orchestras, and bands are perfectly willing to strive for fine performances *in spite of poor conducting*, sum up quite well the reasons for the acceptance of this situation. Most ensemble members have *never* performed under a truly fine conductor. They *don't even know the difference*. Thus, in the conductor's mind, there is really no necessity to improve this dilemma.

In a recent interview with major symphony orchestra players, it was quickly acknowledged that the players would *always* prefer a more precise, skilled, artistic style of conducting — but they seldom get it. Most players have resigned themselves to that fact. The players went on to acknowledge that, as a result, they don't watch the conductor except when absolutely necessary; communication is limited to the conductor's knowledge of the score, expression, and knowing what he or she wants and how to get it. In essence, they have given up on any expectation of seeing clear, precise, disciplined, and artistic conducting in any consistent manner.

VI. The movements and gestures of the conductor should be based on the same kind of pre-determined, highly developed *techniques* for which all performing artists strive.

When it comes to actual conducting movements, they should be as *learned* and *pre-determined* as the pianist, violinist, or singer would learn technique. These people do not spontaneously *improvise* a skill. Conductors should not either. A *technique* is a learned proficiency that, when successfully and consistently employed, results in the perfection of a desired performance — whether in athletics, the arts, or any other physical feat.

The *mastering* of any language will produce a greater potential for the successful communication and expression of one's concepts, thoughts, and feelings. So, too, with conducting — the *visual language* that expresses musical ideas. The level of language proficiency will either hinder or enhance communication. This is as true in conducting as in speaking.

If we are to refine the technical aspects of our conducting "language," what, then, will be the most important concepts for which we will strive? A list will now be presented for your consideration. Some of it may seem elementary; however, be advised not to take anything for granted. *Videotape your rehearsals and concerts.* Be your own best critic. See and *know* yourself as a *conductor.*

A. Assign different and unique responsibilities to each hand.

The right hand:

A consistent *beat pattern* should be its *primary function*; yet it must maintain *full expressiveness* and the ability to occasionally cue *within* a context of clear, concise beating. The right hand *can*, for the most part, be as expressive *within* the context of a beat pattern as out of it. Beat patterns do *not* have to be mechanical, stiff, awkward, or pedantic. It simply takes *practice.*

The left hand:

The left hand, for the most part, *should not duplicate* movements of the right hand. As a concertmaster of a major symphony orchestra put it, "when both hands do the same thing, it just becomes more confusing; we have to look at *two* things instead of *one.*" When *parallel* or *mirror* gestures of the left hand are eliminated, it is free to be instructive and expressive *on its own* — to present *additional* communication, rather than redundantly double the right hand.

Communication of the left hand might include:
  • Cueing

- Dynamic changes and contrasts
- Sforzandi, stresses, accents, and other rhythmic pulsations
- Releases (releases should be done with the *left hand*, not both or the right hand. Any movement of the right hand should be for *making* music, not stopping it.)
- Long-line, flowing phrase indications
- Occasionally, *nothing at all*. The left hand does *not* have to be employed at *all* times. It is very refreshing and clear to view a conductor who, for the moment, is conducting only with the right hand. There are many passages that simply don't need both hands. This is especially true of many solo accompaniments and absolutely true of recitatives. It is also often true of the *beginning* of songs. *One* clearly communicative hand is *often* much better than two.

When not using the left hand, keep it at your side; not hanging straight down, but with a slight angle at the elbow — as though there was a snap on your wrist connected to your waist. Let this be the home-base position for the left hand when it is not in use. The more you insist that your left hand be used independently of the right hand, the more it will find to do — naturally and effectively.

B. Design or formulate your BEAT PATTERNS based upon clarity and overall effectiveness. Get rid of any involuntary idiosyncrasies or habits, such as accents, bounces or rebounds, syncopated up-beat motions on each beat, curly-cued up-beats, etc. All these movements consistently indicate musical (or *non-musical*) ideas that may *not* be indicated in the score.

The physical movements in conducting should, as previously mentioned, be a *true reflection* of the *score*, indicating only *what is there*. The singers and players perform only what is in the score; they don't carelessly improvise without sense or reason. The conductor also must read the score and physically react *accordingly*, expressing only that which is there. To do less is inadequate; to do more borders on "show" and ego-centered "podium drama" that is distracting to both musicians and audience.

Beats should be absolutely clear and discernible by quick flash-like glances from musicians who may have to keep their eyes in the music much of the time — especially in orchestral playing with limited rehearsal time. It is the *upbeat* and *downbeat* that are the most crucial. Thus they should be predominant:

This: **Not:**

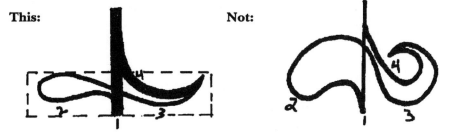

This: **Not:**

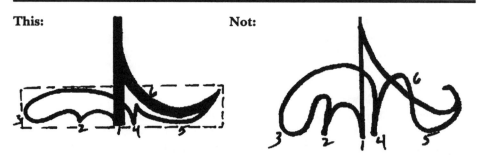

Keep the *action-level* down lower in the conducting zone, allowing the upbeat and downbeat to predominate. If the action rises to the center, the secondary beats begin to resemble the primary motions in length and quality, and there is confusion and lack of clarity. Let the beats be very clearly given, without any extraneous "curling" or movements of any kind. This, as in all "rules," is something from which we may occasionally vary, and then return. Our basic manner of conducting must be one in which the ensemble can *consistently* find *clarity* with *expression* — **one does not need to negate the other**. We might at times go more in one direction than the other, but *seldom* at the *exclusion* of the other.

This: **Not:**

Avoid up-beat conducting. This is a manner of conducting in which *all* beats seem to go up. It approaches the point of the beat (ictus) by means of getting there early, through an ahead-of-time, syncopated manner. It then rebounds *upwards* for each beat.

This: **Not This:**

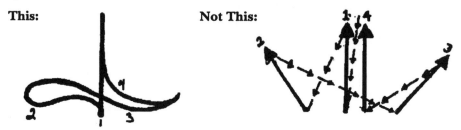

Although this upbeat-style can be very effective in slow tempi, its effectiveness can be negated by carrying it to an extreme, or by using it consistently in *all* tempi.

Be careful that the two-beat pattern is also very clearly discernible:

This: **Not:**   **Nor:**

The "U" formation above makes it impossible to tell the difference between the downbeat and the upbeat. The other extended version is simply too physical and large, unless called for in the music.

The two-beat pattern is often very effective if it resembles a candy cane, or umbrella handle (previously shown); or, simply, a straight, down and up motion (without the small curl at the bottom), and a slight stop at the point of the downbeat (as shown at left). Tempo and style may be the determining factor.

Let us hasten to add that there are almost as many varieties of conducting diagrams as there are conductors and conducting textbooks. It is up to each conductor to spend a great amount of time and effort in seeking out and determining what is practical, economical, clear, and concise — and, at the same time, musically expressive. From the point of view of the musicians in the ensemble, it is worth every minute spent.

C. Establish BEAT STYLES that correspond directly to musical ideas, changing with great flexibility and sensitivity as the musical ideas change, often within a single measure.

The somewhat legato, expressive style is the one that seems to predominate far past its useful boundaries — often reaching, unwarranted, into other styles such as **staccato** and **marcato**. *It is simply used too much.*

1. Legato-expressive:

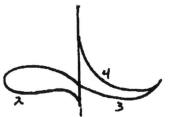

2. Staccato and staccato-like music should receive a special *stop*-beat or *click*-beat:

Stop-Beat: **Click (or Rebound) Beat:**

                             Or:

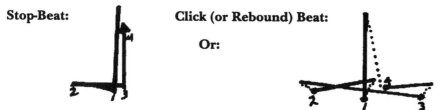

The **stop-beat** is one of the most valuable conducting "tools," yet few use it. It is by far the most concise, clearly distinctive beat in cases where clarity is paramount. It is also very effective in *forte marcato* by simply making the beat *larger* and *more intense*.

Let the size and strength of the stop-beat be determined, of course, by the music. It may dictate that only wrist and/or fingers be used. In other instances, it may be the entire arm. It might be used for either a *dolce* and delicate phrase, or one that is iron-strong and marcato. In any case, when the music needs *precise definement* of conducting motion, the **stop-beat** is great! This is especially true in cases of staccato, marcarto, syncopation, pizzacato, accents (on or off the beat), sudden dynamic changes, and complex rhythmic figures.

3. The *full bounce beat* is effective in rhythmic, dance-like uplifting (bouncy!) music. It rebounds off the point of each beat:

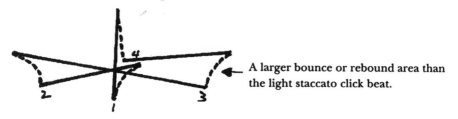

A larger bounce or rebound area than the light staccato click beat.

4. Conducting triple meter (3/8 or 3/4) *in one* should result in a *lift upward* on each beat. Do not think *down*. Everything *lifts*, as though you were touching an iron to determine if it is hot — you would actually touch it on the way up, so as not to burn yourself.

This is similar to the technique percussionists employ when they are taught to play "out of the drum," thereby allowing the head of the drum to more fully vibrate, resulting in maximum tonal output.

5. Subdivision (4/4 = in 8; 3/4 = in 6; 2/4 = in 4; etc.) should be considered only when the original pulse is slower than a metronomic indication of 48. Subdividing in faster tempi tends to negate musical line and phrasing.

Since subdivisions are usually in rather slow, legato music, the conductor's movements/gestures should be very subtle, legato, and *linear* — as opposed to excessive hills, waves, bumps, or jerks. It often reflects *tranquility*.

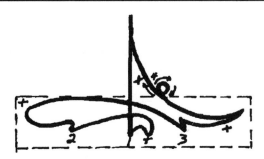

By the same token, reduced beating (4/4 = in 2; 3/4 = in 1; 6/8 = in 2; etc.) should be considered when the tempo is faster than 144. At speeds faster than a metronomic 144, the movement of the hand or baton becomes so fast that it is of little use to those trying to gain something by watching it.

D. Let us briefly say that the conducting of FERMATAS can be problematic if the conductor does not abide by the following rule: The stick (right hand) comes to an absolute *stop* at the point of the beat on which the fermata falls. It *stays* there, absolutely motionless, until it is time to go on. Releases, crescendi, or diminuendi, are all the responsibility of the *left hand*. When it is time to proceed, the *right hand* simply gives the *preparation beat* to do so.

This enables everything musical to be in the complete control of the heart and mind of the conductor, not dependent upon an awkwardly outstretching right hand. It will also avoid the accidental going-on-too-soon of one of the musicians due to right hand movement—to which they are trained to impulsively react.

E. PREPARATORY BEATS must not, through neglect, be taken for granted. They demand practice with each new work, to ensure that they contain within the gesture:

- exact tempo
- dynamic level
- appropriate style

It is important to *think* the preparatory beat before giving it. If there is time, such as at the beginning of a piece, actually *think* a few beats prior to starting. If it is quite slow, it may help to think sixteenths or eighths, even if the music calls for notes of longer duration.

Music: Adagio molto   **Think:**

Given the proper preparatory beat at the beginning of a piece, movement, or new tempo indication, musicians should seldom need a *verbal* explanation of the three points listed above.

F. The SIZE OF THE BEAT is dictated by the dynamic level and, sometimes, by the tempo. Fast-tempo conducting, obviously, cannot be very large. The main point, however, is that *dynamics dictate beat size*. The wrong example would be the large-flailing-beat conductor asking for pianissimo. There are six dynamic levels, ranging from pp to ff. There should be, then, six corresponding *beat sizes*. Consider, for practical application, the following suggestions for the area of the beat-zone:

- *pp* = within the size-span of a softball; finger and minimal wrist movement only.
- *p* = within the size-span of a volleyball or soccer ball; now using some lower arm movement.
- *mp* = within the size-span of a basketball or slightly larger; now using some (but not much) upper arm movement.
- *mf* = size-span now expands into the area outlined vertically by the eyes and the belt and horizontally by the shoulders; full arm employed, plus some shoulder action.
- *f* = Now expand outward from the shoulders, and upwards from the eyes; using full arm and shoulder, as well as some natural upper body movement.
- *ff* = full movement of upper body — everything that feels comfortable and seems sensible.

Practice exercises of 4/4 doing four measures in each of the six dynamic levels. Then practice a crescendo-diminuendo exercise over two 4/4 measures.

Simply be sure that the size of your beat is a true reflection of the indicated dynamic level, crescendo or diminuendo. Do not compromise this (or anything else) due to the size or proficiency level of the ensemble. Rather, raise them to your standards!

VI. Intense, focused, non-stop communication — eyeball to eyeball, from the conductor to musicians — is the essence of effective leadership and inspiration.

First of all, if the conductor doesn't consistently look into the eyes of his or her ensemble, they in turn, will not look back. People tend to respond in like manner.

During early rehearsals, the conductor needs to refer to the score frequently to check mechanical accuracy. Therefore, more emphasis must be placed on *listening* than *physical conducting* — which tends to distract the conductor from being 100% effective as a **listener**.

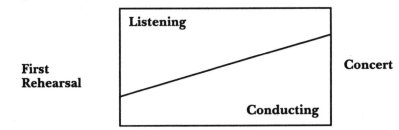

As the rehearsal process continues, more attention can be placed on *conducting, communication*, and *expression*, which can then be done on a pre-built, solid foundation of accurate mechanics as established in previous rehearsals.

Once it is "safe" to begin the emotional communication at a full pace, it is time to begin this eye-to-eye focus of concentration with a *non-stop effort*. "Non-stop" does *not* mean that the conductor must *memorize* the entire score and look up 100% of the time. It means that the score must be known well enough so that, with the aid of occasional quick glances at crucial points of reference, eye contact can be employed *90–95% of the time*.

The conductor should avoid following the score note-for-note or measure-by-measure. If we have done our homework — structural analysis and memorization of key passages — and if our scores are clearly marked, reference glances should suffice. Proper preparation enables the conductor to focus in the musician's eyes *most of the time*.

This direct communication might be thought of as a "yellow highlighted" method of focus. It's as though the conductor has gone through the entire score and *mentally* highlighted, *without interruption*, the primary and secondary themes, cues, and other ideas that need attention:

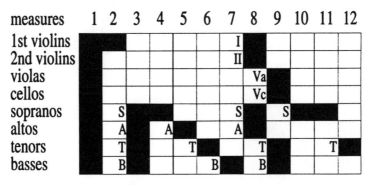

In the above hypothetical situation, we might assume that everyone was singing or playing throughout the entire twelve measures, but the *highlighted* sections are the ones to receive the conductor's main focus of attention.

The goal is to *stay* with a voice or section *until you are needed elsewhere*. Occasionally, but very rarely, *everyone* would be conducted. It should be *one section after another*, without reference to the score, until a major section or long phrase has been accomplished. At that point, a *quick glance* refreshes the memory for the next long phrase or section.

Main point: There should always be something of inspirational value within the heart, mind, and soul of the conductor that needs to be *actively communicated to the musicians* to motivate a *similar response* within them. This, along with teaching fundamental accuracy and expressive interpretation, is the very reason the conductor exists — to enable singers and players to perform at higher levels because the conductor is there to *stimulate them to do so*. Know the music, how to teach it, and then truly *conduct!*

VII. When using a baton, the position of the arm, hand, fingers, and baton should be as natural, relaxed, and free as possible — allowing the baton to truly be an extension, rather than an unnatural, obtrusive, obstacle-like addition to the arm.

When should a baton be used? Anytime it might effectively enhance the *communication* of the conductor, such as in the following instances:

1 Large ensembles, for the simple reason of visible clarity.
2 Intricate or complex rhythmic music in which clarity is paramount.
3 Contemporary music in which mixed meter prevails, again necessitating clarity.
4 Instrumental ensembles that are accustomed to the precision of a baton.

A baton may also be perfectly effective, as a general rule, for the person who simply prefers to use one, and is completely comfortable with one — even in situations when the baton might not be absolutely necessary. It's often a matter of personal preference. It is, however, important that the decision *not* to use one be based solely on musical, logistic, and situational reasoning, *not* on one's inability to use one effectively. We, therefore, need to take the time and extend the effort to become proficient and comfortable with the use of the baton; then base the decision on wisdom and *intelligence*, not fear and insecurity.

The main rationale for using a baton is the need for more precision and accuracy than hands and fingers alone can provide. It is a more *precise* object than the hand, and when this *precision* is needed, use a baton. When it is not, do as you prefer.

Figure 1

Drop the hand to the side in its most relaxed, natural position. The hand will be *slightly angled to the left.* That is, the thumb does not aim *straight ahead*, but rather, aims *slightly toward the left.* The fingers are gently and freely curved; they "breathe," as though you could slip a piece of paper between each one (see figures 3 and 4) — not tightly clenched together. Touch the *tips* of the thumb and index finger — the "pads" — in a relaxed and free manner.

Figure 2

Now, raise the hand *without changing the curved, relaxed position of the fingers,* and place the baton in it, gripping it at the point where the thumb and index finger were previously placed. Slide back easily to the point at which the handle meets the shaft of the baton. This is "the point of the grip." Allow the middle finger to *gently rest* (not grip) on the handle behind the index finger — not pressing tightly against it, but still allowing "breathing" room.

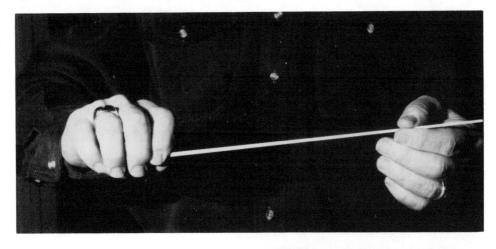

Figure 3

Drop the hand and baton. The hand should be as relaxed and free as before, without the baton — fingers curved, relaxed, and "breathing." The baton will now be slightly pointing to the left, as the hand itself previously did. It is important to point out that if the hand and baton were to aim *straight forward* the wrist would have to turn or twist in an *un-*natural, slightly *forced* position. Remember: the baton and arm must be as natural a collaboration as possible. The physical act of "conducting" must be *natural.*

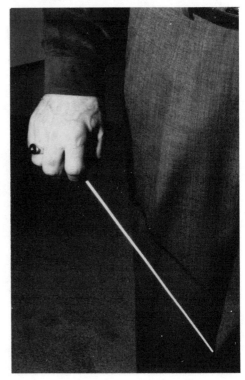

Figure 4

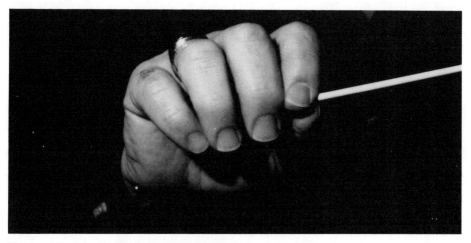

Figure 4 is a close-up of the relaxed hand-baton positioning. Note the following:

- Curved fingers with breathing space between each finger
- Thumb and index finger gently gripping at "pads"
- No tension, tightness, or strain anywhere
- Palm faces the floor; it is not slanted
- Baton points toward the second violins. This is directly related to the slightly-left direction in which the hand and baton were aimed while hanging to the side (see also Figures 3, 7, 8, and 9).

Figure 5 demonstrates the same positioning we've been discussing, but as viewed with the hand inverted, exposing the palm and baton handle. Note that the end of the handle, although aiming toward the palm, does *not* touch it. (The handle is probably too long if it touches the palm.)

Figure 5

Figure 6

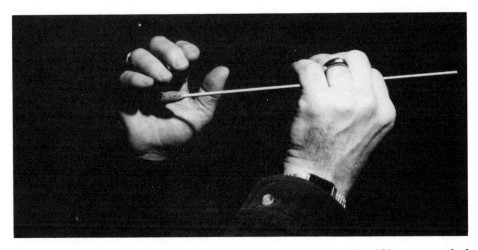

Figure 6 shows where the baton handle *would* touch the palm if it were *pushed* to do so. Pointing out the fact that it would *not* extend out the *side*, as it would in Figure 11.

Figures 7 through 9 demonstrate the following:
• Curved, relaxed hand and fingers
• The baton aimed *slightly* to the left at a 45-degree angle to the body: *not* a 90-degree angle as in Figure 11.
• The wrist is *level* and *parallel with the floor*; not twisted or turned. (Note the coin placed on top of the wrist in Figure 7. For this *basic* positioning, the coin should be able to remain on the wrist, without sliding off due to a turned wrist of the palm facing the left rather than the floor.)

Within the full range of conducting gestures, the wrist and the palm *will move and turn in a wide variety of motions*. This is as it should be. We are, however, simply establishing, at this point, a "home-base" position; one from which you will *depart* for musically expressive reasons and then *return*.

Figure 7

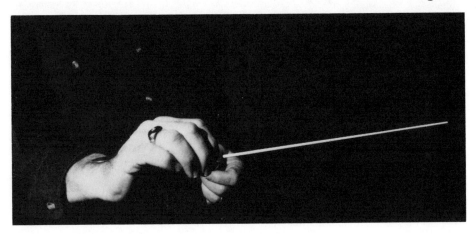

Figure 8

Let's talk further about hand-positioning. With a level wrist and the stick point-ing at a 45-degree angle to the left, you have a natural, *uninterrupted flow* from the right shoulder all the way out to tip of the baton. Try it. Take your left hand, place it on your right shoulder. Now let it follow the natural flow all the way to the tip of the baton. Notice that each of the three angles — at the shoulder, elbow, and wrist — are very similar. To aim the baton straight forward would be an *un-natural interruption* to this flow in the arm and its *natural extension*, the baton. Also, a level wrist (rather than the palm facing left with the thumb on top) allows maximum natural movement *up* and *down*. This enables the two most important beats, the up-beat and the down-beat, to have the greatest potential of visibility — a very important consideration. (Refer to beat patterns, pages 127–131.)

Figure 9

Figure 9: The left hand can move right or left to express a linear flow of the phrase over several beats or measures. Due to its crucial significance, a "responsibility" previously stated is repeated here for emphasis: **the left hand is independent of the beat pattern given consistently by the right hand**. The two hands should, for the most part, be independent of each other. Avoid identical parallel or mirrored movements. The basic function of the right hand is to *musically* and *expressively* display the *beat pattern*. This should be *consistently* available to the members of the ensemble, and this function need *not* be mechanical or limiting; it can be completely *expressive* in addition to being clear and precise.

The functions of the left hand include cueing; all indications of accents, stresses, and dynamic change; phrasing; nuances; releases; and other gestures *not* related to the basic beat pattern.

Figure 10

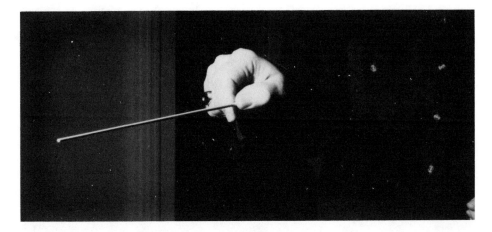

Figure 10 illustrates the straining of the wrist to point the baton straight forward. It, obviously, is *fine* to do this *if specifically needed*, then return to our established "home-base" positioning. It is neither necessary nor natural to conduct in this position *consistently*. Those who may think that the straight-ahead positioning better enables musicians to *see* the beat more clearly fail to realize that:

- The musicians do not look at, nor follow, the *tip* of the baton. They see a *person* -from the waist up. They see the full arm and baton; similarly, they do not look only at the finger-tips when observing a conductor *without* a baton.
- As long as the baton angle to the left is only 45 degrees — as opposed to an extreme 90-degrees — all musicians can see, very well, all that needs to be seen.
- If the straight-ahead position is needed at times for special clarity, do so; then return.

Figure 11

Figure 11 illustrates the extreme 90-degree angle which is to be avoided. Notice that, if pushed, the baton handle would extend out of the side of the hand, rather than into the palm as in Figures 5 and 6.

Figure 12

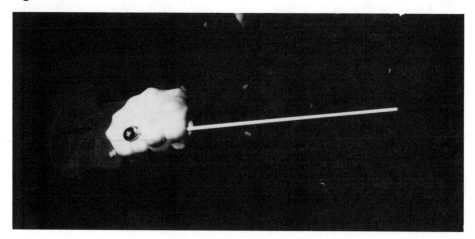

Figure 12 shows a tight-clenched fist. It also shows the index finger over-extended so that it meets the pad of the thumb at its first joint rather than its *pad*. Avoid this display of tension

The *SIZE* OF THE BATON is very important to the *naturalness* of its use. The distance from your shoulder to your elbow, and from your elbow to your hand, is each approximately 12 to 14 inches, give or take, depending on the individual.

If the baton is a *natural extension of your arm*, it should not exceed 14 inches. It should also have a *small, tapered* handle as seen in Figures 5 and 6. This again, will aid naturalness. A bulbous or large handle will stimulate a conscious feeling of *holding on* to something. Ideally, the baton should be thought of as almost weightless — like a feather — balanced so that the weight of the handle is approximately equal to that of the shaft. Anything larger is unnecessary, clumsy, and obtrusive.

Whatever you establish as the best way to hold the baton, give it great thought and consideration. Treat it in the same manner and importance that a violinist gives to the bow and the technique of bowing.

Let your technique be natural and free. Vary from your "home-base" positioning as often as you feel right to do so. Be as *expressive* as you can without becoming a distraction. Demonstrate a comfortable, natural style of conducting that, with great *clarity* and *expressiveness*, allows the musicians to sing or play with confidence, comfort, and musical expressivity. Bring about a successful marriage of clarity and expression. Solid technique with clarity does *not* need to negate musical expression — and vise-versa.

VIII. Checklist for Baton Position:

☐ Hang arm down in relaxed position.

☐ Hand at slight angle.

☐ Touch Thumb to first finger pad.

☐ Place baton in hand at this point.

☐ Drop arm again.

☐ Baton points slightly toward the front of left foot.

☐ Bring baton arm up — as you inhale, leading with elbow and upper wrist.

☐ Point baton toward violin II (45-degree angle), with the tip slightly raised.

☐ Middle of baton in line with buttons of your shirt.

☐ Wrist level.

☐ Arm free, as though floating, with elbow at a "4 o'clock angle."

☐ Fingers and thumb curved — relaxed!

☐ Equal angles at shoulder, elbow, and wrist, with a natural "flow" from shoulder to point of baton.

☐ Basically retain this relaxed position as you conduct through various beat patterns.

IX. Checklist for What Can Go Wrong:

☐ First finger too extended in touching thumb.

☐ Fingers hanging down too far.

☐ Fingers clinched, as a fist.

☐ Thumb or first finger joints pressed inward.

☐ Baton aiming 90-degrees to left, with fingertips on top of baton handle.

☐ Baton aiming 180-degrees straight ahead (wrist bent).

☐ Middle of the baton off to the right, not in line with buttons of your shirt.

☐ Wrist turned over — thumb up, palm to the right.

☐ Elbow either hanging down (5 o'clock or 6 o'clock) as though weighted, or up too high (3 o'clock), rather than the recommended "floating" 4 o'clock angle.

☐ Frozen wrist (let it have the same natural flexibility and slight floating motion as the shoulder and elbow).

☐ Beat pattern conceptually wrong.

☐ Something other than a simple, relaxed clarity indicated as a basic "home base" approach to the baton and arm position.

☐ Hand and/or arm position changes from its original relaxed starting position as it travels through beat patterns. (Remember, though, that this is the *basic* position from which you may *often vary*; then return.

X. The role of the conductor:

Servant
- Serve the *composer* and *score* through integrity, dedication, knowledge and preparation.
- Serve the *choral art* through a relentless effort toward *quality* and *excellence* in *all* things.
- Serve the *singers/players* through technical and musical knowledge, the ability to teach and inspire, artistic musical conducting, and thorough preparation.
- Serve the audience through wise, interesting and varied *programming*.

Teacher
- Teach, with ever-increasing effectiveness, the *right pitch* at the *right time*, and in the *right style*.
- Teach *vocal technique* as a vital part of every rehearsal.
- Teach *comprehensive musicality* in a consistent manner — especially in the

area of *phrasing*, based on the principle that: **no two consecutive notes, words, or syllables should receive equal emphasis.**
- Base rehearsal teaching on:
  - Intense listening
  - Quick recognition and analysis of problems
  - Fast, effective correction
  - Moving on!

Motivator
- Motivate singers/players to *want* to strive for everything that is presented, especially "quality and excellence in all things."
- Motivate singers to *perform* — not simply sing, but to *really perform*, with their *entire being* involved in the presentation and communication.
- Motivate the increased interest (recruitment) of new singers and solid community support.

Leader
- Lead with the realization that the conductor must accept *full responsibility* for the success of the ensemble and the total choral program.
- Lead the ensemble. This is no place for a "democracy." The conductor is the only one trained, knowledgeable, and qualified to make significant musical, vocal, and organizational decisions. Accept this responsibility with respect for the members of the ensemble and with sensitivity for their feelings.

Student
- *Study endlessly throughout life* with musicologists and composers to gain greater knowledge regarding appropriate performance practices and style.
- Study video tapes of your own conducting — as well as the conducting of "professionals" — for continuous growth in the area of *artistic musical conducting*.

Suggested rehearsal techniques and related topics:
- Rehearsal manner:
  - Don't talk much; they're there to *sing* or *play*.
  - Use *musical terminology* at every opportunity, rather than casual, informal, conversational directives.
  - Don't sing with the group; you can't hear them when you sing.
  - Don't mouth the words; they'll follow you *mouth* rather than the *baton*.
- Rehearsal organization:
  - Begin each rehearsal with something they can do well — to immediately build confidence.
  - Next should be the most demanding work while they're still fresh and confident.
  - Close rehearsals with something that is relatively easy and exciting, thereby sending the singers on their way with high spirits and positive morale.

- In the learning process, sing completely through a new song up to tempo, prior to "tearing it apart" later. This gives them an idea of the total "picture" that can be retained when working on details.
- Day-by-day progress is benefited from a structural analysis approach. Occasionally work from the back to the front of the piece in this phrase-structure method.
- Rehearse only those passages that *need* it. Refrain from saying: "Let's go back to the beginning" without a specific reason.
- Correct *one thing at a time*. Hear a problem, correct it, and *go on!*
- Don't mention problems that *might* arise. Wait until they do, then fix them.
- Do, however, give advance warning (and teaching) concerning a *very difficult* or tricky phrase coming up, so they can have a better chance for some degree of success the first time they sing it.
- During early rehearsals on demanding music:
  - Sit or stand in section circles to reinforce group strength as well as improve both accuracy and tone quality.
  - Sing on a neutral syllable such as "doo" or "la" rather than text. Pitch and rhythmic accuracy are learned more easily and quickly by the singers; mistakes are more easily heard by the conductor.
  - Sing no louder than *mp*. There is no reason to sing loudly while developing musical accuracy. Volume and interpretation come later — on a solid foundation of pitch, rhythm, and phrasing accuracy.
  - Speak or clap difficult or complex rhythms until accurate; *then* sing them.
  - Use the next-higher section to provide an example of appropriate sound on a lower section's *high passages* — soprano for alto; unison women for tenor; tenor for bass. This also helps the lower section to learn and perform phrases with greater confidence in their upper range.
  - If one section needs considerable work alone on their part, have *all* singers sing and learn it with them. This adds confidence and keeps boredom at a minimum.
- Keep the pace of a rehearsal incredibly fast! Singers should hardly be able to keep up — not a "hyper" feeling; just really fast-moving. Never stop and think on *their* time. If they can easily keep up with you, they're probably bored.
- Except for early-rehearsal "note-watching," keep your eyes focused in their eyes, not in your score. Maintain a phenomenal communication between the conductor and singer.
- Plan effective warm-up exercises based on sound vocal techniques which thoroughly prepare the voices for singing and are, in part, concerned with demands of the music to be rehearsed.
- Have the singers use body movement as a part of **feeling** the music, as might be dictated by meter, pulse, and phrase: marching, waltz-swaying left and right, leaning forward and back into and out of the phrase, etc.
- As a general rule, don't conduct the pianist during long introductions and

interludes. This is not required; an accompanist does not need to be conducted, and it may be distracting to the audience.

- Each singer should always be in possession of a pencil, and write *all* directives in the music.
- Keep the rehearsal *very business-like*, yet motivated and inspired. Proper discipline and a positive attitude support a consistent high-level of productivity.
- Rehearsal atmosphere must be inspiring and conducive to fine singing.
  - Clean, neat, organized, and cheerful
  - Well-lighted and ventilated
  - Chairs well spaced
  - Risers: 3-4 levels of seating
  - Good piano, in tune
- Lastly, and very importantly, dedicate yourself to phrasing consistently with the "Golden Rule" — that *no two consecutive notes, syllables, or words should ever receive equal emphasis*. Every note has its own special function within the continual process or rise-stress-fall of phrase after phrase. Important: teach this from the *very beginning*, along with the correct pitches and rhythms. To learn the piece *without* phrasing, then re-learn it *with* phrasing, makes the job much harder, and the full phrasing potential seldom becomes a reality. Remember: It is **phrasing** that transcends mechanics into **music!**

XII. Conclusion

We should hasten to concede that there is far more to great conducting than any of us have ever imagined — certainly more than can be expressed in a single chapter. It is a carefully balanced combination of:

- A thorough knowledge of the score and forces.
- A highly focused sense of listening for absolute accuracy, and the relentless pursuit of achieving it.
- A well-developed ability to a) totally understand and personally experience the emotional depth of the music, and b) fully express it to others.
- The possession of a highly skilled, artistic approach to the techniques of physical conducting.
- Continued *growth* in all things for as long as one lives. Unlike most performers, great conductors are usually at their best toward the end of their careers — *if constant growth is present.*

This *begins* to bring within our thinking the potential *comprehensiveness* of conducting — whether it be for an elementary school choir, a high school band, a collegiate chorale, a professional symphony orchestra, or anything in-between. Music is music, and conducting is conducting.

What we're after is

COMPREHENSIVE ARTISTIC MUSICAL CONDUCTING.

Choral Tone

Paul Brandvik

Wherever you find two choir directors, you will find three opinions about choral tone. It is an area in the choral art where strong feelings and preferences abound, generally molded by one's own experience in collegiate choral singing. These preferences cover a spectrum of tonal choices — such as a preference for a dark tone rather than a bright tone or a preference for a blended ensemble tone rather than a soloistic tone. In college it was simple: There was only one way for a choir to sound; others did not exist. As a choral graduate you might have heard only three other college choirs, and from your perspective, they were not nearly as good as your own. Your college choir was the standard by which all other choirs would be judged.

Most of us, at some time in our professional careers, discover there are great choirs that do not sing at all like our college choir, and yet communicate with a style and beauty that is absolutely captivating. The discovery might have come from television performances, recordings, or compact discs. It might have come from live performances at conventions or, because of the ease of travel, at festivals in Europe, South America, Africa, Japan, or Israel. The discovery might have been the stunning sound of a choir from Bulgaria or Yugoslavia that could "out-straight-tone" any midwestern choir of the 50's and melt your earwax at fifty paces; an Italian choir with a full-bodied vibrato that bordered on being terminal; or the extraordinary sound of an African choir with an amazing rhythmic vitality and complexity such as we had never before heard. It might have been the Shaw Chorale or one of the newer professional ensembles which awakened us to the idea that choral tone can be immaculate and exciting at the same time — and that all works need not be sung with the same tone qualities. Whatever it was, it made a profound impact on our perception of the beautiful in the choral art.

So now there are choices in choral tone that did not exist for directors until the last two or three decades. We can experiment and model the tone of our choir after the examples of many great choirs. We have a vast databank of choral sounds from which we can draw. With insight and imagination we can bring the most versatile of instruments — the human voice — to its fullest potential in a choir with a great variety of tonal colors. It is an exciting time to be a choral director!

Two key questions can be asked: What makes the tone of one choir different from another? And, perhaps more importantly, what can the choral director do to make a choir sound better? First let us look at what determines choral tone and later decide which of these determiners we must accept and which we can change.

These determiners can be grouped arbitrarily into four interrelated categories: **Vocal Technique, Mental Attitude, Musical Choice,** and **Environment.** Each have three sub-categories: **The Individual Singer, The Choir and Director,** and **The Music.**

Determiners of Choral Tone

- **Vocal Technique**
  - **Individual Singers:** vocal health, flow of breath, resonance, freedom in the vocal mechanism, vibrato, flexibility, endurance, energy
  - **Choir and Director:** intonation, tuning, use of *falsetto*, breathy tone, *sotto voce*, weight of sound
  - **Music:** range, tessitura
- **Mental Attitude**
  - **Individual Singers:** ego, nerves, tension, relaxation, self concept, personality, imagination, desire to learn, alertness
  - **Choir and Director:** common goals, ability to concentrate, perceived importance of rehearsals, perceived importance of performance, discipline of rehearsals, ambience of rehearsals
  - **Music:** acceptance of style, willingness to rehearse and perform, confidence
- **Musical Choices**
  - **Individual Singers:** knowledge of the music, knowledge of history, understanding of music as communication
  - **Choir and Director:** balance, blend, strength of overtones, sung consonants, vowel spectrum chosen, diphthongs, balance of vowels and consonants, use of sung consonants, articulation, energy and direction of phrases
  - **Music:** dynamics, tempo, harmonic pull
- **Environment**
  - **Individual Singers:** age of singers, musical maturity, general health, intelligence, length of rehearsals, frequency of rehearsals, time of rehearsals, time of performance
  - **Choir and Director:** size of ensemble, singing formation of the choir, conductor's ear, conductors attitude, conductor's intelligence and imagination, acoustics of rehearsal space, acoustics of performance space, activities prior to and following rehearsal or performance
  - **Music:** style of music, difficulty of music, language, amount and rapidity of text in a piece, existence of choral-speaking, existence of humming, length of piece, texture, voicing, length of phrases

The task of creating a good choral sound appears overwhelming with more than seventy-five items affecting the tone of your choir. There are no "quick fixes." Being a choir director is like being a combination organist and organ builder — you must build the choral instrument *as you play.* To be successful, you must be successful at both building and playing.

Of course, there is the age-old trick for making a choir sound good. It was the first rule in *"18 Rules about Tasteful Singing,"* a treatise by Georg Quitschreiber written in Jena, Germany in 1598. He was quoting Heinrich Finck who preceded him by seventy-plus years. The rule is simply: **"Choose good voices."**[1] If you have this luxury, you should be about three-fourths of the way to making a choir with good choral tone. But many do not have this luxury. We must deal with average voices — once in a while exceptional, but most often just basic voices. How, then, can we turn these basic voices into good voices, and the good voices into exceptional voices? How can a director make a mediocre choir sound good, and a good choir sound great?

Vocal Technique

A recent survey disclosed that there are 15,000,000 choral singers in the world.[2] A conservative estimate that at least 95% do not study voice with a private voice teacher, would indicate that 14,250,000 singers worldwide are learning all their vocal technique from their choral directors. What a heady responsibility and a grand opportunity! We can mold the techniques of our singers in a productive and healthy way and create a choral instrument that is at once flexible, free, resonant, and thrilling. All we have to do is know and teach in a manner that is both productive and healthy.

However, most choirs include 1) some singers who study privately with other teachers and 2) singers who learn vocal technique only from their choir director. How do we teach the one without confusing the other? How do we incorporate the *"solo singer"* into a choir whose existence is predicated on the basis of the beauty of *ensemble* singing?

Basically, we must find a safe ground from which we can teach to both extremes, realizing there are different demands on the choral singer than on the solo singer. Some soloistic style must be sublimated in order to be an effective musician in a choral ensemble. These demands are no different than those made on an orchestral musician. If soloistic singers have developed a good technique, they should be able to control or change the voice in terms of volume, vibrato, vowel formations, resonance, and intonation. Anything the individual singer is unable to control should be considered a vocal weakness, not a technique.

Are there vocal concepts that are universal and which can be taught to all singers without fear of contradicting or offending the private voice teachers? Probably not. No two teachers teach exactly alike, and there are as many different approaches to the teaching of singing as there are to the directing of choirs. And like directors of choirs, teachers of singing run the gamut from excellent to poor. However, since 1) the burden of teaching voice to 95% of the world's singers is carried by the choral directors, 2) the quality of your choir depends on the vocal concepts you teach your singers, and 3) you and your singers must share a common language about singing, you must be willing and

---

[1] Dart, Thurston, "How They Sang in Jena in 1598," *The Musical Times*, April 1967, p.316.

[2] Grau, Alberto, "Carte Blanche," International Choral Bulletin, January, 1992, p. 3. International Federation for Choral Music, Namur, Belgium (quoting survey by ICFM World Choral Survey).

able to teach justifiable vocal concepts to *all* the members of your choirs.

In developing your teaching style and in setting your priorities as to the concepts that should be taught, these questions should be asked:

- Are the concepts healthy?
- Are the concepts helpful?
- Are the concepts clear to the singer who studies voice privately *and* to the singer who learns everything about singing from you?
- Are the concepts universally applicable to all the singers you have encountered?

There are four qualities of vocal sound that are found in almost every good singer:

- **Freedom** in the area of the larynx, throat, and head. There are several muscles which hold the tongue and the larynx in suspension. Strain on any of these will affect the pitch and the sound of the voice. Vocal strain and tightness is evident in many choirs, especially younger choirs. We will look at concepts which hopefully can alleviate this problem.
- **Resonance** refers to the production of a clear sound, a sound with focus and ring. It is reported that Enrico Caruso spent his entire life developing a maximum resonance with a minimum amount of breath.
- **Energy** involves the whole body of the singer. It is the magnetism which unites the singer with the song.
- **Expression** is the combining of intuition and intellect in creating phrases. It is the releasing of sound ideas from the singers' imagination into the imagination of the audience.

These four points can be easily remembered: The first letters of each of the words spell **FREE.** Let us examine each in detail:

Freedom

In our conducting and in our teaching of vocal technique, one concept must predominate in our approach to the students' singing development: *The whole body is the instrument of the singer.* The singing mechanism does not exist only in the larynx or from the neck up, but from the bottom of the toes to the top of the head. If, over a period of time, your singers will intellectually and physically understand this feeling of using the whole body to make the sound, your choir will be well on the way to making a sound that encompasses all of the four qualities of sound mentioned above.

Posture

To use this whole body to achieve a FREE sound, we must begin with a positive and active posture. Posture is the foundation upon which the whole structure of good vocal technique is built. Posture should be thought of as *active*, not *passive;* as *free,* not *tense.* Tense muscles are weak muscles.

Good posture results in a freeing of the body to work. To an athlete, good posture provides a freedom of action to the vital organs of the body. We should look at singers as athletes, and singing as an athletic function as well as an artistic expression. Singers must be mentally *and* physically involved in the creation of the music. We must work for a physical alertness in our singers, rather than a rigid, upright, military posture.

Another way of looking at posture is to consider it a reflection of a person's self-image. We must look for ways to build this self-image rather than just repeating *ad infinitum*, "sit up straight, now, boys and girls." No one, including directors, will sit up straight if something inside of them does not feel like sitting up straight. We must develop a pride and a sense of self worth in our singers, so that, from the very core of their being, they *want* to sit up straight. Posture is not an erect support with which we prop up our singers, but a mirror of their emotional state, which we directors should be able to read. Remember, the singer's body language tells you much about the success of your rehearsal.

The following suggestions might be helpful for your singers:

> **Concept:** The whole body is the instrument of the singer.
> **Purpose:** Develop a sense of using the whole body in an active posture to enable vocal production to occur as naturally as possible.
> **Outcome:** The singer will gain an understanding of the best posture for singing. He or she will begin to understand that his or her body is the singing instrument, and that to use it well he or she must use the most efficient, active and productive posture.

Technique #1:
1 A singer should feel as if the top half of his or her body is lifting and floating away, while the bottom half is thrust downward like roots of a large tree extending into the ground. The dividing line should be the beltline.
2 Use one hand in a downward movement from waist level to feel the roots going into the floor; let the other hand extend upward.
3 Feel the lengthening of the body with the visible imagery of the hands.
4 The singers should feel a natural buoyancy, as if springing up and out of the floor.

Technique #2:
1 The singer should be actively involved, not passive.
2 The singer should sing on the balls of the feet rather than on the heels.
3 The singer should feel the readiness to pounce, like a cat.
4 The singer should feel the readiness and energy to return a serve, like a tennis player. Have the singers mime a tennis player.
5 The singer should feel free to move with the phrases and to create the sound with his or her whole body, like a good violin player moves. Mime the moves of a violin player.

Technique #3:
1 The singer should be able to physically lean into the music, not away. The singer should feel a movement forward, not backward.

2 Have the singers put one foot ahead of the other, as you will demonstrate.

3 Lean towards them and ask them to mirror your movement, shifting the weight of their bodies from the back of their feet to the front.

4 Ask them to do this at the high point of the phrase you are singing.

    a Ask them to describe the feeling.

    b Repeat the process after the feeling of strength and energy through the legs and up through the body has been noted.

    c Comment on the change in the sound as the body becomes actively involved in making the sound, and the posture becomes active, not passive.

Breath Management and Airflow

In the same way that we understand posture as being active, we must understand the use of the breath as being an active process, and use active imagery and suggestions rather than constantly reminding our singers to "support." Support is a much misunderstood word. It is doubtful that any two members of any choir would understand it in the same way. Support implies a static structure. Singers should think in the active terms of *airflow* and *breath management* rather than support.

Since everyone learns in slightly different ways, we shall suggest several images, both mental and physical, to help the singers in your choir understand the idea of airflow and breath management. Breathing should be the easiest thing to teach since everyone already does it. But we must help the singers learn to develop the maximum tone with the minimum breath. And to do that we must structure situations in which they experience the best use of the airflow, rather than telling them how they should breathe — first the experience, then the description, then the reinforcement.

> **Concept:** Breathing is a natural process in singing as it is in life.
> **Purpose:** Develop a feeling and understanding of an efficient airflow and breath management.
> **Outcome:** The singer will experience a freer movement of breath through his or her body while singing. Unnatural movements of the shoulders and chest while breathing will be eliminated or reduced. The singer will sing with more strength and the phrases will have more buoyancy and flow.

Technique #1: Exhale first, then inhale:

1 Exhale while bending over, getting rid of all the air in your lungs.

2 Stand up, but do not breathe until your body calls for the breath and it is absolutely necessary to breathe.

3 Breathe very quickly through your mouth with no sound.

4 Notice what happens to your abdomen, chest, and shoulders.

5 Describe the feeling.

6 Repeat the exercise.

Technique #2: Exhale first, then sing:
  1 Exhale completely.
  2 With the residue air left in the lungs, sing a phrase from a song, or merely "ya-ya-ya" on a specified pitch.
  3 Notice how *little* air it takes to generate sound.

Technique #3: Exhale first, then hook:
  1 Exhale completely whispering, "huh......"
  2 Finish the exhalation with an audible, explosion of the last of the breath with, "kuh."
  3 Inhale quickly and notice the feeling in the abdomen.
  4 Describe the feeling.
  5 Repeat the exercise.

Technique #4: Inhale, then...
  1 Mime the blowing up of a beach ball while you exhale.
    a Show the movement and the expansion of the ball as you fill it with air.
    b Let it explode with a, "Pow!" using your last breath.
  2 Mime the cooling of a bowl of hot soup while you exhale.
  3 Exhale while loudly whispering, "My, how time flies..."
  4 Imitate the lip-flapping sound of a winded horse while you exhale.

Notice how the breath flows through your body in each of the above exercises. Describe this feeling and repeat the exercises.

Technique #5: Inhale, then...
  1 As you inhale, imagine you are smelling the wonderful fragrance of a pepperoni pizza fresh from the oven.
    a Exhale
    b With a light, high, head voice, exclaim softly, *"Mama mia, what a pizza!"*
  2 Follow the flow of breath into your body with your hands describing a gesture of going down a large open pipe in front of your body. Exhale with your hands going out of the pipe in a ballet-like gesture.

Technique #6: Inhale, then...
  1 Inhale, imagining the breath being pulled up from the floor through your feet. Mime the movement of the breath with your hands.
  2 Imagine there are several noses around your abdomen.
    a Breathe through these noses as you inhale.
    b Notice the feeling in the abdomen.
    c Describe the feeling.

Technique #7: Sing, then...
  1 When you sing up, sing down.
    a Sing as though the audience were below and behind you.
    b Use your hands to point to the spot behind you where the audience is.

2 Feel a downward thrust of the bottom half of your body when you sing in your upper range.
a The higher you sing, the lower you should feel.
b Let the tone float away from the top half of your body.
3 Point to a spot on the floor about six feet ahead of you.
a Physically take the tone with your hand from your mouth and send it down your arm.
b Feel and hear the strength in the sound.
c Describe the feeling.
d Repeat the exercise.

Technique #8: Move down and sing up:
1 Stand on your tip-toes.
2 Sing the pitches 135875421 in a comfortable range on "yoh."
3 As the pitch rises, slowly lower your body and flex your knees.
4 As the pitch descends, let your body rise again, always remaining on your tip-toes.
5 You may also describe a large circle with your hands extending outward from your mouth and ending up back at your mouth. Make the gesture generous.
6 Describe the feeling. (Most will describe a feeling of strength through their whole body, with the most strength coming when the pitch was high and their body was low.)
7 Repeat the exercise.

If the tone of the choir is free and vital and the phrases are alive with meaning, the air is flowing correctly and the breath management is sound. Teaching your choir good corporate breathing is often a matter of watching for the beginning of bad techniques and suggesting ways to change these before they become bad habits. Watch for these physical signs of trouble:

· Rising shoulders
· Tension in the neck
· Static abdomen
· Inability to sustain phrases
· Audible intake of breath

Remind your singers that if they are to sing with a FREE sound, they must not squeeze the sound out of their bodies, but rather let it fly out from the core of their being.

Keep your rehearsals happy and positive. Keep everything in its proper perspective. Use humor as a tool to loosen up your singers. Laughter promotes a good use of all the muscles involved in breath management. It also helps eliminate the tension that can so easily arise in a rehearsal. Enjoy the choir, delight in their unique qualities, have fun with them — and they will enjoy the rehearsals *and* the music.

Freeing the Throat and the Mouth

If each singer in your choir understands that his or her entire body is making the sound, the posture of each singer is active and alert, and the breath is flowing through the singer's body in a natural, free way, then the stage is set for freeing the area of the throat from all unnatural constrictions. All these aspects of good tone production, however, are connected and can not be taught in isolation. Without a good working habit of breath management, for instance, it is not possible to sing with an open, free throat.

It is important for your singers to accept the concept that their whole bodies are their instruments. It is equally important for you to accept the concept that teaching vocal technique to a choir of singers is different from teaching private voice. It differs in two ways: First, you are not able to hear what each individual singer is doing all the time, so you must make suggestions that are healthy and helpful for all singers. Secondly, you must say things in a variety of ways and make numerous suggestions in the hope that at least one idea will find a home in the technique of each singer.

If there is one important concept to stress in teaching vocal technique to a group of singers, it is the concept of *vocalizing down, not up!* Strain and tightness in the throat occurs when the chest voice is carried too high. Since, when working with a group, you are unable to hear when an individual is beginning to strain by bringing the chest voice up too high, it is far healthier to avoid vocal exercises that go from low to high, even though these might be the mainstay of your private studio. *This concept cannot be stressed too much!*

Another dangerous aspect in teaching a choir of singers to sing with an open, free space in the throat, is that some singers might misinterpret your ideas and try to make the space more open by pushing down the larynx and swallowing the tone. A singer makes resonant space in the mechanism, not by pushing the larynx down, but by feeling the height in the sound.

We now will look at several ideas for making a free, open space in the throat. Some are physical movements which the singers will make with you, and some are images which may help you help a singer understand the process of opening up the back of the throat. The physical movements are suggested because they help involve the whole body of the singer in making sound and they create a physical image outside the body that often translates into an openness in the throat.

Concept: A free, open space in the throat and mouth is necessary for good singing.
Purpose: Develop an open space in the throat and mouth.
Outcome: The singer will begin to understand the concept of freedom in the tone, and to sing with freedom and space in the throat and mouth.

Technique #1: Imagery

1 Think of the mouth as a tunnel, not a cave. It must be open at both ends for the sound to freely move from the body.

2 The mouth has two openings. The important one is the back. Make the back opening bigger than the front.
3 Imagine the vowel that you are singing is standing up on the back of your tongue, rather than lying down.
  a Make this vowel a capital letter.
  b Breathe through this vowel.
  c Now turn the air around and sing through it.
  d Feel the space of the sound.
  e Describe how you feel.
  f Repeat the exercise.
4 Constantly feel as if an umbrella is opening in the roof of your mouth.
5 Create as much distance between your tongue and the roof of your mouth as you can.
6 Feel the air around your teeth and between your cheeks and your teeth.
7 Think of your mouth as a room.
  a Try to make the room completely empty — without any furniture — to allow the sound to permeate the entire room.
  b Make as full a sound as the space you have prepared.
  c Let the tongue lie flat on all the vowels with the front of the tongue against the lower front teeth.

Technique #2: Physical
1 Feel as if you are on the verge of a yawn as you inhale.
2 Let the breath bounce in and out with an open throat.
3 Let the exhaled breath turn into a sustained "hah"; the sound should be breathy and high, in head voice or falsetto, like a high, light sigh.
4 *"Sigh"* the words of a phrase you are singing, or any appropriate sentence, such as, *"My, Minnesota's Muskies are magnificent."*

Technique #3:
1 Stand with good active, singing posture.
2 Make the shape of the top of a barrel in front of you with your hands clasped together. Keep your shoulders back, and maintain good singing posture.
3 As you sing, fill this barrel with so much sound that it wants to break apart.
4 Describe the feeling. (A singer should experience an open, spacious feeling in the back of their throat.)
5 Repeat the exercise.

Technique #4:
1 Mime the holding of a bucket in front of you. Use both hands.
2 Fill the bucket full of air.
3 Lift the bucket to your mouth as you sing a phrase.
4 Drink in the air from the bucket as you sing, until at the end of the phrase you have drained the bucket.

5 Describe the feeling. (Most normal singers will describe the feeling of openness in the back of their throats.)
6 Repeat the exercise.

Technique #5:
Hold your facial cheeks and lips forward with your two hands held flat against your face while singing. This brings the lips and facial muscles into proper action and eliminates excessive throat tension.

Technique #6:
1 Mime the throwing and catching of a frisbee.
2 Let the voice follow lightly and breathily the path of the frisbee; the sound should be high and thin on "oo" or "oh."
3 Divide the choir into two parts. One catches while the other throws.
4 Use your hands to mime the throw and the catch. Have fun. Be creative and uninhibited.

Resonance

The second quality of a good singing voice in our quest for a FREE choral sound is *resonance*. The term simply means the production of a clear tone — nothing more complicated than that.

There are *two* ways for a voice to carry, or to be heard: the voice can be *loud,* or the voice can be *bright* (resonant). In relating this to the production of sound we see that a singer has two options: 1) The sound can be pushed out without optimum resonance, resulting in dangerous muscular pressure on the vocal mechanism, tiring, and a less-than-beautiful sound, or 2) the sound can be allowed to happen and freely resonate, removing — as much as possible — any hindrance to the natural vocal production. A natural sound is made by *thinking* the sound and then *letting it happen.* It is a natural procedure, not artificial. In helping singers discover a natural resonance, there are two approaches that might be used:

I. Vocalize Downward

In the first approach, vocalize the singers downward from the top of the range, bringing the light falsetto or head voice into the middle or lower voice. This helps greatly in extending the singer's range and also is one of the keys to singing with good intonation. It should be *the* technique used almost exclusively in warm-ups that you do with your choir, and throughout rehearsal when the need arises. This technique is not new, but has been used by the greatest voice teachers of the world to train singers for centuries.

> **Concept:** A resonant sound carries better than a nonresonant sound.
> **Purpose:** Help the singer to discover natural resonance.
> **Outcome:** The singer will experience the feeling of head resonance, and sing with a stronger, freer voice.

Technique #1:

1 Sing a descending five-note scale pattern, 54321, on *"mah"* with a lot of breath, but not loud.

2 Use mostly head voice or falsetto, bringing the lighter sound down into the lower range.

3 Let your hands rise, as if floating away as the scale descends. (Remember the "Move down and . . . . sing up" exercise?) Relate this exercise to the childhood experiment of standing in a doorway and pushing your hands against the sides of the door frame, counting to 100 or however high you could count, then stepping away and experiencing your hands rise as if by their own accord. *If you have singers who have not experienced this, have them give it a try before the next rehearsal.*

In a variation of this technique, the director and singers improvise vocal exercises that are accompanied freely by movement of the hands, arms, and whole body. Such exercises should not be loud and should be done primarily with a light head or falsetto voice which descends into the lower register.

Technique #2:

1 Make *light* humming, buzzing, random vowel and consonant, or non-singing sounds. The pitches can slide, skip, be siren-like, staccato, legato, or used in any combination. They can imitate nature sounds — buzzing of bees, twittering of birds, or the high pitched sound of an airplane. Keep the sound moving from pitch to pitch, and let your singers' imaginations run free.

2 Create generous and free movements of the hands, legs, and bodies. The singers might start by forming large circles with their hands; then let their bodies describe the sounds being made.

3 Let your singers create their own vocal/physical improvisations. You might be surprised by their ingenuity. This exercise will succeed — and the singers will lose their inhibitions — only if the director is free of inhibitions. This is great fun for singers of all ages.

Using the body to mirror or describe musical phrases is an excellent way to take your singers' minds off their production of sound and makes that production much more natural and free. Remind them that singing is a natural athletic and creative function. Singers should not be inundated with intellectual concepts of sound production before they have experienced the sensations and made them basic to their singing technique.

In addition to distracting the minds of the singers as to how high they are singing, these exercises free the singers' spirits, and almost always induce laughter, an effective way to loosen the muscles used in singing. This is a great technique to warm up a choir quickly in the morning. *Free the mind from inhibition, free the body from tension, and the voice will be free!*

Another simple technique designed to bring the qualities of the higher resonant sound into the lower range, and connect the entire range, is called the "High-Low Slide."

Technique #3:

1 Have the singers sing a soft, free "oo," "ah," or hum.

2 Instruct the singers to let their voices slide up and down in response to the rise and fall of the director's hand. The voices should slide easily into the piccolo register in a light, free, airy sound. There should be no strain.

3 Without verbally instructing the singers, use one hand to control each side of the choir. Begin by moving the hands in parallel motion, then let the one follow the other or move in contrary motion.

The above exercise is a light non-threatening vocal slide that can be performed by every choir member without fear of their vocal inadequacies being discovered. Everyone is equal in this exercise. Do not allow it to become loud; keep it easy and light.

II. Humming

The second approach to helping singers discover their resonance is to blend a hum into the vowels and the consonants. Humming has several functions; among them are helping the singers discover a clear tone and allowing the singers to feel the resonance of each pitch in their ranges.

The simplest way to incorporate humming into your rehearsal and help your singers feel their humming resonance is to hum a section of one of the songs they are singing in their rehearsal. Move from the hum into a vowel that incorporates the feeling of the hum into the vowel.

Another simple but effective way to help your singers feel resonance and to create a resonant, buoyant sound in your choir, is to balance the actual dynamic level of the vowels and the sung consonants, "m," "n," and "ng."

Technique #4:

1 Listen objectively to the balance of the consonant with the surrounding vowel. For example, if the word in question is "ham," determine if the "m" is projecting as strongly as the vowel.

2 Have the choir sing "ham" with a fermata.

3 Close your hand to indicate that the choir should sing the "m." (Most likely, the consonant will be considerably softer than the vowel.)

4 Have the singers place one of their hands on their abdomen. Ask them to sing the word again, but this time make the consonant as strong as the vowel.

5 Ask them what they felt. (They will probably say that their abdomens srengthened to sing the consonant.)

6 Repeat the exercise, commenting that these consonant sounds need extra strength whenever they are sung, because the mouth is closed. A good choir will balance these sounds with the vowels, thereby making the text understandable and the overall sound of the choir buoyant and resonant.

Humming is basic in English communication and should be as easy as breathing. It can mean "yes," "no," "what?" "go away," or "don't bother me now,

I am planning a rehearsal." We should work to meld the hum into the vowel at all times.

Technique #5:
1 Begin on a comfortable pitch with an "m" hum.
2 Carry that hum into all vowels as you *gradually* change from the hum to a vowel. This is a useful way to help a section in your choir develop a unified, blended, resonant vowel.
3 Feel the *buzz* of the hum and maintain it in all the vowels.

A fun way to check if the hum is actually brought into the vowel is an exercise called the *"Lipo-plucker:"*

Technique #6:
1 With the pitches 555554321, sing mee, may, mah, moh, mu, mu, mu, mu, mu.
2 Next, repeat the exercise, but start slowly with an extended hum with each vowel formed in the mouth behind the hum.
3 Uncover each vowel by plucking the lower lip with a finger, keeping the buzz of a hum in the vowels.
4 On the final "mu," flutter the lips with your finger. This last gesture has no real educational value, but it does induce laughter in most groups and activates the singing muscles.

Another related aspect of humming is to work from the brighter vowels into the darker vowels.

Technique #7:
1 Bring the brightness of the "ee" or "ay" vowel into the "oh" or the "oo".
2 First sing the bright vowel, retain the placement and color, and meld the bright vowel into a darker vowel.
3 Balance the vowels so that the brightness of the one vowel and the space and height of the other vowel enhance each other by working back and forth from one vowel to the other, such as, "ee-oo-ee-oo-ee" or "mee-moo-mee-moo."

If you want your tenor section to sing with more resonance and clarity above middle C, or if you want your altos to be heard, you also might try modifying vowels in that range into vowels that are brighter. Each vowel can be modified to the adjacent brighter vowel. This technique also makes it easier for the tenors to sing in tune when they are above middle C.

Technique #8:
1 Tenors in the mid and upper range, and altos in their mid and lower range can modify the following vowels to achieve more resonance: "eh" becomes "ay", "ay" becomes "ee." This would turn "bet" into "bait," and "bait" into "beet," etc.

2 Ask the section to alternate between the less resonant vowel ("eh.") and the more resonant vowel ("ay"). Have the singers experience these changes so that they hear the difference and are able to make these adjustments automatically. The audience will be unaware of what is happening to the vowels and will hear only an in-tune, clear sound. If this is done with frequency, it becomes a habit for your singers and not only helps them discover a resonant, clear sound, but aids greatly in maintaining good intonation. *Warning: this does not work with sopranos in the upper part of their range, where the problems are considerably different.*

3 Sing a repeated "may, may, may" or "me, me, me." This is very helpful. It brings a hum into the vowel and brightens the vowel.

4 Listen "down the line" to the singers individually so that your suggestions can be specific to each singer. Singers might be shy when this is first done, but it is the only way to guarantee that you are helping each singer.

5 Ask the choir, "What vowel do you hear?" as each singer sings the vowel. It is often difficult for a singer to know exactly what sound is being communicated. This engages the choir in the analysis of the sound and reinforces the perception of the accurate vowel color.

6 Have the singers drop their jaws with a loose, free, untied motion. Listen carefully to the sound to determine if the section is retaining the space in the vowel. Do not let the "ay" or the "ee" become tight or pinched. Also, do not let the sound of the vowel become an affectation without expression or meaning.

With careful use, this technique will generate a natural, resonant sound fitting into the total communication of the musical idea, and not an aberration.

Technique #9:

1 Sing with a slight smile (or lift) in the eyes and upper part of the face. Do not let tension occur in the area of the mouth as you smile. Keep the lower part of your face and jaw completely free.

2 Feel the lift and the airy space below and behind the eyes. It is more important that the smile be felt inside the face than show on the outside.

This technique is one of those simple historical truths in singing which date back to the Italian masters of singing. It is the simplest of all the techniques for increasing resonance, yet one of the most difficult to get shy singers to do.

Energy

The third quality of a good singing voice, in our quest for a FREE sound in a choir, is *energy*. Accepting the concept that the whole body is the instrument of the singer, we must always be alert to ways in which we can infuse energy into this instrument, so that the music we sing will be constantly alive and vibrant.

Humans are meant to move, not to be static. Singers must be helped to develop an awareness of their bodies and how they function in expressive choral singing. They must be alive to the music — flexible, buoyant, and responsive to their own individual resonances. Singing *is* an athletic activity.

Singers in choirs are the most static of musicians. While string players, pianists, pop singers, and professional classical singers all perform with an apparent license to move with the music, choral singers remain as static as statues waiting for their picture to be painted. The resulting sound for many of these choirs is also static and unmoving. We must give our singers license to move and use their bodies, within reason, to create the sound.

Young choirs who sing a variety of music often appear static when singing Bach and buoyant and flexible when singing a contemporary ballad. Because of these extremes in posture and vocal concept, the tone of the latter music is much freer, richer, and more expressive than the music of Bach. It is not Bach's fault. It is the fault of the directors who limit the freedom of movement in the singing of the wonderfully moving music of Bach. We must help singers carry over the applicable ideas of one style to other styles of music by helping them discover the feeling of their whole bodies making the sound in all the music they sing.

A note of caution: Movement is an aid to teaching expressive singing, and not a substitute. The result of movement in a rehearsal should be an expressive, rich, buoyant musical line that is felt throughout the entire body in rehearsal and in performance. It should not an attention-drawing display, but a free reflection of the musical idea. The movements from rehearsals should for the most part be internalized in performance.

Most of the energy-infusing movements are very simple. Some of them have been used by elementary music teachers for decades. You, as a director must be convinced as to their value, and comfortable with your presentation of these ideas, for them to work. Young singers are often inhibited and do anything to avoid looking foolish in front of their peers, so the positive way in which you present these ideas will affect how they are received and performed. Always approach the exercises with the idea that the singers naturally will accept them and do them. Once their inhibitions are conquered, and the singers sense the improvement in their singing, they will enjoy doing the exercises.

In order for the singers to get used to their bodies moving in a rehearsal room and not a gymnasium, you might start with some non-musical natural movements to which they are accustomed. These might include stretching, bending, running-in-place, walking, or simple calisthenics. These help loosen up the body, get the blood flowing and the breathing mechanism working. They are good to use at the beginning of a rehearsal or during a rehearsal when the singers are sluggish. From these we progress to movements associated with the music.

Concept: An energized body is necessary for good singing.
Purpose: Help the singer become aware of the body and how it functions effectively in singing.
Outcome: The singer will sing with greater energy and with an increased understanding of the body as an instrument.

Technique #1: Imagery

1 Feel the movement on the inside of a note. Notes have insides and outsides, just like people. And like people, the inside of the note is more important than its covering.

2 Make the inside of a note fortissimo, even if the outside is pianissimo. Notes are like atoms; the life is on the inside.

3 Sing softly as if silently screaming.

4 Think of long notes as a series of short notes tied together. There are no such things as long notes.

Technique #2: Rhythm

1 Have the singers tap the pulse of the smallest note in the piece lightly with their fingers on their neighbor's shoulder.

    a Start the tapping before the music starts.

    b Make the taps very light with only the finger, not the whole hand. Larger muscles cannot work as quickly or efficiently as smaller muscles.

    c Try singing the music without a director, only with the connected tapping of all the singers.

2 Ask the singers to feel and express the basic pulse and movement of the song in a rocking movement of their bodies.

3 Let the choir represent the rhythm or pulse of the song by tapping their feet or clapping their hands.

4 Instruct your singers to walk or dance in a circle to the rhythm of the song, moving in relation to the size of their notes.

Technique #3: Phrasing

1 Have your singers conduct themselves while they sing.

    a This needn't be fancy and should incorporate a legato pull.

    b Make it a challenge to see which section can conduct and sing most expressively.

2 Have your singers phrase with their arms and hands.

    a Begin with describing a circle; let the circle start rather small and spiral into a larger circle.

    b The movements should be generous, free, and non-restricted.

    c Let the singers create appropriate movements to the phrase: *legato, staccato, crescendo, decrescendo.*

3 Have your singers phrase with their whole bodies.

    a Start simply, such as swaying in the rhythm of the music.

    b Develop the movements into free, spontaneously invented movements. Notice the difference in the music. The music now should have more flow, less restriction, more inner drive and more energy.

4 Ask your singers to experience the sensations of several movements and to notice the difference the movements make in the phrasing and the sound of the music:

    a Put one foot ahead of the other and shift the weight to that foot at the high point of the phrase.

b Flex the knees at places where the energy is needed, such as the high point of a phrase.

c Raise on the toes for the low notes and flex the knees for the high notes.

d Clasp hands in front and pull on the hands as they sing into the phrases. The more the phrase needs strength, the stronger the pull.

e Pull on their neighbor hands in the same manner.

f Have the singers follow the flow of the sound out of their mouths with their hands, starting with the hand near the mouth. Make a large sweeping gesture away from the mouth during the phrase. Develop the feeling of pulling the sound with the hand.

g Mime the playing of a string instrument while singing a phrase. Let the different voice parts be different instruments and work for freedom of movement, as if they were soloists freely moving with the music.

h Mime the landing of a big fish as they sing a phrase. Hook the fish and keep the line taught as you reel the fish in. Use the analogy of hooking the audience with the first note of a phrase and pulling them through to the end of the phrase.

Technique #4: Relationships

1 Have your choir form a circle, with the voice parts mixed into quartets.

2 Have the singers move slowly across the circle so they are on the opposite side when the song ends.

3 They should not attempt to move in a straight line, or there will be a big pile-up in the middle of the circle at about the fifth measure.

4 They should move only when their part has sound.

5 When their part has a rest, they should stop and listen to the sound of the other parts.

6 They should move their bodies in relationship to the sounds they are singing.

7 They should be always aware of the relationship of the other parts to their part.

Note: The above works best with a slower, Renaissance style that has a mixture of notes and rests for each part.

Be careful in using the above exercises. If used effectively, they should benefit your singers in many ways. They are part of a total technique in developing your choir, and should not be used as a crutch for a lack of preparation or an understanding of the other aspects of singing. Instead, use these tools to bring your singers to a better understanding of the singing process. The singers should absorb a physical and visual concept of the high points in the phrases, the movements of the vocal lines, and the relationship of the voice parts to one another.

According to Wilhelm Ehmann, "a by-product of movement in choral singing is its influence on the sonority of the music. The sound loses its rigidity, its spread and lack of focus, and gains freedom, focus, resonance, and beauty."[3] An energized body that has buoyancy and vitality brings the singer closer to the goal of true musical communication in the choir.

Expression

The fourth quality of a good singing voice, in our quest for a FREE sound in a choir, is *expression,* the combining of intuition and intellect in creating a musical communication. This is not just the frosting on the musical cake, but the basic ingredients as well. To paraphrase Vince Lombardi, the former Green Bay Packers football coach who said, "Winning isn't everything . . . but there *is* nothing else," we could say expression isn't everything, but without it, there is nothing else. The most beautiful choral tone without expression is but a hollow shell of the music.

To teach a choir to sing with an expressive tone, one must constantly reinforce good habits of tone production and never allow bad or out-of-tune singing to exist. Everything your choir sings, including the warm-ups, should be musical. Your singers should not merely parrot rote renditions of what you tell them to sing; they must sing with understanding and feeling.

How can you teach your choir to sing expressively?

1 Each singer must understand *what* artistic musical communication in a choir is and be excited by the opportunity to express beauty through singing.

2 Each singer must understand the *text* they are communicating.

3 Each singer must understand that the *body* is the instrument of the singer, and must know how to use it effectively to create beautiful music.

4 Each singer must become *totally involved* in the making of the music and must be able to fully *concentrate* and focus attention on the *"sound idea."*

5 Each singer must *creatively function* as a member of the choral ensemble and clearly understand the relationship of the individual to the ensemble as a complete instrument in order to share in the joyous give and take of choral singing.

Accepting the premise that your singers fit the model of the five points, what do you, as director, do to develop an expressive tone with your choir? Bear in mind that the tone of the choir reflects not only the conductor's intellect, but musical imagination, ability to prepare a score, and personality as well — be it tense or relaxed, vibrant or phlegmatic, compassionate or tyrannical.

With so many decisions concerning expressive tone to be considered, would it not be all right to develop one good sound for a choir and leave well enough alone? For many directors this would be a satisfactory goal. However, there are a few relatively simple things that can be done to vary the tone as needed for

---

[3] Ehmann, Wilhelm, *Choral Directing.* Minneapolis: Augsburg Publishing House, 1968, page 92.

specific pieces or phrases. Some of these involve choices that are made for the entire choir; others involve the technique of the individual singer.

The choices involving the whole choir will be discussed later. These include the type of piece being sung; balance of the voices; predominance of certain vowel colors; tuning and intonation; awareness of overtones; singing formation of the choir; size of the ensemble; use of solo versus *tutti*; the weight of tone in each section; word stress within the phrases; precision of attacks and releases; use of special tone colors such as breathy tone, *sotto voce*, and *falsetto*; emphasis on explosive consonants; and blend within each section and the whole choir. The choices which are directly related to the individual singer's vocal technique are the placement of the tone, the use of voiced or sung consonants, the use of vibrato, and the desire of each singer to produce the best sound possible.

Dark vs. Light Tone

Some conductors ask for an extremely dark tone from their choirs by allowing, or suggesting, that singers swallow the tone by depressing their larynxes. On first impression, the tone is impressive, and a good blend is easily achieved. However, since this technique is based on tension in the neck and throat, it is not a *healthy* way to sing, and is apt to cause vocal problems later.

If a director wants a dark sound, the healthy alternative is to ask singers to sing darker vowels correctly. For instance, if the written vowel is *"oh,"* the singer may be asked to substitute the vowel, *"u."* The singer retains the forward resonance in the vowel, keeps the height in the back of the throat and the freedom in the sound, but sings a darker vowel. The resulting sound is free *and* dark.

On the other side, there are directors who ask singers for extremely bright sounds. This technique makes *fortissimo* sounds possible with any choir, but often produces a harsh, shrill, and brittle sound lacking in depth, blend, or balance. Again the healthy alternative is to use good vocal technique and change vowels when a brighter sound is desired. In the end, always let your ears be the judge of the sound you are eliciting from your singers.

Diphthongs and Vowel Changes

The director must decide exactly how long each part of the diphthong will be sung. Early movement to the second vowel can destroy the line of the phrase you are singing and appear as a self conscious over-pronunciation of text. The technique of sustaining the first vowel as long as possible before a delayed second vowel works well for most music. However, the director must let the actual sound, tempo, and style of the music determine the length of each vowel. In the end, the most important factor might not be the length of each vowel in the diphthong, but rather the ability of everyone to make the vowel movement precisely together.

Practice making vowel changes with freedom, grace, and clarity so that the singers get used to being exact in these movements. Many directors specify the precise length of each vowel within a note, instructing the singers to write the changes in their scores. For instance, a diphthong to be sung on a half note might result in the first vowel being sustained for the time-value of a double-dotted quarter note; the second vowel, a sixteenth note. Bear in mind that the exact length of each vowel is determined greatly by the tempo and articulation preferences in the phrase.

Voiced or Sung Consonants

Choral singing has traditionally been centered on "singing on the vowels." This has been to the almost total exclusion, in some cases, of the warm sound of voiced consonants. We must make sure the voiced consonants are heard, but in so doing not mistake the consonant *length* with consonant *volume*. Make the voiced consonants strong, but not long. They need to be balanced in a vocal phrase so that they project evenly with the vowels. Voiced consonants could be called "semi-vowels" because the vocal cords vibrate in the singing of these consonants. They are important because they 1) form the bridge from vowel to vowel, 2) are the rollers on which the words move forward and 3) give buoyancy and flow to the choral tone.

Vibrato

The use of vibrato in a choral ensemble is a matter of hot debate. Singing *senza vibrato* is common in many countries, especially in northern and eastern Europe, while in America a full range of choirs can be heard — some with a straight tone, some with a good deal of vibrato, and some who tailor the use of vibrato to the music being sung.

A vibrato is a natural phenomena. When a person sings freely with all the small and large muscles of the body working together to create a healthy, energized, and free musical tone, the voice will have a slight, regular pulsation called vibrato. It is a reflection in the human voice of the basic nerve pulse rate. The ability to control a vibrato is an integral part of any good healthy vocal technique. Expressive singing in a choir, or as a soloist, demands control of all aspects of singing, vibrato included. A singer who is unable to control vibrato, whether excessive or non-existent, does not have a good healthy technique.

A vibrato should never interfere with a musical phrase. The audience should be aware of a phrase direction that is horizontal, going to the high point of the phrase and then receding, rather than a vertical fluctuation of the moment that gives no direction to the phrase or meaning to the music. The vibrato should be used as a tool of expression. The director and the choir should decide when vibrato is appropriate, how much is appropriate, and why it is appropriate from a musical and textual basis.

There are four prevalent opinions as to a variable use of vibrato in choral singing. These are in addition to the strict convictions that singers in a choir should always use vibrato, or that singers in a choir should never use vibrato.

1 Vibrato should vary with the dynamics: the greater the volume, the more the vibrato; conversely, the lesser the volume, the lesser the vibrato.
2. Vibrato should vary with the texture of the music. The thicker the texture, the less the vibrato (enabling the harmony to be heard more clearly); conversely, the thinner the texture, the greater the vibrato.

3 Vibrato should be related to the period and style of the music being sung. Renaissance music with its clear lines, sparse texture, and open harmonies demands judicious control of vibrato. Romantic music with vibrant harmonies and full tonal expression often allows for a rich, full-bodied vibrato.

4 Vibrato should be used as an effective tool to delineate the music, ignoring volume, texture, and period. Let the vibrato be expressive of the piece being sung, whether Brahms or Josquin. Should J. S. Bach's *Jesu, meine Freude*, be sung with vibrato, with a controlled vibrato, or with no vibrato? Or because Bach used boy sopranos, should the vibrato in the sopranos be controlled, and the alto, tenor and bass asked to sing with more vibrato because these parts were sung by adult men? These are questions that need to be considered in this school of thought.

Tuning and Intonation

The tone of a choir can be greatly affected by intonation as well as the method of tuning used by the choir or selected for a particular piece. Many choirs, especially when accompanied music is sung or a piano is used for note-learning, use a variation of *Equal Temperament* where all half steps are equal in value.

For choirs that sing Early Music or mostly *a cappella*, it is possible to sing in a modified *Just Intonation*. The simplest approach to this tuning is to sing the fifth scale degree slightly higher, the major third slightly lower, and the minor third slightly higher. The effect will be an exciting experience for your singers when the chords are exactly in tune and the resulting overtones are almost as loud as the sung notes. It can elicit an incredible richness in sound. As singers are taught to listen for these overtones — especially the octave above their voice part — and the choir will be well on its way to singing with good intonation.

Intonation can be affected by several forces, only some of which are under the control of the director. Such things as barometric pressure, weather, day of the week, ball games and proms are beyond the control of the average director. What the director *can* do is:

1 Teach your choir to sing with good vocal technique.

2 Vocalize your singers from the top down, bringing the head voice into the lower range.

3 Work for a FREE sound with a high focus.

4 Do not accept singing that is out of tune.

5 Teach your singers *what* to listen for. Telling them to "listen" is pointless unless they know what to listen for!

6 Give your choir the opportunity to analyze chords that are in tune. Make them aware of what constitutes singing in tune.

7 Make your singers aware of what part of the chord they are singing.

8 Make singers aware of any other section that is singing a unison or octave with them. Have them *listen* and point to the section that has the octave.

9 Try to focus the attention of the choir on the music that is being sung. Concentration is not the only key to good intonation, but it is crucial.

10 Keep the rehearsal room well-ventilated and well lighted, and keep the rehearsals happy and positive.
11 Do not use an out of tune piano!
12 Work for unified vowels in each section.
13 Do not ask your singers to sing with an overly heavy sound.
14 Discipline your singers to hear the pitches before they sing.
15 Compose the rehearsals carefully; be aware that the pacing of a rehearsal can greatly affect the intonation of your choir.

Weight of the Tone

The weight of the tone in each section can greatly affect the overall tone of the choir. Teach the singers to vary the weight of the tone they use relative to the range and volume they are singing. Do not try to bring the full weight of a midrange up to the top of the voice. This is difficult for voices, especially young voices, and gives the impression of a sound being out of control and top heavy. As director, you must have the courage to help the large soloistic voices to gain control of their instruments and learn how to sing with less weight throughout their range — at dynamic levels less than *forte*.

In selecting music, you can cover the inability of your singers to lighten-up the sound by choosing only works of moderate tessitura; but in so doing, you will not be helping them develop the technique of varying the weight of their tone. Look at each piece to determine the weight of tone needed to communicate the composer's idea to the audience.

Desire to Produce the Best Sound

Perhaps the most important aspect of teaching a healthy vocal technique to your choir is to inspire each singer to produce the best sound possible. Whatever you teach, you will be most successful if you can motivate singers to explore their voices, take their voices to the limits, and to extend these limits. The human voice is beyond question the most thrilling of all instruments. Help your singers to get excited about their own voices and their own development as vocal musicians. There is nothing new in singing — except the personal discovery by each individual singer of the joy of singing.

Mental Attitude

The mental attitude of singers in a choir and the mental attitude of a director can greatly affect the tone of a choir. We have all seen average singers with positive and productive attitudes who far outshine those with better instruments and less-positive attitudes.

Ego and Self Concept

A healthy ego is necessary to perform, but it must never be allowed to get in the way of the music. As choral musicians we are truly blessed to be given the ability and the opportunity to perform some of the most inspiring music ever created, and we must impress upon our choirs that each singer also has a responsibility — to share their talent with others and help others see the beauty in music. In this way the self-concept of everyone in the choir will be made more positive, and the tone of the choir will be greatly enhanced.

Personality and Imagination

Every choir develops a personality which usually — but not always — reflects the personality of the director. This choral personality is a composite of the strong and weak points of all the choir members. There are choirs in which the personalities of the members are uniform in their hushed obedience to a visible or invisible choral code; and there are choirs in which the individuals are aggressive in their desire to be persistent individuals. Most choirs are a mixture of personalities —with singers who are *alert* and singers who are *inert*.

How does personality affect choral tone? Singers who are acquiescent are often afraid to take chances with new ways of producing tone; while singers with more aggressive personalities might be more apt to use their imaginations when images are suggested by the director and therefore more willing to change without fear of making a mistake.

The tone, as influenced by a choir's personality, can vary from one full of joy and sparkle to one that is pedantic and dull. Teach your singers to sing with a spontaneous love of singing that is full of joy and life. Inspire your singers with your conducting, your words, and your personality, so that singing with inspiration is a daily occurrence, not an act saved for the audience.

Underlying the personality of a choir are:
- Its ability to set common goals.
- Its ability to collectively concentrate.
- The confidence of the individual singers.
- The perceived importance of rehearsals and performances.
- The self-discipline of rehearsals.
- The general ambience of rehearsals.

All of these points will affect the choral tone in subtle and not so subtle ways. For instance, if the ambience of the rehearsals is tense and adversarial, the resulting tone will not be as good as if the ambience of the rehearsals were positive, challenging, and reaffirming. *The tone of the rehearsal will, in the final analysis, be the tone of the choir.*

Nerves, Tension and Relaxation

Excessive nervous tension — or conversely, complete lack of any nervous energy — can affect the tone of a choir. Any tension in a singer tightens the vocal mechanism, pinches the tone, and often causes sharping. On the other hand, a lack of energy will result in an unfocused, dull, dreary sound that usually is flat.

Directors must be aware of the nervous energy *they* display prior to a performance. Young singers, especially, are apt to be nervous and need a director who exudes confidence and calm. A delicate balance must be maintained between stressing the importance of a performance and maintaining a steady composure as a model for your singers.

The performance should be kept in perspective. Many little things can happen; but they should not interfere with the creative work that you and your choir have done in preparing for the concert. All technical details of the performance should be carefully rehearsed in advance, so that there is not a last minute scramble. Do not panic or be up-tight. At this point in a choir's life, the feeling should be complete confidence and absolute enjoyment of the fruits of their rehearsal labor.

There are some techniques for relaxing a group of singers that work well in stressful situations.

> **Concept:** Ridding the body of unnecessary tension helps to free the mind to focus on making a beautiful sound.
>
> **Purpose:** Relax the singers in your choir to prepare them to sing well.
>
> **Outcome:** The singers will sing with more confidence, a relaxed alertness, and greater mental focus.

Technique #1:

1 Have the singers sit down in the most relaxed, loose way they can.
2 They should feel like rag dolls, or marionettes with loose strings.
3 Their heads should be free to roll very loosely, as if disconnected.
4 They should close their eyes and listen inwardly. There should be complete silence in the room. If possible, lower the lights.
5 Have each singer breathe at his or her own rate.
6 Let the breath fall slowly into the body through the nose.
7 Let the breath fall slowly out of the body through the mouth. The tongue and jaw should be completely relaxed.
8 Their hands should feel very warm.
9 After five minutes or so, have the singers stand and stretch.
10 They should lightly massage their faces and necks
11 They should take a deep breath and do a high sliding sigh, using the head voice or the falsetto.
12 A positive, constructive energy should replace the nervous tension.

Technique #2:

1 Have the singers stand and reach up as high as they can with their hands.
2 Have them roll their eyes up and stare intensely at a spot in the center of their forehead (the third eye).
3 Instruct them to take a deep breath and hold it firmly.
4 Have them feel the tension throughout their bodies as they hold the breath.
5 Slowly let the breath out as the eyes lower and the hands begin to come down.
6 As the hands slowly drop, the eyes lower, and the breath escapes — feel the tension in the bodies leave, from the top of the hands down.
7 The feeling should be warmth flooding your body from the top down.
8 The eyes should lower to a closed position as the hands hang loosely at their sides.

9 Breathe with full silent breaths as you enjoy the relaxed feeling.

10 Shake the last bit of tension out of your hands.

Musical Choices

Many of the musical choices that affect choral tone have been discussed — balance of vowels and consonants, voiced consonants, diphthongs, overtones, dark and light vowels — because of overlapping ideas in the other three areas. We now will look at five determiners which uniquely affect choral tone.

Knowledge of History and Music

At first glance, this topic appears out-of-place, but it involves a conscious choice which should be made in planning your rehearsal. It is important to stress a knowledge of the historical period in which the music was composed and a general social history in order to get a better tone from your choir. If your choir is going to sing musically — with a sense of style and tone appropriate to that style, it is imperative that they understand the music within the context of the historical period in which it was composed.

They should be able to answer these basic questions about each piece they sing:

1 Who is the composer?

2 When and where did the composer live?

3 What was the period in music called and what else do you know from that period?

4 What else was happening in the world then?

5 Why was this work written?

6 What is the style of the music?

7 What is the language?

8 Was it originally accompanied or *a cappella*?

9 How large would the original choir have been and was it mixed, all male, or all female?

10 What was the age of the choir?

11 Was the choir professional or amateur?

12 What else did this composer write?

Articulation

The manner in which a choir attacks each syllable, and concurrently each note, will influence the over-all tone of the choir. Each initial vowel or consonant has its own unique shape and placement in the mouth. The preparation for each sound must come in advance of the actual sound, so that a uniform quality to all the sounds in a phrase can be maintained. Space in the mouth for all the vowel and consonant sounds must be kept at the maximum if a rich and free sound is desired.

The prevalence of many strongly articulated consonants will make the maintaining of space in the mouth for the vowels more difficult. This is true for all voices, especially for sopranos in their upper range. Although the tone will be brought forward into the mask, the repeated action of the tongue, lips and jaw can lead to tension. The effects of this can be minimized by careful planning in rehearsal, so that a piece with many quickly articulated consonants is surrounded by slower, legato works.

Also in the area of articulation, is the question of using a glottal stop. This is the action in which the vocal cords are brought together deliberately to begin a sound without the benefit of air passing through to pull the cords together. While it is not healthy to over-use this technique, it is a helpful tool when words ending with vowels are followed by words beginning with vowels. This situation is found regularly in music in which there are a series of the word, "alleluia." By keeping an open throat and re-articulating each succeeding "alleluia," good tone can be maintained, and the word, "alleluia" can be articulated and, most importantly, be clearly understood.

Intensity and Direction of Phrases

It is important to distinguish between intensity and tension when working with a choir. They are the good and evil twins of our creative vitality. Think of intensity as the product of an energized body; and tension as the product of muscles and minds under stress. Your musical choice as to how much intensity to put into a phrase will affect the sound as it relates to moving the breath and sustaining vocal freedom. Guard against letting intensity turn into tension as crescendos develop. Look at the various techniques noted above for helping your singers experience an open throat, especially the barrel analogy. (See Technique #3 on page 156.)

Enjoy the thrilling effect of a crescendo, but do not sacrifice tonal beauty. Look also at the sound of a decrescendo which needs as much intensity as a crescendo. Each phrase has an obvious or hidden crescendo or decrescendo. Although it is rarely marked by the composer or editor, each part of each note in every phrase must also have a direction which is delineated by volume, intensity, articulation, tempo, vibrato, or color. Look at these elements of phrasing when building a beautiful choral tone.

Balance

One of the easiest ways to change the tone of a choir is to change the balance. Many choirs are top-heavy with sopranos, have almost an equal number of altos, a shortage of tenors, and a few more baritones — some of whom are singing bass. There are some shifts you can make within the personnel of a choir without adding or eliminating voices. Move some of the first sopranos to second, some of the second soprano to alto. *Always* vocalize your choir from the top down, bringing the falsetto or head voice into the lower register, and you are almost guaranteed to find some tenors hiding in the baritone section who had not been helped to uncover their upper range. There is, sorry to say, nothing much that can be done to turn baritones into basses, except to vocalize down to help them find more strength in their lower range.

Along with the shift of people in the choir, you also must let your ear tell you about balance. If the sopranos outnumber all the other sections combined, they should not be allowed to over-sing and obliterate the rest of the choir. Even if their part is marked fortissimo, perhaps they should only sing mezzo forte or even mezzo piano, while the other brave souls sing fortissimo.

If the upper voices are overpowering the lower voices, look at places in the music where they are singing an octave higher than a lower part. This octave is where the first overtone occurs, and the sound of the overtone will augment the sound of the section and make it much louder. You must consciously cut back on the note being sung in favor of the overtone.

If you want to develop a rich, lush sound with your choir, balance the choir with more weight at the bottom than the top, like a pyramid. The overtones from the low notes will augment the upper notes and generate a richness that will never come from a choir that is top heavy with sopranos. If the bass section is weak, let them adjust the tone by modifying the vowels to the bright side, making sure they are all singing the same vowel — thereby strengthening the total sound.

Blend

Perhaps the most significant difference between the sound of one choir in comparison to another is in the degree of blend in each. An absolute blend is humanly impossible, but there are choirs that come very close. The problem of blend for the human voice, with its thousands of permutations of vowel and consonant sounds, is infinitely greater than that for any other instrument. A straight, vibrato-less, white sound from a homogeneous group would probably be the easiest to blend. But that does not define most choirs, nor does it describe what most directors would want.

For most of us with an age, ethnic, cultural, intellectual, and musical diversity of singers in our choir the problem of blend is not easy. If you want your choir to sing with a blended sound, there are four things you and your singers must constantly audit. This is an ongoing process and cannot be limited to the rehearsal plan for the first week and then forgotten. It is a disciplined listening skill that must be practiced consistently.

To sing with a blended sound, singers must listen to those around them and adjust their voices to the following:

- **Pitch:** How close does a pitch have to match to be accurate? Are two singer ever really "in tune" with each other?

- **Vowel color:** Singers must match not only with the written vowel, but with the exact sound of the vowel. The sound of each singer's vowel production can be observed only by letting each singer in your choir or section sing individually. Many singers assume they are producing an accurate vowel when, in fact, they are producing another vowel color.

- **Volume:** A strong voice must exercise control and a smaller voice must sing with as much strength as possible while maintaining a healthy vocal production. *(Be wary of placing smaller voices next to big voices, thereby placing unhealthy demands for volume on the small voice, and causing frustration for the big voice.)*

- **Rhythm:** It is impossible to have a blended sound if the voices are not moving together. This movement is not just at the beginning and end of phrases, but also all the interior moves from sound to sound in each phrase.

It might be helpful to make a poster with these four aspects of a blended sound, and place it where the singers are constantly reminded of listening for blend. If habits of creative listening are reinforced and become routine, the result will be a blended sound that will be thrilling to the choir as well as the audience.

Environment

Let us next look at the determiners of choral tone that fall into the general area of environment. For purpose of our discussion, the term "environment" encompasses all things affecting choral tone which are outside the confines of vocal technique, mental attitude, and musical choices. Included are all elements that seemingly can not be changed — that are considered by many directors and administrators as "givens." But are they?

Intelligence of the Singers
There is the old joke defining singers as having resonance where their brains ought to be. Even though it seems rare that two great talents, a beautiful voice and intelligence, are found in the same person, we do encounter the truly gifted singers in our choirs. Work to create the atmosphere in which the more gifted can help the less gifted. Keep the gifted challenged. Be patient with the less gifted. Look for opportunities for the more gifted to serve as assistant conductors, section leaders, or other types of leadership positions. The general atmosphere of positive learning and shared growth will be as effective as any other factor in helping your choir discover a beautiful choral tone.

Age of the Singers
With a given choir, we can do little to change the age of the singers, except wait. Your mind should always focus on the idea that the beautiful in music knows no age restrictions. Honest beauty in music can sprout in the young, flourish in mid-life, and thrive in the elderly. Cherish whatever age with which you make music.

Although we can not change the chronological age of our singers, we can help the singer, especially the young singer, to match the "vocal age" to the chronological age. So often we find teen-agers who are singing with the same small voice they used when they were elementary students. It is as if they sang a solo for the PTA in the third grade with great success and found no reason ever to change. The following is a useful technique and an interesting experiment with young choirs. It is a wonderful way to play on the imagination of the singers and free their spirits.

Concept: The human voice is a remarkably flexible and constantly developing instrument.
Purpose: Develop freedom and space in the area of the throat.
Promote understanding of vocal development. Provoke laughter and establish a pleasant atmosphere.
Outcome: The singers will sing with greater freedom in the area of the throat and mouth. Muscles of the abdomen will be energized through laughter, and a positive attitude toward singing and choir will be fostered.

Technique #1: Vocal Age Game:
When the tone of the choir is becoming thin because of closed spaces in the area of the larynx and mouth:

1 Ask the singers to sing as if they were two school grades lower then they are. (If they are a high school choir, ask them to sing it as if they were ninth graders.)

2 Then ask them to sing it as if they were sixth graders; then third graders; and finally first graders or pre-schoolers.

3 Notice that the sound thins out and their throats tighten as they perceive the tone of a younger singer.

4 Next reverse the process and go from pre-school to beyond their chronological ages. Ask them to sing like high school seniors; then college seniors; then professional singers who are out of college for ten years, and at last as forty-year old giants, seven foot Wagnerian sopranos with spears, and horns on their Viking helmets, on the stage of the Metropolitan Opera! The vibrato will become a cartoon, the space in the back of the mouth will increase, and everyone will have a good laugh — *which stimulates the breathing mechanism for a singer.*

5 Ask them which sound they like the best, and why. The sound with the most freedom and clarity is usually the college senior sound.

6 Ask them how it feels when they make that sound. (The usual answer is that it feels more open in the back of the throat.)

7 Ask them to make that sound again and put the *feeling of the sound* into their musical memory bank. They have expanded their use of the most incredible musical instrument in the world! Remind them of the great variety of sounds they are capable of making with this glorious instrument!

8 Use the experiment as a point of reference in subsequent rehearsals when the choir's sound becomes thin.

Health of the Singers

Little can be done regarding general health, except to encourage singers to take care of themselves. Vocal health is another matter. Singers can be encouraged to avoid caffeine, alcohol, and other drugs, drink six or seven glasses of water each day to keep the vocal mechanism hydrated, and avoid vocal abuse, such as singing before the vocal mechanism is warmed up, cheerleading and other types of screaming, singing with a sore throat, and over-singing. The latter can be partly controlled by the director *if* it is occurring in the choir. Consider the following points:

• **Frequency of Rehearsals:**

Ideally, in a school or professional choir, rehearsals should be daily so that singers will stay in vocal shape, as opposed to less frequent or weekly rehearsals. But with a church choir, or other volunteer choir, weekly rehearsals are most common. The extremes in rehearsal frequency range from the six-hour-per-day rehearsals of some of the Eastern European professional choirs and the once a month (that last for two days!) rehearsals of the Israel Kibbutz Choir. In both cases, because the singers are adults and have healthy vocal techniques, there have been good results. But it is difficult for a choir to discover a beautiful tone and develop a sound vocal technique if there is not enough *frequent* time to rehearse and learn! If possible, make necessary changes in the rehearsal schedule.

• **Length of Rehearsals:**

The longer the rehearsals, the more carefully the director must plan so that voices are as healthy at the end of the rehearsal as they were at the beginning. If you want your choir to have a good tone, you must listen objectively every minute of the rehearsal and develop a sense that tells you when the voices are tiring. When singers begin to tire, switch to a new piece, a different rehearsal formation, from sitting to standing or standing to sitting, from singing to listening, etc. This is one time when your ingenuity will come into play in a rehearsal. Plan rehearsals carefully — but know your options for changing the plan. Be flexible and adaptable; understand how to save voices.

• **Time of Rehearsals:**

The time of your rehearsals can greatly affect the tone of your choir. If everyone is feeling fresh, the tone will be well along the road to sounding fresh. If rehearsals are at a time when everyone is tired, the choral tone will suffer; this often occurs following lunch or at the end of a day. Try to set rehearsal times when everyone is alert and ready to sing.

Is it really true that singers cannot sing early in the morning? It depends on the nocturnal habits of the choir — *and* the director. In the morning, if the voices are warmed up well, they should be at their freshest — much fresher than at the end of a long, difficult day. But as the director, you must always be positive about an early rehearsal time. If you are not an early bird, pretend you are. In addition to "getting the worm," you might get a great sounding choir! Your attitude will influence the ambience and, consequently, the success of your rehearsals.

· **The Acoustics of the Rehearsal Space:**

If the rehearsal space has no reverberation or feed-back, the tone of the choir can become forced and the singers can tire easily. Conversely, if the space is too live, the tone can become raucous and harsh and the singers will have a difficult time hearing themselves. The sound of your choir is directly related to the acoustics of the space in which you rehearse. It is up to you to make the acoustics as good as possible.

How can you change the acoustics? Several simple things are possible:

- Look for a different space.
- Move your choir so they are facing a different direction.
- Use curtains as an acoustic baffle, or add a carpet, if it is too live.
- Remove a carpet or add hard surfaces if reverberation is limited.
- Contact an acoustical engineer to do an analysis of your room and make suggestions for improving the acoustics.

Activities Prior to and Following a Rehearsal or Performance:

It is difficult for singers of any age to focus attention on making a good choral sound if their minds are more directed to what is happening before or after the rehearsal or performance. In a positive manner, a director must make the choir constantly aware of the importance of the rehearsal or performance.

Conductor's Attitude:

The conductor's attitude is always evident to the singers and very important to the success of the ensemble. Singers will pick up quickly on the small things which will indicate the way in which the conductor views the individual singers, the choir, and their activities. Ask yourself these questions:

- Do you always start exactly on time?
- Are your rehearsals well planned and are you prepared?
- Do you limit your talking in rehearsal?
- Are rehearsals well paced?
- Are you positive about the singers' progress and encouraging about their development?
- Do you teach them to be self-disciplined and self-motivated?
- Do you make them feel important about the work they are doing?
- Do you help them to see the value and necessity for their singing and performance in today's society?
- Do you show them ways to make their most beautiful tone in each piece they are singing?

The Conductor's Intelligence, Ear, and Imagination:

In addition to the conductor's attitude, the conductor's intelligence, ear, and imagination will greatly affect the tone of the choir. Although intelligence is a given, there are ways in which you can focus more of your thoughts on producing a good choral tone. There are books available, workshops to attend, countless opportunities to hear good choirs at festivals, ACDA and MENC conventions, and many chances to talk to directors whose tonal concepts you admire. Do not isolate yourself. Listen to other choirs. Be amenable to change.

The conductor's ear is always in a state of change, either for better or for worse. Notice the difference in your ability to objectively hear your choir in September, after a summer without listening, and at the end of the school year, when listening has been a daily activity. With discipline, a conductor's ability to hear can improve. Try learning your next score away from the piano. Use a pitch pipe or a tuning fork as you sing the individual lines and as you horizontally read the chords.

In your rehearsal, if you are constantly checking the choir's pitches by matching them on a piano, you do not have the freedom to listen objectively to the actual sounds that the singers make. You limit your choir if you always ask singers to match the percussive sound of an often out-of-tune piano, rather than to create a beautiful sound out of their imagination — an imagination that has been seeded with your creative suggestions.

How does a conductor's imagination and creativity expand? Listen to other choirs, talk to directors, seek out people in related arts, develop an appreciation for all literature and art forms, read, visit museums, listen to professional performers, rejoice in the unique qualities of your singers, develop your own voice, invest in yourself, do not hesitate to experiment, and do not be afraid to make a mistake.

Acoustics of Your Performing Space:

If you do frequent performances, the spaces in which you perform can have a positive or negative affect on the tone of your choir. If the space has poor acoustics, your audience will never hear your choir as they should. Performing in a poor acoustical environment is similar to taking a great painting, placing it in a gallery, inviting an audience, then not turning on the lights. The audience will never see the beauty of the painting and likewise will never hear the beauty of your performance. The solution? Sing someplace else.

Time of Performances:

If you are a church choir director, you have little choice about the time of your performances. Directors of school choirs also will perform on occasion in the early morning. If this is your situation, it is absolutely necessary for you to carefully and thoughtfully warm up your choir vocally before the performance. The vocal cords are like any other muscles and have to be carefully loosened up and gently stretched if they are to perform well.

Size of the Ensemble:

The size of your ensemble can greatly influence the tone. One will never achieve a Mormon Tabernacle Choir sound from a small high school chamber choir. These are two different types of ensembles. Although a large choir can sing a delicate pianissimo, a chamber choir's fortissimo will never equal that of a large choir. By forcing a small choir to sing a louder sound than its members are able to technically produce, an unpleasant, strained choral-tone will result. Remind your singers constantly to *sing no louder than beautiful.* When a choral sound ceases to be beautiful, it is too loud!

Is there an optimum size for a choral ensemble? It may be true that mediocre singers sound better in larger numbers than in smaller numbers; the abilities of one singer tends to fill in the cracks in the abilities of another, and together the composite of their voices sounds better. In a large ensemble no one voice is required to carry the entire burden of making a beautiful sound in the section as it might be in a small choir.

The *a cappella* choir tradition, as established in the midwest, favored choirs that were about sixty-five to seventy voices. This size has remained constant for several decades and 1) allows for an evenness of sound in each section, 2) provides enough remaining strength if some singers are ill or missing, and 3) is able to generate fortissimos that are about 6.3 on the Richter scale!

Professional choirs since the 1950's, have placed the optimum number of singers around 24, a size determined partly by economics. However these are professional singers who have developed a sound vocal technique and can easily handle the various demands placed on their voices.

In an ideal world, the music being sung would dictate the size of an ensemble, as it does with many professional ensembles. With chamber works, the size of the ensemble often shrinks to twelve or sixteen singers, while with large choral/orchestral works the size can swell to over one hundred. In a school, church, or community chorus, however, the size of a choir remains fairly static — often more so on the small side than directors desire.

However if one has a choir of 100, all 100 singers are not required to sing 100% of the time. It is interesting for audiences to hear contrasts between solo quartets, small ensembles, and larger choirs, or the contrast between the sound of men or women singing alone. As a director, look for ways to alter the choral tone by changing the size of your ensemble.

The Singing Formation of the Choir:

There is little in the realm of choral music about which directors seem to believe more strongly than in the singing formation of their choirs. Maybe they are right to hold such a strong opinion. The sound of a choir *can* change dramatically with a different singing formation in rehearsal or in performance. But the placement of singers in a choir should be determined by the goals and purposes you have espoused in your conducting. You must set priorities that are appropriate to the ensemble you are conducting, and not to the specifications of the choir in which you formerly sang. Ask yourself these questions:

- Do you want to generate a beautifully blended sound in each section that is unique to that section or do you favor a more generous and unified overall sound?
- Do you want to help the individual singer grow vocally and musically, and develop aural independence?
- Do you want to improve the intonation of the choir in general?
- Do you want the sopranos to stand near the violins and the bass section to stand by the 'cellos and basses?
- Do you want the weaker sections to stand in front?

- Do you want the men and women separated for acoustic reasons in specific pieces?
- Do you want to change the singing formation with each piece thereby giving your singers the challenge of change and giving your audience an aural and visual variety?

Regardless of where the sections are placed in a choir, the basic options in singing arrangements are:

1 Have the sections sing in *blocks*, that reach from the front of the choir to the back of the choir.
2 Have the sections sing in *lines* that go from the center of the choir to the ends of the choir in one or more rows, but with other sections behind or in front of them.
3 Sing in a *mixed* arrangement throughout the choir, either in quartets or in a random pattern.

Each arrangement will elicit a different choral tone from your singers. The determination of the arrangement you use with your choir should come after answering the questions posed above. Bear in mind that each choir is unique, each rehearsal or performance space is unique, and each conductor's priorities are unique. Experiment in various ways of placement and find the formations that best suit your priorities and the sound of the choir that you envision.

Singing in blocks or lines generally will provide a better blend in each section. Singers become accustomed to hearing a specific singer next to them at each rehearsal, and learn to blend and work together as a team. Individual voices in sections tend to reflect and augment the voices that are around them. Block arrangements will also:

- Give greater support to weaker singers singing within their section.
- Allow each section in a large festival chorus to be equidistant from the director with the sound from each section reaching the audience at the same time.
- Enable low voices to be placed near low instruments and high voices near the high instruments.

In contrast, singing in quartets will provide a more homogeneous sound throughout the whole choir, but the individual sections will lose some of their identity. Because the sections are dispersed throughout the choir, a section blend or specific section color is more difficult to accomplish. Secure singers will gain in independence, however, and the intonation will usually improve. It is a great arrangement for strengthening the ears of your choir members, and singers love it.

The best option might be to *vary* the singing formation, depending on the needs of your choir at a specific rehearsal or performance. It can be a psychological boost for a choir to sing in quartets if they usually sing in sections, or vice versa. It can measurably alter their tone while it lifts their spirits.

In addition to the placing of sections in your choir is the issue of placing singers within the section. Where do you place the strongest singers? The brightest voices? The best ears? The best readers?

If you are able to audition the members of your choir from a pool of qualified singers, you can select a homogeneous grouping of voices which all blend perfectly and match your tonal ideal. If you, like most of us, work with a cross section of big and small, bright and dark, musical and non-musical voices, the gifted and the singing impaired, you must decide how you will arrange the voices within each section. Remember, one difference between a choir and a congregation is that choir members have specific, assigned seats within the choir, whereas the members of a congregation can sit wherever they please.

If your choir is arranged in the traditional Midwestern *a cappella* choir formation with the sopranos and altos in front, the basses behind the sopranos and the tenors behind the altos, one way of seating your choir is to place the strongest singers and best ears at the center of the choir. In this arrangement:
- The stronger voices do not protrude from the general sound.
- The singers with the most accurate ears, who can adjust more easily to the pitches of the other sections, are in the center of the choir,
- The weaker voices do not have to over-sing in trying to match the bigger voices.

This usually engenders a well blended sound, with the center of the choir having the strongest sound. If a director wants to use fewer voices in some of the music, the stronger, more soloistic, voices from each section are clustered in the heart of the choir.

Another process of seating singers in sections is to match all voices with adjacent compatible voices. It is a somewhat time-consuming process, but does result in an ideal blend and a feeling of value for each singer. It also allows the singers to listen objectively to their own voices and the other voices in the choir. This method has been advocated by Weston Noble for several years and has been used with success by several directors:

Concept: A variety of voices can be arranged in a manner which enhances the blend of a section.
Purpose: Achieve the optimum blend within each section. Overcome shyness in singing alone.
Outcome: The singers will realize that they are valued contributors to the overall sound of a section. The singers will have opportunity to sing alone in front of the choir and in so doing become less inhibited singers. The sections will sing with a blended sound.

Technique 1: Voice Matching:
1 Have the section to be auditioned stand in a straight line in front of the choir.
2 Have each singer sing a simple phrase such as the first phrase from "My Bonny Lies Over the Ocean," or "My Country 'tis of Thee."
3 Have the choir select the two voices which match most closely in timbre.
4 Have these two singers sing in two arrangements: with singer A on the left of singer B, then on the right.

5 When the choir has decided on the position which exhibits the best blend and the two singers decide which position is the most comfortable for their singing, add one more singer, trying this singer in each of three positions: first on the left of the other two, then in between the two singers, then on the right.

6 When the best blend and ease of singing for each singer has been determined, add one more singer, using the same positioning process.

7 Add the rest of the singers in each section, trying them one at a time in each of the growing number of positions, saving the strongest voices until the last.

8 When the final result is determined, try reversing the whole section. Ask the rest of the choir, "Which do you like best?"

9 Check the final positioning with the original position and again ask the rest of the choir, "Which do you like best?"

10 Use the same procedure with each section.

If your choir is seated in quartets, with the sections scattered throughout the choir, a variation of the above technique is also possible by matching members of each quartet of SATB. Remember that singers generally sing better and more productively when they are comfortable with their placement in the choir. Some voices simply are not compatible with other voices and should not be placed in adjacent positions.

Although this process seems time consuming, the resulting blend and awareness of the unique qualities of individual voices will be of great benefit to the choir. It places importance on every singer in the choir and will provide a tonal foundation on which to grow throughout the year.

Style of Music:

The tone of your choir will be greatly determined by the style of the music that you program. A choir that invests the greater part of the year rehearsing and performing Bach's *Jesu, meine Freude* will sound different from the same choir that spends the time singing Macedonian folk music of the late nineteenth century, or highlights from early Broadway musicals. Setting aside the discussion of whether a choir should consciously fit their tone to the style of music they are singing, it is fairly obvious that certain styles of music elicit specific choral sounds.

The music of Bach, and Baroque music in general, demands and evokes a precision of movement, a clarity and lightness of tone, an absolute inner pulse and integrity of rhythm. A lyrical ballad from a Broadway musical demands a somewhat heavier, lusher sound, with more vibrato and less emphasis on rhythmical integrity and clarity of tone. A wise director will program music that will help the singers grow in their understanding of tone production with various styles of music, and will help the singers apply the universal qualities of tone production learned in one style to the music of another style.

Difficulty of Music:

As well as programming certain styles of music to help your choir develop a concept of choral tone, a director also has the opportunity to program music with various levels of difficulty. Complex and demanding music affects tone quality in two ways: First, if the majority of rehearsal time is spent teaching the notes of an impossibly difficult piece, there will be little time left to teach your singers how to sing. Second, the technical problems of a very difficult piece may be beyond the techniques of your singers and cause them to sing in a forced, tight manner that precludes the development of a free, resonant tone.

Know your priorities in selecting the music for your choir. A simple piece sung with beautiful tone can be more impressive to an audience than a very difficult piece performed poorly. Know what you want your singers to learn from a piece of music and program accordingly.

Language:

The language of a piece can affect the tone of the choir in much the same way as the difficulty of a piece. If too much time in rehearsal is spent in teaching a language, there will be less time available to spend in teaching the choir the other important aspects of a piece. A choir *should* be exposed to various languages, and have the opportunity and joy of singing in a language other than their own. But pieces should be chosen wisely, considering the *amount* of foreign text in each piece. The less experienced the singers are, the shorter the texts should be.

Each language has its own peculiar tonal flavor. Some of these flavors demand different vocal techniques, especially in the shaping of the mouth and the placement of the tongue. It is important to try to capture the essence of each language with your singers and experience the flavors that make that language unique. While you should not be afraid to teach a piece in a foreign language, you might be well advised to bring in a person who is a native speaker to help your choir hear the true flavor of that language.

Amount and Rapidity of Text:

The more text in a piece and the more rapidly the text is sung, the more tension in the mouth and tongue, which decreases the resonating chambers and creates tension in the sound. The more often the tongue and jaw have to move, the less likely they will return to a relaxed open feeling necessary for the creation of a rich sound. This is especially true if the *tessitura* of the rapidly sung text is high.

Choral Speaking and Humming:

The use of choral speaking and humming can also affect the tone, but in different ways. Choral speaking can provide an interesting color to the overall sound and give variety to a choral program. In addition to the variety provided by humming, the use of humming can have a benefit beyond the piece being sung. It has been accepted for centuries that humming can promote a positive resonance in the voice, bringing the sound forward into the mask. This is as true in developing a beautiful choral tone as it is in developing the individual voice. The importance of this experience for your choir is for the singers to transfer the resonance gained from humming into other pieces of music.

Length of the Music:

Each singer has a limit to his vocal, physical, and mental endurance. If demands are placed on a singer which exceed this endurance, the tone of the singer and the choir will suffer as a piece progresses. This should be taken into consideration also in programming an entire concert. You do not want to wear out your singers. They should sound as good on the final cadence as on the first note. Your ear will tell you if their zeal is flagging and limits of good tone have been reached. There are works that are beyond the endurance of all but professional choirs, and which should be left for performance by these choirs.

Length of Phrases:

In the same manner as the length of an entire piece of music can affect the tone of a choir, the length of individual phrases can affect the tone. Listen objectively to the sound that your singers make. Are they still singing with freedom as they end a longer phrase? Singers should never sound as if they are running out of breath. When they do, the tone suffers measurably. Look for logical breathing places within the phrases, or stagger the breathing of a section by having the singers each breathe at a different time, leaving and re-entering the sound as unobtrusively as possible.

Texture of the Music:

It is obvious that music with a thick texture will sound different from music with a thin texture. A director should be aware of this as music is programmed for the choir. If you want your choir to sound rich, with its tonal flaws well hidden, look for music that is more thickly scored. However, you will be helping singers develop more positively if their vocal flaws are not hidden, but rather overcome by the challenge of pieces that rely on a texture that features each section singing alone in a thinner texture. You must establish a balance between what you want the audience to hear and what you want your singers to learn.

Voicing:

The closer the voicing of the chords, the better the choral tone will appear. If you want your sopranos to sound their best, look for music in which the other sections support the sopranos in a close proximity. If the sopranos are separated by more than an octave from the altos, it will be exceptionally difficult for them to sound free and clean.

Observe the difference in the voicing of the *Lenten Motets* by Francis Poulenc and the folk song arrangements for choir by Johannes Brahms. These are extraordinary works from both composers. But the extreme ranges and voicing in the Poulenc makes these works nearly impossible for all but choirs with the most advanced techniques; while the Brahms pieces, with very contained voicing will sound good with most choirs. Know the ranges of your singers, and balance your music selection between that which capitalizes on the most productive ranges of their voices and that which stretches their ranges and expands their vocal techniques.

Conclusion

There are no shortcuts to creating a beautiful choral tone. But do not be dismayed by the amount of material you have just read. Use it as a reference. While it is by no means exhaustive, it is probably more than you need to know to discover a beautiful sound in your choir. In your quest for a good choral tone, listen to as many choirs as you can. Trust your ears and your intellect to tell you what makes the tone of one choir good and another choir less than good. Talk to other directors; be an aggressive listener and learner.

Think about this: The more beautiful the song becomes, the more beautiful the singer becomes. When we discover the beauty in the music we perform, we also discover the beauty in ourselves and, more importantly, in those around us. Choir directing is an exciting and humbling profession. *We must never forget that we who find music in people and mold these people and their music into choirs are among the truly blessed.*

William Byrd has two timeless quotes which should be on every choir director's desk:

> *There is not any Musicke or Instruments whatsoever, comparable to that which is made of the voyce of Men, where voyces are good, and the same well sorted and ordered.*

> *Since singing is so good a thing,*
> *I wish that all men would learn to sing.*

Diction

Richard Cox

Choral directors, singers and listeners agree that diction[1] is important to the success of choral groups. Why is it such an important aspect of choral singing?

- Clear enunciation enables the audience to understand the words.
- Uniformity of vowel sound promotes uniformity of pitch.
- Uniformity of consonant articulation permits rhythmic uniformity.
- The flexibility of lips, tongue, and jaw that makes good diction possible promotes healthy and efficient vocal production.

The principles of diction are best approached through the technical terminology of phonetics and through the International Phonetic Alphabet. These tools, once clearly understood, enable singers to perceive English language sounds precisely and are an invaluable aid in mastering diction in foreign languages. This technology will enable the beginning diction student to sharpen the ear and to gain control over the physical mechanism. What follows is, however, only an introduction. If all this is new to you, I urge you to examine the attached bibliography and, above all, to listen carefully and perceptively to your own diction, to that of your choir, and to that of other fine singers and choruses.

We will begin our discussion with an overview of the consonant and vowel sounds in several of the languages commonly used in singing. After this introduction, we will describe consonant and vowel production in English along with frequently-encountered singing problems. Finally, we will describe ways in which such languages as French, German, Italian, Russian, and Spanish differ from English in sound production and in spelling.

The International Phonetic Alphabet

The International Phonetic Alphabet was devised in 1888 by an international society in an effort to provide each language sound with a symbol that remains constant from language to language. The IPA symbol represents a sound which is consistent even though the spelling may change from language to language or even within the same language. In English, for example, the consonant symbol [f] may be spelled f in **fish**, ff in **taffy**, ph in **philosophy**, or even gh in **rough**. The symbol [ɛ] may be spelled e in **met**, ea in **head**, ie in **friend**, or even ai in **saith**. Symbols are normally placed in square brackets to distinguish them from spelling letters, which they usually resemble. In our charts, however, we will not use brackets since all the symbols on them are IPA symbols, not spelling letters.

---

1 In this chapter we will use this term in the second sense, "Degree of clarity and distinctness of pronunciation in speech or singing, enunciation," as defined by the *American Heritage Dictionary, Second College Edition.* Boston: Houghton Mifflin Company, 1982.

Consonants

Consonants are formed by bringing the lower lip or some part of the tongue into some relationship with the upper lip, the upper teeth, or the palate. Consonants are described by identifying the part of the vocal apparatus used, as

- **labial**, using the two lips;
- **labiodental**, involving the lower lip and the upper teeth;
- **dental**, moving the tip of the tongue between the teeth;
- **alveolar**, using the blade of the tongue and the ridge of gum (alveolar ridge) behind the upper teeth;
- **alveolopalatal**, involving the front of the tongue and the front of the palate, just behind the alveolar ridge;
- **palatal**, involving the middle of the tongue and the middle of the hard palate;
- **velar**, using the back of the tongue and the soft palate (velum); or
- **laryngeal (glottal)**, using the vocal cords.

Consonants may also be described according to the nature of the relationship between the two parts of the mouth, as

- **plosives (stops)**, in which there is complete closure;
- **nasals**, in which the closure is relieved by opening the nasal passages;
- **fricatives**, in which an incomplete closure allows a narrow passage of air between to create a sound of friction;
- **affricates**, combinations of plosives and fricatives;
- **glides**, vowels articulated quickly enough to be perceived as consonants; and the
- **lateral**, in which the tongue is held in such a way as to permit air to escape on the sides of the tongue.

Finally, a consonant is described as **voiced** or **voiceless**, depending on whether the vocal cords vibrate during its articulation. A consonant that can be whispered is by definition voiceless. So a consonant may be described, for example, as a **voiceless dental fricative** or as a **voiced velar stop**, and we know exactly how it is made. Even if we have never heard the **voiceless uvular stop** used in Arabic, we can pronounce one by following the description.

Here is a chart showing the IPA symbols for the consonants sounds used in English and the major singing languages. To save space, the descriptive adjectives **labial**, **labiodental**, **alveolar**, etc. are abbreviated. The left-to-right organization of the chart shows the relationships among the consonants from the front of the mouth on the left to the back of the mouth on the right. When two symbols occupy the same position, the upper one is voiced, the lower one voiceless; e.g., under "labial plosives" [b] is voiced, [p] is voiceless.

	lb	lbdn	dn	al	alpl	pl	vl	gl
Plosives	b			d			g	
	p			t			k	ʔ
Nasals	m	ɱ		n		ɲ	ŋ	
Fricatives	β	v	ð	z	ʒ	j	ɣ	
	f		θ	s	ʃ	ç	x	h

	lb	lbdn	dn	al	alpl	pl	vl	gl
Affricates				dz	dʒ			
		pf		ts	tʃ			
Glides	w					j	ɹ	
Lateral				l		ʎ		
Tap				ɾ				

Vowels

Vowels are also described in terms of the relationship between the tongue and the roof of the mouth. Thus, a vowel is "high" or "low" depending on the distance from the tongue to the roof of the mouth. "Front" or "back" describes the point at which the tongue is closest to the roof of the mouth. Vowels may also be described as "round" if the lips are rounded during their articulation. Here is a chart showing the IPA symbols for the vowel sounds used in the major singing languages:

The parentheses ( ) indicate lip rounding. The lip-rounded front vowels are no less forward than the unrounded front vowels to their left.

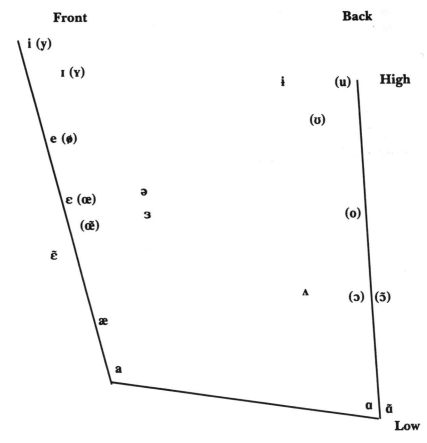

The charts that follow show the spellings for the symbols used above.

Plosives (Stops)

	Labial		Alveolar		Velar	
	voiced	voiceless	voiced	voiceless	voiced	voiceless
	[b]	[p]	[d]	[t]	[g]	[k]
English	baby	poppy	deed	tot	go	clock
Latin	Sabaoth	pax	Deus	Sabaoth	gloria	cujus
Italian	bambino	pizza	dardo	Torelli	Guido	cosí
French	bébé	pays	dindon	toute	gaz	coucou
Spanish	baja	Pedro	donde	tia	gusto	Cuba
German	Bach	hab	du	Tod	gegen	decken
Russian*	Boris	Piotr	Vladimir	ty	Gorbachev	Kiev

*Russian spellings represent standard transliterations.

Nasals (all voiced)

	Labial	Alveolar	Palatal	Velar
	[m]	[n]	[ɲ]	[ŋ]
English	mummy	none	—	singing
Latin	meus	nova	Agnus	Sanctus
Italian	mio	Norina	ogni	lungo
French	moi	non	agneau	—
Spanish	Madrid	niño	niño	angel
German	mich	nein	—	Finger
Russian	Moskva	nashikh	—	Glinka

Fricatives

	Labial	Labiodental		Dental	
	voiced	voiced	voiceless	voiced	voiceless
	[β]	[v]	[f]	[ð]	[θ]
English	—	vivid	fifty	this	thin
Latin	—	vivos	factorem	—	—
Italian	—	Verdi	farfalla	—	—
French	—	vive	effet	—	—
Spanish	Cuba	—	Falla	nada	hacer
German	—	Wagner	von	—	—
Russian	—	slava	Kiev	—	—

	Alveolar		Alveolopalatal	
	voiced	voiceless	voiced	voiceless
	[z]	[s]	[ʒ]	[ʃ]
English	rose	success	vision	shore
Latin	miserere[2]	Sanctus	—	viscera
Italian	rosa	santo	—	scena
French	rose	son	je	chose
Spanish	mismo	rosa	—	—
German	Rose	ist	Orange[3]	Schubert
Russian	zima	slava	Bozhe	Khrushchev

Fricatives (continued)

	Palatal		Velar		Laryngeal
	voiced	voiceless	voiced	voiceless	voiceless
	[j]	[ç]	[ɤ]	[x]	[h]
English	—	—	—	—	hand
Spanish	—	—	agua	jota	—
German	ja	ich	—	Bach	Hand
Russian	—	—	—	Rakhmaninov	—

Affricates

	Labiodental	Alveolar		Alveolopalatal	
	voiceless	voiced	voiceless	voiced	voiceless
	[pf]	[dz]	[ts]	[dʒ]	[tʃ]
English	—	—	—	judge	church
Latin	—	Lazaro	etiam	agimus	pacem
Italian	—	mezzo	pizza	Giorgio	Puccini
Spanish	—	—	—	—	muchacho
German	Pferd	—	zu	—	Kitsch
Russian	—	—	Tsar	—	Chekhov

Glides   Tap   Lateral

	Labial	Palatal	Retroflex	Retroflex	Alveolar	Palatal
	[w]	[j]	[ɹ]	[r]	[l]	[ʎ]
English	we	yes	red	three	love	—
Latin	qui	—	—	gloria	gloria	—
Italian	uomo	ieri	—	cantare	la	egli
French	oui	fille	—	amour	la	—
Spanish	nuestro	vaya	—	pero	la	Falla
German	—	Lilie	—	regen	Lied	—
Russian	—	Yeltsin	—	Boris	Volga	—

Front Vowels (high to low)

	[i]	[ɪ]	[e]	[ɛ]	[æ]	[a]
English	see	in	chaotic	met	cat	—
Latin	in	—	—	Deus	—	—[4]
Italian	in	—	volere	sebben	—	—[4]
French	ici	—	été	aile	—	la
Spanish	in	—	pero	ver	—	—[4]
German	ihn	in	den	denn	—	—
Russian	Boris	—	eti	etot	—	Tsar

Rounded Front Vowels (high to low)

	[y]	[ʏ]	[ø]	[œ]
French	tu	—	queue	jeune
German	für	hübsch	böse	Götter

Back Vowels (high to low)

	[u]	[ɨ]	[ʊ]	[o]	[ɔ]	[ɑ]
English	too	—	book	obey	dawn	calm
Latin	tu	—	—	—	dona	pacem
Italian	tu	—	—	amore	donna	la
French	tout	—	—	haut	donne	âme
Spanish	tu	—	—	corto	corto	la
German	du	—	Mutter	ohne	dort	Bach
Russian	dush	ty	—	—	Levin	Boris

Central Vowels

	[ɜ]	[ə]	[ʌ]
English	sir	government	done
French	—	je	—
German	—	liebende	—
Russian	—	kolokol	—

English Sounds in Detail

Consonants I: Plosives

Spellings

[b] bubble   [p] pepper
[d] daddy   [t] totter, tossed
[g] goggle, ghost, guest, exact ([gz])
[k] cat, chorus, kick, quick, accept, except ([ks]).

There is also a voiceless glottal (laryngeal) plosive whose phonetic symbol is [ʔ]. Although this sound is not spelled in English, it is often used to precede

---

[2] Not all authorities agree that **s** between vowels in Church Latin should be voiced. Of the sources cited in the bibliography, Hines, May/Tolin and Wall prefer the voiced **s** between vowels, while Moriarty insists that it should always be voiceless. Singers should pronounce this **s** as instructed by the conductor, but conductors should be consistent. Singers also need to be aware that, whereas the pronunciation of Church Latin common throughout the United States is based on Italian, a very different system of pronunciation, based on German, is current in Germany and Austria. Many conductors prefer this pronunciation for the Latin works of, for example, Mozart, Haydn, and J. S. Bach.

[3] The sound [ʒ] does not exist in native German words, but is used in some borrowings from the French, such as **Orange**.

[4] The **a** sound in these languages is transcribed by most authorities as [ɑ]. The vowel sung by Italian and Spanish singers, however, sounds brighter and more forward than the vowel in the English word **father**, also transcribed [ɑ], except that this vowel is higher in the English spoken in the Midwest than it is in the East and the South. Since French makes a distinction between [a] and [ɑ] but the other languages under consideration do not, it really makes no significant difference whether the **a** in these other languages is transcribed [a] or [ɑ]. Some authorities, too, distinguish the two sounds in German, though most consider the two pronunciations of the German **a** to differ in length rather than in vowel quality.

words beginning with vowels. Most of us use it in the expression **uh-oh**; speakers of Cockney English substitute it for [t] between vowels.

Description
The plosives (stops) are different from other consonants in that there is no sound while the consonant position is maintained; all the sound comes as the lips or tongue separate.

Advice for Singing
Because the sound of the plosives involves bringing two parts of the mouth absolutely together, it is important for singers to make firm contact with, for example, the two lips for [b] and [p], and with the blade of the tongue and the alveolar ridge for [d] and [t]. At the same time, nothing is gained by pressing the two parts of the mouth excessively, or by prolonging the contact. What is important is that the contact be firm, deft, and brief. The little explosion that accompanies the release of the consonants does not need to translate into an accent on the following vowel; that is another useless effort sometimes made to clarify stops.

Consonants II: Nasals

Spellings
[m] **mummy**   [n] **nanny**   [ŋ] **singer, finger, sink.**
Note that **n** before [k] is normally pronounced [ŋ], unless the **n** is part of a prefix.

Description
Nasal consonants are pronounced with the same organs of articulation as the stops, but with air passing through the nose.

Advice for Singing
Unlike the stops, the nasals, unless preceded by a consonant, may be sustained briefly; and they are more expressive as well as more clearly audible if they are sustained briefly, provided the dynamic level matches that of the surrounding vowels. Singers need to be careful not to allow the nasal quality to creep into the preceding vowel or to linger into the following vowel. Nasal consonants often become voiceless before voiceless stops in speech; this unvoicing should be avoided in singing.

Consonants III: Fricatives

Spellings
[v] vast, of, Stephen   [f] **fluff, philosophy, cough**
[ð] **then**   [θ] **thin**
[z] roses, reads, zone, exact ([gz]) [s] city, scene, so, class, except ([ks])
[ʒ] vision, beige, azure, pleasure
[ʃ] **ship, sure, mission, nation, ocean, precious, machine**
[h] **he, who.**

Description

Fricatives are formed by bringing two parts of the mouth close together so that a sound of friction occurs when air passes between.

Advice for Singing

Like nasals, voiced fricatives may be briefly sustained unless preceded by other consonants. Like a nasal, a fricative is more expressive and clearer if singers energize the sound that characterizes it, in this case a sound of friction between two parts of the mouth held very close together but not quite making contact. The sounds [z], [s], [ʒ], and [ʃ] are referred to as "sibilants." Because of their buzzing or hissing quality they should not be prolonged, and choruses need to be even more careful than with other consonants to articulate them precisely together.

Consonants IV: Affricates

Spellings

[dʒ] **George, judge,** e**du**cate   [tʃ] **church, ditch,** righ**teous.**

Description

An affricate is a combination of a plosive and a fricative pronounced in the same place in the mouth.

Advice for Singing

Singers should be sure both elements are in place, with a firmly articulated plosive at the beginning and a clearly-sounded fricative at the end.

Consonants V: Glides

Spellings

[w] **we, q**u**ick, lang**u**age, _one**   [hw] **which**
[j] **you, _u**nion   [ɹ] **red.**

Description

The glides [w], [j], and [ɹ] are vowels (respectively, [u], [i], and [ɜ] shortened before another vowel to the extent that they are perceived as consonants. The sound [hw] is, in a sense, the voiceless equivalent of [w], but is really [h] and [w] articulated simultaneously. Not all English-speaking people make the distinctions between **why** and the letter **Y**, or between **which** and **witch**. However, careful soloists and choral singers do make this distinction. Note that in words like **one** and **once** there is an unspelled [w]. Similarly, the "long **u**" in English includes an unspelled [j], except after some alveolar consonants. It appears in **union, cube, music, view, repute,** but not in **flute** or **rude.** Its usage after alveolar consonants will be further considered in the next section under [u].

Advice for Singing

Be careful in singing initial glides not to sustain the vowel even briefly, but to place the vowel which follows on the rhythmic value of the note. With the initial **w**, be sure to round the lips before beginning the sound, so that the listener doesn't hear, for example, "a-wee" instead of "we."

In *The Singer's Manual of English Diction* (New York: Schirmer Books, 1953), Madeleine Marshall refers to the glide [ɹ] as the "American **r**." Note that, like the other glides, this sound appears **as a consonant** only before vowels. When preceded by vowels, the English consonant letters **w, y,** and **r** do not result in consonant sounds unless they are also followed by vowels. Usually they turn the preceding vowel into a diphthong, but they should not be given consonant quality. To attempt to pronounce the **r** in words like **Lord** or **star** as consonants of any kind is as un-English as trying to pronounce the **w** in **dawn** or the **y** in **boy** as a consonant.

The style of **r** favored by the British, especially between vowels, is a voiced alveolar tap whose phonetic symbol is [ɾ]. Although this sound, called a "flipped **r**" by Madeleine Marshall, is not often used in North American speech, North American singers should cultivate it since it is necessary in virtually all foreign languages. In choral singing its use between vowels produces cleaner rhythmic focus than the glide **r** can do. Although it should not be used after alveolar consonants, its use after other consonants is often appropriate in opera or oratorio or in other dramatic contexts.

North American singers often have trouble finding a flipped **r**. Yet many Americans use it regularly in words like **three**, where the tongue naturally falls behind the alveolar ridge between the [θ] and the [i]. And almost everybody uses it in place of a [t] when **t** or **tt** appears between two vowels. Try it with words like **city** or **better**. Needless to say, these words should be sung with a pure [t]. However, speaking these words as you normally do may help you discover how to articulate the [ɾ]. Try, for example, moving rapidly from your normal pronunciation of **better** to a British-sounding pronunciation of **berry**.

Consonants VI: The Lateral

Spelling
[l] lullaby

Description
The [l] is called a lateral because its characteristic sound derives from a somewhat flattened tongue position, air escaping on the sides of the tongue.

Advice for Singing
The ear will perceive an **l** almost no matter where the tongue approaches the roof of the mouth, so long as the tongue is in the lateral position. The vocal tone is certainly better if the approach between the tongue and the roof of the mouth is made with the front rather than with the back of the tongue. In practice, we tend to use an alveolar **l** before a vowel but a more velar one after a vowel. The result often is a swallowing of vowels before **l**, in which an **o** or a **u** may actually disappear, and in which front vowels become lower and more diphthongal, so that we may hear **sell** for **sail**. Of course, the **l** has indeed disappeared in many combinations such as **alm, olk,** and **ould,** and should not be restored in singing.

Consonant Sounds in Phrasal Contexts

All the previous observations are intended primarily to apply to consonant sounds within words. What singers should be communicating, however, is not individual words, much less vowel and consonant sounds, but rather phrases and complete thoughts. When young children read aloud, they often read word by word, not connecting them into phrases and sentences. Occasionally we hear adults read this way, making it clear they are reading, not conversing. Certainly we want to avoid this when singing by connecting words and notes in such a way that words fall into sentences and notes into musical line. How words are finished depends to a considerable degree on what follows. Let us consider three possibilities: 1) consonants before a breath; 2) final consonants before vowels; and 3) final consonants followed by words beginning with consonant sounds.

1) **Final consonants before a breath**: since we hear only the end of a stop, but the beginning, middle, and end of other consonants, it is obvious that a final stop must be treated differently from other consonant sounds. The listener needs to hear the lips part or the tongue leave the roof of the mouth. An "audible release" is required; that is, a continuing of the sound until the action is complete. In the case of final nasals or fricatives, such a release is not required, and would in fact be intrusive. An audible release is especially intrusive at the end of a nasal and even moreso when [ŋ] is provided with a concluding [g]. What is needed with a final nasal, fricative, or lateral is a brief sustaining of the characteristic sound of the consonant — briefer in the case of a voiceless fricative then in the case of a nasal or a voiced fricative or a lateral, all of which can be sustained on pitch.

Failure to execute the kinds of consonant-completing motions suggested in the previous paragraph is symptomatic of an all-too-common tendency, especially of young singers, to allow the energy that launches a word or a breath-group to dissipate before the end. Another symptom of this "running-out-of-gas" finish is allowing voiced consonants to end voiceless. Too often we hear **ice** for **eyes**, **etch** for **edge**, or **height** for **hide**.

2) **Final consonants followed by vowels**: As a choral director, I have a strong preference for joining final consonants directly to words beginning with vowels in most English-language contexts. I am aware that not all choral directors agree, but my own experience suggests several strong justifications for this practice. To begin with, the attempt to finish a word with a final consonant and then start the next word with a detached vowel may result in the total disappearance of the consonant (especially in the case of a plosive) and in a rather harsh attacking of the vowel, often with a glottal stop ([ʔ]). A more important consideration is that this kind of separation is likely to result in the listener's perception of words rather than sentences and of individual tones rather than musical phrases. The result too may suggest reading rather than direct communication, because careful listening to 1) casual conversation, 2) good actors portraying casual conversation, and 3) reading by newscasters, preachers, and other public speakers reveals more connecting of words in 1) and 2) than in 3). To be sure, there are some kinds of vocal and choral music in which a kind of heightened

declamation may be a desirable effect. There are probably many more occasions, however, in which an unforced, natural communication is in order.

Obviously in any context there are some words that require separation because of special emphasis on a word beginning with a vowel (the climactic "It is enough" in Elijah's aria) or simply to avoid creating unintended new words ("cease not"). Choral directors and singers must exercise some discretion in these matters, neither mindlessly connecting nor mindlessly separating. Always bear in mind that a central goal in developing good diction is the communication of thought, both verbal and musical, not the focussing on individual units of that thought whether consonants, vowels, words, or notes.

3) **Final consonants followed by words beginning with consonant sounds**: There are a number of possibilities here. If both consonants are the same (**deep peace, cease sorrow, had done, with the, in need**), there should be a slight lengthening of sound but no separation.

A similar technique may be used if the two consonants are "homorganic;" that is, pronounced with the same organs of articulation (**in time, had not, well done, big country, help me**). Here the singer needs to make the adjustment in the mouth that clarifies each sound without separating them.

When the second word begins with a glide (**great war, red rose, beg you**), the connection may be made as with an initial vowel, since glides are vowels used as consonants. Be careful, however, to avoid the kinds of intrusive sounds that have become acceptable within words. The combination [tj] has been reduced to [tʃ] in **righteous**; in **let your** each sound should retain its integrity so as to avoid changing it to **lecher**. Similarly, [dj] should remain pure in **did you, miss you** should not rhyme with **issue**, and the sounds in **sees your** should be more distinct than those in **seizure**.

If the combination of consonants is different from any of those above, it is best to treat the final consonant as though it were the end of a phrase; that is, provide an audible release for a plosive, and energize the characteristic sound of a nasal, fricative, or lateral.

Finally, a few comments about placing consonants in terms of rhythmic notation: It is of utmost importance for singers to be fully aware that the rhythmic notation in every instance must **begin with a vowel**. This means that any initial consonant must precede the written rhythmic notation by a fraction of a beat in order for the vowel to be heard on time. The rhythmic placement of final consonants varies widely with context. In general, when a final consonant is followed by a rest, a plosive is articulated on the beat on which the rest begins. Other consonants, if they are preceded by vowels, may begin a little earlier and finish precisely on the rest. There are of course exceptions to this practice, especially when one or more voice parts continue while others rest.

Vowels in English

Singing is sometimes described as "sustained speech." What is sustained is of course the vowel sound. This sustaining of vowel sound is indeed the hallmark of someone who is really singing as opposed to speaking on pitch, chanting, or crooning. What should be the very first thing singers learn to do — sustain the vowel — is sometimes one of the hardest concepts to instill in young, inexperienced singers. Obviously, it is necessary for singers and choral directors to have a clear idea in mind as to precisely what vowel is to be sustained. In English, spelling may help a little, but not much. How do foreigners deal with discrepancies like **heat, head, hear, heart, learn**? Fortunately, those of us who grew up speaking English usually have long exposure to guide us. Sometimes, however, that exposure is to regional pronunciations which may or not be considered standard. When in doubt, consult a reliable dictionary, such as *Pronouncing Dictionary of American English* by John Samuel Kenyon and Thomas Albert Knott (Springfield: Merriam-Webster, 1953). This dictionary uses IPA symbols. Most dictionaries do not, although with a little effort the knowledgeable reader is able to fathom whatever phonetic system is used. Often dictionaries will provide two or more choices in pronunciation. A soloist may then select what he or she is comfortable with. A chorus must, however, conform to a single pronunciation in order to unify pitch and tone quality. In my small church choir, for example, there are probably at least six pronunciations of the vowel in **on**, most of them standard, acceptable, readily identifiable pronunciations. When we sing this word I usually have to remind them to decide on a single pronunciation — mine.

Once a vowel sound has been identified, singers must sustain it to the end of the note, or very nearly so. In the case of diphthongs and triphthongs, secondary sounds should be delayed until the last possible moment. Singers must not begin moving the organs of articulation toward a following consonant prematurely, either, so that the vowel will continue to sing unimpeded throughout the notated rhythm. Development of this manner of dealing with vowels is really central to the development of good vocal and choral habits. Inexperienced singers seem to want nothing so much as to keep some organ of articulation constantly in motion, and they need to be convinced that singing demands maintenance of a steady center for every vowel sound.

Vowels in Stressed Syllables

One of the distinctive characteristics of English, not always found in other languages, is that vowel letters completely alter their pronunciation from stressed to unstressed syllables. Consider, for example, the three related words **prophecy, prophesy**, and **prophetic**. The noun **prophecy** has stress only on the first syllable. The verb **prophesy**, using the same vowel letters, has secondary stress on the third syllable resulting in a different vowel sound. The adjective **prophetic**, with the same vowel letters in the first two syllables, shifts the accent to the second syllable and has different vowel sounds in both the first and second syllables. We will begin with a consideration of **vowels in stressed syllables**.

Front Vowels

Spellings
[i] me, meat, meet, field, receive, machine, people
[ɪ] it, been, England, women, myth

[ɛ] met, head, any, said, says, friend
[æ] mat, laugh.

Advice for Singing; Regional Problems

Notice the progressive lowering of the front of the tongue for these four vowels. The tip remains behind the lower teeth for all vowel sounds, but the front is almost behind the upper teeth for [i] and almost at the bottom of the mouth for [æ]. The mouth is somewhat wider for front vowels than for back vowels. However, there should be no tension in the corners of the mouth. This tension results in the edgy tone often associated with front vowels. As the tongue is lowered for [ɪ] and [ɛ], be sure it doesn't pull back away from the teeth. This pulling back results in indistinct vowel sounds and the unfocussed vocal tone often associated with unclear vowels.

In the southern United States, there is often no distinction between syllables spelled **im** and **em** or **in** and **en**. This confusion is due to a tendency to lower the [ɪ] as well as raising the [ɛ] before nasals. Pronunciations like **min** for **men** or **thim** for **them** are substandard and should be corrected for singing. At the same time, singers should be careful not to overcorrect to [æ], and should bear in mind that **England** and **English** are properly pronounced with [ɪ], and that **been** may be pronounced **bean** or **bin** but not **Ben**.

Some English speakers use a lower front vowel, represented [a], in a variety of ways. In parts of New England and New York it is often used as an alternative to [æ] in words like **half, laugh, ask,** and **can't**. Singers who do this should be careful not to apply it inappropriately to words like **at** or **land**. Madeleine Marshall, on pages 188 and 198 of *Singer's Manual of English Diction*, lists words in which [æ] may be "broadened" appropriately to [a] or [ɑ].

The sound [a] is often used in the Midwest and West as a substitute for [ɑ] in words like **father** and **hot**. In the South, a long form of [a] is often substituted for the diphthong [aɪ] as a final sound (**eye**), before a voiced consonant (**ride**), and sometimes even before a voiceless consonant (**write**). These substitutions are substandard and should be avoided in choral singing unless a regional accent is desired for some reason.

Back Vowels

Spellings

[ɑ] father, calm, hot
[ɔ] all, taut, taught, dawn, ought
[ʊ] book, put, woman, would
[u] lose, loose, blew, blue, group.

Advice for Singing; Regional Problems

Except for [ɑ], all back vowels are pronounced with lip-rounding, which varies from slight for [ɔ] to extensive for [u]. This lip-rounding is an essential part of the pronunciation of these vowels. Singers should take care that it involves projecting the lips outward away from the teeth so that the resonance in the mouth is not affected. Singers should begin the lip-rounding before the vowel sound begins rather than gradually altering the vowel in mid-note.

The lip-rounding is one aspect of the vowel [ɔ] varying widely throughout the country. As a matter of fact, this vowel, so far as the English language in North America is concerned, definitely belongs on the Endangered Species list. In most of the West and Midwest we hear **don** for **dawn**, **tock** for **talk**, and **dotter** for **daughter**. While these pronunciations are substandard, there are many words such as **on, off, gaunt, want, cough**, and **dog** in which both [ɑ] and [ɔ] are acceptable. In the Southeast (where **on** is usually pronounced **own**), the vowel often begins with [ɑ] and then rounds slightly in midcourse. This is presumably the sound that cartoonists have in mind when they write **aw**, as when my favorite Texan proclaims that his "muscle aches are lawng gawn." In New York and parts of New England we find the opposite effect: the sound begins round and then opens. All these sounds are (so far) substandard. Singers should cultivate a pure [ɔ] vowel, higher than [ɑ] and slightly rounded throughout its duration. Singers should also study lists of words in which this is the preferred vowel. Such lists may be found on pages 196–7 of the Madeleine Marshall book cited above, and on pages 57 through 61 of *Singing in English* by Richard Cox (Lawton: American Choral Directors Association, 1990).

The vowel [ʊ], like [ɪ], is often subject to lowering and centering of sound. Both should be avoided in favor of a round vowel almost as high as [u], but not so high as to create confusion between, for example, **pool** and **pull**.

In many contexts where [u] is spelled **eau, eu, ew**, or **u**, the sound often begins with the palatal glide [j] (**use, beauty, cure, few, hue, music, pew, view**). This glide is normally present unless the vowel is preceded by one of the alveolar consonant-letters **th, d, t, n, s, l**, or **r**. In the latter cases, most North Americans pronounce words like **enthusiasm, dew, tune, neutral, suit, lute**, and **rude** with [u] rather than with [ju]. Many North Americans, however, use [ju] after **d** (**due, dew**), **t** (**tune, stew**), and **n** (**neutral, new**), and after **s** when a prefix precedes (**pursue, presume**). This usage is preferable for formal singing. My recommendation would be to use [u] rather than [ju] after **th**, initial **s**, or **l** unless a British accent is required, and never to use [ju] after **r** or after **l** preceded by another consonant (**flute, blew**). For a somewhat different opinion, the reader might wish to consult Madeleine Marshall, *op. cit.*, ch. 36.

Central Vowels

Spellings

[ʌ] **up, won, flood, touch** and
[ɜ] **earth, her, bird, word, journey, fur, myrrh.**

Advice for Singing; Regional Problems

Because these vowels are central in the vowel diagram, they are pronounced in an astonishing variety of ways. For singing, they should be as open as possible. The sound [ʌ] is the unrounded form of [ɔ], and should be at least as low and open as that is, though preferably not quite [ɑ]. I have heard choral directors ask for such pronunciations as **lahv** for **love** or **wan** for **one**, but I think this is a desperation request that should be avoided if possible.

The spellings of [ɜ] all involve the letter **r**. In many parts of the U.S. and Canada, this vowel is spoken and sung very high, with a strong retroflex action of the tongue before the end of the vowel sound. For singing, this vowel too should be as open as possible, as open as [ɜ]. Since the **r** is always there in the spelling, there is no need to exaggerate the **r** color by moving the tongue before the end of the vowel sound. Bear in mind that **r** in English, like **w** and **y**, is a consonant sound only when it precedes a vowel. Otherwise these consonant letters are only vowel colors; in the case of the vowel [ɜ], the color can be minimal because the **r** is a clearly-understood part of the spelling.

Vowels in Unstressed Syllables

When English vowels are absolutely unstressed, they should not be sung with stressed vowel sounds. They are never spoken that way except by foreigners, and singing them that way suggests a foreign accent. Singers sometimes sing stressed vowels in unstressed syllables because they fear losing resonance if they sing unstressed vowels. Rather than applying Italian speech patterns to English, however, they should find ways to sing unstressed vowels with focus and resonance. We will try to suggest some ways of doing this.

I. The Schwa [ə]

There are two vowel sounds most frequently used in unstressed syllables in English. The more common is the so-called "schwa," whose phonetic symbol is [ə]. It is frequently found in unstressed monosyllables, including **a, an, the** (before a consonant), **for, of, from, or,** and. Except for the articles, these monosyllables may sometimes acquire secondary stress in certain contexts; they would then take stressed vowel sounds.

The schwa has a large variety of spellings in polysyllabic words: **a**lone, **gov**ernment, opp**o**se, hon**o**r, joy**ful**, natu**re**, mart**yr**, no**ble**, did**n't**.

This vowel should not be thought of as an unstressed [ʌ], the latter vowel being farther back and more open. The schwa is closer to [ɜ], especially when the spelling involves an **r**, but it is ideally a little higher and of course unstressed. To find a resonant focus for it, begin with [ɛ], then retract the front (not the tip) of the tongue just a little while relaxing the corners of the mouth. With the spellings involving the **r**, there will be a tendency to move the tongue into a retroflex r-colored position. This is unnecessary; the words can be understood without this potentially unattractive vowel color. At the same time, singers should avoid opening the final **er** or **or** all the way to [ʌ] or even [ɑ], as sometimes heard in the South where the two vowels in **mother** or even the two in **father** may become identical.

Note the spellings **noble** and **didn't**. In spoken English these words have no real vowel in the second syllable, but what is called a "syllabic" **l** or **n** respectively. Except in very informal vocal music, singers should use the schwa in such words.

II.

The other common vowel in unstressed syllables is [ɪ], found in these spellings:

- **i:** imagine
- final **ace, age, ate:** palace, image, palate. Note, however, that in verbs the final **ate** may acquire secondary stress, requiring a full vowel sound, as in pla**cate**, propa**gate**, etc.
- **e** in suffixes: added, suffixes, dearest, goodness. In this context, [ə] is an alternative; avoid [ɛ]!
- **e** in prefixes: become, desire, prevent, restore. Sometimes these prefixes have secondary stress and are pronounced with [i]: dethrone, prearrange, reconsider (*cf.* Marshall, *op. cit*, p.157–158).
- **e** before **a** in separate syllables: create, ethereal
- **the** before a word beginning with a vowel
- final **y, ied, ies:** city, cities, married.

In the last three contexts, as well as in **i** before [ŋ], the vowel is really a little higher than the [ɪ] normally used in stressed syllables, but it is laxer and less forward than [i]. Still, it is clear that the two vowels in **city** and **cities** are not quite identical, and that in a context like **the initial**, the vowel in **the** is a little higher than the first two in **initial**.

III.

In a few cases, [e] (nativity, fatality) or [o] (obey, follow), which are diphthongal in stressed syllables, may appear in pure form in unstressed syllables. Otherwise, English unstressed vowels should be sung as slightly retracted, relaxed front vowels. Sung as [ə] or [ɪ] they may retain vocal resonance and avoid the artificial stress or foreign-accent flavor that comes with applying full stressed vowel sounds to them.

Diphthongs and Triphthongs

The Five Principal Diphthongs

Spellings

[ɛɪ] make, maid, may, break, they, weigh
[aɪ] write, right, by, aisle, height, either (also acceptably pronounced [i])
[aʊ] out, how   [ɔɪ] voice, boy
[oʊ] beau, boat, bone, blow, toe, though.

Advice for Singing; Regional Problems

Diphthongs are combinations of two vowels on the same note. In English all diphthongs have the stress on the first vowel, the second becoming almost a glide sound. In singing diphthongs, therefore, it is important to sing a long first vowel, moving to the second as late but as clearly as possible. Choral directors may wish to provide exact rhythms for the two vowels. For example, the quarter-note "How" that opens Brahms's "How Lovely Are Thy Dwellings" might be thought of as consisting of a dotted eighth on [ha] followed by a sixteenth on [ʊ].

In all these diphthongs the second vowel is a little higher than the corresponding stressed vowel, but laxer and more central than [i] or [u]. The [ɛ] of [ɛɪ] is higher than some North Americans pronounce it in such monophthongs as **set** or **said,** especially in the South. It is, on the other hand, definitely neither as high or as tense as the [e] of French and German, though many phoneticians, such as Kenyon and Knott in the dictionary cited above, use [e] for this English sound, and [o] for the sound that we will describe as [oʊ]. The pure [e] and [o] vowels may be heard in Scotland, Ireland, and some areas of the northwestern United States and southwestern Canada. Voice students will, however, probably have a clearer understanding of the pure high [e] and [o] of French and German if they recognize the diphthongal quality of the English sounds [ɛɪ] and [oʊ].

Here are some regional problems associated with most of these sounds:

• [ɛɪ]: In the South, the [ɛ] is often so low as to be almost [æ]. In much of the Northwest and West we hear the pure [e] or Scotland and Ireland. The singer wishing to avoid a regional accent should strive for a pronunciation of the [ɛ] lower than [e], but not more than halfway to [æ], and finish the diphthong with a clear high [ɪ], close to [i] but laxer and less forward.

• [aɪ]: In the South, the second vowel is often omitted; when it is present, it is often too low, closer to [ɛ] than to [ɪ]. Southerners might do well to think of the second vowel as [i], which is how some phoneticians transcribe it. In other parts of the country, however, the second vowel really is a high, tense [i] and needs to be relaxed and retracted a little.

• [aʊ]: In most of the country the first vowel has become [æ]. Choral directors may want to work for [ɑ] rather than [a] in order to correct this tendency. The second vowel is often not round enough. In Virginia and Eastern Canada the first vowel tends to be [ʌ] or [ɜ]. All these pronunciations are substandard for singing.

• [oʊ]: Like round-vowel monophthongs, this diphthong is often not round enough. In England, the first element is usually [ɛ] or [ɜ]. In standard North American pronunciation, this diphthong should begin round and rather high and move higher at the end. There should be no tension in the corners of the mouth for this or for any other lip-rounded vowel.

Diphthongs and Triphthongs with *R*

Spellings

In discussing r as a glide consonant, we made the point that the letter **r** in English, like the letters **w** and **y**, represents a consonant sound only when a vowel follows either in the same word or in a closely-connected following word. When a vowel precedes but does not follow **r**, this letter becomes a vowel color. We have already seen how the **r** turns a preceding vowel into [ɜ] or [ə]. Here are the diphthongs and triphthongs that are created by the **r**:

[ɪə] **here, hear, hero, cheer, pier**	[ɛə] **bear, fare, fair, there, their**
[ɑə] **far, are, heart**	[ɑə] or [ɔa] **sorrow, quarrel**
[ɔə] **war, hoarse, horse, door, four**	
[ʊə] **poor, your, sure, pure** (=[pjʊə])	[aɪə] **hire, higher**
[aʊə] **flour, flower.**	

Advice for Singing; Regional Problems

A number of variant pronunciations exist. To begin with, several of the diphthongs, like some of the other vowels, have higher pronunciations in the North and lower pronunciations in the South. In Minnesota, **here** may be [hiə] and **poor** [puə], whereas in Georgia the first vowel in each may be so low and centralized as to be very close together. A "happy medium" is surely preferable for singing.

In parts of the country where r colors are strong, the second element in these diphthongs may be very high, followed by a strong retroflex gesture by the tongue. In the South, conversely — although not in Texas where the r color is very strong — the final element may approach [ʌ] or even [ɑ]. Again a happy medium is preferable; a strongly burred r is generally considered not very aesthetic in a singing tone, especially if it comes early enough to spoil the purity of the vowel preceding. The tongue motion should be slightly down from [ɪ] or [ʊ] to [ə], sideways from [ɛ] or [ɔ] to [ə], and upward from [ɑ]. This slight acknowledgment of the r is sufficient for an audience to identify the word without the intrusion of a burred r. Of course, a flipped r is totally unnecessary unless a vowel follows. In this case (**hero, Mary, soaring, curate**), both the diphthong and the r are necessary.

The diphthongs [ɛə] and [ɔə] have variants which are standard in various parts of the country. Not everyone pronounces **horse** and **hoarse** the same. Many North Americans use a lower initial vowel for the first than for the second; and the British use a pure [ɔ] rather than a diphthong in the first. These variants are perfectly acceptable. Similarly, if you find your speech uses a lower initial vowel in **air** than in **heir**, you are not alone. Pronunciations like **sher** or **sho** for **sure**, or **yer** or **yo** for **your**, are, however, definitely substandard.

Triphthongs can be tricky, especially in choral singing. Often we hear pronunciations like **are** for **our**, or **tar** for **tire**. To prevent this, make sure that the second element of the triphthong is clearly audible. At the same time, avoid turning the [ʊ] into [w] or the [ɪ] into [j] so that the triphthong is not heard as a two-syllable word.

For further information and varying opinions about English diction, the reader is encouraged to explore the additional materials found in the Bibliography at the end of the chapter.

Singing in Foreign Languages

Foreign-language singing has become very popular in the United States. In most countries of Europe, singing is done largely in the native language or in some familiar liturgical language, except in a few major opera houses. In this country, all regional opera companies feel obligated to sing standard operas in the original languages. Choral groups in universities and conservatories, and in many high schools and even some churches, are expected to sing in foreign languages. And of course voice students are expected to learn standard fare at least in Italian, German, and French. There can be no doubt that successful performances of vocal music in the original languages bring everybody closer to the music itself, **provided** the singers know what they are singing and make **every**

effort to convey the meaning of the text to the audiences, both through expressive singing and through written translations. Too often, however, people sing with little idea what the words mean and audiences are rightfully resentful. In some kinds of music (baroque arias, fugal choruses), meaning of individual words seems less critical to musical understanding. In other kinds of music (secco recitative, songs by Debussy and Wolf), the music is almost meaningless without a clear understanding of text. Therefore, the first recommendation to a vocal musician wanting to perform in foreign languages is: Understand what you are singing! Even a general idea of meaning won't really suffice; you must know enough syntax to know what words are important and expressive and what words are not. In a chorus, perhaps not every member needs to have this level of understanding, but certainly the conductor does.

Consonants

General Concerns

There are some features of foreign-language consonants that differ from English pronunciation. Singers who wish to sing with authentic pronunciation need to master these.

In Romance languages, all the alveolar consonants ([d], [t], [n], [z], [s], [l], and [r]) are pronounced with the tip of the tongue at the front rather than at the back of the alveolar ridge. Because the tongue touches the top of the upper teeth, these consonants are sometimes referred to as "dental"; this term, however, should not be interpreted to mean, as with the English dental fricatives, that the tongue passes between the upper and lower teeth.

In English and in German the voiceless stops are accompanied by a slight explosion of air, more prominent before a stressed vowel than after a stressed vowel or before a consonant. In Romance languages and in Russian these consonants must be pronounced without this aspiration.

In English and in French the doubling of a consonant seldom makes a difference in sound. In Italian, however, doubled consonants must be prolonged. This is done not by repeating the consonant, but by lingering on it slightly. This is the way we pronounce English combinations like **deep peace, full load, roommate**. Treat the Italian words **Beppe, farfalla, mamma** similarly. In German and Russian lengthening of doubled consonants is more apparent after than before a stressed vowel.

In Romance languages syllables normally begin with consonants and end with vowels. For singing, this means that consonants must be carried forward, even between words. In Italian, of course, most words end with vowels. In French, many words end with silent consonants; when the next word begins with a vowel sound, however, the consonant is sometimes carried in *liaison*. This means that a normally silent final consonant is pronounced at the beginning of the following word. Liaison is a very tricky aspect of French diction. In many cases it is mandatory, and in some it is forbidden. Liaison is applied more frequently in singing than in conversational French. The best help available is in the Introduction to *The Interpretation of French Song* by Pierre Bernac (New York: W.W. Norton, 1970). A related matter of French diction is the *elision* of the final e before a word beginning with a vowel, again insuring that the syllable begin with a consonant. Note that the two words *liaison*, meaning "linking," and *elision*, meaning "omission," have very different meanings and should not be interchanged.

The glottal stop [ʔ] is a more distinctive feature of German than of English. In German speech, most words beginning with a vowel will begin with this sound. German singers, however, use it more sparingly for expressive emphasis and for clearly-indicated word separations.

In German, voiced plosives become voiceless at the end of words or syllables (Tod, weg, obgleich) or in a final voiceless cluster (hübsch, Siebs). In Russian, this is the case with voiced fricatives as well as stops (Prokofiev, vodka).

Consonant Sounds not Found in English

Some of the familiar foreign languages contain consonant sounds not found in English. Romance languages contain a palatal nasal [ɲ], spelled **gn** in French and Italian and **ñ** in Spanish. The sound is similar to the **ni** in the English word **union**, but with the [n] and the [j] articulated simultaneously, the tongue in the [j] position.

In Spanish, the voiced plosives [b], [d], and [g] become voiced fricatives between vowels, even between words within a breath group. The voiced labial fricative [β], spelled **b** or **v**, is close in sound to [v] but made with the two lips rather than the lower lip and upper teeth. The voiced dental fricative may be represented [ð] but, when spelled with a **d** in Spanish it is pronounced at the top rather than at the bottom of the upper teeth. The voiced velar fricative [ɣ], spelled **g**, is the voiced equivalent of [x], which we will describe below.

German has two additional voiceless fricatives, both spelled **ch**. The symbol [ç] represents the palatal fricative found in such German words as **ich, breche, Mädchen, Bücher, euch.** To find this sound, put the tongue in a position for the vowel [i] and blow air across it. The German [j] (jeder, ja) is really a voiced palatal fricative, pronounced with the tongue closer to the palate than in English. The symbol [x] represents a voiceless velar fricative, the voiceless equivalent of [ɣ]. The sound is made by air passing between the raised back of the tongue and the hard palate. This is the sound found in such German words as **ach, Buch, noch,** and **auch.** It is also the pronunciation of the Spanish **j** (jota, mujer and **g** before **e** and **i** (gente, Gilda). In Russian, [x] is usually transliterated **kh** (Khrushchev, Rakhmaninov).

Several foreign languages have affricates not found in English. In German the [pf] (Pferd, Schwarzkopf) is an affricate, the two consonants pronounced almost simultaneously. The affricate [ts], with the [t] and the [s] closer together than in the English word **gets**, appears in Italian (pizza), German (Mozart), Russian (tsar), and other Slavic languages. The voiced equivalent [dz] appears in Italian, where it is also spelled **z** and **zz** (zefiro, mezzo), requiring the use of a dictionary to distinguish it from [ts].

The common North American **r** as a retroflex glide is absent from most other languages. And in most other languages **r** has a consonant sound after vowels. English singers must be especially careful not to use the retroflex glide, or any English-sounding r-colored vowels, after vowels in other languages.

Nothing is more intrusive than the **r** color in such Latin words as **morte æternam**, such Italian words as **cor, languir,** such French words as **amour, vers,** and such German words as **werden, für.** Nor should the "uvular **r**" often found in conversational French and German be used in formal singing. Most foreign languages require a tongue-tip **r** flipped or trilled off the front of the alveolar ridge. Students of foreign languages need to master this sound and then know where a single tap is appropriate and when a roll is required in each language. It has already been suggested that the sound regularly substituted for **t** between vowels in North American speech (better, got to) is a voiced alveolar tap. The difference between this [r] and a [d] is really the direction in which the tongue moves across the alveolar ridge. For [d] it moves down and out, with [r] it moves back and up.

Spanish and Italian have a palatal lateral [ʎ]. Spelled **ll** in Spanish (**llama, Falla**) and **gl** in Italian (**Gigli, Pagliacci**), this sound closely resembles the **lli** in the English word **million** except that the [l] and the [j] are pronounced simultaneously, with the tongue in the [j] position. In Latin America, the **ll** has in most locations been reduced to [j] (the German fricative in parts of Argentina and Uruguay, but the glide elsewhere). This appears to have been the historical development of the French [j] in words like **fille, travail;** it is also the usual fate of [lj] in English words like **million** and **William** in most casual speech of North America.

Russian has palatalized forms of most consonant sounds, used preceding the five "soft" vowels. When these vowels are initial, the word begins with the palatal glide [j] (**Yalta, Yeltsin**). Within a word, however, the effect is similar to that of the [ɲ] or the [ʎ] in that the consonant and the [j] are articulated not successively but simultaneously.

Vowels

General Concerns

Of major concern is the absence of any concept of vowel purity on the part of many English-speaking singers. Although our short vowels maintain some semblance of purity during their brief duration, virtually all our long vowel sounds become diphthongs. We have observed this with the "long **a**" and the "long **o**." Even [i] and [u] as used in English speech begin a little more open than they end. It's very hard for English singers to maintain the vowel purity required to sing in other languages. At the same time, one of the reasons voice teachers like to use foreign languages, especially Italian, is that the vowel purity required is beneficial in developing vocal resonance and legato musical line.

Of special difficulty for English-speaking singers is avoiding the rather vague treatment of unstressed syllables that characterizes our language. Of all the foreign languages used for singing, only Russian has different pronunciations of the same vowels depending on stress. The Russian **o**, for example, has three different pronunciations depending on whether it has full stress, secondary stress, or no stress. The English-speaking singer must exercise great care that vowels in Latin, Italian, and Spanish have precisely the same quality whether stressed or unstressed — another reason voice teachers favor Italian. In French and German, only the **e** varies between [e] or [ɛ] in stressed syllables and [ə] in unstressed ones. The German schwa is essentially identical to the English one if the latter is properly focussed. The French schwa should be more forward and more rounded than either the English or the German.

Combining vowels in foreign languages can be bewildering. The appearance of two vowels side by side can mean two separate syllables, as it usually does in Latin, or some newly-spelled single sound, as it usually does in French. More often such a combination means something in-between — an articulation in which each vowel is sounded but one is predominant in length and/or dynamics. The problem for the singer is to determine which vowel is the predominant one, especially when the composer has provided a single note. In Italian, most of whose words end in vowels, the appearance of two or more vowels between words, all on one note, can be especially puzzling. It helps to realize that in Romance languages **i** and **u** are weak vowels, as is **y** in Spanish. This means that if **i** or **u** precedes another vowel it usually becomes a glide except in many Italian three-letter words. It also means that when **i** or **u** follows another vowel in Italian, or when **u** or **y** follows another vowel in Spanish, a diphthong is formed in which the first vowel is predominant. The problems of the vowels between words in Italian can often be resolved too by following the normal stress patterns of the words in isolation, or by observing the syntactical importance of the words, monosyllabic prepositions and conjunctions being weak. For more details, consult *Singers' Italian* by Evelina Colorni (New York: Schirmer Books, 1970).

Vowel Sounds not Found in English

Most languages have two forms of **e** and **o**. Typically, both vowels will be lower, laxer, and shorter when followed by a consonant in the same syllable and higher, tenser, and longer when ending a syllable. This can be a helpful generalization, but the singer must master the exceptions for each language. Of greater importance is establishing the basic ability to make the distinction. In English, although "long **e**" and "long **o**" are sometimes represented by [e] and [o] respectively, we have seen that they are really diphthongal in standard pronunciation. This makes it difficult for English-speaking singers to avoid pronunciations like [mizeɪreɪreɪ] for the Latin **miserere** and [oʊmoʊn] for the French **aumône**. Listening carefully to native-speaking singers suggests that the distinctions between [e] and [ɛ] and between [o] and [ɔ] are greater in French and German than in Italian and Spanish, but the distinctions exist in these languages as well. Latin is usually sung with the open [ɛ] and [ɔ]; English-speaking singers still need to be on guard against singing diphthongs.

French and German have a system of front vowels pronounced with lip-rounding. Each of these vowels has the tongue position of a front vowel combined with the lip position of a back vowel.

[y] has the tongue position of [i] and the lip position of [u].
> French: **du, dû, eut**
> German: **für, Asyl.**

[ʏ] has the tongue position of [ɪ] and the lip position of [ʊ].
> German: **hübsch, Myrthe.**

[ø] has the tongue position of [e] and the lip position of [o].
   French: Dieu, nœud
   German: Gœthe, höhe.
[œ] has the tongue position of [ɛ] and the lip position of [ɔ].
   French: cœur, jeune, orgeuil
   German: Götter.

The French schwa is essentially an unstressed [œ]. The French [y] is also used as a glide when it precedes another vowel (lui, juin, nuage). The phonetic symbol is [ɥ]; it has the lip position of [w] and the tongue position of [j]. The tongue position is hard for English-speaking singers, who tend to substitute [w], or, worse yet, [u].

Opposite to the rounded front vowels in French and German is the un-rounded back vowel [ɨ] of Russian, with the lip position of [i] and the tongue position of [u]. In the usual Russian translation, the Cyrillic letter is represented by a y. When it stands alone in a syllable, as in Baryshnikov or Chernobyl, the y usually means [ɨ]. If the y precedes a vowel, as in Yeltsin or Yalta, it represents [j].

Finally, French contains four nasal vowels:
   [ɛ̃] vin, bien, symphonie, saint, hein
   [ɑ̃] dans, en, jambe, empire
   [ɔ̃] bonbon, bombe
   [œ̃] un, parfum.

To make these sounds, simply lower the soft palate to allow some air to pass through the nose while singing the corresponding vowel. Nasal vowels are in order only when the following n or m is final or when it precedes another consonant, **not** when the n or m is doubled or when it precedes a vowel. When the nasal consonant precedes a pronounced consonant, be especially careful not to pronounce the n or m. The result should resemble the way most of us pronounce English words like **jump, can't**, or **think**, with a nasal vowel and no really consonantal m or n. Avoid this in singing English; it's legal in French.

Obviously, no attempt has been made here to provide detailed rules for pronouncing any of these foreign languages. For such rules, the reader is referred to the sources listed noted in the text, especially the works by Carnellada/Madsden, Colorni, Cox, Grubb, Hines, Jones/Ward, Moriarty, and Wall.

Bibliography

Carnellada, Maria Josefa and John Kuhlmann Madsden, *Pronunciación del español*. Madrid: Editorial Castalia, 1987.

Colorni, Evelina, *Singer's Italian*. New York: Schirmer Books, 1970.

Cox, Richard G., *The Singer's Manual of German and French Diction*. New York: Schirmer Books, 1970.

Cox, Richard G., *Singing in English*. Lawton, Oklahoma: American Choral Directors Association, 1990.

De Boor, Helmut, Hugo Moser, and Christian Winkler, ed., *Siebs, Deutsche Aussprache*. Berlin: Walter de Gruyter & Co., 1969.

Grubb, Thomas, *Singing in French*. New York: Schirmer Books, 1979.

Hines, Robert S., *Singer's Manual of Latin Diction and Phonetics*. New York: Schirmer Books, 1975.

Jones, Daniel, and Dennis Ward, *The Phonetics of Russian*. Cambridge: Cambridge University Press, 1969.

Kenyon, John Samuel, *American Pronunciation*. Tenth Edition. Ann Arbor, Michigan: George Wahr Publishing Company, 1958.

Marshall, Madeleine, *The Singer's Manual of English Diction*. New York: Schirmer Books, 1953.

Marshall, Yale, *Singing Fluent American Vowels*. Minneapolis: Pro Musica Press, 1993.

May, William V., and Craig Tolin, *Pronunciation Guide for Choral Literature*. Reston, Virginia: Music Educators National Conference, 1987.

Moriarty, John, *Diction*. Boston: E. C. Schirmer Music Company, 1975.

Odom, William, *German for Singers*. New York: Schirmer Books, 1981.

Pfautsch, Lloyd, *English Diction for Singers*. New York: Lawson-Gould Music Publishers, 1971.

Tiffany, William R., and James Carrell, *Phonetics: Theory and Application*. Second Edition. New York: McGraw Hill Book Company, 1977.

Uris, Dorothy, *To Sing in English*. New York: Boosey & Hawkes, 1971.

Wall, Joan, *et al.*, *Diction for Singers*. Dallas: Pst...Inc., 1990.

Wall, Joan, *et al.*, *International Phonetic Alphabet for Singers*. Dallas: Pst...Inc., 1989.

Wise, Claude Merton, *Applied Phonetics*. Englewood Cliffs: Prentice Hall, 1957.

Rehearsal Technique:
A Guide for Planning the Choral Rehearsal.

James M. Jordan

Introduction

An efficient rehearsal technique is a marriage of two basic skills — analysis and listening. First, a conductor must be able to identify the major technical and musical "stumbling blocks" that the choir will encounter as it goes about the work of learning a new piece of music. Therefore, analysis might be better labeled as the art of prediction, where one anticipates ahead of the rehearsal those spots and specific vocal technique issues which will inhibit the singing of the piece. The conductor, prior to the rehearsal, needs to spend considerable time studying each voice part for every conceivable problem that may lurk within the score. The conductor's task is not only to identify the technical/musical problems, but to arrive at a way of giving "tools" to the singers so that they can master those technical/musical challenges within the score.

Mastering the rehearsal procedure, however, goes beyond the identification of technical/musical problems and their solutions. The most challenging aspect of rehearsal procedure for the young conductor is listening. One must become comfortable with the myriad details of that analysis so that there is, in reality, no "analytical thinking" going on by the conductor as the music is being made by the singers. The conductor needs to be able to breathe for and with the choir and to open himself to listen to the sounds being made by the ensemble: to receive sounds being made by the singers and to, in effect, "store" them for "analysis" after the ensemble has completed singing. A common fault of new conductors is to concurrently listen and analyze while the music is being created by the ensemble. If this occurs, the amount of music that is accurately heard and retained as well as the conductor's ability to give the choir needed tools, will be greatly diminished. A common concern expressed by young conductors after their initial rehearsals is that "there is so much to listen to; I don't know what to focus on." The problem is one of simply trying to "think" too much while the music is being sung, instead of concentrating complete energies and focus upon listening. A conducting student once characterized the experience of listening in a rehearsal as having "ears as big as my body." That analogy is not far from the truth.

While it is important that the beginning conductor focuses on the *what, why* and *how* of rehearsing, it is even more important while conducting (rehearsing) to develop the skill of total listening *without* concurrent analysis. Students who temporarily "shut off" the cognitive side of their brain discover, to their amazement, that they can "hear" better as they conduct. They also are amazed that after the music ceases, the wonders of the cognitive/thinking side of the brain continue to function well and that the musical "mind" is able to quickly "replay" to the cognitive side of the brain the music that has just been sung. It is at that moment that effective rehearsal procedure is born. If the potential problems have been identified before the rehearsal through score study, the cognitive mind has little difficulty matching a previously identified problem with the sound in the conductor's "ear." When the two processes are developed separately, the hopeless listening/pedagogical muddle that usually plagues young conductors will not exist. A conductor who intensely listens at all times during the music making process and then applies a pedagogical solution to the musical problem at hand is well on the way to achieving a rehearsal technique mastered by many of the great choral conductors.

This chapter will attempt to identify the issues which should be located and studied before the rehearsal. The pedagogical solution—the techniques of actually teaching and fixing problems—will not be found here; but this chapter will tell you where to find solutions. While it looks like an enormous list, the suggestions that follow are designed to help you prepare a score for rehearsal and to allow listening to occur. One *listens* by *listening*. One does not listen by thinking. Nor does one think by listening. Listening is of the moment and is spontaneous. It is similar to play in childhood! Listening is the conductor's major technical asset. Score study provides solutions to potential problems, but those problems must be identified through active hearing. Rehearsal procedures merely provide the "how" of fixing problems after they have been heard.

The author will attempt to identify as many possible choral "problems" along with their solutions or tools as space will allow. The problems are grouped under headings such as "rhythm," etc. The format is designed to allow user "friendliness" and to allow the beginning conductor to be guided through the process of identifying various rehearsal technique issues. While many solutions are provided in the text, the reader is referred to the text by Frauke Haasemann and James Jordan, *Group Vocal Technique* published by Hinshaw Music (1991) — hereafter referred to as "GVT."

At the conclusion of each section, the reader will find the following: (**RR 1, 18, 22**). This is a cross reference to the References and Resources bibliography at the end of the chapter. Numbers listed after the **RR** refer to the number of the book in the list that can provide further background and information concerning information discussed in that particuliar section.

Preparing and Marking the Score

The first step in preparing for the rehearsal is the obvious step of preparing the score. The learning of the notes and the rhythms of all the parts is prerequisite to the other levels of score preparation. The following steps should be followed.

   1. Hum or moan through the piece. This technique allows the conductor to actively participate in and make decisions concerning the phrase direction of the work. The humming or moaning establishes a connection between the notes on the page and the sensation of a musical line in motion. It is during this activity when breath locations are established.

   2. Play and sing all parts. Play and sing all parts individually. Then, play one part and sing another until all combinations of parts have been experienced. Finally, begin by singing one part and then switching immediately to another part. This procedure is especially helpful in contrapuntal music.

3. *When preparing a score, always prepare it from a sitting or standing position that is reflective of the singing process.* There is an intimate but unseen connection between body posture and the music learning process. When a piece of music is performed the body's "muscle memory" will recreate the posture and body alignment that was in evidence as the score was being learned. The conductor should view score preparation as both an aural and kinesthetic exercise. The kinesthetic attitude of the body is established at the time the initial note learning of the score takes place. (**RR** 5, 14)

One of the most obvious "helps" in rehearsal technique is often overlooked by both experienced and novice conductors. Marking the score in an organized manner will assist both the preparation for rehearsal and serve as a visual reminder for the conductor in rehearsal. While such score marking may be time consuming, most conductors find that it ultimately hastens the score learning process.

The key to score marking is to establish a consistent procedure for marking the score. That is, establish standard color codes for the most important aspects of the score. Below is a suggested color coding system that may be used as a model. Unless otherwise indicated, colors refer to a colored pencil.

red	circle all forte dynamics
green	circle all piano dynamics
dark green	circle all mezzo forte dynamics
light green highlighter	trace over all crescendi and decrescendi
orange	enlarge all meter changes
yellow highlighter	trace and track thematic and immitative material
blue	indicate textual words that receive stress
purple	connect notes between voice parts that are in suspension or create a dissonance
pink highlighter	trace over accents
maroon	place harmonic analysis underneath score; use highlighter to draw attention to unusual harmonic progressions
turquoise	circle thirds in triads and other intervals which may cause intonation problems
light green	underline all tempo changes
pencil	indicate necessary possible vowel modifications above voice part and trace over with blue highlighter; draw arrows where necessary to track entrances

Breathing With And For The Singers

Breathing is often overlooked by conductors because it is such an obvious part of the singing process. The conductor should not only breathe with the choir, but for the choir. However, when conducting, most conductors cease to breathe as singers. The result is that 1) the conductor is unable to "set" the color of the sound for a particular piece of music; 2) a lack of breathing with the accompanying "opening" process that allows breath to fall into the body is directly proportional to a conductor's ability to hear well, and the less one breathes, the less one will hear; and, 3) the less that one breathes, the more one will find that his conducting gesture becomes "locked" and rigid. The result is that a choir is not able to sing freely and that the conductor is able to hear less. Generally speaking, if a muscled or pressed gesture is "held," the less the conductor will be able to hear. A held gesture is one which does not allow for a release of energy, sometimes called a natural rebound. A "held" gesture is many times worsened because the conductor holds the breath in the body after it has been inhaled. Such "held" air results in a heavy and pressed gesture. The lack of breathing by the conductor coupled by overly physical gesturing by the conductor that is not borne out of listening will most certainly make listening for the conductor a difficult, if not impossible task.

When learning scores, it is important to have a clear sense of where the choir will breathe within the phrase structure and between phrases. This serves several important functions. The consistent tempo of a piece is often altered by the conductor because he does not breathe with the singers and hence rushes the tempo. One of the most important factors in maintaining a consistent tempo is to make sure that the breath process of the singers is rhythmic. In the initial stages of the score preparation process it is very important for the conductor to not only breathe where the choir breathes, but to exhale air constantly in the motion of the piece to simulate the forward motion of the phrases. One can also "moan" or "hum" in a monotone. Regardless of the rhythm of the work, the "humming" or "moaning" should be *continuous* and should not echo the melodic rhythm (exact rhythm) of the piece. This encourages the conductor to always be connected with the "sound" of the piece while learning the score. One should avoid learning a piece of music without connecting oneself and one's singing mechanism to the ongoing rhythmic motion and flow of the work. Moreover, if the conductor does this, it will help to free the conducting gesture. (**RR** 3, 5, 20, 30, 35)

Breathing the "color" of the style and affect of the piece. While programatic approaches to music-making can be dangerous, it is very helpful to consider the character of the breath for each piece that you conduct and rehearse. The vocal "color" of a piece is set through the inhalation process. Consequently, the conductor must pre-determine the color and mood of the breath that is taken to start phrases so that the color of the ensemble is set in the breath that they take. It is often effective to ask the choir to "inhale the color purple." Such a technique will elicit a darker sound than if one asks the choir to breathe "red," and so on. The reader is referred to Chapters 5,6 and 7 in *GVT*.

Teach the breath process that connects phrases. Do not conduct a phrase ending; rather, breathe for the next phrase. When teaching a piece, take special care to teach how the breath begins simultaneously with the end of a phrase. Amateur singers tend to finish the phonation of the tone and then start the breath process for the start of the next phrase. If one examines the process as a singer, the inhalation of breath happens at the same moment as the finishing of the tone. When conducting, the conductor should not conduct the end of the phrase, but simply breathe for the next phrase — cue the breath. By doing so, the previous phrase ending will "take care of itself" and the tone color, pitch and forward rhythmic motion of the phrase will be maintained. (**RR** 11,12)

Neutral Syllables for Rehearsal: Why, When and What Ones?

One of the rehearsal decisions that conductors are faced with when rehearsing a piece concerns the choice of what syllables should be used in the initial rehearsal/reading/learning of the piece. Many conductors choose a favorite rehearsal syllable and begin rehearsing the piece without considering why a syllable is chosen. In actuality, the choice of a syllable or syllables is one of the most important pedagogical decisions that a conductor makes in preparing for the rehearsal.

Before a discussion of neutral syllables for rehearsal can take place, the conductor must understand why it is very inefficient to begin the rehearsal of a work with text. There are both vocal pedagogical reasons and learning efficiency reasons for using neutral syllables.

First, a discussion of the use of text versus neutral syllables. Without entering into a lengthly discussion of the psychology of music learning, suffice it to say that to begin rehearsing with text confounds the music learning process for the choir. Research in the psychology of music has proven the value of neutral syllable teaching for children through adults. By using a neutral syllable, the conductor, in essence, limits the number of variables which may cause problems for the choir both musically and vocally. Moreover, the neutral syllable focuses the hearing of the choir on the basic elements of the music, i.e. rhythm, pitch, line and tone quality. Without the "crutch" of the text, the choir must commit to memory those basic elemental music ideas within the score. Perhaps an analogy will clarify this point. Have you ever asked a person with little music experience to sing the National Anthem without words? In all likelyhood, they cannot. The reason for this is because they learned the tune in association with the words, and the tune is forever bound to the words. The person is unable to separate the music from the words and focus upon the music. Hence, adjustments in pitch, rhythm, etc. are almost impossible to make. An amateur choir which learns a piece immediately with text will find it difficult to separate out music elements for repair, such as accurate pitch and rhythm, because the notes and rhythms of the piece are psychologically married to the text. Teaching text too early inhibits music expression and spontaneous music making. It also does not allow for accurate pitch and accurate rhythm in a consistent tempo to be "schooled in." Pitch, rhythm and the stylistic colors of the piece must be in the choir's ear before text is added. To do otherwise is a serious rehearsal oversight by the conductor in preparing for the rehearsal.

Second, delay text as long as possible until the music elements of the score have been learned. The choice of learning a piece on one or two vowels is central to the rehearsal process. Neutral syllables chosen for the correct reasons can build a choral sound with the appropriate breath support from the initial stages of learning a piece. If the choices are made correctly on one or two vowel sounds, when text is added, the conductor will find that a consistent "sound" has been built into the choir that transfers easily and immediately to other vowels. Rules to consider are as follows:

1. *Rehearse only on pure vowels; no diphthongs!* A choir should always rehearse on pure vowels. Diphthongs such as "doe," "tay" will produce unclear sounds, many times manifested as pitch problems. Because it is a challenge to get a choir to sing a diphthong correctly, virtually each person in the choir places the second vowel at a different time, hence the choral color and pitch problems. While diphthong execution must be taught to the choir, they are best handled after the music has been learned on a neutral syllable!

2. *Be careful with the vowel sounds chosen when they move into extreme high and low ranges for all voice parts.* No matter what pure vowel is chosen for rehearsing, caution must be used when those vowels move out of middle register for each voice part. The conductor should give "helps" to the choir when the part moves into those extremes according to the suggestions below. See GVT, Chapter 18.

3. *Choose a consonant to proceed the vowel that reflects both the rhythmic spirit of the piece and will assist with the correct vocal production of the sound for a particular music style period.* The choice of what consonant should proceed the chosen vowel is also very important. The choice of the consonant can quickly establish the rhythmic style (legato, marcato, staccato, etc.) of the piece. The choice of the consonant can also "launch" the appropriate resonance (bright vs. dark) for the style of the piece.

4. *When in doubt about what vowel to choose, select "oo," "ee" or the German "ü."* The vowels which build a choral sound with head tone are the "oo," the "ee" and the German "ü." The choir should be asked to perform these vowels with rounded lips, like a fish. This seemingly ridiculous analogy brings immediate focus to the vowel and also promotes frontal resonance!

5. *Avoid the "ah" vowel!* While the choir may have an easier time producing the "ah" vowel in various registers, the ease of execution does not outweigh the vocal problems it may foster. The vowel is a dangerous one to use because 1) it encourages the use of lower or "chest" register singing in amateurs; 2) it flats easily because of the possible lack of head tone in the vowel by amateurs; 3) the vowel requires a free and open vocal tract; 4) it requires consistently low breath support which is difficult for amateurs and 5) it is more difficult to adjust intonation with this vowel. (**RR** 9,10, 11,12,13,19)

Choosing a vowel for rehearsing.

Below are listed the possible vowels for rehearsing with explanations for choosing one vowel over another (Note: vowels are spelled phonetically). *The rule below should be observed for all vowels:*

Foundation Rule for All Vowels: Open the mouth like "ah" in the high range and maintain a fishmouth! In going up, drop the jaw gradually; when descending, close the mouth gradually.

Vowel and Explanation for Use

oo

Is a healthy vowel for general vocalization because it fosters head tone for all voice parts. Should be performed with a slight fishmouth. In upper ranges, women should continue to sing pure "oo" with a fishmouth with the space of "uh"; men should sing the "oo"vowel that is in the word "foot."

ee

Is also a very good vowel for learning a piece. This vowel also fosters head tone for all voice parts and should be performed with a slight fishmouth. In upper ranges, women should continue to sing pure "ee" with a fishmouth with the space of "uh." Men should sing the vowel that is in the word "him." Use of this vowel fosters a brighter sound in the choir.

German "ü"

This vowel is the most desirable vowel for most circumstances because it combines the best qualities of both of the above vowels: the head quality of the "oo" vowel with the the brightness of the "ee" vowel. This vowel is especially useful in initial readings of works sung with the beginning voiced consonant combination of "ny." The use of the voiced "ny" demands the singer "connect" the vocal sound to the support mechanism. The "nyee" should be sung very bright so that the center of the pitches can be heard and the choir can begin to hear and develop appropriate intonation. Once the accurate pitches have been "schooled in" through this brighter (almost French) vowel sound, rehearsal can progress to other vowel sounds. For both voice parts, the jaw should be dropped when ascending. Maintain a fishmouth! Use of this vowel fosters a brighter sound in the choir.

o

Generally should be avoided because of its diphthong.

i (as in "night')

Generally should be avoided because of its diphthong.

ah

While this vowel can be used, it should be used with caution. This vowel fosters chest quality in all voice parts and is difficult to monitor in a choral situation. If it must be used, it should be sung very bright, with a fishmouth. The choir should also be reminded that "ah" lives in the same "house" that "oo" does. In upper ranges, the women should think "oo" into the sound; men should sing the vowel that is in the word "but." This vowel is useful in building a darker choral sound.

Choosing a consonant for rehearsing

Non-Legato Consonants. In selecting a consonant or consonants to pair with vowels for rehearsing, the style of the music is a major determining factor that helps to determine what consonant or consonant combinations should be used. The conductor should choose a consonant which will most closely re-create the rhythmic style of the music. For example, for a piece that is very rhythmic such consonants as t, p, b, and d could fit your needs. The choir should be instructed to spring quickly into the vowel with the shortest possible consonant, thus creating a long vowel.

Legato Consonants. For works that are more legato that need a consistent approach to continuous line and continuous sound, voiced consonants should be used, such as m, n, ny, v and z. The choir should be told to voice the consonant and lengthen it so that it has time to sound the pitch before moving to the vowel sound. The voiced consonants are also useful to build a "connection" between the "support" and the voice. If the conductor insists on the voicing of these consonants, he will be insuring that support is connected to the following vowels. It is also very helpful to intersperse humming and chewing of a sustained sound between long periods of rehearsing with the above consonants. "Humming and chewing" with "thick lips" (that are slightly touching) helps bring continued relaxation to the jaw and vocal mechanism in addition to continuing to foster a healthy and resonant forward placement.

Tip of the tongue "l" cautions. If the consonant "l" is selected, care must be taken to instruct the choir concerning the correct articulation of a "tip of the tongue 'l'." Many American choirs articulate this consonant by humping the middle of the tongue and touching the middle portion of the hard palate. This will immediately place the tone farther back than desired and most likely will produce a flatness on the pitch, plus considerably slow the rhythm of the piece. The choir should be instructed to articulate the "l" with the portion of the tongue immediately behind the tip, touching that area to the gumline above the upper front teeth. This simple adjustment will insure that the sound maintains a forward placement, in addition to maintaining rhythmic integrity.

Alternate neutral syllables and consonantal combinations to reflect changing textures. When working through the initial reading of a piece on a neutral syllable, it is possible to establish the texture of sections within the piece by alternating neutral syllables. For example, if one begins a work that has a rhythmic, marcato quality, "du" may be used. For a contrasting legato section, the choir could be asked to sing "noo." (**RR** 11,12, 13, 23,34)

Rhythm

After a decision has been made concerning what syllables would best establish the character of the piece, it is important to establish how the piece moves, it's forward motion, and the nature of the forward rhythm which carries the line. It is important to remember that each singer will bring his or her "personal"tempo to the reading and learning of a piece. That is, each singer will hear the tempo of the piece slower or faster than the tempo that the conductor has chosen. The establishment of "communal" tempo must be undertaken for each new work rehearsed.

Establishing Consistent Tempo

Consistent tempo may be established using several different techniques. Regardless of the technique chosen, several cognitive elements concerning the pedagogy of consistent tempo must be kept in mind before any techniques can be used and be expected to be retained by the ensemble.

1. *Large body movement should be used as the basic starting point for establishing consistent tempo.* As the "beats" of the piece are chanted or played, the choir should be able to move their bodies in free response to the basic rhythmic pulse of the piece. Body movement can take the form of swaying from side to side; clapping hands across the body midline as if tossing dough from hand to hand; moving the hands and arms in an outward circular motion. It is important to remember that basic rhythmic impulse is learned through what amounts to a disturbance of the body kinesthesia. Swaying from side to side upsets the equilbrium of balance due to the movement of fluid within the inner ear. It is that disequilibrium which first establishes pulse in its broadest sense. Regardless of the activity chosen, the choir should chant on a neutral syllable on each major pulse of the piece until the ensemble does not rush or slow the tempo.

If the ensemble cannot hold a consistent tempo, they must be taught by rote and experience, through conductor example, the feeling of a consistent tempo in the following manner. The conductor should first demonstrate rushing or slowing. The choir should listen, perhaps with eyes closed. The conductor should then demonstrate a consistent tempo to the choir . The choir should keep the large beat in their feet while the conductor chants (using a neutral syllable) in a consistent tempo. The choir should then echo, on a neutral syllable (such as "bum") the rhythm of the piece.

2. *After large body movement has been established, the large beat (macro beat) should be performed with the feet.* The first subdivision (micro beat) should be performed with a light clapping motion in the hands. The rhythm of the piece (melodic rhythm) is spoken simultaneously with the action of the feet and hands. A consistent teaching strategy is important in teaching consistent tempo and the melodic rhythm of the piece to the choir. If the procedure for teaching the rhythmic structure is altered with each piece, it will take longer for the choir to musically understand and retain the rhythm of the work. Rhythm learning is most efficient when the same "input" mechanism is used, i.e. the combination of feet, hands and mouth, each always performing the same element of the

rhythm, macro beat, micro beat and the melodic rhythm. One may view the action of the feet and hands as the "input and filing mechanism" for the rhythmic patterns of the piece.

3. *Always perform the melodic rhythm of the piece with neutral syllables first before employing other techniques such as counting, etc.* It is important to remember that before any rhythmic syllable system is used by the choir, that the melodic rhythm of the piece should be chanted in a monotone syllable such as "bum," "du-bee-du-bee " (useful in passages using eighth note or sixteenth note runs), "tee," "tah," "pum," "pah," "nyee," "nu," "du," etc. By limiting the choir to such neutral syllables until the pitches and rhythm have been stabilized, the choir will focus on listening without the cognitive confusion that ensues when a rhythm syllable system is added. Amateur singers, especially those who do not read music, will complain. In fact, at first, rehearsals may move slower. The conductor will find, however, that the "ears" and overall listening ability of the choir will show a marked improvement. In general, follow the following sequential procedure when rehearsing a piece. Remember that if you skip a few of the steps, and difficulty results, you should return to step one.

• *Have the choir locate the "large beat" of the music with large body movement,* i.e. rocking, swaying, swinging, etc.

• After the choir has been able to move with their bodies to the "large beats," then have the choir put the macro beat in their feet, the micro beat in their hands. Make sure that the choir is in a consistent "communal tempo."

• After the choir is able to locate the macro beat with their feet, and the micro beat with their hands, have them chant the melodic rhythm of their part on a neutral syllable simultaneously with keeping the macro and micro beat in their feet and hands.

• After the choir is able to perform the melodic rhythm in the above fashion in a consistent tempo, the conductor may ask them to use any syllable or number counting system that is preferred.

Remember that before any number or counting system is used with the choir, the choir must have demonstrated to the conductor an ability to perform the rhythm of the piece on a neutral syllable in a consistent tempo. A number system used prematurely will inhibit the choirs ability to hear and learn the rhythm of the piece!

The Use of Numeric Counting Systems

Many different counting systems that use numbers are employed by conductors as means of establishing and re-establishing rhythmic pulse within a work. It is also a valuable technique to teach the forward motion and internal rhythm pulse of a work to a choir. It is additionally useful to clearly establish those points within the music for rhythmic breath and phrasing. The most commonly used technique is to count the music with the numeric syllables " One and Two and Tee and Four and." (Note that the word "tee" is substituted for the word "three." The consonantal combination of "th" tends to slow the tempo of the piece.) Aside from the usual use of the counting system by all members of the choir, some variations in the technique add to rehearsal variety and maintain interest.

1. Use numeric syllables, but leave all rests silent.

2. Divide the choir in half by asking those whose last name begins with A-M to be in the first group, and those with the letters N-Z to be in the second group. Have half the choir chant the melodic rhythm of the piece, while the other half of the choir counts numbers aloud.

3. Have half the choir perform macro and micro beats in their feet and hands (tapping macros in feet, clapping micros in the hand) while the other half of the choir counts the music. Have the choir reverse their task on your direction.

4. To further anchor the consistent tempo, have the choir count numerically but accent the offbeat after each pulse. (**RR** 7,11, 15, 24,26,32,40,41)

The Initial Reading:
Correcting Note and Rhythm Problems During Rehearsal

Initial reading of a work. It is recommended that, when a piece is being introduced to the choir for the first time, the choir be allowed to hear it played from the keyboard while they listen. Too often, conductors underestimate the ability of the ear to absorb considerable musical information about the piece from listening. If the choir is focused and directed toward listening, they can glean the following from the initial playing of the work: 1) the rhythmic direction and shaping of the work; 2) the tonal and harmonic nature of the work; 3) changes of key or mode; and 4) the style of the work. After the work has been played by the keyboardist, it should be played again by the keyboardist, but this time the choir should be asked to "hiss" each phrase, using an inforced and low supported double-s consonant. The conductor should hear, regardless of the music style of the work, a continuity of air flow (support). If one hears the melodic rhythm of the piece, this indicates that the choir is incorrectly supporting the tone. Continuous air should be sounded with an increase of air flow to parallel the rise of phrases. Any break in that flow will indicate that the support of the singers has lessened. Hence, the tone will not be supported, which will lead to many other problems. It is important to establish in the first reading the support feeling necessary to sing the work, which grows out of how the piece moves. After the choir has "hissed" through the work, they can then begin to sing it on a neutral syllable. It is also recommended that the choir "moan" through a work on "mm" or "nn." The moaning provides a tool for the conductor to hear and teach the concept of the line for that piece in addition to connecting the support "system" to the singing voice.

Correcting Tonal and Rhythm Problems. The conductor must realize that when a mistake is sung by a choir, that mistake could be the result of one of two problems: either a tonal or a rhythmic error. Can you recall the times when sightreading that you made a tonal mistake because you encountered a rhythmic problem, or vice versa? When you come upon a musical stumbling block, ALWAYS rehearse the tonal aspects separate from the rhythm. That is, rehearse the "tune" or parts devoid of rhythm, and rehearse the rhythm devoid of the melodic materials. Isolation of either the tonal or rhythm problems will more effectively and efficiently correct the problem.

Initially begin the rehearsal of a new piece at a slow tempo. Many conductors make the mistake of beginning to rehearse a work at "performance" tempo. While this certainly can be done, rehearsing using a modified or slower tempo can be beneficial: 1) to allow for the exact intonation to occur; moving at a fast tempo does not allow the choir time to hear the pitch, let alone make adjustments to it; 2) to guide the choir toward hearing the subtleness of the harmonic movement, further assisting tuning; 3) to allow for exact placement and musical execution of artistic and deep seated breaths; 4) to establish articulation issues, i.e. length, color of pitches, style of the piece and the direction of the musical line more efficiently than rehearsing at a fast tempo. (RR 11, 15, 40, 41)

Identifying Vocal Technique Problems within the Score.

Aside from preparing the tonal, rhythmic and harmonic aspects of the score so that you can "hear" the score you are to conduct, it is valuable for the conductor to study the score with respect to the vocal technique problems that one may encounter in amateur choral singers. In many cases, a tonal or rhythmic error may be evident that is caused by the singer's inability to technically execute the pitch they are hearing. Obviously, the space allotted to a summary such as this does not allow for a detailed explanation or solution of this problem. However, below you will find a list of problems to look for. In some cases, short solutions or tools will be offered. In all cases, you will be given a reference to seek out the pedagogical solution to the problem by consulting GVT.

List of Vocal Problems

- Maintaining Posture for Correct Singing: The Foundation for the Inhalation Process
- Diaphragm Activity (for diction and for articulation of the rhythm)
- Breathing: Exhalation, Inhalation and Support
- Appropriate Resonance for the Style of the Music
- Five Pure Vowels (without diphthongs, to maintain pitch and tone color)
- Finding Head Voice (yawn-sigh, to maintain proper tone color)
- Expanding the Vocal Tract (to insure a free, open singing sound)
- Range Extension and Register Consistency (as required by the piece)
- Flexibility (runs)
- Resonance and Placement (to execute a specific style)
- Martellato
- Staccato
- Legato
- Dynamics

- Accents/Sforzati
- Crescendo/Decrescendo
- Execution of Leaps
- Vowel Modification (for blend and intonation)

When preparing a score for rehearsal, one should sing each vocal part and search each part for technical problems in the above areas. By familiarizing oneself with these problems before rehearsal, in addition to the proper solutions, the conductor will be able to keep the rehearsal pace moving and also to provide the choir with tools to fix them. Many times new conductors may hear some of the problems, but often lack the pedagogical expertise to correct the problem. Hence, the rehearsal pace is slowed. (**RR** 4, 11,12, 21, 25, 27, 29,34)

Maintaining Posture for Correct Singing (the foundation for the inhalation process). Examine the score meticulosly for those points where the breath must be taken. Rehearse the inhalation process as one counts through the work. Make sure that the breath is being taken low enough and is not shallow. Make sure that the choir is able to set the sound with the breath. This can only be done if the body is able to accept air through correct posture and alignment. (See GVT, p.37-42).

Diaphragm Activity (for diction and for articulation of the rhythm). The process of using the breath for singing should be taught to the choir as a two-step process. Diaphragmatic activity is not support; it is is used only for cleaner, sharper diction and accents. If air is only taken into the body to the perceived level of the diaphragm, shallow breathing will result. Moreover, if the diaphragm is used to propel the air through the vocal mechanism rather than the lower "support" mechanism, a harsh, pushed sound will certainly result (See GVT, p.48-56).

Breathing: Exhalation, Inhalation and Support. It is important to establish the manner in which the breath is allowed to fall into the body, and the sensation of support for the particular piece of music you will be rehearsing . The choir members need to "feel" what the support sensation is like for that piece of music. They need to "connect" the feeling of support for that piece to their bodies (See GVT, p. 48-56).

Appropriate Resonance for the Style of the Music. The conductor, before entering the rehearsal room, must have a clear concept of an appropriate color or sound for a particular piece to be rehearsed. That sound is borne out of his own experience and tone preference. An initial decision, however, must be made concerning whether the piece to be rehearsed will require a bright tone color or a dark one (See GVT, p. 64-71).

Five Pure Vowels (without diphthongs, to maintain pitch and tone color). As was stated earlier, rehearse the piece using the five recommended pure vowels. Do not use diphthongs when rehearsing a piece. Because the choir is not skilled in diphthong execution, poorly executed diphthongs will manifest themselves as a veiled or unusual tone color or a variance in pitch. After the choir has learned the piece on neutral syllables, then move the choir to the text of the piece. Locate all diphthongs in the text and be prepared to teach the proper performance of the diphthong (See GVT, p. 108-110).

Finding Head Voice (yawn-sigh, to maintain proper tone color). The conductor must be vigilant that the appropriate amount of head tone is maintained in each respective voice part, regardless of the tessitura of the work. Often parts that lay low in the tessitura for a voice part, sung without the proper amount of head tone, will immediately result in pitch difficulties, inability to perform a wide range of dynamics, and obvious tone color inconsistencies (See GVT, p. 57-63; p. 82-88).

Expanding the Vocal Tract (to insure a free, open singing sound). If a variety of vocal ranges are required to perform the work, maintaining a free vocal tract will present some problems to the conductor (See GVT, p. 43-47).

Range Extension and Register Consistency (as required by the piece). If extremes of tessitura are required by the work, an approach to range extension, and more importantly, register consistency should be addressed. In fact, a choir's ability to maintain register consistency (the same relative color throughout the entire range) is a major determinant of choral tone (See GVT, p. 82-92).

Flexibility (runs). For certain styles of music, especially those pieces in the Baroque and Classical Periods, the ability to execute runs is important to the rhythmic clarity of the piece. The choir should be taught the technique of singing "martellato." *Martellato* comes from the Italian word *il martella,* "the hammer." It is an articulation style that is between staccato and legato. The technique required to sing *martellato* can be easily acquired by the amateur choir. When *martellato* is taught, the conductor will find that the choir is able to sing extended melismas with ease (See GVT, p.98-104).

Rhythmic Styles. In studying the score, the conductor will make a determination based upon his concept of the piece of the inherent rhythmic styles that are included in the piece. As was stated earlier, much work can be accomplished toward that end through the correct choice of neutral syllable and consonant combinations when the work is introduced and taught. To further rehearse the inherent rhythm style of the piece in the following areas: Staccato, Legato, Dynamics and Accents/sforzati, see GVT, p.96-103).

Crescendo/Decrescendo and Messa di voce. This may seem like an over simplification, but amateur choirs need to be instructed as to the proper execution of crescendi and decrescendi as they are required by the score. Most amateur choral singers will provide more air (support) to sing a crescendo without dropping the jaw. This results in a harsh, unrealistic crescendo (See GVT, p. 77-81). The use of *messa di voce* (crescendo/decrescendo on one pitch) heightens the expressive color and range of emotional expression of the choir. Choirs should be made very familiar with messa di voce and how it is produced. This technique is especially necessary in contrapuntal music.

Execution of Leaps. Leaps within all voice parts should be located. The choir should be given the tools concerning the execution of leaps. Basically stated, the choir should be taught to drop the jaw and to use a "fishmouth" for every ascending leap. This technique also is the foundation for vowel modification (See GVT, p. 93-95).

Vowel Modification (for blend and intonation). Help must be given to the choir when their voice parts approach extremes in range. This is especially important in both female and treble parts. Failure to deal with vowel modification issues will result in poor tone color in addition to pitch difficulties. In many instances, problems which appear as inacurate pitches can be solved by employing vowel modification. (See GVT, p. 126-136).

Standing (Seating) Arrangements (to help with blend and intonation). Great improvement in choral intonation and tone color can often be affected by the standing arrangement of a choir. After the music has been rehearsed, and the issues above have been taught, the "polish" can be a standing arrangement that will enhance the choirs sound and their ability to hear each other, regardless of their age or expertise (See GVT, p. 145-151).

Diction Pitfalls

Pages could be devoted to diction issues which must be considered in the rehearsal process. There are some very important diction concerns which should be addressed from the beginning. Four are specifically vital:

Vocalise on pure vowels only; no diphthongs! Use only the pure vowels when vocalising and rehearsing the choir. Because the choir is unsure of how to sing a correct diphthong, the variation in their execution will produce both pitch and blend problems. It should be noted that many rhythmic and blend problems occur in choirs as a result of rushed or poorly executed diphthongs. Many choral singers inadvertently make a diphthong from a pure vowel sound. When diphthongs must be sung, instruct the singers to sing only the first vowel and not even to think the second one (See GVT, p.104).

Teach the "tip of the tongue 'l'." Many conductors do not realize the vocal confusion that the American "l" causes for amateur singers. Generally, the consonant is articulated with the middle or rear portion of the tongue touching the middle or rear of the roof of the mouth. By doing so, forward placement is lost and pitch suffers. The choir should be taught to produce the "l" with the area of the tongue that is just behind or shy of the tip. When the "l" is articulated in singing, the area of the tongue just shy of the tip should contact the area just above the upper front teeth gumline (See GVT, p.112).

Relative length of vowels and consonants. In general, musical line is lost or hidden within choral textures because of the undue length of consonants. When rehearsing, the conductor should constantly implore the ensemble to make the consonants as short as possible so that they can spring to the vowel very quickly. To do so will improve both intonation and placement of the tone.

Observance of the neutral vowel, the Schwa. The Schwa, categorized as an unstressed, neutral sound, is often found in words with more than one syllable. A basic guide for the sound of the basic schwa is that it shares the same sound with the vowel that is in the English word "learn." The schwa is always unstressed and gives the word, and consequently the musical line, a shape. It should be noted that in solo singing there exists a great variation concerning the color of the schwa. It is important that the choir be taught a single sound for the schwa because of the blend requirements of choral ensemble singing. Some examples: (ə=schwa) fathər, mothər, nevər, presənce, sistər, gardən, televisiən, lowəst, cornər (See GVT, P. 113). (**RR** 1, 22, 28, 31, 33)

Marking the Score

A number of years ago when the author was teaching in a high school, students were urged to mark their scores in rehearsal so that errors would be corrected or phrasing concepts established that would be remembered in subsequent rehearsals and performances. Finally, a grading system was devised to make sure singers would mark their scores. One young woman, who received a failing grade came to me and said, "I'd be happy to mark the score if you would teach me what and how to mark!"

That dose of reality brought home the point that how to mark a score, something we often take for granted, is not so obvious. Rehearsal efficiency will be improved if 1) scores are marked prior to singing the piece and 2) that the markings go beyond the traditional breath and simple diction issues. Many vocal technique suggestions, vowel modifications and rhythmic ideas can be marked in the score. Theoretical ideas that need to be aurally apparent to the listener such as imitative material and suspensions can be marked in the singers' scores. One should devise a system of markings. For suggestions and ideas, see GVT, p. 137-140.

The "Warm-Up": Pedagogical Help or Hinderance?

A choir is most attentive at the beginning of a rehearsal. Yet, many of us lose valuable teaching time at the beginning of each rehearsal when we have the choir perform a ritual of vocal exercises that will "warm-up" the voice. Consider making the warm-up the time during which pedagogical information and tools are given to the choir in order to rehearse the music that day.

The choral conductor should organize a series of vocal exercises for use at the beginning of each choral rehearsal that accomplish a number of objectives. Those objectives are obtained through score study procedures which require the conductor to study the issues listed in this chapter. While the format may vary from conductor to conductor, the overall organization of exercises is suggested below. Each rehearsal should begin with a general warm-up which leads the choir through familiar concepts and attempts to create a body that is ready for singing. In the general exercises (see below for categories), it is the responsibility of the conductor to listen and correct vocal problems. It may also be the time to re-teach or reacquaint the choir with previously taught concepts, or to introduce new ones. In the specific warm-up, exercises should be designed to accommodate a particular piece of choral literature to be rehearsed that day. It is in this portion of the warm-up that the singer can make a direct connection between vocal technique and its relationship to the music. While the general warm-up exercises should occur at the beginning of the rehearsal, the specific exercises can occur immediately following it, or smaller specific warm-ups can be distributed throughout the rehearsal as each new piece is rehearsed. The latter procedure tends to break the monotony of a rehearsal and allows the choir to readjust to the new piece of choral music to be rehearsed. A warm-up that is constructed with the above principles in mind will greatly increase the productivity of the choral rehearsal that is to follow. Because the choir has been given the tools to sing the music at hand, mistakes that are caused because of a lack of vocal technique are lessened. With vocal technique problems minimized, spontaneous music-making in the rehearsal comes closer to being a reality!

Space and Core: Two Important elements in Organizing the Warm-Up Sequence . In planning the warm-up sequence, an overall plan for building the choral tone must be kept in mind. As the exercises for the warm-up are being planned, the conductor should be certain that exercises are not only grouped into the categories of general and specific as listed below, but must also contain: 1) exercises that provide "space" within the vocal instrument and 2) exercises which provide "core" color to the voice. These principles are discussed in the resonance chapter in the GVT book. Those exercises which "open" and create "space" for the voice can be found in the exercises in the following categories: yawn-sigh; expanding and opening the vocal tract (especially exercises which use the "call"); range extension exercises; and flexibility exercises. Those exercises which create "core" for the choral sound are those exercises which create a specific resonance (and "placement") for the style of music being rehearsed. A warm-up which contains only exercises that create "space" will yield a choral should which is very "open" and perhaps, "round." The pedagogical difficulty, however, with this sound for the conductor is that a sound with all "space" and no "core" will foster intonation problems because the "center" of the pitch cannot be clearly heard due to a lack of "core" in the voice which contains the fundamental of the pitch being sung. Most importantly, choral sound which has a spacious quality without core also indicates choral tone which is undersupported and not "connected" to the breath. The ideal choral warm-up builds spaciousness into the voice that is well prepared by inhalation/exhalation and support exercises. Exercises are also contained in the warm-up after spaciousness is created to build "core" into that sound.

General Exercises
- Exercises for awakening the mind and imagination
- Relaxation of the body
- Posture
- Diaphragm activity (also use to improve consonants)
- Breathing: exhalation, inhalation and support
- Resonance and dynamic
- Relaxation of the jaw, tongue and lips
- Five pure vowels (without diphthongs)
- Finding head voice (yawn-sigh)
- Expanding the vocal tract
- Range extension and register consistency
- Flexibility (runs)

Specific Exercises
Vocalises should be designed for specific vocal techniques that will be required of the singers. Those techniques may include the following categories.
- Resonance and placement to execute a specific style
- Legato
- Staccato

- Martellato
- Dynamics
- Accents, sforzati
- Crescendo/decrescendo (Messa di Voce)
- Execution of leaps
- Vowel modification (for blend and intonation)
- Diction
- Rhythm skills development
- Tonal skills development (ear training)
- Use of falsetto for men
- Use of head voice for children and women
- Sounds for different styles
    (**RR** 9,11,12,13,21, 25, 34, 36)

Intonation

Intonation is a cause for concern and pedagogical worry for conductors. Many conductors approach intonation problems as a cause rather than an effect or effects of other factors. That is, intonation problems many times are the result of other choral issues. Granted, if one is rehearsing Stravinsky, Schoenberg, etc. where the harmonic and/or the melodic idiom is unfamiliar, the learning of notes for notes sake may be necessary to get the pitches in the "ears" of the choir.

Intonation is an attitude. That attitude is influenced and pre-determined by an interaction of the processes surrounding inhalation, depth and seating of the breath in the body, vowel color and musical line. When intonation problems occur, the reader should reinforce the concepts presented in this chapter. Further, when intonation problems occur, rehearse the tones of the work devoid of the rhythm of the passage. It is pedagogically more efficient to rehearse rhythm devoid of tones and tones devoid of rhythm. (**RR** 11, 13, 23).

Some Final Reminders:
The Importance of the Consistency of Pedagogical Language

If one examines the life work of those choral conductors who have been labeled as "successful," a certain pattern emerges. Whether it be Roger Wagner, John Finley Williamson, Fred Waring, F. Melius Christiansen or Robert Shaw, there is a consistency to their pedagogical language and their approach to a wide range of choral rehearsal problems. At the risk of over-simplifying the complex pedagogical act of teaching, certain tenets remain that can be valuable guides for both new and experienced conductors.

1. Always demonstrate; sing and experience before explaining. A conductor should never explain something that the choir has not yet experienced. Sing first, label later! Good rehearsal technique requires that once the choir has experienced a singing sensation, that sensation can then be easily labeled. Done in this way, the choir will use terminology, and understand terminology because it is based upon their experience. For example, the choir should be taught the process of singing *martellato* by being taught the technique to sing *martellato*. After the choir has correctly sung a passage using *martellato*, the conductor can then label that sensation as *martellato*. Many young conductors try to explain the theory of vocal techniques to their choirs with the desperate hope that the singers will be able to produce the desired results with verbal explanations. Remember, sing first, label later!

2. Do not use several different terms to label the same vocal technique. It is very important that the conductor not adapt many different terms to describe the same outcome. Using many words to describe the same experience — such as focus, placement, core, point, etc. — can lessen the conductor's effectiveness within a rehearsal. Conductors assume that amateur singers can transfer and infer meaning from previously learned concepts. While some can, there are many who cannot. Hence, some vocal confusion may abound within the ensemble. Consistency of spoken language is a hallmark of great conductors.

3. Develop and adopt some systematic approach to teaching the pedagogy required to sing choral literature. This may sound obvious, but another hallmark of great conductors is that they have a system for teaching all the aspects of a piece. They have decided for themselves on how they will approach rhythmic, tone, and pitch issues, etc. Once they have decided on a direction, they continue in that direction. They do not change their approach to the pedagogy of a piece with each new work. Their "system" or "approach" or "philosophy" is taught in the same way with the same language to all the choirs they conduct. The rehearsal efficiency is greatly improved because they are consistent in their approach to the score. Granted, a choir can certainly learn a piece of music with a scattershot approach to the rehearsal, but valuable time will be wasted in the process. With a pedagogically focused approach, a choir will begin to understand the pedagogy involved and, in turn, will begin to teach themselves before the conductor hears the need to become involved.

4. Trust the choir to make a beautiful sound. While there are many pedagogical aspects of rehearsal technique, one of the most overlooked points rests with the conductor's ability to create a correct ambiance for sounds to be made. If one begins a piece worried that the choir will not be able to sing it, in all likelyhood they probably will not. If, however, the conductor hears a beautiful sound before the piece begins and trusts the choir to make that sound, in all likelyhood it will be beautiful. Above all, trust your choir to make a beautiful sound.

There are two ways one can approach the rehearsal process—"outside-in" or "inside-out." If one employs the outside-in approach, one rehearses and fixes details incessantly. Stoppings and startings are frequent in order to repair problems along the way. Such a process is not unlike producing squares of different fabrics for a quilt. While each of the squares may possess beauty in and of themselves, they lose their importance because they do not fit into a larger shape or whole. Like the quilt, music created by merely correcting a series of problems will not have an essence; it will not give the "big picture" to the listener. It is the difference between "performance" and "piece." A *piece* is when a work is sung and its component technical aspects intrude upon the ear and prevent the listener from hearing the work as an indivisible whole. A work that is *performed* each time it is rehearsed comes from the inside-out of the conductor. That is, the conductor's ear and spirit allow the work to speak. A *piece* consists as tones written being reproduced in an exacting repititous manner for performance. A *piece* rather than a *performance* results when the conductor listens only for "things," i.e. the correct note, the correct rhythm, the correct vowel, etc.

On the other hand, a *performance* is able to transform tones written into tones sounded. The conductor in rehearsal must lose oneself and become the sounds of the piece which then create a *performance*. This magical and fantasy experience can only result from open listening from the "inside out," with one's ear being the guide through the performance journey. Rehearsal techniques that are guided by ear, rather than the cognitive brain, infused with the spirit of the music through the conductor , will lead to artistic music-making for a choir at any stage of development. (**RR** 2,3, 30, 35, 39)

> *We must not cease from exploration. And at the end of all our exploring will be to arrive where we began and to know the place for the first time.*
> — T. S. Eliot

References and Resources

Below are listed resources to assist the conductor in exploring various pedagogical problems concerning rehearsal technique as presented in this chapter. While it is not an exhaustive list, it can provide the basis of a personal library of resource materials for the choral conductor.

1. Adler, Kurt, *Phonetics and Diction in Singing.* Minneapolis: University of Minnesota, 1967.

2. Bamberger, Carl, *The Conductor's Art.* New York: Columbia University Press, 1965

3. Buber, Martin, *I and Thou.* New York: Macmillan Publishing Company, 1987.

4. Bunch, Meribeth, *Dynamics of the Singing Voice.* Springer-Verlag: New York, 1982.

5. Caplan, Deborah, *Back Trouble.* Gainesville, Florida: Triad Publishing Company, 1987.

6. Copland, Aaron, *Music and Imagination.* Cambridge, Massachusetts: Harvard University Press, 1977.

7. Gajard, Dom Joseph, *The Solesmes Method.* Collegeville, Minnesota, 1960.

8. Cone, Edward T., *Musical Form and Musical Performance.* New York: W.W. Norton, 1968.

9. Cooksey, John M., *Working with the Adolescent Voice.* St Louis: Concordia, 1992.

10. Decker, Harold A. and Julius Herford, *Choral Conducting Symposium.* (Second Edition) Englewood Cliffs, New Jersey: Prentice-Hall, 1988.

11. Ehmann, Wilhelm, *Choral Directing.* Minneapolis: Augsburg Publishing House, 1968.

12. Ehmann, Wilhelm and Frauke Haasemann, *Voice Building For Choirs.* Chapel Hill, North Carolina: Hinshaw Music, Inc., 1982.

13. Finn, William J., *The Art of the Choral Conductor.* Evanston, Illinois: Summy-Birchard Company, 1960.

14. Gelb, Michael, *Body Learning.* New York: Henry Holt and Company, 1981.

15. Gordon, Edwin E., *Learning Sequences in Music.* Chicago: G.I.A. Publications, 1993.

16. Gordon, Edwin E., *The Nature, Description, Measurement and Evaluation of Music Aptitudes.* Chicago: G.I.A. Publications, 1987.

17. Haasemann, Frauke and James M. Jordan, *Group Vocal Technique.* Chapel Hill, North Carolina: Hinshaw Music, Inc, 1991.

18. Haasemann, Frauke and James M. Jordan, *Group Vocal Technique: A Video.* Chapel Hill, North Carolina: Hinshaw Music, Inc, 1989.

19. Haasemann, Frauke and James M. Jordan, *Group Vocal Technique: The Vocalise Cards.* Chapel Hill, North Carolina: Hinshaw Music, Inc, 1991.

20. Highwater, Jamake, *The Primal Mind.* New York: Penguin Books, 1981.

21. Huff-Gackle, Lynne Martha, "The Adolscent Female Voice: Characteristics of Change and Stages of Development," *Choral Journal,* 31-8, 1991, March, p. 17-25.

22. Jeffers, Ron, *Translations and Annotations of Choral Repertoire, Volume I: Sacred Latin Texts.* Corvalis, Oregon: earthsongs, 1988.

23. Jordan, James M., "Choral Intonation: A Pedagogical Problem for the Choral Conductor," *The Choral Journal,* April, 1987.

24. Jordan, James M., *The Effects of Informal Movement Instruction Derived from the Theories of Rudolf von Laban Upon the Rhythm and Performance Discrimination of High School Students.* Diss. Philadelphia: Temple University, 1985.

25. Kemp, Helen, *Of Primary Importance.* Garland, Texas: Choristers Guild, 1989.

26. Laban, Rudolf von, *Modern Educational Dance.* Boston: Plays, Inc., 1980.

27. Lamperti, Giovanni Battista, *Vocal Wisdom.* New York: Taplinger Publishing Company, 1957.

28. Marshall, Madeline, *The Singer's Manual of English Diction.* New York: Schirmer Books, 1953.

29. Miller, Richard, *The Structure of Singing.* New York: Schirmer Books, 1986.

30. Moore, Thomas, *Care of the Soul.* New York: HarperCollins Publishers, 1992.

31. Montini, Nicola A., *The Correct Pronunciation of Latin According to Roman Useage.* Chicago: G.I.A., 1973.

32. Moore, Carol-Lynne and Kaoru Yamamoto, *Beyond Words: Movement Observation and Analysis.* New York: Gordon and Breach, 1988.

33. Moriarty, John, *Diction.* Boston: E.C. Schirmer Music Company, 1975.

34. Phillips, Kenneth H., *Teaching Kids to Sing.* New York: Schirmer Books, 1992.

35. Richards, Mary Caroline, *Centering.* Middletown, Connecticut: Wesleyan University Press.

36. Rotermund, Donald, *Children Sing His Praise: A Handbook for Children's Choir Directors.* St Louis: Concordia, 1985.

37. Thakar, Markand, *Counterpoint–Fundamentals of Music-Making.* New Haven: Yale University Press, 1990.

38. Thurmond, James Morgan, *Note Grouping.* Camp Hill: JMT Publications, 1989.

39. Toch, Ernst, *The Shaping Forces of Music.* New York: Criterion Music Corporation, 1948.

40. Walters, Darrel L., ed., *Readings in Music Learning Theory.* Chicago: G.I.A. Publications, 1989.

41. Weikart, Phyllis and James Froseth, *Movement to Music.* Chicago: G.I.A., 1981.

The Tools of a Choral Musician

Guy B. Webb

Madeleine Marshall, author of *A Singer's Manual of English Diction*, had a unique manner for starting the first day of class in Beginning English Diction. Aware that students thought they knew everything they needed to know about singing in English (especially after mastering more difficult courses in French, Italian, and German), she established her ground quickly: marching over to a large sash-hung window, she threw it open violently and let in a cold gust of January air, fresh from the Hudson River. "There," she exclaimed, "that won't hurt you a bit! It's good for you singers!" From this shock-treatment, she challenged anyone to stand up and sing an English song with perfect diction.

If anyone could do so — and it was reported only two had in all the years she had taught — that person would pass the course and be excused from class. Not a soul volunteered. Having succeeded in convincing the class that there just might be more to learn about the subject, she went on to explain:

1. A singer must have tools to work with — very much like a carpenter who builds a house.

2. These tools evolve from usage and "good taste" and should be thoroughly mastered through practice and experience until they become involuntary.

3. Tools form the foundation for successful performance.

The same precepts should guide a choral musician. Through one's training and experience certain "rules" are established, which in turn become effective tools in achieving choral excellence. While they may not be entirely evident in a Messiah "sing along" or when a large audience sings the National Anthem, these tools are crucial in our attempts to transform a vocal ensemble. To strive for perfection in our vocal ensembles — and as true Romantics we strive whether or not we ever achieve! — means that we must be extremely meticulous over details. Every component of articulation, textual stress, intonation, tone, style, interpretation, and choral ensemble demands attention. If we are thoroughly familiar with the "tools" and how to use them, then surer are the steps toward choral excellence.

Of course, tools are not the end but the means of achieving choral excellence. Often, while everything can be "correct," music fails to happen! So, while no interpretation was ever hampered by correct notes and accurate rhythms, artistic choral singing demands much more; above all, it demands imagination and a desire to express the unique beauty of the text. As choral directors we must keep a proper balance between mere technique and imaginative expression. Tools are best viewed as helpful subservients to artistic goals; but without certain basics of good choral singing these goals are difficult if not impossible to achieve.

Indeed, a choral tradition can be thought of as an accumulation of successes with a choir made up of singers who know what to do ahead of time. In the United States strong choral traditions have evolved, as they have in England, Sweden, Canada, and other countries. In England a distinct cathedral and choir-school legacy has evolved from a long history of choral music and, in particular, from the unparalleled successes of nineteenth century English music festivals. You feel, when hearing a fine English choir sing, that the singers are living a tradition they have known all of their lives; that each singer is thoroughly grounded in the fundamentals — the tools — of making beautiful music within an ensemble. Likewise with a professional choir, where the members are paid and expected to possess the fundamentals of good singing — to be able to achieve results with a minimum of rehearsal time. (If not, they can be replaced by one who can!) Clearly it is a desirable goal to train singers in the fundamentals of good singing so that they know beforehand how to approach the music and, most important, how to attain the desired results.

Our job would be much easier if at the first meeting of a choir — or even at the end of two or three weeks of rehearsals — the tools of singing were clearly established. This goal can only be realized through effective rehearsal techniques. Vocal warm-ups should include practice on these fundamentals, for it is the involuntary action that is crucial to good singing. No one can think of every detail while singing — how to sing repeated notes without scooping, how to approach a lower interval, when to anticipate a penultimate stress. It takes concentrated effort and knowledge of what is expected to make consistent use of these tools. How often after a special concert or when we come to the end of a successful tour do we think, "Now is when we should start to rehearse!" In other words: "We've reached the point where everyone is in agreement on all aspects of the performance, and there is a sense of ensemble unity — we're ready to go a little bit deeper into the music now!" Tools take us to this point more quickly and efficiently. The author finds it helpful to publish a choir manual so that singers will know in advance what is demanded of them. This chapter is an expansion of that manual.

From the beginning, then, demand attention to detail from your singers and set goals for mastering basic concepts. Some principles will be derived directly from voice study, many from the personal experience of singing in a choir, and others from reading everything available about choral techniques; most, however, will come from intense listening — by attending choral concerts and conventions and listening to any recording you can get your hands on, both instrumental and choral. We learn from the "good" as well as from the "not so good" — the latter can be helpful in establishing our priorities for good singing.

And our priorities must evolve, finally, from our own understanding and experience. Attempts to imitate another conductor's style or technique can lead to frustration; imitation cannot take the place of honest and thorough investigation. The tools that follow are the author's. They are to be challenged, and, by doing so, perhaps one's own set of principles will be verified and strengthened; if not, then perhaps new ideas will emerge to make one a better listener — to explore alternate ways of approaching choral skills.

The following, then, are the tools of the choral musician: I. Articulation — Precision of Attacks/Releases; II. Accent/Negation in music; III. Intonation; IV. Vocal Concepts; V. Diction; VI. Style/Interpretation; and VII. Riser Formations.

I. Articulation — Precision of Attacks/Releases

Barn Door

One of the most pernicious habits that must be overcome to achieve good choral ensemble is the "barn door" attack into each note. Like a heavy barn door that is sluggish to open, it is an attack that is slow to develop: the consonant is not placed ahead of the precise moment the note occurs, and the vowel is slow to evolve into its full size and beauty. This habit pervades most of a singer's pre-training experience, and it is most evident in casual singing, or even when choral directors sing in a reading session! Listen carefully to choirs, as well as professional singers. Analyze how a clean attack is achieved. Demand absolute purity and fullness of vowel sound precisely on the moment of attack. In most styles, particularly in the Baroque, it is essential to have the fullness of tone at the beginning of the attack. Without this precision legato is difficult to acquire, and a corrugated "nuance" style of singing pervades. Challenge the choir to get rid of all "barn door" singing, say, within the first two weeks of rehearsals. Quickly work for a "guillotine" approach and include exercises with a variety of initial consonants to help the choir overcome the unwanted "barn door" effect. The correction of this one habit will do much to improve your choir's precision and ensemble.

Attack *senza* "Scoop"

A nasty accomplice of the "barn door" is the scoop! The habit of varying the pitch on the attack requires constant vigilance to be overcome, unless of course a scoop or "slide" is desired, as in show and jazz styles.[1] Initial notes, as well as repeated notes within a phrase, are crucial points to watch. Voiced consonants can be culprits too, both at the beginning or end of a word. All elements connected with a syllable should be produced on the same pitch without variance, and this takes constant perseverance to achieve. Technically, when the breath fails to move on the attack, a scoop results — very much like turning on a pipe organ with a key depressed. Good singing habits include vowel formation **prior** to the intake breath. Indeed, when the vowel is formed — that is, thought in all its purity — through an open, relaxed throat, the intake breath is involuntarily achieved. Any tension on the attack — or the release at the end of a phrase — tends to cause a pitch variation. Describe, with microscopic approach, exactly how you want a note to begin and end — until your choir involuntarily sings each note on pitch without any scoop or pitch variation. This is the essence of good articulation in singing.

---

[1] Singers who are asked to mix classic with show/jazz styles, particularly within the same ensemble, have a difficult time avoiding scooping when it is *not* desired. Hence, the importance of absolute clarity of the attack when singing in a classic style. To scoop is easy; not to scoop requires much effort.

Attack Following a Rest/Breath

A common problem of ensemble singing is failure to negotiate a breath or pause in the music and then enter precisely together on the next phrase. There are two primary reasons this occurs:

a. The singers — or perhaps just one! — fail to plan ahead and are caught off-guard. A successful professional singer was asked what he thought about while singing. After thinking a moment, he replied: "What I'm going to do next!" If we fail to plan ahead for what comes next, the moment will be gone and the ensuing entrance ragged.

b. Tension on the release contributes to a faulty re-entrance. As a vocal coach explained: There are three main parts of the breathing-sustaining process — the intake breath, the flow of breath through the tone, and relaxation on the release. This feeling of complete freedom from tension at the end of a phrase — particularly when the pause is very brief — is very important to a clean new attack.[2]

As usual, the cure comes through practice. Invent exercises that have built-in pauses, and pauses without a breath (marked in the following exercise with a small circle) can alternate with pauses with a breath. The sensation of a relaxed open throat and low, non-tense breath should be the same, whether or not one breathes during a brief pause.

Through repetition, the "correct" way becomes involuntary, and singers are able to retain in concert the sensations achieved over and over in rehearsal. It is the director's responsibility to demand absolute togetherness on all phrase beginnings.

Clarity of attack.

There are times when a precise attack is difficult to achieve. Though problems can occur with initial vowel or consonant attacks, remedies include 1) moving the breath through an imperceptible "h" on the initial vowel, and 2) a quick release or flip of initial consonants. A **pianissimo** attack can likewise present a special problem to a choir, for it often lacks the energy required to cleanly bring all voices into action at the same time. A **forte/piano** attack can be effective in solving this problem. A very brief **forte** attack followed by a sudden **diminuendo** will, if judiciously applied, 1) supply the energy needed and 2) create a hushed effect that gives the illusion of an extremely soft attack. For example, consider the opening of Victoria's "O vos omnes":

---

[2] While individual singers can contribute undesirable techniques within the composite sound of a choir that can go undetected by the director, tension on the cutoff can be *seen* when (1) the lip formation changes on the end of a vowel ending or (2) there is visible tension in the throat and the upper chest heaves on the ensuing intake breath. A third result is *heard* – an audible intake breath.

Or the beginning of "Since by man came death" from Handel's *Messiah*:

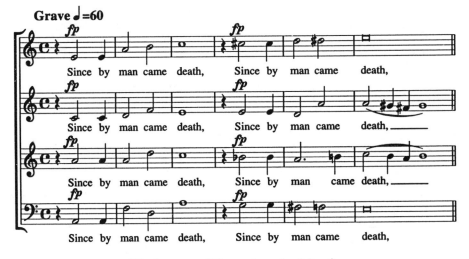

II. Accent/Negation in Music

The Three Types of Accent

There are three basic types of accent in music: a note can be made 1) louder (dynamic accent), 2) higher (pitch accent) or 3) longer (agogic accent). Dynamic accents are more within our control — we can at will make a note louder or softer. Pitch and agogic accents are inherent to the vocal line and require careful attention; high notes and long notes exert a very powerful influence in terms of accent, and quite often they do not conform to textual accents. A choral director must constantly make decisions in favor of the natural word stress and not allow singers to place accents which take precedence over the textual stress. This seems like a simple concept, yet it is perhaps the most frequently violated rule of good singing and of expression of feeling in the music.

a. **Pitch Accents.** We can learn much from a fine instrumental soloist who approaches a high note with extreme care. High-notes tend to be "loud-notes," and when a high-note accent occurs on an unstressed syllable singers must be cautioned **not** to accent a syllable or word which should be negated. (Note: accent or stress marks are indicated below by / and negations by **u** .)

a. *Away in a Manger —* arr. Paul Sjolund

b. *Flow Gently Sweet Afton —* arr. John Leavitt

c. *Der bucklichte Fiedler —* Johannes Brahms

d. *Zion's Walls* (Revivalist Song) — Aaron Copland

e. *All Men Draw Near* — Peter Williams

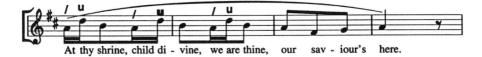

Agogic Accents

Notes that are longer tend to receive a stress. A decision should be made to determine if this stress is desirable or if it should be negated to conform to the textual stress:

a. *He's got the whole world in his hand* — arr. Malcolm Sargent

b. *Hear the Lambs A-Cryin* — Spiritual, arr. Robert DeCormier

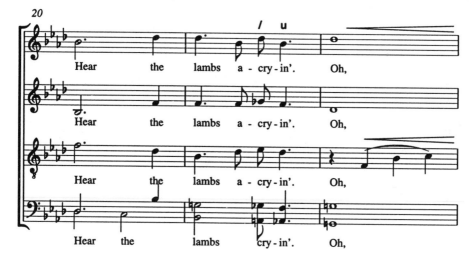

c. *Done made my vow* — Spiritual, arr. Wendell Whalum

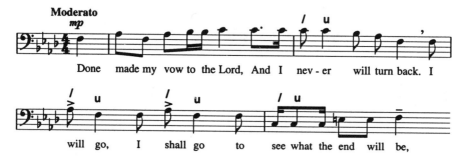

Often pitch and agogic accents occur simultaneously:

a. *Drink to me only with thine eyes*

b. "Time and Concord" from *Gloriana* Choral Dances — Benjamin Britten

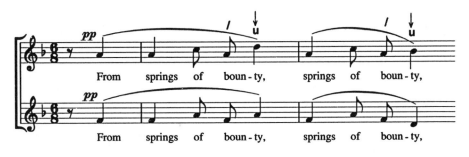

c. *Away from the Roll of the Sea* — arr. Diane Loomer

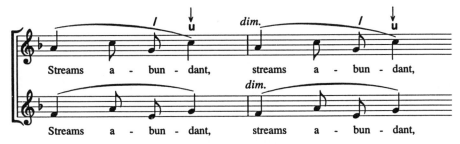

Textual Emphasis.

Text is unique to vocal music; it communicates thoughts and emotions directly to the listener through words. In Richard Strauss' "Capriccio," Op. 85 (a "Conversation piece for Music in One Act") Olivier, the poet, and Flamand, the musician, argue which is more important — the words or the music — in wooing the heart of the Countess.[3] In a skillfully forged vocal work the music and the words amplify each other. Thus the interpreter's job starts with the meaning of the text. If the text is in a foreign language, it starts with an accurate literal translation of each word and then moves to a poetic translation, with a clear understanding of word stress in the original language.

Harry Robert Wilson's primary rule was: "The poetry should be marked up more than the music." If we are striving for a fine choral performance, we must pay close attention to the meaning of the text; word stress largely determines the meaning of the text, while vowel coloration and clarity of consonants intensify this meaning. *Nothing can bring more intensity of expression to the music than singing with correct textual accents.*

Selecting important words in a vocal line can be likened to an earlier time when sending a message in a telegram was the norm — something which is rarely done today with our modern telephone system, FAX machines, etc. At fifty cents a word, which words would be essential to convey the message to the receiver? Below is an example of how key words can be stressed. In "Isaiah 43" by Z. Randall Stroope, a ten-word telegram could be sent to convey the meaning of the first eleven bars: *"LORD CREATED JACOB [stop] FORMED ISRAEL [stop] REDEEMED [stop] SUMMONED NAME [stop] YOU MINE [stop]"*

"Isaiah 43" — Z. Randall Stroope

---

[3] While music may have won out, Strauss was adamant in setting each word in his fifteen operas and many solo songs so that audibility of text was paramount.

sum - moned you by name, you are mine. _____

In the above example, one should avoid agogic stresses in m's 6 and 9. So often choirs are heard stressing unstressed syllables, so that the result is "JaCOB" and "IsraEL"

Penultimate Stress.

When two notes end a phrase — especially if they are of equal value — usually the note before the last receives the stress. This is called the "penultimate stress" [*paene* almost + *ultima* last]. The resultant "lift" to the end of the phrase is often heard in instrumental music. The penultimate stress normally coincides with the word stress, as in Handel's *Messiah*:

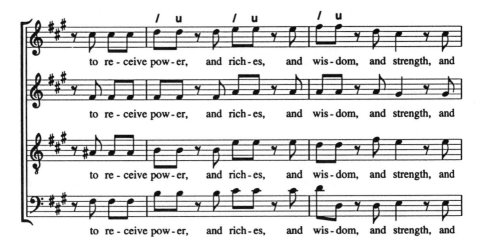

to re - ceive pow - er, and rich - es, and wis - dom, and strength, and

In the following, also from *Messiah*, the penultimate stress occurs over two slurred notes:

For un - to us a child is born, __

Negations.

Accents are made stronger when negations occur; very rarely if ever are notes given equal stress, especially a series of notes of equal value. Some of the opportunities for non-accents are a) anacruses, b) slurred notes, and c) syllabic non-stress. The difficulty is to achieve a decided non-stress on a note that should be negated and at the same time support that note with breath and energy. Otherwise the note is "out of the phrase or line" and it becomes an expression-less nuance.

a. **Anacrusis.** An anacrusis or upbeat has the effect of carrying the melody over the barline and giving a lift or "arsis" to the character of the music. An anacrusis most often pervades a piece, with each phrase starting with this lift. Any weight or stress that occurs on the upbeat tends to destroy this effect, and careful attention should be given these preparatory beats, to make sure they are not unduly stressed.

b. **Slurred notes.** There are two basic points in handling slurred notes: 1) Very simply, two or more notes that are marked with a slur should be slurred without any "h-ing" between the notes and 2) the "Baroque sigh" is achieved with the first note stressed and a negation on the second. This applies to all styles; it is most often violated when the second note is a higher pitch (pitch accent) or a longer note (agogic stress). Devise exercises such as the following which prepare the singers for this technique:

c. **Syllabic non-stress.** The role of the neutral vowel or "schwa" — indicated phonetically by an upside-down e [ə] — should be clearly understood. Its primary difference from all the other vowels is that it is **unstressed** and should not be stressed. There is a major difference between the pronunciation of an "ʌ" and an "ə" vowel, which determines when a note will be stressed or unstressed.

III. Intonation

There are many popular excuses for poor intonation, ranging from tone-deafness, to the weather, the key of a piece and lack of energy or support. There are, however, two basic causes for poor intonation, and they are often over-looked: 1) failure to prepare intervals and 2) improper vowel concepts.

1. **Failure to prepare intervals.** If intervals are not properly prepared correct pitch as well as a legato line are hindered. Analogies abound: "Giant steps going up — baby steps down," or "Think low going high — high, low" are two commonly used. Upward intervals demand energy in their preparation; repeated notes, as discussed above, are often sung with a slur or pitch-alteration. However, downward intervals present the greatest challenge to maintaining good intonation in the vocal line. They can best be approached by 1) moving the breath to the lower note — where the energy is often relaxed, and 2) increasing the lift of the velum (soft palate) to the lower pitch. These two techniques, occurring simultaneously on the lower note of an interval, will do much to cure

faulty intonation and an uneven vocal line.

2. **Improper vowel concepts.** It is difficult to sing on pitch when the vowel is improperly conceived or produced. A mouth-oriented tone, i.e. one which is primarily produced in the oral cavity without sufficient head resonance or laryngeal relaxation, lacks true intonation or "overness" to the tone to be on pitch. In short, good principles of vocal production are required for a choir to sing in tune. Choral warm-ups should be based on vocal principles which in turn enable the choir to sing with good intonation.[4]

IV. Vocal Concepts

In order to be a fine choral director, one must possess a good understanding of vocal principles and a whole bevy of tools that can be called on to build the choral sound desired. While there are many successful non-singer directors, often a lack of vocal concepts limits the accomplishments of a choral musician. Here are a few major vocal principles that are crucial to good singing:

1. The Breathing/Supporting Mechanism.

Intake Breath

The intake breath should be void of any stress; **tension** on the intake means there will likewise be **tension** in the tone. To be free of tension the intake breath must be **inaudible.** The practice of using an audible breath to assure togetherness on the attack inhibits good vocal technique. Pre-humming the pitch is also a deterrent to a relaxed intake breath. Formation of the initial vowel through a relaxed open throat **is** the intake breath — air automatically fills the lungs as a result of the descending diaphragm, and in good singing these actions become **simultaneous.**

Breath Flow

The ecology of breath to tone is crucial in producing a good vocal sound and in the movement of breath that supports the vocal line. A choral director who knows how and where a vocal tone is produced reflects this understanding by conducting where the singers breathe. A high beat tends to induce shallow breathing. The power and energy of the choir will benefit from the conductor who essentially keeps the beat within the area of the supporting mechanism where the support must evolve and from which the breath flows.

Demonstration

Stand before a group of singers and conduct a simple unison song. Start in a high position with the point of the ictus well above the torso. Stop. Change the hand position to a lower point and conduct the same song. Do you hear a difference in the tone coming from the singers?

---

[4]Warm-ups can include several basic principles that aid intonation and vocal development: 1) vowel changes to practice the modifications required in moving from one vowel to the next, 2) starting and ending on the same vowel, so that the intake breath is unencumbered by any need to change vowels, 3) slurred notes to avoid "h'ing" in the transition to the slurred note, and 4) downward intervals to practice breath flow and lifted soft palate (velum) on the lower note.

Relaxation on Cut-off.

The release of the phrase should be as free of tension as the attack. Singers should achieve an "open-throat release." They should avoid closing the mouth immediately on the cut-off—until well after relaxation takes place. The sensation is one of almost incredulity! Very much like driving ten miles from home, only to be asked by a family member if the stove was turned off! To accomplish this total relaxation before the next attack is an important vocal principle. Likewise, final consonants should be produced crisply and efficiently, as on the attack, in order not to interfere with relaxation on the cut-off. The frequently heard practice of having the choir move up to the next pitch level — before the intake breath at the end of an exercise — causes tension and discourages relaxation on the release. The principle of relaxation on the ends of phrases must be inherent in vocal warm-ups.

2. Tonal Concepts.

Singers are called upon to produce a variety of sounds and colors in the choir. Basically, there are three types of choral tone: 1) **a solo sound,** each singer using a full sound with ample vibrato; 2) **an ensemble tone,** a full sonority, yet with each singer controlling the vibrato and listening well for blend and vowel agreement; and 3) **a cathedral tone,** a light, pure sound with almost complete absence of vibrato.

The cathedral tone is most useful for the Renaissance style, as well for contemporary music when the texture is thick and harmonic clarity is required. Opera choruses and robust choral works demand a full solo style; the solo style is also useful when, for balance purposes, a section has a fugue subject that must be heard. Otherwise, a full ensemble sound remains the primary sound of a choir. Singers who can produce only **one** sound are limited (and this is true in solo as well as ensemble singing), in which case the choir has only a small palette of colors to offer an audience. Singers can quickly be taught to produce and hear the difference between the three sounds; they should have a clear concept of **when** a particular sound is required.

3. Identification of Vowel Sounds.

Vowel agreement determines, to a large degree, choral blend; correct vowel identification is thus a part of good vocal technique. To agree on a vowel, that vowel must be accurately identified, and the IPA phonetic symbols for the vowels are an invaluable aid to helping singers to consistently produce pure vowel sounds.

The author has had much success with a system of hand signals — similar to the Kodaly hand signals for tuning the steps of a musical scale — to remind the choir of what vowel is being produced or, most important, anticipated. It has proven effective in adjusting vowel inequities, as well as tuning and building a choral sound; it also facilitates changing vowels at will during vocal warm-ups — visually communicating directions to the choir without having to stop and speak. On command, the choir can "sign" together the vowels while singing a work — which makes the singers intimately aware of the phonetic symbol that must be reproduced in tone and, very importantly, what must be produced next. This takes practice; and they will be slow at first. But confidence is soon gained as they watch and coordinate their signals **with the director**, who forms the vowels within the conducting pattern of the right hand (they are designed to be produced with one hand). By anticipating the next vowel in the time line and producing it accurately on the ensuing ictus, agreement on exact placement of the vowel sound is achieved. This timing is also helpful in placing diphthongs or vanishes to the vowels precisely in the time line. Primarily, signing the vowels makes the choir **think** phonetically, physically etching the multitude of complicated changes a text demands.

In the following chart each vowel is represented by a hand position that attempts to duplicate the phonetic symbol or the manner in which the vowel is produced.

Chart of Vowel Hand Signals

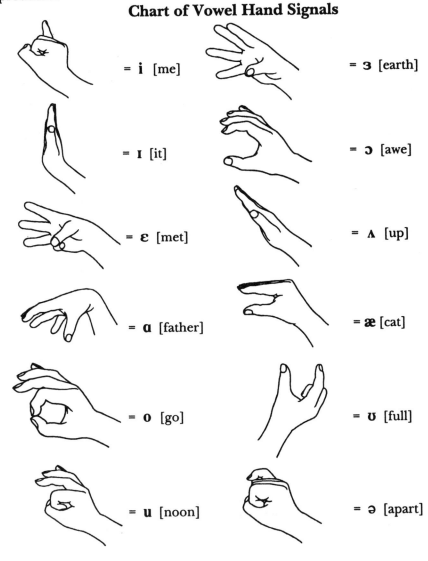

= **i** [me]

= **ɜ** [earth]

= **ɪ** [it]

= **ɔ** [awe]

= **ɛ** [met]

= **ʌ** [up]

= **ɑ** [father]

= **æ** [cat]

= **o** [go]

= **ʊ** [full]

= **u** [noon]

= **ə** [apart]

Explanation of Vowel Hand Signals

1. All the vowel hand pictures show the hand from the view of the director. The ε vowel will appear to the choir as facing to the right, as the phonetic symbol – not to be confused for the ɜ which is represented by a different hand symbol. By closing or opening the fingers of the ε vowel the choir will change from a closed form (almost "ay") to the more desired sound of the pure (and tall) "eh" vowel.

2. The "ah" hand position represents the roof of the mouth (soft palate or *velum*). By raising the hand the singers imitate the lifting of the *velum*. A flat left hand (palm down) can be added below to show the role of a flattened, spineless tongue required to obtain a pure "ah" vowel.

3. Three vowels require some lip consideration: o, u, ɜ (as in "earth"). The "oh" and "oo" vowels are produced the same, one with a large roundness and the other with a very small opening, about the size of a pencil. Both have a slight lip protrusion, without tension. By changing the size of the opening, the singers glide between the two vowels effortlessly and smoothly. Two hands can also be used to demonstrate the large roundness of the "oh" vowel.

4. The ɜ (sometimes represented by œ or ø) requires flared lips, similar to a morning glory or a horn bell. This hand signal attempts to imitate the outward flaring of the lips, relaxed and free of tension.

5. The ʌ signal represents one side of the phonetic symbol. Two hands can also be used with the finger tips coming together in the shape of a roof top.

6. The æ hand signal shows the tongue position as it widens and hugs the upper back teeth to produce the "ae" vowel. This is a vowel that often escapes vocalization and is susceptible to regional pronunciations.

There are twelve pure vowel sounds in the English language. Madeleine Marshall also lists the "First Five Diphthongs" (which she originally referred to in her classes as "vowels with glides or vanishes") and the "Diphthongs and Triphthongs Ending in the Neutral Vowel.[5]

First Five Diphthongs:

oʊ	=	o (no)	ɔɪ	=	o (boy)
εɪ	=	a (ate)	aʊ	=	o (now)
aɪ	=	a (night)			

---

[5] In *A Singer's Manual of English Diction* (New York: G Schirmer, 1955). Dorothy Uris in *To Sing in English* (New York: Boosey and Hawkes, 1971) claims sixteen vowels in the **American** English language, which includes vowels with glides and combines ʌ and ə as the same vowel. The latter are formed alike. Marshall lists them as separate since ʌ is a stressed vowel and ə is an **unstressed** vowel.

Diphthongs and Triphthongs Ending in the Neutral Vowel:

ɛə	=	air	ɔə	=	ore
ɪə	=	fear	uə	=	sure

ɑɪə	=	fire
ɑuə	=	sour

Unison Singing

It is cause for amazement how a children's choir can stand before an audience — as elite as a choral director's convention! — and sing a unison song so well that there is not a dry eye left in the hall. We delight in complicated textures and rich harmonic sounds, program esoteric music that "looks good on the program" — yet forget the simple and the beautiful. The skills of a vocal ensemble are tested in unison singing. Ensemble is the culmination of a variety of achievements — the ability to think and execute together all aspects of articulation, rhythm, style, diction, and vocal tone with a high degree of precision. It is through unison singing that vocal ideals are solidified.

Unison singing presents opportunities and challenges:

1. Short folk or art song fragments can be used in vocal warm-ups.

2. Accompanied art songs or unison choral works can be effectively programmed.

3. Unison points in a multi-voiced work require attention; singers must quickly make adjustments in the transition from harmonic complexity to unison "oneness," often for short fragments of one note or more. Tuning to unison points is crucial to the tone and intonation.

V. Diction

The training of a choral director must include a strong foundation in languages and diction. Both are required. In-depth study of a language provides the ability to understand the grammar and character of a language; courses in singing diction give needed skills in pronouncing a foreign language text so that the director is able to train the choir to sing with clarity, as well as aid expression and vocal tone. Rules of singing diction are often not the same as for spoken diction. However in singing — which can be defined as "beautiful sustained speech" — the singer must have a microscopic approach to words and how to make them legible when sustained in song. The choral director should expand his knowledge of singing diction through language courses, coaching sessions, and workshops with diction experts.

The tools of diction are many, and they all must be based on legibility and naturalness of the text. The following are a few basic tools to deal with what the author has found to be common diction problems which plague singers and choirs (see the chapter on "Diction" by Richard Cox and the bibliography at the end of that chapter for a more definitive study of the subject):

German:

1. German is not a guttural language when sung; keep the **a** vowel pure and forward, with a flat, spineless tongue.
2. German is a "falling language;" stress is usually placed on the first syllable.
3. Never elide a final consonant into an initial vowel sound.
4. Make all **r**'s audible with a flip; in a choir, a rolled **r** is often required.

French:

1. All vowel sounds are pure and without diphthongs. Watch the lips carefully in a mirror to make sure there is no change of the mouth position while sustaining a vowel, especially on the release.
2. Nasals: no "n" or "m" is sounded at the end of a nasal. Keep the tongue from rising to the roof of the mouth on the release.
3. The uvular **r** is not used in singing French; flip with the tip of the tongue.
4. Avoid strong textual accents; strictly observe composer's markings, especially in regards to ritards.

Italian:

1. Flip or roll all **r**'s; never use an American **r**.
2. Vowels are pure without any vanish. Diphthongs are formed by combining vowels (**miei, tuo**). This is the difficult part in singing Italian — to know which vowel should be stressed in a combination of vowels.[6]
3. Three vowels are invariable — **i, a, u**; two [**e** and **o**] have open and closed forms; know when they are closed and when they are open.
4. Avoid aspirating the dental consonant t by stopping the air with the tongue against the upper teeth.

English:[7]

1. Never sound an **r** before a consonant; flip an **r** when between vowel sounds in opera, oratorio, arts songs with classic texts, and songs with an English dialect.
2. Know when to sing **ae** and when to sing **a**. [**Dance, laugh, ask, answer** are **a** words in opera, oratorio, art songs and classic texts, and songs with an English dialect; all forms of **have** are **ae** words.]
3. Final consonants **b, d, and g** require a voiced "uh" sound to be heard.
4. Prefixes with **e** are usually **I** [**deliver, remember, receive**]; in words where action is changed, an **i** vowel is required [**renew, reheat, decode**].

---

[6] See "Italian is So Easy to Sing – Or is it?" by Evelina Colorni in *The NATS Bulletin*, Nov./ Dec., 1979.

[7] The reader is referred to Madaleine Marshall, *Op. cit.* for a more definitive study of these and many other basic rules of English diction.

VI. Style/Interpretation

Tempo

A noted composer was once asked in a clinic session if the metronome markings printed in his music should be faithfully obeyed. He replied: "My goodness no. I put those markings on my music for five years before I discovered my metronome was broken!" A musician has some flexibility in choosing a tempo, and there are many considerations. A tempo may be too fast for the smallest notes to be articulated, or too slow for phrase movement and expression. Often, especially in the driving rhythms of the Baroque style, there are both macro and micro considerations; that is, if a piece can be conducted in two ways the tempo will be correct.[8] Choice of tempo is crucial to the performance. Yet, it is and must remain a highly individualistic subject.

Dynamic/Tempo Variations

Gradations in dynamics or tempo should be carefully and precisely planned; they are often treated lightly or as separate from what the text is expressing. Loudness can lack fullness and quality of tone; a **ritardando** many times loses energy and vitality. A **crescendo** means to start softer; a **decrescendo**, begin louder. Likewise, an **accelerando** means to start slower; a **ritardando**, begin faster. Interpretative markings not provided by the composer need not — most often **should not** — be carefully observed, depending on the quality of the edition. A director should refer to an **urtext** edition, if available, for original markings. He also has license to add "hairpins" or any interpretative marks, **depending on the style**. Again, we learn much from fine instrumental performance. In an exceptional performance — say by a professional artist or a piano trio — interpretative decisions are very clearly stated. An analogy might be a theatre make-up class, where strong colors and bold lines are first applied; then, in the final step, powder is applied to temper the starkness. **But the basic, bold colors are still there!** Interpretative marks in music represent bold expressive decisions; they are at the base of performance, planned carefully and clearly stated to the audience. They meld into a composite expressive sound in performance.

Cadential Treatment

One of the distinctive characteristics of a fine ensemble — whether it be a children's chorus, a professional choir or a string quartet — is the careful attention given to bringing a work, a section, or phrase to a close. Cadences should not be tossed off casually; how the audience perceives the close of a piece is crucial to the effectiveness of the performance. Attacks receive much attention; cadences, almost a perceptible "whew, it's over!" Treatment of ritards, final notes, and the degree of blend are a few cadential tools:

a. **Ritards.** A ritard is most effective when it is well-proportioned over the inner-rhythm — a slowing of **the smallest note value**.

---

[8] In "For unto us a child is born" from Handel's "Messiah," it can be sung comfortably in two and in four; if the tempo is increased, it is uncomfortable in four.

"Come again, sweet love" — John Dowland:

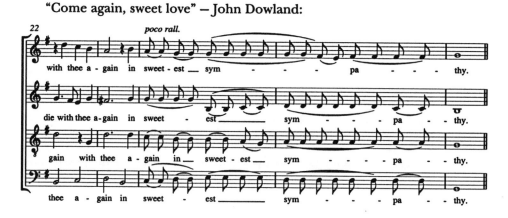

b. Final Notes. There are no rules for how long a final note should be held, but there are a few considerations:

1. Savor a final fermata; it is often an effective way of maintaining the mood of a piece through to the final cutoff. When a composer places a fermata on a final note, there is often a reason for its existence! Even if there is no fermata, the number of beats in the final note should be observed.

2. Maintain energy and flow of breath through the final note. Singers should be taught how to breathe imperceptibly during a long note before supportive air is exhausted.

3. Timing of the final note release can be effective. The conductor has the ability to maintain a mood and delay applause as desired. The softest **pianissimo** or the most thunderous climactic moment can be maintained effectively long after the cutoff.[9]

c. Blend. Vowel unanimity, clarity of harmony, intonation, control of vibrato should come together at cadential points to achieve a perfect blend of sound. This takes much practice and thought. Every phrase is conceived as a destination to an end, and each closing of the sound should be carefully prepared. When there is a specific difficulty at a cadence — or in any place in a work — go back a few beats and pause on the problem chord or unison sound. Repeat this process several times until each singer feels the sensation of the unified ensemble sound. This is an effective technique in improving cadential points.

Phrasing/Structure

There are a few aspects of phrasing and structure which demand attention:

a. Where to breathe? The text and the phrase structure usually dictate where the chorus should breathe. Repeated words are effective when punctuated with a breath. Staggered breathing is enhanced when breaths are avoided over the

---

[9] All who attended the final performance of the 1991 ACDA national convention at Phoenix vividly recall the effect achieved by Helmuth Rilling on the final cutoff of Bach's *Mass in B Minor*. His baton held the audience spellbound long after the final note had ended, until emotions burst into applause.

barline or before/after long notes. A short pause without a breath can also be effective in maintaining the onward flow of a phrase — marked in the music by a small circle over the staff.

b. Arsis/Thesis. *Arsis* means "to lift"; *thesis*, to "lower." So much of music — particularly that with a strong sense of melodic flow — is a continual lifting of the line achieved by a constant flow of energy to the tone. The technique of a "silent clap" is effective in teaching "lift." It is demonstrated by attempting to clap the hands together, and, as they almost touch, let them deflect each other as two protons repelled and bounding up and into the air, devoid of gravity. Gregorian chant and all linearly conceived music, as well as rhythmic clarity, are aided by *arsis*; marcato style by *thesis*.

c. Phrase movement. A phrase must go somewhere, fed by a continual supply of energy and breath movement. An analogy to a well-spun phrase might be the manufacture of wire. Heated metal is **pulled** through a small aperture, not pushed! Similarly, a beautifully sung and fully supported "vocal line" is created by a continual flow of breath. As one teacher once put it, "The breath leads the tone as a locomotive pulls a train."[10] Attempts to *crescendo* a note to achieve phrase line through what the author terms the "unwanted crescendo" results in an awkward accordion effect to the phrase. A long note will have movement and line if the breath is moving, impelled by low support; a *crescendo* can disturb this phrase movement, especially when it is without an expressive reason.

d. Nuance. The manner in which one note moves into the next note is crucial to a legato line, assisted by the exact agreement on diphthong placement and final/initial consonants. Singers often sing with too much nuance — with "hairpins" on each note. A "vocalized line" means a line where vowel changes are achieved with the least amount of muscular change possible. Warm-up exercises should include a combination of related and unrelated vowels so the singers will know how to get from one vowel to another — an incredible degree of muscular change — with the least amount of nuance or change.

e. Strophic vs. Through-composed. A strophic piece, where all stanzas of a text are sung to the same music, as in a hymn, demands not-so-subtle shades of expressive and dynamic changes for each stanza. Repetition means change; rarely is a repeated passage sung the same way, let alone whole verses set to the same music. A choral director must be aware of a strophic form, in contrast to a through-composed work that has different music for each stanza of text. Examples of strophic songs abound. In "Waldesnacht" by Johannes Brahms, the following is offered as one way to achieve variety in each verse, unique to the meaning of the text:

---

[10] The analogy can be taken further. As a youth, the author recalls watching steam locomotives stop to take on water. If it was a long train, the conductor would back up the train before starting forward in order to compress the space in the couplings between cars. Therefore, when starting forward, the locomotive only had to start one car at a time, not the entire train! Singing is similar; the singer must only start the first part of the tone, and the breath leads the rest through a continual flow of energy.

German Text:	Literal Translation	Interpretive Ideas:
Waldesnacht, du wunderkühle,	Forest-covered night, you marvelous coolness,	**Emotion:** youthful enthusiasm, joy
die ich tausend Male grüß;	which I a thousand times greet;	
nach dem lauten Weltgewühle,	after the loud worlds tumult,	**Tone:** free, full solo
o, wie ist dein Rauschen süß!	O, how sweet is your rustling!	voice
Träumerisch die müden Glieder	Dreamily I shelter my tired limbs	
berg ich weich ins Moos,	softly in the moss,	**Tempo:** quarter = 66,
und mir ist, als würd ich wieder	and it seems to me as if I would	with rubato
all der irren Qualen los.	be free again from all confusing torments.	
Fernes Flötenlied, vertöne,	Fade away, distant flute-song.	**Emotion:** reflective,
das ein weites Sehnen rührt,	That a vast longing stirs,	pensive, trancelike
die Gedanken in die schöne,	which thoughts in the beautiful,	
ach, mißgönnte Ferne führt.	O, begrudging distance leads.	**Tone:** airy, controlled
Lass die Waldesnacht mich wiegen,	Let the forest-covered night rock me,	vibrato
stillen jede Pein,	still every pain,	**Tempo:** quarter = 86,
und ein seliges Genügen	and a blessed satisfaction	limited rubato
saug ich mit den Düften ein.	I absorb with the fragrant breezes.	
In den heimlich engen Kreisen	In these hidden narrow places	**Emotion:** both
wird dir wohl, du wildes Herz,	you are well, wild heart,	intimate and brash,
und ein Friede schwebt mit leisen	and a peacefulness floats with	urgency, giving way to
Flügelschlägen niederwärts.	gentle wingbeats downwards.	inner peace.
Singet, holde Vögellieder,	Sing me, tender birds,	**Tone:** Full ensemble
mich in Schlummer sacht!	to soft slumber!	blend; exaggerated
Irre Qualen, löst euch wieder,	You confusing torments, vanish	vowel colors on key
wildes Herz, nun gute Nacht!	again.	words
–Paul Heyse	Wild heart, now good night!	**Tempo:** quarter = 78, free, greatly increased rubato, much ritard to ending

Pulse

The heart-beat, dripping water, a clock ticking are all examples of pulse — a steady re-occurrence of short sounds or beats. There are variations of the pulse, such as **accelerando, ritardando,** and **rubato.** However, all too often the pulse is allowed to stop or wait in order to accommodate a breath, place a final consonant, or some other misbegotten reason. Great caution should be taken **not** to interrupt the pulse of a song when the continuation of the pulse is crucial to the flow and emotion of the text.

6. Rhythm

There are three facets of rhythm that pose difficulties to a performer:

a. **Dotted notes.** Execution of dotted notes demands a brief "lift" to the dot.

In Baroque music this is particularly important: ♩· ♪ becomes ♩ 𝄾 ♪ , or

♩·· 𝄾♪ , when double-dotting is desired. This principle holds true for all styles, legato or non-legato. If there is not a lift to the dotted note, the second note is invariably delayed. Listen carefully to dotted-notes in instrumental as well as vocal music and decide how dotted notes can best be articulated. Singers tend to sing lazy dotted rhythms.

b. **Triplets.** Triplets easily become ♫♩ if not carefully produced as three equal subdivisions of the note value. They have a sensuous languid quality when correctly accomplished.

c. **Rests.** Rests are active points, responsible for keeping the pulse of a piece and the precision of the ensemble. They must be accurately planned as an important part of the phrase; they should not be left indeterminate in length — except, perhaps, for the **Grand Pause [G.P.]** of the Baroque style.

Legato vs. non-legato

Legato can be defined as smooth, connected music. Singers correctly spend much time in vocalizing to achieve a full legato vocal line. However, there are important non-legato considerations as well, and the choral musician should know the non-legato styles, their markings, and how to conduct them:[11]

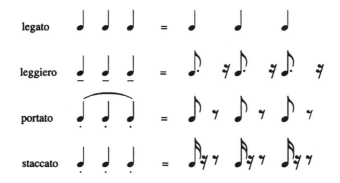

VII. Riser Formations

How a choir is placed on the stage can directly influence the sound of the choir and the success of a choral ensemble. Choral placement of voices can also amplify the style or form of a composition.[12] The choral director should be aware

[11] Apel, Willi, *Harvard Dictionary of Music.* 2nd Edition, Cambridge, Massachusetts: Belknap Press, 1969, p. 465.

[12] See Ray Robinson and Allen Winold, *The Choral Experience.* Prospect Heights, Illinois: Waveland Press, 1992, (re-issue of Harper-Collins, 1976), pp. 177–192, for a detailed discussion of performing arrangements and seating plans.

of factors that determine good choral placement: 1) aural considerations, 2) blend, 3) style, and 4) balance of parts.

Aural considerations.

a. **Open or closed formation.** Using the traditional 3-step choral riser, the distance between singers can affect the sound of the choir and each singer's ability to hear. An open formation — with each singer spaced comfortably apart — allows space for the sound; a closed formation — with each singer standing as close to each other as possible — inhibits the sound.

Demonstration

Place the singers in a tight four-row formation with each singer as close as possible and the heels against the back of each step. While singing, instruct the front row to step forward eight inches and the next two rows to stand forward on the riser steps, creating a space between each row. **Do your hear a difference?** Next, expand the choir — while singing — so that there are six to eight inches between each singer. **Did the sound change?** Repeat this process several times; go to the back of the room and listen. Decide what spacing works best for a specific piece and for the performance hall.

---

b. **"Windows."** Each singer should be able to see the conductor and, most important, able to project the voice to the audience through "windows," rather than into the back of the head of the person standing in front. This seems like a small point, but it is actually very important to the sound of the ensemble.

Demonstration

In a four-row formation align each singer directly behind the other in an open formation; leave a space on the stage-left end of the risers. On cue while singing, have the first and third (or second and fourth) row move a half-step to their left. Clear "windows" should be achieved. Repeat and listen. **Do you hear a difference?**

It is difficult to achieve clear "windows" when back rows enter the risers first, especially in a closed formation where there is no room for adjustments and singers are fixed in place. The adjustment, ideally, should be from front to back — with the front row entering first on the risers; each succeeding row will know exactly how to stand so as to have accurate "windows." This makes for some awkwardness for the back row mounting the tall last step. A director will discover the best way to achieve "windows." Singers can assist the row in front, as they enter the risers, by reaching out with their hands and guiding those immediately in front exactly where to stand. Or, as in the above demonstration, perfect "windows" are achieved by aligning singers vertically, with the front row evenly spaced; at a cue from the conductor (or the choir president, before the conductor enters) alternate rows move a space left (or right) — being careful that the end singer does not step off the riser! The main point is: some plan must be devised for achieving good "windows" or there will be confusion and inaccurate spacing.[13]

The author has found it helpful to duplicate the following master diagrams for planning choral formations on the risers, using a numbering system for the singers (see "Individual Placement" below). By looking at it the singers can easily tell exactly where they are placed on the risers, and how to make good "windows."

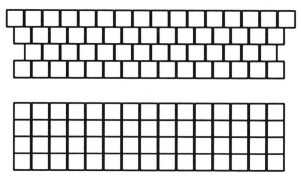

c. Height.

Height differences **can** affect the sound.

Demonstration

Alternate three tall and two short singers of similar vocal timbre in a row. Have them sing. Then equalize the height with boxes or books for the shorter singers. Have them sing again. **Do you hear a difference?** Repeat and listen. Or, stand two singers of equal height so that one is on a chair and the other on the floor. Have them sing. Then have both stand on the floor. **Do you hear a difference?**

Many have found success in equalizing height through the use of small individual boxes. Aside from the rather dramatic aural difference when height is equalized, the ensemble also looks and feels good about itself with everyone of equal height. However, the primary reason for equalizing height is aural; there is a dramatic difference in blend and sound when all ears and sources of sound emission (mouths) are approximately at the same level.

---

[13] The precision and style of the Robert Shaw Chorale entering the stage is well-remembered. The Chorale travelled with square platforms of varying heights to accomodate each individual singer; good "windows" were automatically achieved, with spacing of at least three to four feet between each singer. Some choirs use seated risers (three-feet wide) which allows for great flexibility for placement of the choir and good space between each row.

Placement with Instruments

Voices can be placed near instruments of like timbre when performing with instrumental forces — sopranos near the violins and the basses over with the cellos and string basses. In theory, this seems like it would work well. In practice, how the choir sounds best within itself may be the determining factor. As with all formations the key principle is: **Experiment — change the formation and go to the back of the performance hall and listen.** The director must make the decision which sounds best and be willing to make changes in favor of the best sound for a particular hall.

Soprano/Bass Relationship

As a general rule, blend is enhanced when the outer voices are placed in close proximity on the risers, and the altos and tenors together.

Demonstration

Place the soprano and tenor sections on one side of the risers; the basses and altos on the other side. Sing two short phrases or sections of varied styles and dynamics. Change the formation so that the sopranos and basses are together; altos are next to the tenors. Sing again and listen carefully. **Do you hear a difference?**

Individual Placement

Riser placement in terms of how individual singers blend is crucial to a choir's balance of sound. Aside from height considerations discussed above, the size of voice and ability to blend are important factors to consider. This area is very subjective; a director must make personal decisions on individual placement. Nothing in the following is scientific; nothing can be proven — except by listening — but is offered from the experience of the author.

Demonstration

Determine within a section which voices are **blending** voices (perhaps smaller voices, with ability to hear and a high degree of musicianship) and which voices are **non-blending** (larger voices or those with aural problems or excessive vibrato). Place them in a straight row with the blending voices on one end and the non-blending on the other end. Have them sing a unison song that they all know. Next alternate blending voices and non-blending voices in the row, place a blending voice on each end, if possible. **Listen.** Have them change back and forth. **Do you hear a difference?**

How singers stand in relation to each other has an influence on blend; there seems to be a "favorite" way two singers sound as they attempt to blend that is apparent both to the singers and to anyone listening.[14]

---

[14] This phenomenon is further complicated by the fact that the sympathetic or ideal side changes according to the time of the day! It appears to be linked to the autonomic nervous system which determines many functions of the body – including how we breathe. This can

---

Demonstration

Stand two singers of equal height next to each other and have them sing a unison song they know. **Listen.** Then switch their placement and have them sing again. **Listen carefully.** Alternate positions several times. **Do you hear a difference? Is one side easier for the singers to blend?** Try the same experiment two to four hours later and see if the results are the same.

The author has found success with a numbering system which classifies each singer by degree of blending ability within each section. By using blending numbers — based on the blending quality of singers, according to personal tastes and concepts of choral placement — formation charts can be formed, recalled, and adapted in a clear, efficient system. Through these charts a director is able to see at a glance where the blending voices and non-blending voices are located on the riser formation.

Key to Numbering System

10's — Sop I	50's — Ten I
20's — Sop II	60's — Ten II
30's — Alto I	70's — Bass I
40's — Alto II	80's — Bass II

In the above numbering system, the lower number in each section is the best blending voice; the higher the number, the larger and least blending voice. Example: No. 20 is the best-blending second soprano; No. 58, one of the least-blending first tenors.

This numbering system is illustrated by the following chart for a choir of 60 voices (17 sopranos, 14 altos, 13 tenors, and 16 basses) arranged in an "Olaf" formation:[15]

80	85	81	86	82	87	83	84	63	66	62	65	61	64	60
70	75	71	76	72	77	73	74	53	52	55	51	54	50	
20	25	21	26	22	27	23	24	43	46	42	45	41	44	40
10	15	11	16	12	17	13	18	14	33	36	32	35	31	34	30

In the above chart, notice that the better blending voices are placed on the ends of the rows and the non-blending singers are interspersed with the better-blending voices. Adjustments can be made to put the largest voices nearer to

---

be demonstrated by closing off one nostril with a finger pressed against the side of the nose and breathing; next, the other nostril, and breathing. One side is felt easier to breathe through than the other, and this changes every two to four hours. This principle appears to transfer to how we listen and blend with other voices; the sympathetic side changes every two to four hours. Further research is required to explain this curiosity.

[15] An "Olaf" formation is identified by Robinson and Winold, *Op.Cit.*, as that made famous by F. Melius Christiansen with the St. Olaf Choir; it has basses behind the sopranos on stage-right; the tenors in back of the altos on stage-left.

the center — but always with blending voices on either side. Again, this is an area that involves personal taste. The director must experiment, and be willing to adjust when the ear — **not theory** — confirms which way sounds better.

The chart/numbering system has several advantages. It gives the singers a visual picture of the riser formation and clearly shows where each singers stands. (It is helpful to include a listing of singers' names with choir numbers along side the chart so that the singers know where they are placed in relation to others.) In theory, once a director decides where the blending voices and non-blending voices will be placed in this numbering system, the same chart is valid each year, providing there are the same number of singers on a part. If not, simple adjustments can be made. Also, choir numbers based on section assignment are useful when assigning music to new singers at the start of the year; they assure that music will be assigned with markings and translations as previously rehearsed for the same part. (For instance, music marked "No. 61" would always be assigned to a second tenor.)

Singers who have less blending voices should understand that a higher choir number is not a "put-down"; it should be explained that blending considerations, as well as voice quality, intonation, musicianship, and confidence on a part, take precedence over the size of the voice.

Sectional or mixed

Decisions on whether to use a sectional or a mixed (quartet) formation should be based on sound as well as style, and they should be arrived at through experimentation and listening.

Advantages of quartet style formations:
· Sound is more rich and homogeneous.
· Part independence and musicianship is encouraged.
· Strong social and musical pressures are established.
· Singers are able to hear the complete chord structure.

Disadvantages to a quartet style:
· Contrapuntally conceived music suffers from homogeneity of parts.
· Less mature voices tend to reduce sound output, resulting in a tonal blandness.
· Individual voices predominate in <u>forte</u> singing.
· Stereotyped sound results from exclusive use of quartet style.

Advantages with a sectional formation:
· Clarity of sectional strength is intensified, especially in contrapuntal music.
· Blending and tuning within a section
· A dramatic impetus is given to music with opposing forces; men vs. women, for example.

The above is subject to hot debate. In recent years many directors have come "full-circle" in their use of quartet and sectional arrangements. However, many feel that there is no **one** way to sing **all** music — that formations must be based on the music first and foremost. Again, the director's ear is all-important. Also, the audience must be considered; listeners deserve a variety of sounds during the course of a concert. This does not mean that choirs have to "hop around like jackrabbits" after each number. Ehmann advises "grouping compositions of similar types" as an important principle of good programming. He also states that "the musical form of the work determines the formation of the choir."[16]

Quartet Variations.

A "pure quartet" formation attempts to achieve as much variety as possible with no voice standing next to another of the same section:

B	A	T	S	B	A	T	S	B	A	T
	T	S	B	A	T	S	B	T	S	B
A	T	S	B	A	T	S	B	A

A "modified quartet" formation places singers so that there is some sympathy with a like voice while still retaining a basic quartet style:[17]

B	A	S	T	B	A	B	T	S	A	B
	T	A	S	B	T	T	B	S	A	T
A	T	S	B	S	B	S	T	A

Some directors capitalize on the basic soprano/bass relationship as a principle in the following formation:

S	B	S	B	S	B	S	B	A	T	A	T	A	T
B	S	B	S	B	S	B	S	T	A	T	A	T	A
S	B	S	B	S	B	S	B	A	T	A	T	A	T
B	S	B	S	B	S	B	S	T	A	T	A	T	A

It is also possible to achieve vertical quartets by placing sections across on the same row:

B1	B2
T1	T2
A1	A2
S1	S2

The above formation can be modified to move the sopranos from the front row, which some feel[18] is advantageous to the sound; it also places the sopranos next to the basses.[19]

---

[16] Wilhelm Ehmann, *Choral Directing.* Minneapolis: Augsburg, 1968, pp.7–14.

[17] This is the formation used by the Robert Shaw Chorale with seven quartets plus two extra singers arranged in mirror fashion, as reported in Robinson and Winold, *Op.cit.*, p180.

[18] Riser formation opinions in this chapter are based on surveys taken by the author with choir directors of performing choirs at ACDA divisional conventions in 1988 and 1990.

[19] If height adjustments are made with boxes and there is open spacing with clear "windows," shorter singers will be able to stand in rows behind taller singers.

Section Formations

A variety of sectional arrangements are possible. Most common is the "Olaf" arrangement given above. An "SBTA" formation is also possible, which places the men in the center of the choir:

S	B	T	A
S	B	T	A
S	B	T	A
S	B	T	A

Some directors modify the above into a "Vertical BSTA" formation:

S	B	S	B	S	B	S	B	A	T	A	T	A	T	A
S	B	S	B	S	B	S	B	A	T	A	T	A	T	A
S	B	S	B	S	B	S	B	A	T	A	T	A	T	A
S	B	S	B	S	B	S	B	A	T	A	T	A	T	A

While it appears the above is a scrambled formation (especially when recommended "windows" are achieved), sectional strength is retained by singers of like voices in vertical rows. The above can be modified further by having the first two rows rotate with the last two rows to form a "Modified BSTA" formation:

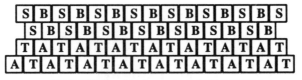

Large festival choirs can make use of an arrangement which divides the predominating sound of stronger sections – most often, the sopranos and altos:

S	S	S	A	A	B	B	B	B	B	A	A	S	S	S
S	S	A	A	B	B	B	B	B	B	A	A	S	S	
S	S	A	A	T	T	T	T	T	A	A	S	S		
S	S	A	A	T	T	T	T	T	A	A	S	S		

Imbalance of Parts

Choice of formation is crucial for a choir with an imbalance of parts. A weaker section is often found placed on the back row where hearing is difficult; it can be strengthened by more favorable placement within the body of the choral sound.

Imbalanced Formation A:

Imbalanced Formation B:

Optional Arrangements

With a little imagination and experimentation several optional arrangements are possible — with or without the use of the traditional three or four-step risers:

a. In a two-row arrangement with a chamber choir, consider a curved, multi-level formation, instead of straight lines, so that the singers may hear others at the far end and relate to each other better:

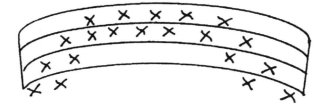

b. Black boxes of various heights (constructed so that three fit within each other for transporting) can be effectively utilized as a substitute for choral risers. They are useful when singing in a choir loft on tour and there is not room for traditional risers. They allow for level variations in a variety of arrangements — here, one more traditional and the other more abstract:

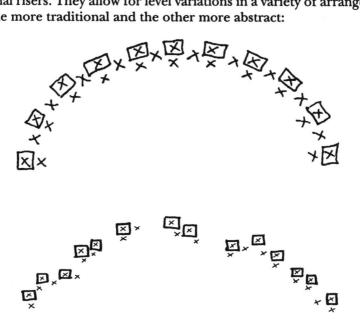

Appearance/Discipline

How a choir looks and relates to an audience is very important to a choral presentation. Good stage etiquette is a **must**, and it should be planned carefully. From the moment the singers appear on stage they are saying something very important to the audience: "We know what we're doing. We love to sing, and we respect the art of making music. We're here to give our best — to represent the composer(s) well and the music that we have selected to sing for you." Any talking, casualness, itching is out of place. Individual hand movements bring attention to a singer and distract the audience. We can take our cue from artists and professional groups who enter the performing area with all grace and respect for the audience. Spend some time talking about concert decorum; let the singers and the officers of the group get involved. Video-tape a performance and analyze how the choir looks as well as sounds.

Conclusion

In our growth as musicians we learn and are inspired by our teachers. Along the way we may have been "turned on" to music through a first-grade rhythm band; an elementary or junior high chorus; a high school, then a college choir; professors who cared and gave us their best; a voice teacher who guided progress — both vocally and otherwise! And then, how much was learned in that first unforgettable year of teaching. The educational process continues, still after teaching for many years, if we are growing in our field as choral directors. The quote attributed to Pablo Casals, the world-renowned cellist/composer is legend. When asked why he still practiced five and six hours a day, he replied, "Because I think I'm getting somewhere." The demand is clearly to continue learning — to ask questions, listen for new concepts, sacrifice all for the best performance possible.

The techniques in making music are difficult to discuss. The "tools" used to hone conducting skills and choral methods are extremely personal. There is no "one" way to approach how music is put together — otherwise music would be a science and not an art form. Most of what we know comes from someone else — what we read and hear from others. We literally "steal" — then we assimilate, toss about, and come up with our own ideas and way of thinking about things. It is within this spirit that this chapter is offered.

If we become more careful about every facet of choral music, we grow as choral directors. This "pickiness" is requisite to artistic expression. There is no other field exactly like choral music. We make music, yes, just as a fine violinist or pianist makes music. We conduct an ensemble, as a band or orchestra director also directs large groups of musicians. (Many of our tools are learned from instrumental musicians.) But we also deal intimately with **texts** — and this makes choral musicians a very special breed.

The job is awesome! An inquisitive mind and explorative persistence show the way. To repeat, tools are not the end, only the means. A choir composed of singers who are able to recognize ahead of time when a specific tool is required reaches a higher level of ensemble more efficiently. Tools form the basis for the process of achieving choral excellence.

Effective Choral Programming

G. Roberts Kolb

Degree in hand, you look forward with great eagerness to your initial employment as a *conductor*. You can now confidently conduct mixed meters, know seventeen different reasons that your choir might sing under pitch, and have a database file on your computer that contains over 13K of powerful imagery that will inspire your singers to new and exciting choral heights. But then you find yourself staring at a sheet of paper that is blank save for its heading: "Repertoire for Next Year."

The first impulse of most of us in this situation has probably been to program all of those works that were our favorites in our college chorus. "I loved singing it — can't wait to conduct it!" This is a noble impulse. It is natural and appropriate that the most lasting part of our education in choral literature comprises those works whose study involved actual performance. One hopes, however, that a conducting career will be of sufficient length that programming needs will extend beyond the list of personal old favorites. Besides, few of us will start out with an ensemble that can handle the same repertoire we loved as collegiate singers. (Is your ninth-grade chorale really up to Bach's *Singet dem Herrn*? Yes, Brahms's *Schaffe in mir, Gott* is a wonderful piece, but it is unlikely that it will work well for your women's glee club.)

What, then, are you to do?

Happily, there is not a single correct path to good programming. Many conductors produce interesting programs, yet they certainly do not all follow the same model. There is opportunity here for experimentation — for creativity. There are a few basic considerations, however, that underlie effective programming — whether consciously or intuitively — over a period of time:

· Consider for whom you are programming.
· Include variety.
· Seek unity.
· Know why you program each piece.
· Stay abreast of what others are doing.

These seem self-evident, but each conceals more complexity than we might at first assume.

For Whom Do We Program?

It is easy to overlook the most fundamental of programming questions: For *whom* are you programming? The answer to that question will have a major impact on repertoire decisions.

As you make decisions about repertoire, there are three constituencies whose interests you have at least some obligation to consider: the singers, yourself (the conductor), and the audience. All should be considered, but individually they will not always lead to the same choices. Although the relative weight given will vary with the nature of the ensemble and its performances, *effective programming recognizes the importance of each.*

Programming for the Singers

The conductor is a teacher. Whether singers are students, or adult singers in community or church choirs, or even professional singers, all need instruction to enable them to progress as an ensemble, to learn and to interpret the music, and to communicate that music to an audience. The level at which that instruction takes place will vary enormously from ensemble to ensemble, but instruction there must always be, and the repertoire we select is the vehicle for that teaching.

In rehearsing and performing a piece of music, singers learn not only the musical qualities of that particular work, but also characteristics of the composer's style and of the historical period in which it was composed — all relevant to their approach to other works. Vocal and musical skills are also taught, and the music is the vehicle through which the teaching can happen. If you plan to help your singers learn how to handle *forte* passages while maintaining good vocal production, you must not provide a musical diet that consists only of Renaissance motets and madrigals. Similarly, if a goal is to improve the choir's ability to handle complex rhythms, you must do something other than a Haydn mass. Music should be selected that will fully develop a choir's potential.

Such selection can involve a clear link between a piece of music and a specific teaching objective. In a recent year, anticipating a young and inexperienced tenor section, the author programmed William Byrd's *Look Down, O Lord* because its opening tenor phrase (Fig. 1 below) seemed ideal for teaching the tenors to use their head voices and to let that production influence the production of lower notes as well. Once achieved for this phrase, this technique was then applied to other literature.

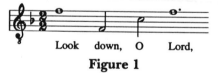

Look   down,   O   Lord,

Figure 1

Pedagogical objectives, then, are a factor in repertoire selection. Other questions should be considered as well:

· Who are my singers?
· Why are they singing in this chorus?
· What musical experience do they bring with them?
· How has this shaped their musical taste?

If we let the answers to such questions influence our programming decisions, it does *not* mean that our repertoire will be no different than if we left its selection to a committee of singers, for that would be to abandon our responsibility as teachers. It *does* mean that we will try to include pieces that will be immediately attractive, as well as those that will be "an acquired taste." For most ensembles, early rewards in the rehearsal process are important to ensure that there are still singers left to reap those rewards that come at the end of the process. If a work is programmed that singers will enjoy singing and rehearsing from the beginning, they will be more likely to work to learn and appreciate another work that is not so accessible and whose worth becomes manifest only after an investment of time and toil.

In the end, of course, whatever repertoire you choose must be appropriate for your ensemble. The question of "fit" can be an obvious one: You will not program a piece with an important tenor solo if you have no tenor soloists. There are less obvious considerations as well, such as the vocal maturity of the singers. You may, for example, wish to avoid a work with a high tessitura if your voices are young.

We must also consider the level of skill of the ensemble. No one is well-served — not the singers, not the conductor, and certainly not the audience — if we consistently program music that is beyond the capabilities of our singers. On the other hand, we want to provide music that will challenge the ensemble and enable it to grow. Finding that balance will require continual evaluation. Flexibility is the key, for while planning is essential, we should be willing to make changes in our intended repertoire as we discover strengths or weaknesses that were unknown to us as at the initial planning stage.

Programming for Self

We do in fact program for ourselves. Some may pretend that this is not so, but such pretence is clearly false. We are choral conductors because we derive pleasure from rehearsing and performing worthwhile choral literature — from performing on the choral instrument, if you will. *Of course* we will select music that we like, music that we want to perform. *Of course* our own taste in music will be reflected in the repertoire of our ensembles.

There is danger here, however. We cannot continue to grow as conductors and musicians unless we stretch ourselves occasionally, experimenting with styles and composers that are new to us or that have never been our favorites — but perhaps are admired by colleagues whom we respect. It has been debated whether or not a conductor can properly teach and conduct a piece that he or she does not like. The answer is probably "yes," but this question ignores the more fundamental and important one: Can a conductor develop an appreciation for works (or composers, styles, genres, etc.) that he or she "doesn't like"? The answer here is certainly "yes." The author still remembers the dislike once held for the music of Henry Purcell — a dislike that was cured when Purcell's songs and anthems became the subject of a seminar presentation in graduate school. All of us, no doubt, believe that our students would learn to love our favorite works and composers even as we do if they would just be patient and "give it a chance." How unfair these two-edged swords!

Programming for ourselves, then, is more than simply selecting pieces that we like. It is also selecting pieces that we need to do in order to continue our own growth as teaching musicians.

Programming for the Audience

At some point your chorus will perform, and performance implies someone to listen, someone to whom we will try to communicate through choral song: the audience. What is the nature of our responsibility to the audience as we choose our repertoire? The answer to this question will vary somewhat with the nature of the ensemble and of the audience.

An audience comprising mostly parents and family of the singers will be different from a paying audience that comes for love of music alone. Some may encounter great pressure to program music that will entertain such an audience. In such situations, however, we should not hesitate to point out that entertaining the audience is not our ultimate goal. In an educational setting, performance is the principal motivational tool for achieving another, more important objective: enabling our students to grow as singers and musicians.

This is not to say that there is never a place for "pops" pieces artistically performed, but simply that a perceived need to provide entertainment for our audiences should not override any obligation to our singers and ourselves. In fact, the principles of variety and unity discussed below serve an audience as well as the performers.

Variety in Programming

Our discussion of the "who" of programming has led us to a simple idea that underlies effective programming — variety, in a number of guises:
· variety of musical styles and historical periods
· variety of moods
· variety of languages
· variety of keys
· variety of difficulties
· variety of performing forces

Variety of Musical Styles and Historical Periods

Good programming will include a variety of works from different style periods. This principle follows directly from our educational responsibility to our singers. If your choir performs only nineteenth century music, your singers may become very proficient and wise in the performance of Brahms and Mendelssohn, but what will they learn of the musical style of Schütz or Josquin? Thus, unless the ensemble is one that is specifically geared to music of a particular period, the conductor's responsibility to the musical development of the singers seems to require a repertoire that includes a diversity of musical styles.[1]

---

[1] It is worth noting that even professional ensembles whose initial repertoire is essentially drawn from a single historical period tend over time to enlarge that repertoire to include a greater variety of musical styles. As a case in point, the author recently heard a splendid concert by the Scholars of London, an ensemble that has evolved from its all-male beginning to now include a female soprano and to perform repertoire that includes Mendelssohn part-songs and commissioned twentieth century works, as well as the music of Josquin, Palestrina, and Lassus.

Whether this means that there is such a variety in any given program depends on the nature of that particular concert and on how it fits with other concerts in a given academic year or season. Obviously, an ensemble that performs major works will not perform works from different periods on each concert. Over a period of time, however, the repertoire of such an ensemble should reflect this diversity.

Variety of Moods

Effective programming will involve the singers and the audience in a variety of emotional experiences. An unrelenting diet of "Ay me, alas!" can exhaust singers and listeners alike. After singing of unrequited love, let it be requited for awhile! Let both life and death, joy and sorrow, find musical expression in your program. Follow a group of Lenten motets with some English madrigals. (Of course, if the program is a sacred Lenten program, this option is not available, so find some Lenten texts that contain an occasional "alleluia!")

A corollary to this principle is never to make repertoire decisions in a single sitting, lest singers and audience both become victims of a single day's dark humor. There will be those days when anything even remotely cheerful will seem unworthy, even as there will also be days when music that portrays suffering will seem an unnecessary blight. Neither is true, and the wise programmer will ensure that passing moods are not preserved in the repertoire of an entire year.

Variety of Languages

We work and perform in an era when singing in the original language has become expected, when most are no longer willing to accept the sacrifice of so much of the composer's original intentions that singing in translation necessitates. This introduces another variable that we need keep in mind as we program literature for our choirs. It is all too easy to choose a tentative repertoire for a tour program only to realize that the program is in German from beginning to end. For all the reasons that variety of style and period are important, so is variety of languages. And don't forget to include works in English! (This is not as obvious as it sounds, and audience and singers alike will be grateful.)

Variety of Keys

There is a potential monotony to unchanging tonal centers that should be avoided. The author well remembers a concert early in his conducting career that was a model of variety, with several style periods and languages represented. After the concert a colleague said the obligatory kind things, but then observed: "It was a very long time before we escaped the key of F." The program was arranged chronologically, and we changed keys only when we left the Renaissance!

Consideration, then, should also be given to tonal variety in a concert.

Variety of Difficulties

Everything in a program need not be a tour de force — nor should it be. Technical difficulty is not a prerequisite for artistic worth. In the author's experience, a performance by Iva Dee Hiatt and the Smith College Glee Club at a college chapel service will never be forgotten. They sang a two-voice Schütz motet from the *Kleine geistliche Konzerte* with lovely tone, beautifully shaped phrases, and sublime ensemble, and it is this piece that is long-remembered, while performances of other works much more complex and difficult have been forgotten.

While we should certainly program works that are technically difficult and that challenge the singers, we should never forget simplicity — works that allow for shaping a phrase and touching the audience with that which is beautiful.

Variety of Performing Forces

Finally, it is not necessary that every work on a program be performed by the entire ensemble. One section of the concert can be performed by a smaller "madrigal" ensemble. Soloists or solo ensembles can be effectively interspersed.

Neither is it necessary for a mixed ensemble to deprive itself and its audience of some of the splendid music for men's or women's voices. It is consistently popular with both singers and audience when men and women perform separately within a mixed-choir concert.

Unity in Programming

While variety seems to be the essential element, the most effective programming also looks for connections, for ways to bring unity to the program or to sections of the program. There are many ways to do this. One can design programs around a particular theme or the music of a single composer or group of composers. The year 1985 saw many concerts of the music of Schütz, for example — not just Bach and Handel! — as musicians celebrated the 400th anniversary of his birth. In the same way, 1992 was an appropriate year for music of Les Six, as both Honegger and Milhaud were born in 1892.

Often, of course, our concerts cannot adhere to a single theme. Connections can still be made within groups, however, whether textual, stylistic, or thematic.

It may be helpful to look at a few models. These are not set forth as ideal or beyond improvement, but they may help to suggest ways in which these dual principles of variety and unity can be realized.

Figure 2 shows two different programs, each built on the works of a single composer. By their very nature then, a basic unity is embodied in these programs. In the Schütz program, the linking of separate motets with three strophes of the *Becker Psalter* setting of Psalm 23 provides greater unity to the first half. Although not readily apparent from the printed program, greater variety is achieved in that the second and third *Kleine geistliche Konzerte* are performed by solo voices. In the second half, further variety in the performing forces is provided naturally by the music, which calls for a solo trio separated from the full ensemble for the final section.

Similarly, the Monteverdi program, with its sacred first half and secular second half, achieves variety within the context of a single composer by varying the performing forces: The second and fourth motets are for solo voices, the final madrigal adds continuo and two violins, and in our performance, the *Lamento d'Arianna* was performed by a solo quintet.

Music of Heinrich Schütz (1585-1672)	Music of Claudio Monteverdi (c. 1567-1643)

Ist Gott für uns, SWV 329
    from *Kleine geistliche Konzerte II*
    (1639)
	Confitebor all francese

	Laudate Dominum
Psalm 23 (strophe 1), SWV 120 from *Beckerscher Psalter* (1628)	Nisi Dominus

Wohl dem, der nicht wandelt, SWV 290
    from *Kleine geistliche Konzerte I*
    (1636)
	Confitebor tibi

	Beatus vir
Psalm 23 (strophe 2)	**Intermission**
Ich liege und schlafe, SWV 310 from *Kleine geistliche Konzerte II*	*Madrigals*
Psalm 23 (strophe 3)	Ecco mormorar l'onde (Book II)
So fahr ich hin zu Jesu Christ, SWV 379 from *Geistliche Chormusik* (1648)	A un giro sol (Book IV)
	Sfogava con le stelle (Book IV)

Intermission	Lamento d'Arianna (Book VI)
	    Lasciatemi morire
	    O Teseo mio
	    Dove, dove è fede
	    Ahi ch'ei non pur risponde

Musikalische Exequien (1636)
    Concert in Form einr teutschen
    Missa, SWV 279
    Motet: Herr, wenn ich nur dich
        habe, SWV 280
    Canticum B. Simeonis, SWV 281
	Hor ch'el ciel e la terra (Book VIII)

Figure 2: Two "Composer" Programs

William Byrd (1543-1623)	Mass for Four Voices (c. 1592)
Kyrie, Gloria, Credo, Sanctus, Benedictus, Agnus Dei	

* A Brief Intermission *

Frank Martin (1890-1974)	Mass for Double Chorus (1922)
Kyrie, Gloria, Credo, Sanctus, Agnus Dei	

* A Brief Intermission *

Ariel Ramírez (b. 1921)	Misa Criolla (1963)
Kyrie, Gloria, Credo, Sanctus, Agnus Dei	

Figure 3: A "Theme" Concert

A "theme" concert is illustrated by Figure 3. The unity here is obvious: three settings of the Ordinary of the Mass. But each setting is quite different from the other two, both in style and in performing forces: The Byrd Mass is in the contrapuntal style of the late Renaissance; the Martin Mass combines Gregorian-like melodies, post-Romantic harmonies, and frequent rhythmic intricacies in a setting for double choir; and the *Misa Criolla*, based on the melodies and rhythms of South American folk music, employs solo voices as well as chorus to the accompaniment of keyboard, guitars, and several percussion instruments.

Music of the People

Bela Bartok (1881-1945)   *Four Slovak Songs*
             Zadala mamka, zadala dcéru
             Na holi, na holi
             Rada pila, raja jedla
             Gajdujte, gajdence

Ralph Vaughan Williams (1872-1958)   from *Five English Folk-Songs*
             The Dark-Eyed Sailor
             The Lover's Ghost
             Just as the Tide Was Flowing

Johannes Brahms (1833-1897   *Zigeunerlieder*
             He Zigeuner
             Hochgetürmte Rimaflut
             Wißt ihr, wann mein Kindchen
             Lieber Gott, du weißt
             Brauner Bursche führt zum Tanze
             Röslein dreie in der Reihe
             Kommt der manchmal in den Sinn
             Horch, der Wind klagt
             Weit und breit
             Mond verhüllt sein Angesicht
             Rote Abendwolken

Intermission

Canadian Folk Songs

arr. Stephen Chatman   John Kanaka
arr. Imant Raminsh   Doukhobor Lullaby
arr. Harry Somers   Feller from Fortune

American Folk Songs

arr. William Penfield   Minstrel Boy
arr. James Erb   Shenandoah
arr. Gail Kubik   Oh Dear, What Can the Matter Be!
arr. G. Roberts Kolb   Mary Wore Three Links of Chain
arr. Jester Hairston   Hold On!

Figure 4: Music of the People

"Music of the People" is the theme that ties together the concert of Figure 4, a program that demonstrates that "lighter" fare can be a filling meal indeed!

A final illustration of thematic programming is found in Figure 5. The music is arranged according to the sequence of events in the Christmas story. Within each group, the texts have a common theme, and these are set forth visually for the audience in the guise of verses of scripture. Within this thematic unity, there is considerable variety of styles, with music ranging from Gregorian chant (the alternate verses of the Lassus *Magnificat*) to Power and Josquin to Distler and Duruflé to lighter carol settings. Once again, there is also some diversity in the performing forces employed: *Beata progenies* is sung by the men alone, even as the Duruflé *Tota pulchra es* is sung by the women. *Hymn to the Virgin* calls for a solo quartet separate from the tutti ensemble, and of course the audience is involved as performers on the carols that conclude most thematic sections.

I

O beatum et sacrosanctum — Peter Philips (c. 1561-1628)

Audience Carol — "All My Heart This Night Rejoices" — No. 123

II

And there shall come forth a rod out of the stem of Jesse, and a branch shall grow out of his roots: and the spirit of the Lord shall rest upon him...

Beata progenies — Leonel Power (d. 1445)

Surge illuminare — William Byrd (1543-1623)

Wachet auf, ruft uns die Stimme — Johann Christoph Friedrich Bach (1732-1795)

Audience Carol — "O Come, O Come Emmanuel" — No. 110

III

And the angel Gabriel was sent from God to a virgin espoused to a man whose name was Joseph, of the house of David; and the virgin's name was Mary. And the angel came in unto her, and said, "Hail, thou that are highly favored, the Lord is with thee; blessed art thou among women."

Hymn to the Virgin — Benjamin Britten (1913-1976)

Ave Maria — Josquin des Prez (c. 1440-1521)

Total pulchra es — Maurice Duruflé (1902-1987)

Audience Carol — "From Heaven Above to Earth I Come" — No. 121

IV

And Mary said, "My soul doth magnify the Lord, and my spirit hath rejoiced in God my Savior..."

Magnificat primi toni — Orlando de Lassus (1532-1594)

V

And so it was that the days were accomplished that she should be delivered. And she brought forth her first-born son, and wrapped him in swaddling clothes, and laid him in a manger, because there was no room for them in the inn.

Infant Holy, Infant Lowly — Polish Carol, arr. Willcocks

Hodie Christus natus est — Jan Pieterszoon Sweelinck (1562-1621)

Rocking — Czech Carol, arr. Willcocks

Audience Carol — "On This Day Earth Shall Ring" — No. 136

VI

And lo, the star, which they saw in the east, went before them, till it came and stood over where the young child was. And when they were come into the house, they saw the child and Mary his mother, and fell down, and worshipped him.

Singet frisch und wohlgemut — Hugo Distler (1908-1942)

Audience Carol — "Angels We Have Heard on High" — No. 116

Figure 5: A Christmas Program

I	
Deutsches Magnificat	Heinrich Schütz (1585-1672)
Singet frisch und wohlgemut	Hugo Distler (1908-1942)

II

Super flumina Babylonis	Giovanni P. da Palestrina (1522-1596)
Super flumina Babylonis	Guillaume Bouzignac (fl. c. 1630)
Baruch Haba B'shaym Adonai	Salomone Rossi (1570-1628)
Laus Dei creatoris	Samuel Pellman (b. 1953)

Intermission

III

Il bianco e dolce cigno	Orazio Vecchi (1550-1605)
El Grillo	Josquin des Prez (c. 1440-1521)
Sweet Honey-sucking Bee	John Wilbye (1574-1638)

IV

Three Shakespeare Songs	Christopher Brown
Tell Me Where Is Fancy Bred	(b. 1943)
Come Unto These Yellow Sands	
Come Away Death	

V

The Turtle Dove	English Folk Song arr. Kolb
Ezekiel Saw de Wheel	Spiritual arr. Dawson

I	
Recordare, virgo Mater	attr. to Josquin des Prez (c. 1440-1521)
Si ignoras te	Cipriano de Rore (1516-1565)
Duo seraphim clamabant	Tomás Luis de Victoria (c. 1549-1611)

II

As Fair as Morn	John Wilbye (1574-1638)
Come Shepherd Swains	John Wilbye

III

Dixit Dominus	Jean-Baptiste Lully (1632-1687)

IV

Gott ist mein Hirt	Franz Schubert (1797-1828)
Ständchen	Franz Schubert

Intermission

V

Petites Voix	Francis Poulenc (1899-1963)
La petite fille sage	
Le chien perdu	
En rentrant de l'école	
Le petit garçon malade	
Le hérisson	

VI

Three Madrigals (1960)	Ernst Krenek
Fairies' Song	(b. 1900)
The Four Sweet Months	
Summer Again	

VII

Ain'-a that Good News!	arr. Dawson
Mary Wore Three Links of Chain	arr. Kolb
Little Innocent Lamb	arr. Bartholomew

Figure 6: Two Tour Programs

We conclude this brief look at some programming examples with two programs that are not thematic in nature (Figure 6). These are two tour programs, the first for a mixed chorus, the second for a women's chorus. While both represent a variety of styles and composers, the organizing principles are different. The program for a women's chorus (on the right) is arranged chronologically, whereas the program on the left is not. While the chronological organization itself gives a certain unity, the author has come in later years to prefer the asynchronous arrangement, if for no other reason than the principle of varieties of key areas discussed above.

Thus in the mixed-chorus program, we begin with the double-choir *Deutsches Magnificat* of Schütz and follow it immediately with a Distler motet, recognizing implicitly in our programming the direct line of Lutheran musical style from Schütz through Bach to Distler. The second group includes four psalm settings, beginning with two very different yet nearly contemporaneous settings of verses of Psalm 136 (137), followed by yet a third setting from the same era, this one in Hebrew, and concluding with a commissioned setting of Psalm 19 for chorus, piano, and brass.

After the intermission, a smaller ensemble sings three Renaissance secular works, which have an additional connection in that all three are about animals! Three twentieth century settings of English texts are then followed by a concluding group of folk song arrangements.

Know Why You Program Each Piece

And so now the decisions have been made, and your repertoire for next year is set. The thoughtful programmer may well have quite different reasons for programming each piece in a concert, and so this piece of advice: Make a brief note to yourself on why you have selected each piece, whether it be because it gives you the opportunity to work with your ensemble to develop some particular skills, or because it provides a good emotional counterfoil to the piece right before it in the program, or because you want to explore the stylistic links between two or three different composers.

Why such a note? As you work through the rehearsal process, you can then occasionally remind yourself why you chose any given piece in the first place. It is very easy, in the "heat of battle," to overlook our initial priorities. When the notes and rhythms take longer to learn than we imagined possible, we can lose sight of the beautiful phrasing we hoped to create, or the tone color we were going to develop, or the emotions that we hoped to convey. There is never enough time, and if we discover that we cannot accomplish everything that we hoped, we must make choices. Those choices ought to be informed by the reasons for programming a particular piece, lest we find ourselves having included a work because of its powerful text, only to have the text remain unintelligible to the listener because we never found the time to work on diction!

Stay Abreast of What Others Are Doing

We learn from colleagues, and we can gain ideas for new works by learning from others. For the author, one of the most important benefits from attending conventions, such as those of the American Choral Directors Association, is the opportunity to hear good choirs and a variety of literature. Later we come back to these programs and discover marginal notations we had made about the worth of a particular piece, and find new works for our choir.

This, then, is the final word of advice: Do not be complacent, content with self-immersion in your own programming ideas. Seize the opportunity to listen to other choirs. Look at all the programs you can. It is in this way that we can continually refresh and renew ourselves, as we discover new repertoire and new ideas about how to create interesting programs that are at the same time diverse and unified.

Resources for the Choral Conductor

Scott W. Dorsey

Among the factors which determine one's success as a choral musician is the ability to find information and materials. The choral conductor must serve in many different capacities — conductor, musicologist, music educator, vocal coach, educational psychologist, music theoretician, administrator, to name but a few. It is thus reasonable that one should have the widest possible array of resources at one's disposal. The familiar adage, "It's not what you know, it's who you know," could be paraphrased "It's not what or even who you know, it's knowing where to look."

The most obvious place to locate resources and information pertinent to the choral musician is the music library at a college or university. While the specific holdings will vary depending upon the primary thrust and resources of the institution, a university music library is the major resource for the choral musician. Of the many important resource volumes in a collegiate music library, one crucial resource is Anna Harriet Heyer's, *Historical Sets, Collected Editions and Monuments of Music: A Guide to Their Contents* (Chicago: American Library Association, 1957). For an in-depth discussion on proper use of music library facilities, consult commentaries by both V. Duckles and R. Watanabe, listed below under "Suggested Readings for the Choral Conductor." Despite the importance of the university music library, however, many choral conductors do not reside in an area convenient to a major institution of higher learning. It is important, then, that the choral director develop a personal collection of holdings that will enable the conductor to carry on the basic study and research necessary in any choral conducting position.

This chapter will endeavor to outline general types of study and research resources that might be useful to the choral conductor. Specific materials will depend to a great extent on the conductor's area of specialization and the requirements of an individual position. Also included in this discussion are methods through which one may obtain resources without excessive financial burden.[1]

Professional Publications

There are a number of professional organizations devoted to choral music and to the enrichment of musical culture; many of these associations produce publications of high quality and intellectual depth. Among the best resources available to the choral conductor are professional journals. These publications

---

[1] Names and addresses are provided in this chapter solely as an aid to the student and by no means constitute an endorsement for selected commercial firms or organizations by either the author, the editor, or the publisher. It is an ongoing responsibility of the choral musician to update and expand a list of publishers, firms, and organizations that produce useful resources.

provide the conductor with articles on a wide variety of topics, many of which offer the latest scholarly findings on vocal health, performance editions, historical discoveries, and numerous other related subjects.

Professional publications also offer a wealth of information concerning recent publications of scores and musical texts, and other developments of interest to the choral conductor. Advertisements found in such publications make known the availability of a wide range of valuable services from the music industry, such as music publishers, tour agencies, management firms, festivals, choir risers and performance attire. Journals can also alert the choral professional to important career information concerning graduate school opportunities and job openings. The following is a list of several professional journals that might prove particularly useful to the choral conductor:

American Choral Review. Journal of the American Choral Foundation. Administered by Chorus America, Inc.. 2111 Sansom Street, Philadelphia, PA 19103. This publication provides useful, scholarly articles on choral literature and related writings on such subjects as new choral scores, the release of choral recordings, and concert reviews. The *Research Memorandum Series* is another important publication of the American Choral Foundation. Each issue of the *Research Memorandum Series* is devoted to a single topic of discussion. Prior to September, 1991, the *American Choral Review* and the *Research Memorandum Series* were released separately. After that time, the two journals were incorporated into a third publication, *Voice* the quarterly newsletter of Chorus America, Inc. Back issues of the *American Choral Review* and the *Research Memorandum Series* are available from Chorus America.

Choral Journal. Journal of the American Choral Directors Association. P.O. Box 6310, Lawton, OK 73506. Published ten times annually, the *Choral Journal* is the foremost American publication devoted to the choral art. It presents a wide assortment of articles, from motivational "how-to" approaches to improving rehearsal technique to scholarly discussions of historical issues related to choral music. Regular features include reviews of new books and choral scores, research reports, and interviews with significant choral conductors.

Choristers Guild Letters. Official publication of the Choristers Guild. 2834 West Kingsley, Garland, TX 75041. Produced primarily for the church musician, the *Choristers Guild Letters* offers appropriate news items as well as articles on children's choirs and handbell ensembles.

Chorus! 2131 Pleasant Hill Road, Suite 151–121, Duluth, GA 30136. Published monthly since June, 1989, *Chorus!* is printed with a newspaper format. It features interviews with notable choral figures, writings on various topics of research, and other items of interest to "the choral music enthusiast."

Journal of the American Musicological Society. 201 South 34th Street, Philadelphia, PA 19104-6313. Published thrice annually, *JAMS* is devoted to scholarly research on significant musical and historical topics. The American Musicological Society also publishes a substantial catalog of research monographs.

Leadership in Church Music. 3773 West 95th Street, Leawood, KS 66206. Released on a bi-monthly basis, this publication provides the choral musician with insightful commentary on recent developments in the church music field, including performance, research, and transition. The work is written in a scholarly, unbiased manner.

Music and Letters. Journals Subscription Department, Oxford University Press, Pinkhill House, Southfield Road, Eynsham, Oxford OX8-1JJ, UK. Founded in 1920, this publication is a leading British journal of musical scholarship. Its coverage embraces all fields of musical inquiry, and its authorship is international.

Music Educators Journal. Journal of the Music Educators National Conference. 1902 Association Drive, Reston, VA 22091-1597. This publication addresses issues relevant to all areas of music education. The choral art is represented equally with band, orchestra, and most other areas of musical pedagogy. In addition to those articles that directly address choral issues, choral musicians can gain useful insight into the methodology used by colleagues in other musical disciplines.

Musical Quarterly. Published by Oxford University Press, 200 Madison Avenue, New York, NY 10016. Devoted to articles on a variety of musical topics, this publication offers the latest scholarship on issues of historical importance.

NATS Journal. Published by the National Association of Teachers of Singing, Inc., 2800 University Boulevard N., JU Station, Jacksonville, FL 32211. Though written primarily for the voice teacher, the *NATS Journal* has much to offer the choral conductor. Articles focus on practical use of the voice, and recent scholarship on singing.

Being an important resource, professional journals should be kept for further reference and research. It is recommended that journals be stored in hard-cover binders for ease of storage. Maintaining an index of journal articles, ideally with some form of cross-reference, will prove invaluable as an aid to future study and research.

In addition to their regular publications, professional organizations make available a variety of supplemental publications designed to address specific topics. Several of these supplemental resources are discussed below.

While it is not devoted exclusively to choral music, the Music Educators National Conference provides a number of valuable materials and resources to the choral music educator. Among the titles which might be of particular interest to the choral musician are *Music for Children's Choirs*, *Pronunciation Guide for Choral Literature*, and *Religious Music in the Schools*. Another supplemental resource available from MENC is the *Journal of Research in Music Education*. A comprehensive catalog of MENC materials may be obtained from the MENC National Office.

The American Choral Directors Association has produced a series of monographs which could be of particular usefulness to the choral conductor.

Listed below, these are available through the ACDA National Office:

Guide for the Beginning Choral Director, by the ACDA National Committee on High School Music (1972), Gordon H. Lamb, Chair (Monograph No. 1). Prepared to provide guidance of a practical nature to the college senior, the beginning choral director. The information is designed to supplement either the course work the student may have completed, or other early choral experiences.

An Annotated Inventory of Distinctive Choral Literature for Performance at the High School Level, by Margaret Hawkins (Monograph No. 2). This monograph is designed as a useful supplement to the choral director's own knowledge of choral repertoire. The publication is concerned primarily with literature for the mixed choir.

The Choral Journal: An Index to Volumes 1–18, by Gordon Paine (Monograph No. 3). This is an important source of annotated information on nearly every topic of concern to the choral profession. It was developed to make the *Choral Journal* more accessible to researchers.

A Classified, Annotated Bibliography of Articles Related to Choral Music in Five Major Periodicals Through 1980, edited by Lynn Whitten (Monograph No 4). This volume was compiled as a source of data retrieval for choral conductors seeking to strengthen their rehearsal and performance routines in stimulating and scholarly ways. It contains annotation of articles for the following periodicals: *American Choral Review*, *Church Music*, *Journal of the American Musicological Society*, *Music and Letters*, and *Musical Quarterly*.

Singing in English: A Manual of English Diction for Singers and Choral Directors, by Richard Cox (Monograph No. 5). This publication applies phonetic principles, including the International Phonetic Alphabet, to the performance of English-language vocal texts, with special reference to choral singing. Language sounds are grouped systematically; for each group of sounds there is discussion of singers' problems and of acceptable regional variants, and illustrative word lists for practice in phonetic transcript.

A Classified Index of American Doctoral Dissertations and Dissertation Projects on Choral Music Completed or Currently in Progress Through 1989, by Michael J. Anderson (Monograph No. 6). This volume is designed to assist the choral musician in locating research on various topics related to the choral art. Includes entries listed in *Doctoral Dissertations in Musicology* and *Dissertation Abstracts International*, as well as doctoral documents which, for a variety of reasons, are cataloged only by the awarding institution.

The Choral Journal: An Index to Volumes 19–32, by Scott W. Dorsey (Monograph No. 7). In the years since the publication of Dr. Paine's original index the *Choral Journal* has grown in size, depth, and stature, thus making the development of a second index all the more necessary. This publication is designed to be used in concert with the first index.

In addition to journals and monographs, both ACDA and MENC publish a variety of newsletters on the state and divisional or regional level. While these often focus primarily on current events in a specific geographic region, such publications contain a variety of articles and commentaries relevant to the choral art. Organizational membership includes an annual subscription to one's respective state and divisional publications. Student members of ACDA also receive *The Student Times*. This publication is designed to address the various issues facing the student of choral music, and can serve as a resource for those involved in ACDA student chapter activities.

Most professional choral music associations host annual conventions or conferences for the purpose of sharing information and research. These conventions generally include concerts by performing ensembles selected by audition in advance of the event. While attendance at such a convention is an unsurpassed musical and learning experience in itself, the printed convention "book" or "program" should not be overlooked as an exceptional resource. Often the length of a small book (approximately 50 to 150 pages), the convention book contains valuable information on choral literature, publishers, leading figures in the choral field, performing ensembles, and a variety of organizational insights. These documents should become a part of the conductor's personal library.

Books

The most obvious resource available to the choral musician is one's personal library of books. This is often comprised primarily of text books which one was compelled to purchase for specific classes (the clearest illustration being the well-known text, *A History of Western Music* by Donald J. Grout, commonly known to the music student and most active choral professionals simply as "Grout"). Such books will serve as the nucleus around which one builds a library. As the conductor advances into an area of specialization, texts are added to one's library which will provide more focus than survey texts. By way of example, Willi Apel's text, *The Notation of Polyphonic Music 900–1600*, is a well-chosen library addition for the specialist in early music. The titles of specialty texts may be located in a variety of ways, including the bibliography in the back of general survey texts, professor's libraries, graduate libraries, or the book review section of the *Choral Journal*. The following is a partial list of publishers and distributors of music-related texts:

Alfred Publishing Company, Inc., P.O. Box 10003, 16380 Rosco Boulevard, Suite 200, Van Nuys, CA 91406. (818) 891-5999.
Augsburg Publishing House, Music Department, 426 South Fifth Street, Box 1209, Minneapolis, MN 55440. (800) 328-4648.
ECS Publishing, 138 Ipswich Street, Boston, MA 02215. (617) 236-1935.
Mark Foster Music Company, Box 4012, Champaign, IL 61820.
G.I.A. Publications, Inc., 7404 South Madison Avenue, Chicago, IL 60638. (708) 496-3800.

Harcourt Brace Jovanovich, 6277 Sea Harbor Drive, Orlando, FL 32887. (407) 345-2000.

Harper & Collins Publishers (formerly Harper & Row), 10 East 53rd Street, New York, NY 10022. (212) 207-7000.

Harvard University Press, 79 Garden Street, Cambridge, MA 02138-9983. (617) 495-2577.

Hinshaw Music, Inc., P.O. Box 470, Chapel Hill, NC 27514-0470. (919) 933-1691.

Houston Publishing, Inc., 224 South Lebanon Street, Lebanon, IN 46052. (317) 482-4440.

W. W. Norton & Company, Inc., Customer Service Department, 500 Fifth Avenue, New York, NY 10110. (800) 223-2588.

McGraw-Hill School Division, A Division of MacMillian Publishing Company, Inc., 866 Third Avenue, 3rd Floor, New York, NY 10022. (212) 702-7922.

Oxford University Press, Inc., 200 Madison Avenue, New York, NY 10016. (212) 679-7300, ext. 7165.

Prentice-Hall, Inc., U.S. Highway 9 West, Englewood Cliffs, NJ, (201) 592-2000.

Schirmer Books, A Division of Macmillan Publishing Company, Inc., 866 Third Avenue, New York, NY 10022. (212) 702-2000.

Wadsworth Publishing Company, Ten Davis Drive, Belmont, CA 94002. (415) 595-2350.

In addition to these companies, many publishers of choral music also release books written by composers who regularly produce choral works for that specific company. Most major universities also maintain some form of publishing concern, many of which produce fine scholarly texts on musical issues (i.e. David Wulstan's *Tudor Music*, published by the University of Iowa Press, 1986). Building a library of books can be an expensive undertaking, but it does not necessarily have to be so. There are several inexpensive methods for building a library.

1. **Library Sale**. For a variety of reasons, libraries periodically "thin" their collections through book sales. Very often this is done to replace older books with more recent scholarship. While up-to-date research is most desirable, few can afford to turn down a valuable, albeit older, resource offered at a low price.

2. **Bookstores**. Frequent the "cut-out" bin at local bookstores. Book merchants are in the business of selling books. When a particular title is not "moving," a dealer may opt to lower the price in order to clear inventory. While most "mall" book stores are unlikely to have a wealth of specialized musicological texts, they will have music dictionaries, biographies of notable musical figures, and historical texts which would be of value to the choral conductor.

3. **Music Faculty**. Professors occasionally receive free texts, known as desk copies, from publishers hoping for class adoptions by the faculty member. After

a period of time, desk copies may begin to take up valuable shelf space, which can compel a faculty member to give these books to interested students or colleagues. Also, professors planning a move or nearing retirement frequently wish to clean out their libraries and may give unneeded books to students.

A valuable addition to any library is a set of general encyclopedias. An encyclopedia makes, quite literally, a world of information available at one's fingertips. Though an encyclopedia is typically an expensive item, pre-owned sets can be obtained from owners planning to upgrade their collection. Occasionally, the Encyclopedia Britannica will have pre-owned sets available. Of course, the standard encyclopedic resource for the musical arts is the *New Grove Dictionary of Music and Musicians*, edited by Stanley Sadie. While this would be an exceptional addition to a conductor's library, it would not be an inexpensive acquisition. Further information may be obtained from any of the following corporations:

Encyclopedia Britannica, 310 South Michigan Avenue, Chicago, IL 60604. (800) 767-1613 or (312) 347-7000.

Grove's Dictionaries of Music, Inc., 15 East 26th Street, New York, NY 10010. (212) 481-1332.

World Book Encyclopedia, 101 NW Point Boulevard, Elk Grove Village, IL 60007. (800) 433-6580.

The development of a personal library of books is a highly individual matter. Holdings will be determined by any number of seemingly unrelated factors, including types of course work undertaken, subjects of specific interest, professional and educational aspirations, the scope of one's conducting/teaching position, and even the availability of shelf space. Therefore, no one "suggested readings" list will meet the needs of all conductors. However, the following lists a variety of basic texts, many of which would be of particular use to the young conductor.

Suggested Readings for the Choral Conductor

Achtert, Walter, *MLA Style Manual*. New York: Modern Language Association of America, 1985.

Ades, Hawley, *Choral Arranging* (expanded). Delaware Water Gap, Pennsylvania: Shawnee Press, 1983.

Adler, Samuel, *The Study of Orchestration*. New York: W.W. Norton, 1982.

Apel, Willi, *Harvard Dictionary of Music*. Cambridge, Massachusetts: Belknap Press, 1969.

Apel, Willi, *The Notation of Polyphonic Music 900–1600*. Cambridge, Massachusetts: The Medieval Academy of America, 1942.

Backus, John, *The Acoustical Foundations of Music*. New York: W. W. Norton, 1977.

Brown, Howard M., *Music in the Renaissance*. Englewood Cliffs, New Jersey: Prentice Hall Publishing Company, 1976.

Busch, Brian R., *The Complete Choral Conductor: Gesture and Method*. New York: Schirmer Books, 1984.

Carlisle, Marsha, and Betty Roe, *Something to Sing About*. New York: G. Schirmer, 1982.

Cassell's Compact German Dictionary. Ed. by H.C. Sasse. New York: Dell Publishing, 1966.

Collins Italian-English Dictionary. Ed. by Catherine E. Love. Berkley: Berkley Books, 1982.

Conscience of a Profession: Howard Swan. Ed. by Charles Fowler. Chapel Hill, North Carolina: Hinshaw Music, Inc., 1987.

Dart, Thurston, *The Interpretation of Music*. New York: Harper Books, 1954.

Davidson, Archibald T. and Willi Apel, *Historical Anthology of Music*. Volume I: Oriental, Medieval, and Renaissance. Cambridge, Massachusetts: Harvard University Press, 1946.

Davidson, Archibald T. and Willi Apel, *Historical Anthology of Music*. Volume II: Baroque, Rococo, and Pre-Classical. Cambridge, Massachusetts: Harvard University Press, 1946.

Decker, Harold A. and Julius Herford, *Choral Conducting: A Symposium*. Englewood Cliffs, New Jersey: Prentice Hall Publishing Company, 1973.

Decker, Harold and Colleen J. Kirk, *Choral Conducting: Focus on Communication*. Englewood Cliffs, New Jersey: Prentice Hall Publishing Company, 1988.

Donnington, Robert, *Baroque Music: Style and Performance*. New York: W. W. Norton, 1982.

Duckles, Vincent, *Music Research and Reference Materials*. New York: Free Press of Glencoe, 1964.

Ehmann, Wilhelm, *Choral Directing*. Minneapolis: Augsburg, 1968.

Einstein, Alfred, *The Italian Madrigal* (Three Volumes). Princeton: Princeton Press, 1949.

Emmons, Shirlee, and Stanley Sontag, *The Art of the Song Recital*. New York: Schirmer Books, 1979.

Five Centuries of Choral Music: Essays in Honor of Howard Swan. Ed. by Gordon Paine. Stuyvesant, New York: Pendragon Press, 1988.

Fowler, Charles, *Conscience of a Profession: Howard Swan*. Chapel Hill, North Carolina: Hinshaw Music, Inc., 1987.

Garland Composers Resource Manuals. Ed. by Guy A. Marco. New York: Garland Publishing, Inc.

Garretson, Robert L., *Conducting Choral Music* (Fifth Edition). Boston: Allyn and Bacon.

Glenn, Carole, *In Quest of Answers: Interviews with American Choral Conductors*. Chapel Hill, North Carolina: Hinshaw Music, Inc., 1991.

Grout, Donald Jay, and Claude V. Palisca, *A History of Western Music* (Fourth Edition, Longer). New York: W. W. Norton, 1980.

Henry, Earl, *Fundamentals of Music*. Englewood Cliffs, New Jersey: Prentice Hall Publishing Company, 1988.

Hindemith, Paul, *Elementary Training for Musicians*. New York: Schott, 1949.

Hoffer, Charles R., *Teaching Music in Secondary Schools*. Belmont California: Wadsworth Publishing Company, 1991.

Jones, Archie. *Pronouncing Guide to French, German, Italian and Spanish*. New York: Carl Fischer, Inc., 1945.

Juilliard Repertoire Library. Ed. by Paul A. Harry. Cincinnati: Canyon Press, Inc., 1970.

Kamien, Roger, *Music: An Appreciation* (Brief Edition). New York: McGraw Hill, 1990.

Kaplan, Abraham, *Choral Conducting*. New York: W. W. Norton and Co., 1985.

Kennedy, Michael, *The Oxford Dictionary of Music*. London: Oxford University Press, 1985.

Kennan, Kent W., *The Technique of Orchestration*. Englewood Cliffs, New Jersey: Prentice Hall Publishing Company, 1952.

Kirk, Theron, *Sure You Can! Extra-Musical Guidance for the Young Choral Conductor*. Champaign, Illinois: Mark Foster Music Company, 1978.

Kjelson, Lee, and James McCray, *The Conductors Manual of Choral Music Literature*. Burbank, California: Belwin-Mills.

Komar, Arthur, *Music and Human Experience*. New York: Schirmer Books, 1980.

Lamb, Gordon H., *Choral Techniques* (Third Edition). Dubuque, Iowa: William C. Brown Publishers, 1988.

Larousse Encyclopedia of Music. Ed. by Geoffery Hindley, New York: Excalibur Books, 1981.

Larousse French-English Dictionary. Ed. by Marguerite-Marie Dubois. New York: Pocket Books, 1971.

Longyear, Rey M., *Nineteenth Century Romanticism in Music*. Englewood Cliffs, New Jersey: Prentice Hall Publishing Company, 1969.

Lovelace, Austin C., and William C. Rice, *Music and Worship in the Church*. Nashville: Abingdon Press, 1960.

Machlis, Joseph, *The Enjoyment of Music* (Sixth Edition). New York: W. W. Norton & Co., 1990.

Machlis, Joseph, *Introduction to Contemporary Music*. New York: W. W. Norton & Co., 1979.

Malm, William P., *Music Cultures of the Pacific, the Near East and Asia*. Englewood Cliffs, New Jersey: Prentice Hall Publishing Company, 1967.

Meister, Barbara, *An Introduction to the Art Song*. New York: Taplinger Publishing Company, 1980.

Miller, Phillip L., *The Ring of Words: An Anthology of Song Texts*. New York: W. W. Norton, 1973.

Moe, Daniel, *Basic Choral Concepts*. Minneapolis: Augsburg Publishing House.

Moe, Daniel, *Problems in Conducting*. Minneapolis: Augsburg Publishing House, 1968.

Moses, Don V., *Face to Face with an Orchestra*. Princeton: Prestige Publications, 1987.

New Grove Composer Biography Series. Ed. by Stanley Sadie. London: Macmillian LTD.

Norton Anthology of Western Music (Second Edition; Volume 1: Medieval, Renaissance, and Baroque). Ed. by Claude V. Palisca. New York: W. W. Norton, 1990.

Norton Anthology of Western Music (Second Edition; Volume 2: Classic, Romantic and Modern). Ed. by Claude Palisca. New York: W. W. Norton, 1990.

Norton Scores: An Anthology for Listening (Fifth Edition; Volume 1: Chant to Beethoven). Ed. by Roger Kamien. New York: W. W. Norton, 1990.

Norton Scores: An Anthology for Listening (Fifth Edition; Volume 2: Schubert to Crumb). Ed. by Roger Kamien. New York: W. W. Norton, 1990.

Ottman, Robert, *Advanced Harmony: Theory and Practice*. Englewood Cliffs, New Jersey: Prentice Hall Publishing Company, 1972.

Ottman, Robert, *Elementary Harmony: Theory and Practice*. Englewood Cliffs, New Jersey: Prentice Hall Publishing Company, 1970.

Palisca, Claude V., *Baroque Music*. Englewood Cliffs, New Jersey: Prentice Hall Publishing Company, 1968.

Pauly, Reinhard G., *Music in the Classic Period*. Englewood Cliffs, New Jersey: Prentice Hall Publishing Company, 1965.

Randel, Don M., *Harvard Concise Dictionary of Music*. London: Belknap Press, 1978.

Randel, Don, *The New Harvard Dictionary of Music*. Cambridge, Massachusetts: Harvard University Press, 1986.

Robinson, Ray, *The Choral Experience*. New York: Harper's College Press, 1976.

Routley, Erik, *The Music of Christian Hymns*. Chicago: G.I.A. Publications, Inc., 1981.

Rudolph, Max, *The Grammar of Conducting*. New York: Schirmer Books, 1950.

Seay, Albert, *Music in the Medieval World*. Englewood Cliffs, New Jersey: Prentice Hall Publishing Company, 1965.

Shaw, Watkins, *A Textual Companion to Handel's Messiah*. Kent: Novello, 1965.

Sheil, Richard F., *A Manual of Foreign Language Diction*. New York: Palladian Company, 1979.

Simons, Harriet, *Choral Conducting: A Leadership Approach*. Champaign, Illinois: Mark Foster Music Company, 1983.

Sloboda, John A., *The Musical Mind: The Cognitive Psychology of Music*. London: Oxford University Press, 1986.

Ulrich, Homer, *A Survey of Choral Music*. New York: Harbrace/HBJ, 1973.

University Carol Book. Ed. by Erik Routley. London: H. Freeman and Company, 1961.

Watanabe, Ruth T., *Introduction to Music Research*. Englewood Cliffs, New Jersey: Prentice Hall Publishing Company, 1967.

Wormhoudt, Pearl Shinn, *Building the Voice as an Instrument*. Oskaloosa, Iowa: Arthur Wormhoudt, 1991

Audio Recordings

Modern technology has affected virtually every area of life. Certainly, high quality recordings are a technological resource which were unavailable to the conductor of old. Recordings can serve a variety of uses; as an aural guide to the exploration of unfamiliar literature, as a sampler of choral tone, or as an aid to the preparation of concert material (However, the use of choral recordings should never be considered a substitute for thoughtful, thorough score study).

Obviously, a library of choral recordings would be of considerable use to the choral professional, but developing such a collection can be a challenge. Choral recordings do not seem to have the wider appeal afforded the standard orchestral repertoire, and are therefore not readily available in general record stores. By way of example, a five-album set titled *Mozart Masterpieces* (Capriccio, LC 8748) includes only one choral selection, his motet, *Ave Verum Corpus*; movements from his Masses and the *Requiem* are completely ignored.

As is the case in acquiring books for one's library, building a collection of choral recordings could prove to be an expensive endeavor. Like before, there are ways to limit the financial strain of developing this important resource.

1. **Record Stores**. Spend time browsing through the "3-for-$10" bin at a local record store. Although record merchants in malls tend to aim toward the pop music market, they frequently have available a selection of classical recordings, usually on cassette, which are reasonably priced at about $3.99 each or three for $10. One can find a variety of musical gems in such offerings — from gregorian chant, through great opera/oratorio choruses, to the occasional recording of motets or perhaps vocal jazz.

2. **Libraries**. The advent of new recording technologies, such as compact disc, digital audio tape, digital compact cassette, mini disc, etc. has sent many libraries and private record collectors scrambling to "update" their holdings. Often, they will decide to eliminate their LP holdings altogether. In this case, a stereophile may sell their holdings at a garage sale, or, as was the author's experience, they might choose to donate their entire LP collection to music students at a local college. Libraries might sell selected recordings at their annual book sale. A classical radio station in the process of an upgrade may eliminate their LP holdings in much the same manner. In any event, one could easily and inexpensively acquire a wealth of priceless recordings, albeit on vinyl. Predictably, future developments in recording technology will certainly move collectors and libraries to unload "old" recordings in favor of the latest audio fad.

To locate recordings of specific interest, the choral conductor will, in all likelihood, be required to contact dealers which specialize in the genre. Listed below are a sample of companies which have a considerable number of choral recordings as a part of their catalog[2]:

---

[2] For additional detailed information on discography, including an in-depth discourse on journals related to new recordings, consult the following articles in the *Choral Journal* by Richard J. Bloesch: "Choral Recordings: Resources for Discography," March, 1990: 5–16; and "Choral Recordings: Retail Sources," May, 1990:15–22.

American Gramophone Records, 9130 Mormon Bridge Road, Omaha, NE 68152. (402) 457-4341.

Augsburg Publishing House, Music Department, 426 South Fifth Street, Minneapolis, MN 55440. (800) 328-4648.

Bradford Consultants, P.O. Box 4020, Alameda, CA 94501. (415) 523-1968.

CBS Special Products, P.O. Box 4450, New York, NY 10101-4450. (212) 445-3596.

Collegium Records, P.O. Box 31366, Omaha, NE 68131. (800) 367-9059. FAX: (402) 597-1254.

Discount Music Club, Inc., 481 Main Street, P.O. Box 1748, New Rochelle, NY 10801.

DJ Records, P.O. Box 95, 813 South Davis, McMinnville, OR 97128. (503) 472-6971.

Duwars, P.O. 6662-D, Greenville, SC 29606.

Educational Record Center, 1575 Northside Drive NW, #400, Atlanta, GA 30317. (800) 438-1637.

Ethel Enterprises, P.O. Box 1069, Murphy, NC 28906.

Mark Foster Music Company, Box 4012, Champaign, IL 61820.

Haverstick & Ballyk, 2186 Jackson Keller, San Antonio, TX 78213. (800) 222-6872.

Mark Records, 10815 Bodine Road, P.O. Box 406, Clarence, NY 14031-0406. (716) 759-2600.

Maildisc, P.O. Box 131588, Staten Island, NY 10313-0005.

Musical Heritage Society, 1710 Highway 35, Ocean, NJ 07712.

Oxford University Press, 200 Madison Avenue, New York, NY 10016.

OZ Warehouse Outlet, 1575P Highway 29, Lawrence, GA 40244.

Recordmasters Classics, 711 West 40th Street, Baltimore, MD 21211. (800) 727-DISC (3472), FAX: (301) 235-0534.

Rose Records, 214 South Wabash Avenue, Chicago, IL 60604. (800) 955-ROSE (7673).

St. Olaf Records, St. Olaf College Bookstore, Northfield, MN 55057. (507) 663-3048.

Video Recordings

Video cassette recordings would be a resource of tremendous usefulness to the choral conductor. Like audio recordings, video cassettes could serve a variety of important functions, including studying the physical techniques of noted conductors, analyzing the visual performance practice of exceptional ensembles, and as an introduction to such visually active choral functions as the madrigal dinner setting and the show choir. An example of a video recording that would serve as an excellent learning tool is, *Robert Shaw: Preparing a Masterpiece* (A choral workshop on Brahms' *A German Requiem,* available from Carnegie Hall Professional Training Workshops, (800) 683-7846).

A number of valuable documentary films are available on videocassette. One particularly important set of music history videos has been developed by the noted European film maker, Hans Conrad Fischer. The Fischer series includes four videos, *The Life of Wolfgang Amadeus Mozart* (1968), *The Life of Ludwig van Beethoven* (1970), *The Life of Anton Bruckner* (1974), and the latest in the sequence, *The Life of Johann Sebastian Bach.* These videos have been produced by Hänssler-Verlag, and are available through Antara Music Group, 211 Whitsett Rd., Nashville, TN 37210, (800) 546-1546.

ACDA has produced a series called *ACDA on Location.* This three-volume set makes available the expertise of distinguished choral conductors as they lecture, rehearse and perform. Listed below, these are available through the ACDA National Office:

Volume 1: The Children's Choir focuses on the children's choir with the Glen Ellyn Children's Chorus and its immediate past conductor, Doreen Rao, who shares her "artistic approach" to the music education of children.

Volume 2: Howard Swan is an interview with one of the "deans" of the choral profession, Dr. Howard Swan. Dr. Swan reviews the history of American choral music during the first half of the twentieth century, discusses the present state of choral music in church and school, and gives learned advice to the young choral conductor.

Volume 3: Jester Hairston features the internationally renowned composer, arranger and conductor, Jester Hairston. In this interview, Mr. Hairston traces the history of the black spiritual in America, gives suggestions for interpretation, and demonstrates the use of rhythm and dialect in the music.

Scores

Perhaps the most important resource needed by the choral musician is a collection of choral scores. A well organized library of quality choral compositions will serve not only for study and research, but will also be invaluable should one take a teaching/conducting position that includes a poor choral library, or no choral holdings whatsoever.

Personal choral holdings can be arranged in any manner that one deems appropriate. By way of example, the author's personal library is built around historical periods, alphabetized by composer, with an accompanying series of cross-referenced indices. The important factor in establishing the score library is ease of access for the primary user.

Unlike books or recordings, acquiring choral scores is not an inherently expensive process. While major works with full choral/orchestral scores can be somewhat costly, octavo scores are rather reasonably priced and in some cases, can be obtained for free. Many music companies go to great length to place scores in the hands of choral conductors and are often willing to provide single copies in the hope that the conductor will adopt a work and purchase multiple copies. There are a variety of methods for obtaining scores at little or no cost.

1. **Attend reading sessions.** Choral music reading sessions are often sponsored by a regional or national music distributor interested in introducing their product to a group of choral directors. Reading sessions are usually of two

types: 1) A choral clinician or committee of choral directors selects music to be read, which is in turn supplied by a music store or publisher(s), or 2) A music store or publisher sponsors the reading session and makes decisions on what music will be read in the session. Reading sessions provide the choral conductor with the opportunity to hear a work performed and to peruse a variety of repertoire.

2. **Attend conventions.** Free materials are often available at professional music conventions. Most choral music conventions feature a considerable area devoted to product displays, including publishers and distributors of choral scores. Their sales representatives are usually prepared to provide free copies of a select list of titles. Frequently, their complimentary offerings are directly related to works being performed during the convention. Most conventions also include some form of a choral literature forum, often in the reading session format.

3. **Read advertisements** found in the various professional music journals discussed above. Advertisements from publishing companies frequently offer free samples of their wares simply for the asking. Such advertisements may also offer the merchant's catalog, again at no cost.

4. **Contact music publishers** or distributors directly to request sample copies of choral literature. In most cases, they will be glad to provide the conductor with perusal materials, at little or no cost. This will understandably cause one's name to find its way onto the firm's mailing list, which, if one is seeking a variety of sample scores, is a desirable outcome.

The list of choral music publishers and distributors is far too long for inclusion here. However, there are various organizations who maintain current lists of firms that specialize in the publication and distribution of choral music. Three of these concerns are listed below. Additionally, the November, 1990 edition of the *Choral Journal* includes the "Music Publisher's Sales Agency List," a copious roster of 433 companies dedicated to providing the choral musician with materials and resources. For further information on matters concerning music publication, consult the chapter on page 17 by Timothy W. Sharp: "Research References, Current Sources, and Future Directions."

Music Publishers Association of the United States, 205 E. 42nd Street, New York, NY 10017.

National Music Publishers Association, 205 East 42nd Street, New York, NY 10017.

Church Music Publishers' Association, P.O. Box 158992, Nashville, TN, 37215.

Computers

Computer technology is such a common factor in everyday life that to mention it seems almost passé. Computers are cited briefly here not as a resource, but as a tool which should be used in conjunction with the conductor's library.

Among the computer's many functions, data storage could be the most useful to the choral conductor. Countless reams of information on everything from personnel lists to concert program notes can be stored on a single disk. Entire libraries can be indexed and cross-referenced in any conceivable manner via a personal computing system.

Beyond simple storage, the computer also has some uses as a research tool. Specialized encyclopedic resources and references that utilize the computer medium are being developed, and in some cases, resources which were once available only in printed form are also being offered in a software format. This will become increasingly common, particularly as mass production of this technology makes it more affordable.

When combined with an electronic keyboard instrument and the proper MIDI equipment, the computer becomes a powerful tool for music composition. The computer will, quite literally, notate on the monitor screen any musical notes played on the interfaced instrument. Thus, the composer/arranger can save untold hours of laborious copying and editing by use of the computer music program.

Perhaps the most common use of the computer is word processing. From the inter-office memo, to a massive dissertation project, the word processing function of a computer reduces hours of arduous labor to a few minutes, or even seconds, at the computer keyboard. The use of graphics in the word processing program allows the choral conductor to construct attractive, eye-catching designs, which could be used in concert programs, posters, newsletters, etc.

A variety of personal computing magazines are regularly available at local newsstands. These publications provide information on the latest equipment, new software, and computing techniques. Articles which relate this technology to the specific needs of the musician have appeared in many of the professional music publications discussed above. A brief sampling of firms that offer specialized music-oriented software is listed below.

Advantage Software, 239 Southland Drive, Suite B, Lexington, KY 40503. (800) 666-2764.

Bureau of Electronic Publishing, 141 New Road, Parsipany, NJ 07054. (201) 808-2700.

Claris, 5201 Patrick Henry Drive, Santa Clara, CA 95052-8168. (408) 727-8227.

EduCorp, 7434 Trade Street, San Diego, CA 92121. (619) 536-9999.

Edugraphics, P.O. Box 356, Lafayette, IN 47902. (800) 331-4564.

Maya Computer, P.O. Box 680, Waitsfield, VT 05673. (800) 541-2318.

Musication, Bay Bridge Avenue, Brooklyn, NY 11219. (718) 680-5500.

Passport Designs, 625 Miramontes Street, Half Moon Bay, CA 94019. (415) 726-0280.

Pygraphics, P.O. Box 639, Grapevine, TX 76051. (800) 222-7536.

Sound Management, P.O. Box 3053, Peabody, MA 01961. (800) 548-4907.

Temporal Acuity Products, Inc., 300 120th Avenue N.E., Building 1, Bellevue, WA 98005. (800) 426-2673.

Voyager Company, 1351 Pacific Coast Highway, Santa Monica, CA 90401. (800) 446-2001.

Warner New Media, 3500 West Olive Avenue, Suite 1050, Burbank, CA 91505. (818) 955-9999.

To be certain, installation of a computer is not quite as simple as plugging in a toaster, and it will take the new user some time to learn how to operate a particular system. However, in response to the needs of the general public, computer designers have made computer programs more accessible by removing long-winded explanations and technical jargon. Without question, the time invested in learning to use a computer system will be repaid many times over.

Additional Resources

In addition to that which is discussed above, there are a variety of less obvious resources available to the choral conductor that are, nevertheless, valuable in the performance of the conductor's widely divergent duties.

Program file. This includes the printed programs of concerts which one attends either for enrichment or simply for pleasure. The printed program can serve as a valuable, multifaceted resource, though far too often these handbills find their way into the trash bin at the close of a particular concert presentation. The concert program can provide a conductor with information on literature, and on programming techniques. The program might also serve to update the conductor on the activities of colleagues and associates. The program file can further serve as an artwork sampler by giving the choral conductor ideas for future program and poster design layout. Programs might be filed by ensemble category (choral, orchestra, band), age level (children, high school, collegiate), or chronologically.

Clipping file. As discussed above, most professional organizations produce newsletters or supplementary publications containing a variety of relevant articles and commentaries, many of which do not find their way into larger publications such as ACDA's *Choral Journal* or MENC's *Music Educator's Journal*. Often, newsletter articles tend to be written in a concise "how-to" format and can be among some of the most inspirational "battery chargers" available. Articles that relate well to the individual conductor's particular situation should be "clipped" and saved in some sort of clipping file for later retrieval and use. Several titles from organizational newsletters included in the author's clipping file are listed below:

"We are the Winners (An Attitude Exam)" — ACDA Nevada
"Building Your Own Support System" — ACDA California
"The Well-Tempered Conductor" — ACDA Nebraska
"In Pursuit of Perfection" — ACDA Western Division
"Musicology and the Music Major — CMS Symposium
"Errata in the Poulenc *Gloria*" — ACR Memorandum Series
"Church Music: Amateur vs. Amateurish" — ACDA Utah
"20 Ways to Irritate the Singer" — ACDA Kansas
"Art Where There was None Before" — ACDA North Dakota
"Musical Athletes" — MENC Iowa

Organizational newsletters are not the only venue of important information for the choral conductor; other sources include newspapers and magazines. For example, *Newsweek* seems to have a special affinity for news items on contemporary artistic and musical figures. This coverage has included admirable coverage of conductors and composers such as Bernstein, Levine, Rostropovich, Slatkin, and Tilson-Thomas. Additionally, the Sunday edition of the *New York Times* features an extensive performing arts section, highlighting important musical premieres and performances by notable musicians.

Class notes. Though it may seem too simple to be true, the notes one has taken in various music classes can be a valuable resource. The author has, on many occasions, been thankful for the availability of old class notes, either as a guide to developing a syllabus, as a source of specific information, or for its bibliographic content. It is suggested that class notes be organized in three-ring binders by single class or specific subject.

Rolodex. In all likelihood, the best resources available to any choral conductor are other choral professionals. If, for instance, one is not an expert on choral literature for women's voices, a telephone call or letter written to a recognized expert in that specific area can produce answers in a relatively short time. Despite the hectic schedules inherent in any conducting position, choral musicians are, by-and-large, willing to answer student questions and provide assistance to young conductors. The author has never experienced any difficulty in locating information or answers when enlisting the assistance of a colleague.

Beyond scholarly considerations, one's colleagues constitute an unparalleled professional support structure. Who understands better the many challenges, frustrations, and joys of being a conductor than one who is in a similar situation? Often, a conductor's work can be hampered by feelings of isolation, irritation, helplessness, and a sensation of being the only conductor to have faced a particular situation. To use a rather hackneyed expression, "Help is only a phone call away." A telephone call to, or a visit with a colleague can do wonders for the spirit, leaving both conductors feeling refreshed, and ready to face whatever challenge lies ahead. Keep the names, addresses and phone numbers of former teachers/professors, mentors, colleagues or others who might be of assistance in a rolodex file for easy access.

This brief discussion was intended to outline some of the general materials that might serve the various needs of the choral professional, including professional publications, books, recordings, and scores. Many additional resources needed by the conductor will be determined by specifics such as age of ensemble members, availability of staff support, ensemble goals, and institutional guidelines. While the information presented here represents a reasonable survey of current resources for the conductor, it is by no means the final word in building a personal library. The conductor must constantly reach for new, innovative ideas by listening to latest recordings, reading the newest books, and searching for the most recent research in any given topical area.